T5-AQT-731

MAINSTREAMING

A Practical Approach for Teachers

JUDY W. WOOD
Virginia Commonwealth University

Merrill, an imprint of
Macmillan Publishing Company
New York

Collier Macmillan Canada, Inc.
Toronto

Maxwell Macmillan International Publishing Group
New York • Oxford • Singapore • Sydney

To my sons, Eddie, Scott, and Jason
  and
to my husband, Greg Wheal

Cover Photo: Kevin Fitzsimons

This book was set in Quorum

Administrative Editor: Vicki Knight
Production Coordinator: Carol S. Sykes
Art Coordinator: Vincent A. Smith
Cover Designer: Brian Deep

Photo Credits: All photos copyrighted by individuals or companies listed. Lloyd Lemmerman/Merrill, pp. 1, 299, 321, 349, 380, 393; Blair Seitz, pp. 4, 95; Merrill, p. 16; Bruce Johnson/Merrill, pp. 33, 228; Jean Greenwald/Merrill, p. 35; Kevin Fitzsimons/Merrill, pp. 65, 105, 113, 141, 149, 195, 285; David Strickler, p. 100; Steve Takatsuno, p. 131; Photo Edit, p. 249; and Celia Drake/Merrill, p. 274.

Copyright © 1989 by Macmillan Publishing Company. Merrill is an imprint of Macmillan Publishing Company. All rights reserved. No part of this book may be reproduced in any form, electronic or mechanical, including photocopy, recording, or any information storage and retrieval system, without permission in writing from the publisher.

Library of Congress Catalog Card Number: 88–61798
International Standard Book Number: 0–675–20535–2
Printed in the United States of America
2 3 4 5 6 7 8 9—93 92 91

Preface

Mainstreaming, the effort to provide an appropriate education for handicapped children in the same setting as their nonhandicapped peers, is a reality of today's educational system. For many years parents of handicapped students fought unsuccessfully to have their children placed in the same educational setting that other children enjoyed. With time and the creation of laws, parents and educators saw mainstreaming become a reality. Today, educators are working together toward the goal of providing the most appropriate educational setting possible within regular and special education for handicapped students. Meeting this goal has brought about changes in education and has merged the skills of regular and special educators as they work cooperatively to provide an education that is appropriate for all students.

The focus of *Mainstreaming: A Practical Approach for Teachers* is to assist regular and special educators in providing appropriate services for the handicapped student within the mainstream environment. In addition, the text is intended to help educators design and implement educational services in regular classes that will eliminate the need to label many students as in need of special services. With the current trend to provide support teams within schools, we are seeing an increasing number of handicapped students being served within regular education.

Chapter 1 provides the reader with an overview of mainstreaming; Chapter 2 describes the functions, roles, and responsibilities of the multidisciplinary team; and Chapter 3 identifies the various characteristics of the major handicapping conditions. A discussion of the unique characteristics of culturally diverse handicapped students is presented in Chapter 4, and to assist educators in designing an appropriate mainstreamed environment, Chapter 5 discusses the learning environment, classroom management, and the instructional process in depth. Chapters 6–8 present recommended teaching strategies for individualizing for language arts, arithmetic, and science and social studies, respectively. In Chapter 9, instructional approaches and models for career and vocational education are presented. The final chapter is unique to textbooks on mainstreaming. Chapter 10 discusses a survey, conducted by the author, of regular and special educators in the United States. It presents educators' views on how best to teach the handicapped student, identifies the problems they most often encounter, and explores the techniques they find most useful in mainstream classrooms.

The text is supplemented by special features designed to assist readers in developing a better understanding not only of handicapped students but also of your future role as educator of these students. Most chapters include a case study that illustrates important points discussed in the text and a boxed feature, entitled "What You Can Do," that summarizes the educator's responsibilities in the various topic areas. Further, each chapter includes numerous illustrations and tables that expand on text discussion as well as discussion questions that promote understanding of the material presented. Most chapters conclude with a "Resources" section that enables interested readers to pursue topics further. Finally, at the end of the book are an appendix of relevant organizations and associations and a list of references.

The ultimate goal of *Mainstreaming* is to assist readers who will teach handicapped students in mainstream classrooms by providing them with useful information. It is hoped that this goal will be realized. Readers are encouraged to convey their comments or suggestions for improvement to the author, as successful mainstreaming is the result of a collective effort and the sharing of ideas. Cooperating, learning, sharing, and growing are worthy goals for us all.

Acknowledgments

Appreciation is extended to the wonderfully talented and patient educators whose contributions to this book are immeasurable: Jerry Aldridge, University of Alabama at Birmingham; Katherine E. Andre, Department of Defense Schools; Deborah A. Bott, University of Kentucky; John Kregel, Virginia Commonwealth University; Jennifer Miederhoff, Virginia Commonwealth University; James R. Patton, University of Hawaii at Manoa; Carolyn K. Reeves, University of Southern Mississippi; and Alice V. Watkins, California State University, Los Angeles. I am also grateful to Jennifer Kilgo, Virginia Commonwealth University, for the excellent development of the Instructor's Manual.

I am indebted to the reviewers who provided valuable comments and suggestions: Virginia J. Dickens, Fayetteville State University; Steve Graham, University of Maryland; Marleen Pugach, The University of Wisconsin-Milwaukee; Joan Safran, Ohio University; Tommie Sellers, San Francisco State University; George Shepherd, University of Oregon; Paula J. Smith, Illinois State University; and Kay Stevens, University of Kentucky. Thank you for many months of assistance.

To Vicki Knight, a very special and talented editor at Merrill Publishing Company, thank you for your many years of patience and friendship. To my production editor, Carol Sykes, to my copy editor, Wendy Polhemus-Annibell, and to the staff at Merrill, thank you. As always, it has been a great pleasure to work with Vicki and the Merrill staff.

I am grateful to my friends and colleagues for their support, encouragement, and endless love throughout this endeavor. Ruth Dickinson, Dolly Thomas, and Beverly Watson were always ready to help when needed. Trish Nichols, Barbara Wright, and Alice Whittaker assisted in providing research. Reginald Tinsley typed the manuscript with care and with a positive attitude during a difficult time. To Ginny Padgette and Wendy Crandall, my very special friends, thank you for always seeing the rainbows. To Jack Corazzini and Theresa May, I am thankful for your insight into life. To John Oehler, Dean of the School of Education, Virginia Commonwealth University, and to Richard Vacca, Acting Head of the Division of Educational Services, Virginia Commonwealth University, I thank you for your encouragement and support, which made this project a reality. To Paul Wehman, my friend and mentor, thank you. And to John O'Bannon, my friend and physician, I am grateful for your humanistic approach to healing.

To my lifelong friends I cannot convey in words the measure of your influence on my life—Len Hughes, Kay Christian Morse, and Buster Bounds, I thank you. I am also indebted to my second parents, Charlie B. and Maxine Christian, whose lifetime of influence is hard to assess.

Appreciation is extended to Billy Rogers of Hattiesburg, Mississippi, an outstanding educator who helped me to start my educational endeavors. His immeasurable influence has given me the courage to face the challenges of my choices.

A very special acknowledgment goes to my friends and colleagues Jenny Miederhoff, Debra Gibson, and Beth Holcomb Davis, whose time, love, talent, and support helped in so many ways to make this book a reality.

The ongoing faith and support of my best friend and sister, Sandra Foutz, will always be remembered. To my mother, Ercyle Walker; to my brother, Ford Walker, II; and to the loving memory of my father, Ford Walker, thank you.

To my husband, Greg Wheal, whose love I can always count on, thank you for enduring and for supporting me through trying times. To my sons and God's greatest blessings, Eddie, Scott, and Jason, thank you for your unconditional support and love, and for once again sharing your mother so that other children may have a better life. No mom could be more proud, no sons could be finer, and life does not hold a greater treasure than each of you.

Contents

5 **Designing a Mainstreamed Environment**
Carolyn K. Reeves

6 **Individualizing for Language Arts**
Jerry Aldridge

7 **Individualizing for Arithmetic**
Deborah A. Bott

Chapter 1

Mainstreaming: An Overview

JUDY W. WOOD

CAROLYN K. REEVES
University of Southern Mississippi

Chapter Objectives

After reading Chapter 1 the student will be able to

- Define mainstreaming
- Provide suggestions for setting the stage for mainstreaming into regular classes
- Discuss the importance of positive attitudes as they relate to mainstreaming

M ainstreaming is a way to teach handicapped students in environments that do not restrict their educational potential, including placing handicapped students in the regular classroom with their nonhandicapped peers. Mainstreaming is not only a reality of today's educational system but an educational standard as well. Responding to this mandate requires cooperation between regular and special education personnel as well as the ability to adapt to new roles and responsibilities. Sharing resources, skills, and time are now commonplace within regular and special education. In Chapter 1 we examine mainstreaming definitions, the handicapped population, how services developed, a model for delivering services, and how to set the stage for successful mainstreaming.

Mainstreaming Defined

Most definitions of mainstreaming share similar goals for the education of handicapped students. Some common elements of the definitions include (1) the involvement of handicapped students as part of the regular educational program and (2) an emphasis on the social and instructional aspects of the integration process. Other components of the definition of mainstreaming are the inclusion of special services, placement in the least restrictive environment, and cooperation among educators. Whether for social or instructional purposes, mainstreaming requires that the handicapped student be educated with nonhandicapped students and that services be made available to supplement the educational process for mainstreamed students. In the mainstream, the handicapped student receives special supportive or related services as needed.

School personnel involved in a mainstreamed program must work closely to place students appropriately. An *appropriate placement* is one in which the social, emotional, and educational growth of the student is not restricted. Frequently, it may be necessary for the handicapped student to return to the special classroom for a portion of the day to receive instruction from the special education teacher. Mainstreaming requires planning, preparation, and instructional consideration designed to meet the needs of the student. It is a shared responsibility of regular and special education. (Figure 1.1 presents various definitions of the concept of mainstreaming.)

What Mainstreaming Is and Is Not

Among educators confusion has developed over the term *mainstream* and over the role it plays in the educational system. Mainstreaming is

- Identifying the student's strengths.
- Learning about the characteristics of handicapped students and how they relate to their education.

2

Mainstreaming is "the provision of an appropriate educational opportunity for all handicapped students in the least restrictive alternative, based on individualized education programs, with procedural safeguards and parent involvement, and aimed at providing handicapped students with access to and constructive interaction with nonhandicapped peers" (Johnson & Johnson, 1980, p. 90).

Mainstreaming is "the process of bringing exceptional children into daily contact with nonexceptional children in an educational setting" (Kirk & Gallagher, 1983, p. 15).

Mainstreaming "means helping people with handicaps live, learn, and work in everyday settings where they will have the greatest opportunity to become as independent as possible. . . . It gives handicapped children the chance to join in the 'mainstream of life' by including them in the regular preschool experience, and gives nonhandicapped children the opportunity to learn and grow by experiencing the strengths and weaknesses of their handicapped friends . . ." (Hayden, Smith, von Hippel, & Baer, 1978, p. 4).

Mainstreaming "refers to the temporal, instructional, and social integration of eligible exceptional children with normal peers. It is based on an on-going, individually determined educational planning and programming process which requires clarification of responsibility among regular and special education, administrative, instructional, and supportive personnel" (Kauffman, Gottlieb, Agard, & Kukic, 1975, p. 9).

FIGURE 1.1
Definitions of Mainstreaming

- Providing educational opportunities for handicapped students equal to those of their nonhandicapped peers.
- Teaching handicapped and nonhandicapped students how to appreciate similarities and differences among individuals.
- Sharing resources, skills, and time.
- Sharing the educational responsibilities for the handicapped student.
- Providing a climate in which positive attitudes prevail.
- Realizing that the handicapped student belongs within the regular classroom environment and should receive support services outside this environment as needed.
- Creating change, and realizing that change will not occur instantly.

Mainstreaming is *not*

- Serving the handicapped student in regular classes without a well-planned support system in place.
- Presenting regular class instruction to handicapped students without allowing for modifications when necessary.
- Placing all handicapped students, regardless of the degree of handicapping condition, into the regular education program.
- Placing at risk the progress of the nonhandicapped student.

Mainstreaming is a joint venture of both regular and special education personnel. The focus of mainstreaming is to provide instructional options for the special student within the regular classroom and to provide special education only when this is the best educational practice. In the mainstream, educators share their skills and time to develop an educational climate designed for success.

Who Is the Mainstreamed Student?

Children with handicaps are different from other children in some important aspects of human functioning. For various reasons (physical, psychological, cognitive, or social), it is difficult for handicapped children to reach their full potential. The extent of time that needs to be spent with the mainstreamed student depends on the degree of the student's impairment. Frequently, these children require a specially designed environment in which to function to their

Handicapped students are as unique as their nonhandicapped contemporaries.

fullest. Thus, an instructional climate that can meet the intellectual demands of handicapped students needs to be provided.

Handicapped students are as unique as their nonhandicapped contemporaries, varying in learning patterns, behavioral aspects, sensory areas, or physical aspects. Our focus here is on the special characteristics of handicapped students with mild learning problems and how they are best served in the regular classroom.

One of the largest groups of handicapped students found in the mainstream are those with mild learning problems, representing 7.36% of school enrollment. These students have difficulty learning the traditional curriculum and may encounter problems in one or more academic areas, as with the learning disabled (LD) student. The mentally retarded (MR) student is often delayed in all academic areas, while the student with emotional or behavioral disorders (ED/BD) may need academic assistance as well as help with inappropriate behaviors. The mildly handicapped student needs a closely monitored curriculum within both regular and special education.

Another large group of handicapped students are those with speech and language disorders (2.86%). Speech disordered students experience difficulty with articulation, voice, or language. They visit a speech pathologist for therapy on a regular basis. Further, students with visual and/or hearing impairments (0.22%) are frequently served in regular classes. Hearing impaired students are provided special equipment and materials for mainstreaming. More and more we are seeing blind or deaf students being served in regular education as well. Students with physical and health handicaps (e.g., orthopedically and other health impaired students, representing 0.32%) may have limited abilities that may require specially designed equipment or facilities. For the most part, the limited physical or health condition has little or no effect on academic achievement. (Table 1.1 presents the percentage of handicapped school enrollment by condition for 1985–1986.)

Increasingly, our schools are seeing large numbers of students who come from different cultures. The culturally diverse student brings to the class languages, customs, and other cultural-specific characteristics. Although some of these children need special education services, the vast majority of them do not qualify. More often, these students need special considerations within general education. Another group of exceptional students is that of the gifted and talented. Although gifted and talented students typically do not experience learning problems, they need a specially designed curriculum to help them meet their fullest potential. This text does not specifically address this group.

The specific educational characteristics of each handicapping condition are presented in Chapter 3. How we address the characteristics of these students and in which educational setting are determined by the characteristics themselves and the severity of the handicapping condition. In general, students with less severe handicapping conditions spend more time in the regular classroom than students with more severe handicaps. Students with mild handicaps often can be served within the regular classroom exclusively.

TABLE 1.1
Percentage of Handicapped School Enrollment by Condition (United States, in 1985–1986)

Handicapping Condition	Percentage (1985–1986)
Learning disabled	4.73%
Speech or language impaired	2.86
Mentally retarded	1.68
Emotionally disturbed	0.95
Other health impaired	0.17
Multihandicapped	0.22
Hearing impaired and deaf	0.14
Orthopedically impaired	0.14
Visually impaired	0.07
Deaf and blind	0.01
Total	10.97%

Source: Data from U.S. Department of Education (1987), To assure the free appropriate public education of all handicapped children, *Ninth annual report to Congress on the implementation of the Education of the Handicapped Act* (Washington, DC: U.S. Government Printing Office), p. 5.

Mainstreaming: The Law

In the past, students with handicaps were not afforded the opportunity to participate in regular classroom settings. The mainstream movement, designed to provide quality education to handicapped students in the least restrictive setting, was first formed during the 1950s as an extension of the civil rights movement, which pursued equal opportunities across racial boundaries. The civil rights movement, slowly entering the arena of public education, gave way to numerous court decisions and legislation supporting handicapped persons. In the 1950s and 1960s, momentum began to build.

In 1950, the National Association for Retarded Children (presently known as the National Association for Retarded Citizens [NARC]) was formed. Public schools began to be pressured by parents who were organizing and supporting the rights of their handicapped children. In 1954, the United States Supreme Court decision in *Brown v. Board of Education of Topeka*, ruling against segregation, set a precedent for equality in education for handicapped children. Other suits followed. The 1967 landmark decision of *Hobson v. Hanson* ruled that using a tracking system to place children is discriminatory. In 1972, a federal decision in the *Pennsylvania Association for Retarded Citizens v. Commonwealth of Pennsylvania* case ruled that retarded children have the right to a free and appropriate public education and that parents dissatisfied with their children's placement have the right to a hearing. Shortly thereafter, the federal courts ruled in *Mills v. Board of Education* that handicapped children have the right to an education. Further, testing abuses with non-English-speaking students were attacked (Diana, 1970, 1973), and the *Larry P. Riles* case (1972) ruled against abuses with minority students.

As attention to the individual rights of the handicapped student continued to grow, legislation was passed. Section 504 of the 1973 Rehabilitation Act, Public Law 93–112, disallowed the exclusion of any handicapped person from vocational programs receiving federal funds. In 1974, Section 111a of Public Law 93–516 amended this act, requiring any recipient of federal funds to provide equal employment services for handicapped persons. (Figure 1.2 presents information on Section 504 of the Vocational Rehabilitation Act.)

These first federal civil rights laws protecting the rights of handicapped persons are probably the most important ever written for the handicapped (Berdine & Blackhurst, 1985). Section 504, which prohibits discrimination against the handicapped, applies to preschool, elementary, and secondary schools; institutions of higher education; and state, county, and other local governments. Section 504 states:

> When otherwise qualified handicapped individuals in the United States . . . shall solely by reason of his handicap, be excluded from participation in, be denied the benefits of, or be subjected to discrimination under any program or activity receiving Federal financial assistance. (29 U.S.C. 5 794)

As a result of this legislation, several changes have occurred:

1. Employers are required to provide equal recruitment, employment compensation, job assignments, and fringe benefits for the handicapped.
2. All nonpublic facilities are required to be accessible to the handicapped.
3. School-aged handicapped children are entitled to a free and appropriate public education.
4. Institutions of higher education are prohibited from denying admission to the handicapped on the basis of discrimination in regards to their limitations.
5. Discrimination is forbidden in providing health, welfare, and other social-service programs. (Berdine & Blackhurst, 1985, p. 24)

FIGURE 1.2
Section 504 of the Vocational Rehabilitation Act of 1973

The legislation movement culminated with the passage of Public Law 94–142, The Education for All Handicapped Children Act of 1975. Recognized as a landmark in legislation for education, Public Law 94–142 provides a free, public education with related services for handicapped individuals, ensures the protection of those rights, assists states and localities in providing for the education of all handicapped children, and ensures the effectiveness of these efforts. Figure 1.3 includes more detailed information on Public Law 94–142 and its five major components.

FIGURE 1.3
Public Law 94–142: The Education for All Handicapped Children Act

Important Legislation

Public Law 94–142 provides for the educational rights of the handicapped and explains procedures for the distribution of federal resources in establishing and maintaining special education programs. States must provide evidence that they are meeting the intent of the law in helping handicapped children receive appropriate education. States must comply with specific requirements of the law as follows:

1. State and local educational agencies must insure that all children who are handicapped and in need of special education and related services are identified, located, and evaluated.
2. Parents are provided a number of procedural safeguards that protect the handicapped child's right to a free and appropriate education, including the right to:
   a. review the educational records of their child.
   b. an independent evaluation of the child.
   c. a written notice before the school initiates a placement process.
   d. a hearing before an impartial officer to challenge the placement of their child if they so desire.
3. A comprehensive educational assessment is required, one that goes beyond single IQ tests. It requires the attention of a multidisciplinary team and should include teacher recommendations, data relating to sociocultural background and adaptive behavior, and standard school measures. Also, a reevaluation is required at least every 3 years.
4. A written individualized education plan (IEP) is to be developed and annually updated. The IEP documents the child's current performance, the long- and short-term educational goals, and the specific procedures and services to be provided to the child, plus a means for evaluating the success of the plan.
5. Children must be placed in the least restrictive environment compatible with their handicap. This means that if they can receive an effective program in a regular setting, they should not be placed in a special class; if they can receive their education in a special class, they should not be placed in an institution (Kirk & Gallagher, 1983, pp. 17–18).

Public Law 94–142 establishes the following major components, which have a direct effect on the handicapped child:

- Right to a free and appropriate public education
- Nondiscriminatory evaluation
- Procedural due process
- Individual education program (IEP)
- Least restrictive environment

Right to a Free and Appropriate Public Education

P.L. 94–142 grants all handicapped children the right to a free and appropriate education at public expense. Although this fundamental freedom has always been afforded to the regular student, the handicapped student was frequently denied this right in the past. Handicapped students can now attend their neighborhood schools and receive necessary services to accomodate their regular education. These services may include, for example, an instructionally modified curriculum within the regular classroom or one that requires students to spend portions of the school day in the regular and special class. Special students can no longer be denied the right to attend school, and support must be provided to help them receive an education that equals that of regular students.

Nondiscriminatory Evaluation

In an attempt to eliminate errors in the classification and placement of children who have suspected handicaps, the law requires nondiscriminatory evaluation of students. The fundamental intent of this provision is to eliminate discrimination based on cultural background, race, or handicapping condition (Haring & McCormick, 1986). According to the law, the evaluation process works

> to determine whether a child is handicapped and the nature and extent of the special education and related services that the child needs. The term means procedures used selectively with an individual child and does not include basic tests administered to or procedures used with all children in a school, grade, or class. (34 C.F.R. 330 500)

The law requires that agencies involved with the evaluation of handicapped students ensure the following:

1. Trained personnel must administer validated tests and other evaluation materials, and provide and administer such materials in the child's native language or other mode of communication.
2. Tests and other evaluation materials must include those tailored to assess specific areas of educational need and not merely those designed to provide single, general intelligence quotients.
3. Trained personnel must select and administer tests to reflect accurately the child's aptitude or achievement level without discriminating against the child's handicap.
4. Trained personnel cannot use a single procedure as the sole criterion for determining an appropriate educational program for a child.
5. A multidisciplinary team must assess the child in all areas related to the suspected disability. (Wood, 1984, p. 8)

Procedural Due Process

Handicapped children and their parents are guaranteed procedural safeguards in all areas relating to the identification, evaluation, and educational placement of the handicapped child. These safeguards include:

1. Written parental permission for the evaluation of the handicapped child for special education services.
2. Written parental permission prior to the placement of a handicapped child in a special education program. This permission may be withdrawn at any point.
3. Parents have the right to review and question any records on their child.

(*continued*)

FIGURE 1.3 (*continued*)

4. Parents have the right to an independent evaluation of their child.
5. Confidentiality in all matters relating to the handicapped child must be maintained.
6. Parents, as well as school officials, have the right to a hearing, to present evidence, to have a lawyer present at the hearing, and to call and confront witnesses.
7. Both parents and school authorities have the right to an appeal.

Individualized Education Program (IEP)

The Individualized Education Program (IEP) is a communication tool used by parents and school personnel. The IEP is a major vehicle for resolving differences between the school and the parents, a written commitment of resources to be used, and a management tool that assures special education and related services are provided. It also serves as a compliance/monitoring device for governmental officials and an evaluation device that determines a child's progress toward stated outcomes. The law specifies that certain components be included in the IEP:

1. a statement of the present levels of educational performance of each child
2. a statement of annual goals, including short-term instructional objectives
3. a statement of the specific educational services to be provided to each child and the extent to which such child will be able to participate in regular educational programs
4. the projected date for initiation and anticipated duration of such services and appropriate objective criteria and evaluation procedures for determining . . . whether instructional objectives are being achieved. (Kirk & Gallagher, 1983, p. 19)

Least Restrictive Environment

The law requires that handicapped children be educated with nonhandicapped children when appropriate. The removal of a handicapped child to a special class or separate schooling can be done only when the severity of the child's handicap limits the possibility of an education in a regular class. The concept of the *least restrictive environment* is "based on the premise that many creative alternatives exist to help the regular educator serve children with learning or adjustment problems within the context of a regular class setting" (Wood, 1984, p. 11).

Mainstreaming—A Model for Service

With federal mandates and a national movement in place to provide an appropriate education in the least restrictive environment, models for mainstreaming began to evolve. Today, after many years of trial and error, educators strive to keep the handicapped student in regular classes—moving the once

TABLE 1.2
Handicapped Students Served During the 1984–85 School Year

Environment	Age Group							
	3–5 Years		6–11 Years		12–17 Years		18–21 Years	
	Number	Percentage	Number	Percentage	Number	Percentage	Number	Percentage
Regular classes	107,952	36.8%	726,308	35.4%	300,533	17.0%	26,374	11.4%
Resource room	65,990	22.5	813,481	39.7	847,254	47.9	80,726	34.9
Separate class	68,939	23.5	406,397	19.8	482,939	27.3	74,023	32.0

Source: Data from U.S. Department of Education (1987). To assure the free, appropriate public education of all handicapped children, *Ninth annual report to Congress on the implementation of the Education of the Handicapped Act* (Washington, DC: U.S. Government Printing Office), p. 22.

homogeneous responsibilities of educating the handicapped student to a shared responsibility of both regular and special education.

Special education, designed especially for handicapped children and youth, provides several placement options for the special needs student. Vast numbers of handicapped students are served in the regular class setting, the regular class setting with partial special class placement (the resource class), and in full-time special class placement. Table 1.2 presents by age group the number and percentage of handicapped students served in these educational environments during 1984–1985.

Figure 1.4 presents five placements in which services may be provided within the public schools. It is hoped that students can remain in the regular class setting where modifications can be made, as appropriate, to the curriculum. If students still experience difficulty in the regular class after instructional modifications are made, then other options should be considered. Such options include keeping the special student in the regular class, with the special education teacher serving as a consultant, or placing the special student in the special class for varying periods of time depending on the student's educational needs.

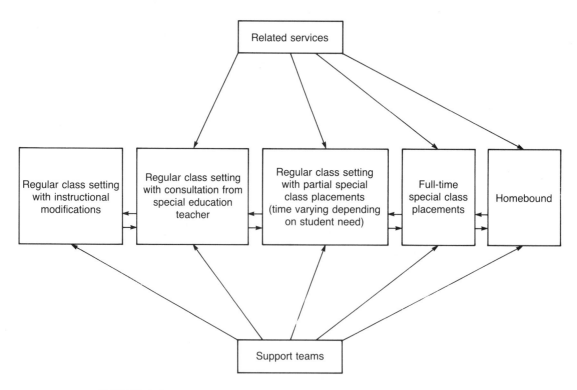

FIGURE 1.4
Model for Educational Options

Receiving full-time education in the special class is reserved for students who do not benefit instructionally in the regular class. Even with full-time special class placement, we strive to mainstream students into other noninstructional school activities. Homebound placement is reserved for students who must remain at home temporarily while recovering from a serious illness or other condition.

Related services are those provided to students that help them obtain an appropriate education. These services may include counseling, speech and language therapy, physical therapy, occupational therapy, special transportation, and other services necessary for the student.

All services and placements are monitored and supported by school-based teams, which provide direction, suggestions, and guidance to the personnel instructing the special needs student. Chapter 2 discusses the team and its roles in more detail.

Benefits of Mainstreaming

The numerous benefits of the mainstreaming effort are realized by special students, regular students, and teachers alike.

Benefits for the Regular Student

Through contact with handicapped students, regular students acquire a realistic view of heterogeneous society. Learning from an early age through adulthood that physical, intellectual, and emotional differences are acceptable produces more mature adults, able to accept the weaknesses of being human. Regular students who associate with their handicapped contemporaries learn what it means to be different and to accept others, as well as themselves, as they are.

Benefits for the Handicapped Student

The benefits of mainstreaming for the handicapped student are many. Special students have the opportunity to remain with their nonhandicapped peers, thus allowing them to participate in normal school activities. The labels often attached to the handicapped student no longer play an important role in the school.

Other benefits of mainstreaming for the handicapped student include academic achievement and social-emotional outcomes. In an extensive review of research on the effects of mainstreaming on the academic achievement and social-emotional outcomes of the mildly handicapped student, Madden and Slavin (1983) concluded that (1) the achievement of the mildly handicapped student is higher in the regular class placement as compared to the special class placement when individualized instruction is used; and (2) on outcomes such as self-concept, classroom behaviors, and school attitudes, the regular classroom placement with support was found to be superior to the full-time special class placement.

Benefits for the Teacher

The educator of today is one of the best-prepared educators of all time. Emphasis is placed at the preservice and in-service levels on developing competencies for working with handicapped children. Many states require that the regular educator take a special course in mainstreaming the handicapped student. Frequently, the special educator is required to take course work in regular education. Course emphasis is on individualizing instruction, which benefits nonhandicapped and handicapped students alike. The methods and materials used with handicapped students frequently may be used with their nonhandicapped peers as well.

Regular and special class teachers must work together to provide appropriate services in the mainstream. The communication process must be clear and the educational responsibilities shared. Both gain benefits from the sharing of ideas and skills. The special educator acquires knowledge of the competencies necessary for regular education. The regular educator learns new skills specifically related to special education. Through sharing, special and regular educators can develop new perspectives on educating children.

Suggestions for Assisting Handicapped
Students in the Regular Classroom

This text assists educators with special needs students in either the regular class setting or the special class setting. Specific suggestions for helping to keep special students in regular classes include the following:

1. Reduce the class size of regular classes to serve the needs of special students.
2. Provide the regular class teacher with an aide to assist in any additional tasks that may be required.
3. Provide in-service training to all teachers in how to adapt and modify instruction to meet specific needs.
4. Provide in-service training to all teachers in how to identify the characteristics of specific handicapping conditions.
5. Help teachers understand how specific characteristics may manifest themselves in the classroom.
6. Provide time during the school week for the regular and special class teachers to work together on specific educational concerns.

7. Develop programs for the handicapped and nonhandicapped student to help facilitate peer relations.

With support most handicapped students can be successful in general education.

Setting the Stage for Mainstreaming

Setting the stage for mainstreaming is important to a successful outcome. Preparing students (both regular and special), principals and administrators, and teachers is a vital component in providing the emotional/social foundation of a mainstreamed environment. It is from this foundation that we can begin to develop our curriculum. Here we examine the foundation stones of attitudes, preparation, and peer relations and suggest ways to set the stage for mainstreaming.

Attitudes

The attitudes of administrators, regular and special class teachers, and regular and special students toward the mainstreaming effort and mainstreamed students are significant in the success or failure of mainstreaming. When administrators and teachers are supportive of and prepared for mainstreaming, and when regular and special students have received adequate preparation, there is a greater chance that a successful experience will result.

School Principals and Administrators. In the past, school principals and administrators as a group have tended to be somewhat skeptical about mainstreaming (Payne & Murray, 1974). However, the results of recent studies indicate that their attitudes toward mainstreaming are becoming more positive (Carlberg & Kavale, 1980; Center, Ward, Parmenter, & Nash, 1985; Pieterse & Center, 1984).

Among the individual traits of principals and administrators that seem to affect their attitudes toward mainstreaming are (1) number of years in the position; (2) educational degree or qualifications; and (3) degree of administrative or teaching experience with special classes. Principals and administrators who have served more than 7 years in these positions and who have a special class at their schools or have been actively involved with a special class tend to be the most resistant to mainstreaming (Center et al., 1985). These principals and administrators feel that special classes best serve the needs of special students in that only special education teachers possess the required expertise to provide adequate support services. Also, they believe that regular teachers lack

Attitudes are as expressive as words.

the knowledge and ability to mainstream special students successfully and that the current level of resource support for mainstreaming is inadequate.

However, principals and administrators who have had some formal training in special education are less resistant to mainstreaming efforts. Their more positive attitudes toward mainstreaming also seem to be related to having established and maintained successful mainstreamed programs (Carlberg & Kavale, 1980; Center & Ward, 1984; Johnson & Johnson, 1981; Madden & Slavin, 1983). Awareness of the variables critical to successful mainstreaming and effective use of available formal and informal resources reflect the special education expertise of these principals and administrators.

The attitudes and perceptions of principals and administrators regarding mainstreaming affect the attitudes of teachers and students; that is, when teachers sense a positive attitude, they feel they can depend on administrative support to ensure success of the program. Students, in turn, benefit from teachers who not only display a positive attitude but who also strive to provide an appropriate educational setting. Deno (1973) maintains that the attitudes of teachers and administrators are more important to successful mainstreaming than are physical facilities and organizational structure within the school.

Regular Teachers. Research indicates that teachers' attitudes about mainstreaming are becoming more positive. Initially, teachers were reserved about mainstreaming, mainly concerned that the integration of special children into regular classrooms would be too time-consuming and that they lacked adequate preservice training to work with special students (Flynn, Gack, & Sundean, 1978; Johnson & Cartwright, 1979; Middleton, Morsink, & Cohen, 1979). They also worried about such matters as increased paperwork, accountability, and possible conflict with special education teachers (Ryor, 1978), and they wanted to be assured that if special students were placed inappropriately there would be an appeal procedure to correct the errors (Morsink, 1984). Studies have also revealed that, in general, regular classroom teachers tend to underestimate the abilities of special children (Final, 1967; MacMillan, Meyers, & Yoshida, 1978), be less tolerant of maladaptive classroom behaviors than are special education teachers (Doris & Brown, 1980), and believe special education class placement to be more appropriate for special children (Barngrover, 1975).

The results of more recent studies seem to indicate that elementary schoolteachers' attitudes toward mainstreaming are becoming more positive (Marston & Leslie, 1983; Reynolds, Martin-Reynolds, & Mark, 1982; Schmelkin, 1981). However, positive attitude changes among secondary schoolteachers toward mainstreaming appear to be developing at a slower rate. Reports by Post and Roy (1985), Powers (1979), and Young and Shepherd (1983) indicate, respectively, that secondary regular teachers (1) believe that special students should be taught in special classes, (2) are subject-matter rather than learner-centered oriented and less willing to use consultancies and support services, and (3) perceive special students' performance in social, emotional-psychological, and academic areas as weak.

It has been documented repeatedly that teachers' attitudes toward students are a major force in determining the nature of the interaction between teachers and students, and in turn, affect students' achievement (Cazden, 1976; MacMillan, Jones, & Meyers, 1976; Schulz & Turnbull, 1984). Not only do teachers' attitudes set the tone for the student-teacher relationship but they also influence the attitudes of regular students toward special students. Thus, because teacher attitude is so crucial to the success of mainstreaming, it should be the first area dealt with as preparations are made to place special students in regular classrooms. As teachers explore their attitudes about teaching special students, they are likely to discover that their concerns stem from fear of the unknown.

Teachers who feel that they lack knowledge about handicapping conditions and the competencies required to teach special students view these unknowns with a great deal of anxiety.

Special Education Support Personnel.   Although attitudes of special education support personnel toward mainstreaming are usually positive, they do have some concerns about mainstreaming. Among their concerns are (1) clarifying their role changes as a result of mainstreaming, (2) interacting and communicating effectively with the regular teacher, (3) preparing the special student for the transition process, (4) the ability of regular teachers to work with special students, (5) the pressure to be an expert about all types and degrees of handicapping conditions, and (6) having to serve in an itinerant capacity rather than being school-based. Some of these concerns can be alleviated through appropriate preparation of all personnel and students who will be involved in a mainstreamed program.

Regular Students.   Research studies of regular students' attitudes toward special students, at both the elementary and secondary school levels, have reported conflicting evidence (Asher & Taylor, 1981; Brown, 1982; Drabman & Patterson, 1981; Goodman, Gottlieb, & Harrison, 1972; IRUC Briefings, 1977; Prillaman, 1981; Reese-Dukes & Stokes, 1978; Siperstein, Bopp, & Bak, 1978; Yaffe, 1979). However, the bulk of evidence indicates that regular students tend to reject special students. Historical practices, lack of knowledge about the nature of handicapping conditions, and the attitudes and behaviors of school personnel toward exceptionalities have been identified as factors that contribute to regular students' rejection of special students.

Historical practices placed special and "problem" students in self-contained special classrooms, and they were taught by special education teachers. This kind of isolation and special treatment helped to create the myth that special students were too different to be included in the mainstream educational program. Lack of knowledge about the nature of handicapping conditions has been perpetuated through isolation of special students. The unknown has created fear, incorrect expectations, hostility, prejudice, and ridicule toward students with exceptionalities and has been a major impediment to the implementation of successful mainstreaming programs in many schools. Negative attitudes and behaviors displayed by school personnel toward special students have adversely influenced regular students' reactions to mainstreamed students (Clark, 1980; Garrett & Crump, 1980; MacMillan, Jones, & Meyers, 1976). Regular students tend to model behaviors of school personnel toward special students.

Deviant social behaviors, sometimes displayed by special students, understandably have a negative affect on the attitudes of regular students. Research by Van Bourgondien (1987) indicates that the attitudes of nonhandicapped females toward handicapped females are influenced more by deviant social behaviors than by a label such as *mentally retarded*. However, when nonhandicapped females were paired in peer-tutoring situations with handicapped females, they did not react negatively to a label or to deviant behaviors.

Studies and reports of strategies used to improve regular students' attitudes toward special students indicate that positive attitude changes result from increased knowledge about handicapping conditions and gradual, structured interaction experiences with special students (Clore & Jeffrey, 1972; Donaldson & Martinson, 1977; Fiedler & Simpson, 1987; Guralnick, 1976; Simpson, 1980; Van Bourgondien, 1987). Also, teachers' attitudes toward special students seem to be a major factor in producing positive attitudes among regular students.

Special Students. The focus of research studies has been how mainstreaming affects special students' self-esteem and academic skills rather than on the total process. Although special students' self-esteem and academic skills are important, knowledge about their attitudes toward regular students as well as the other aspects of the mainstreaming process is necessary to plan and implement successful, comprehensive mainstreamed programs.

Most special students have a negative self-image, which is the result of rejection by the "normal" population and their feelings that a handicap makes them unreliable—a sense of being unable to depend on themselves (Heron & Harris, 1982). Although a difficult task, teachers and students can facilitate the development of more positive self-concepts among special students by accepting them as people and by helping them to achieve success in both academic and social contexts. As an outgrowth of a negative self-image, most special students have mixed feelings about being mainstreamed. These feelings are the result of conflict between the need for security (i.e., remaining with the known) and the need for increased independence (i.e., exploring and succeeding in the unknown).

The attitudes of both regular and special students play a significant role in successful mainstreaming. Students in both groups may have negative, or unrealistic, views about themselves as well as about their classmates; poor self-esteem, insecurity, and lack of knowledge about each other are factors that interfere with regular and special students' abilities to interact successfully. Most research studies addressing the social aspects of regular and special student integration have focused on improving the attitudes of regular students toward special students. Studies are needed that examine the attitudes of both regular and special students toward each other as well as toward themselves. School programs that emphasize the similar needs and desires of handicapped and nonhandicapped students and that are designed to improve the self-esteem and interaction skills of all students are likely to experience success in their mainstreaming efforts.

Preparation

Ideas for helping special and regular students, school administrators, regular teachers, and special support personnel prepare for the implementation of a mainstreamed program are presented here. Although the emotional and social preparation of each group is discussed separately, often the suggested preparatory experiences should involve all groups simultaneously.

School Principals and Administrators.   The principal or administrator is the key figure in the successful implementation of any new program in a school. Schools that display successful mainstream programs have involved the principal or administrator in the groundwork, implementation, and supervision of the program (Deno, 1973; Mandell & Strain, 1978). The first step in creating and maintaining a positive attitude is to *devise a preparatory plan* to help reduce potential problems in management and teaching arrangements. Such a plan should include

- Consultation with other principals and administrators who have implemented successful mainstreamed programs.
- Visits to mainstreamed classrooms that have been designated successful.
- Interaction experiences with handicapped people.
- Participation in special education workshops for administrators.
- Consultation with experts in the field of mainstreaming and/or course work in special education.
- Arrangements for in-service training activities for all personnel who will be involved in mainstreaming.
- Consultation with parents of mainstreamed students.
- Identification of available formal and informal support services.
- Development of a procedure that will provide ongoing support and supervision of the mainstreamed program once it is in place.
- Development of a procedure that supports members of the professional team, thereby reinforcing the team approach to mainstreaming.

School administrators responsible for designing and implementing a mainstreamed program need to recognize that regular teachers may be insecure and uncertain about teaching special students, to acknowledge the source of teachers' anxieties (i.e., fear of the unknown), and to develop strategies to help teachers feel more confident about functioning in their newly established roles. By participating in in-service training activities with teachers, principals and administrators demonstrate their interest in making the mainstreamed program successful.

Regular Teachers.   Donaldson (1980), in studying research on the results of attitude change related to handicapped people, has concluded that the negative attitudes of regular teachers and students can be made more positive by providing interaction experiences with handicapped people supplemented by structured instructional activities in which accurate information is presented and discussed. Thus, the preparation of regular teachers for teaching special students should include in-service training and the experiences of (1) getting to know handicapped people; (2) obtaining knowledge about specific handicapping conditions and special student capabilities; (3) identifying the roles of professional team members and planning for the use of available resources; and (4) adapting materials and instructional methodologies to the needs of special students.

Getting to know handicapped people as *people* enables teachers to overcome many of their initial fears. As teachers discover the likes and dislikes, strengths and weaknesses, hobbies, interests, and future plans of handicapped students, they come to view them as individuals with needs and interests similar to their own. Leyser and Lessen (1985) have assessed the effectiveness of two training models on the attitudes of preservice regular education teachers toward mainstreaming. They compared three groups: (1) preservice teachers who received both information on and field experience with special students; (2) preservice teachers who rec ived only information about handicapping conditions and mainstreaming; and (3) a control group of preservice teachers who were enrolled in a course on human development and learning. Following treatment, the two experimental groups, in comparison with the control group, showed significant positive attitude changes toward mainstreaming but were not significantly different from each other, even though one of the groups also had participated in a field experience. The results of the study indicate the importance of providing teachers at the preservice and in-service levels with information and experience related to special students prior to the implementation of a mainstreamed program.

Obtaining knowledge about specific handicapping conditions and special student capabilities is helpful to teachers as they prepare to teach special students. Since the focus of this book is on mainstreaming the mildly handicapped, each of the three handicapping conditions that compose the mildly handicapped category—the educable mentally retarded (EMR), the emotionally disturbed (ED), sometimes referred to as behavior disorders (BD), and the learning disabled (LD)—is addressed in Chapter 3. Teachers preparing to teach or who are teaching special students need to learn as much as possible about these specific handicapping conditions as well as about the levels of special student capability associated with them (also discussed in Chapter 3). However, the information presented in Chapter 3 concerning special student capabilities is intended to serve as general guidelines for regular teachers and should *not* be interpreted as representative of *all* students' capabilities. Variations in special student capabilities do occur and, as with regular students, positive teacher expectations can influence their achievement.

Identifying the roles of professional team members and planning for the use of available resources are helpful to regular teachers as they work with special students. The resource teacher has many roles to fill—diagnostician, remedial teacher, materials specialist, and advocate and administrator of various services that relate to mainstreaming. Teachers hired as resource teachers may or may not have training in special education, but they should be able to demonstrate through previous teaching assignments that they possess the skills needed to work effectively with special students. (Chapter 2 describes the roles of the professional team members in more detail.) Other human resources that may be available to the regular teacher include (1) itinerant teachers, who travel from one school to another to work with individual students; (2) special education consultants; (3) the principal, who can be called on to arrange in-service training, locate appropriate instructional resources, establish a volunteer program to help with individualization, and work toward reduction of the student-teacher ratio in mainstreamed classrooms; (4) school counselors and psychologists; (5) librarians, who can identify textbooks and other supplementary materials appropriate to student achievement levels and interests; (6) therapists in areas such as speech, physical development, occupational development, dramatics, art, and music; (7) paraprofessionals, who function as teacher aides to help individualize instruction; (9) special and regular students, who can provide teachers with information about their instructional needs as well as the classroom climate; (10) parents of special students, who can share their ideas about motivational strategies and possible classroom adaptations and who may be able to serve as volunteers in the classroom; and (11) community volunteers.

Teachers need to keep their principals informed about their mainstreaming needs so that appropriate resources can be identified and made available. Prior to mainstreaming, teachers in collaboration with their principals should devise a plan for using all available support services and resources so that management of the resources does not become burdensome.

The task of *adapting materials and instructional methodologies to the needs of special students* adds to regular teachers' anxieties when they lack training and experience in such procedures. Fear and anxiety related to the instructional process can be alleviated by in-service training designed to provide quality hands-on activities in adapting materials and instructional techniques as well as interactional experiences with special students.

In-service training in adapting materials and instructional methodologies for use with special students may occur in small-group sessions or in one-to-one consultant-teacher sessions. Although small-group sessions are more cost efficient, one-to-one consultant-teacher training sessions can produce greater initial and long-term effects. Langone, Koorland, and Oseroff (1987) investigated the effects of one-to-one consultant-teacher in-service instruction on the behaviors of three classroom teachers of moderately and severely mentally handicapped students. The major goal of the in-service training was to improve the quality of the teachers' use of (1) verbal instruction, (2) demonstration (modeling), (3) physical prompting, (4) physical guidance, and (5) consequences of verbal or tangible stimulus presented immediately on completion of a student's response. The magnitude of change in the correct use of the teacher behaviors from pre- to posttreatment was significant for all behaviors except physical guidance (i.e., manually assisting a student through an entire task while repeating the instructions). The investigators pointed out that the use of verbal instructions, modeling, physical prompts, physical guidance, and consequences of stimuli are as appropriate for teaching regular students as they are for teaching special students.

The results of another type of one-to-one in-service instruction, referred to as the *consultation-collaboration model,* have been reported by Cochrane and Ballard (1986). During the study, Cochrane worked with the teacher in a consultant-collaborator role to establish a remedial reading program for five special needs children placed in the teacher's regular class. Cochrane assisted the teacher in the collection of baseline data and the development of intervention strategies (i.e., material adaptations and instructional techniques). Not only did the teacher benefit from the experience but the five children "showed a mean gain of 6.4 reading recovery levels" after 22 weeks of intervention (Cochrane & Ballard, 1986, p. 100).

Although one-to-one in-service training is a promising alternative to traditional in-service models, it is not as cost effective, requires extensive interaction between consultant and teacher prior to implementation of learned skills, and may require frequent classroom visits by the consultant during intervention. However, it may be possible to train a small cadre of teachers using one-to-one in-service instruction, who can in turn train other teachers. The effectiveness of this approach needs further study. (Some specific instructional methodologies and techniques are described later in the chapter, and suggestions for adapting materials by academic area are described in Chapters 6–9.)

Special Support Personnel.   A national survey has indicated that members of special support teams receive little, if any, preservice interdisciplinary team training (Courtnage & Smith-Davis, 1987). Therefore, special support personnel and regular teachers of special students need to be brought together to systematically study and practice teamwork and the skills of collaboration. The concerns of special support personnel about their changing roles and responsibilities must be communicated to persons responsible for implementing the mainstreamed program, so that appropriate in-service activities can be planned. (Chapter 2 contains more information about the professional team.)

Regular Students.   Positive social integration of regular and special students in mainstreamed classrooms does not occur spontaneously. Schools that have engaged in advanced planning and preparation for mainstreaming have been successful in reducing rejection and alienation of special students and in increasing acceptance and knowledge of special students among regular students and teachers. Research concerning the attitudes of regular students toward special students suggests that 4-year-old children are aware of handicaps, younger students are less negative than older students, and contact is not sufficient by itself to bring about attitude changes (Barclay & Kehle, 1979; Cook & Wollersheim, 1978; Keogh, 1976; Wylie, 1976).

Suggestions for preparing regular students for mainstreaming, at both the elementary and secondary school levels, abound in the literature. Designed to increase regular students' knowledge and information about handicapping conditions, most suggestions fall into one of the following categories: (1) understanding the nature of handicapping conditions, (2) instructional units, (3) simulation activities, or (4) structured interaction strategies.

Understanding the nature of handicapping conditions can be the focus of a series of lessons. Popp (1983) has designed lessons to help elementary students understand disabilities. Six of his lesson titles are Individual Differences; Wheelchairs and People in Wheelchairs; Devices that Help People Walk and People Who Use These Devices; Amputation, Artificial Limbs, and Amputees; Visual Impairments and People Who Are Visually Impaired; and Hearing Impairments and People Who are Hearing Impaired. Popp provides suggestions for modifying and expanding the lessons to make them appropriate for use with older students.

Fiedler and Simpson (1987) have compared the effectiveness of two curricular approaches for modifying nonhandicapped high school students' attitudes toward their handicapped peers. The curriculum of one approach is structured around the categories of disability whereas the other focuses on generic concepts such as individual differences, effects of labels, and disability versus handicap. After 10 weeks of instruction, the results of a pencil-paper attitudinal measure revealed that both curricula positively modified students' attitudes but that students exposed to the categories of disability curriculum demonstrated significantly greater attitudinal changes.

Classroom discussions also can be used to help regular students gain knowledge about the nature of handicapping conditions. Baker, Dixon, Englebert, Kahn, Siegel, and Wood (1982) have emphasized that discussions can enable regular students to identify the similarities and differences between themselves and special students. With appropriate teacher guidance, discussions centered on the feelings and activities of students (e.g., their favorite after-school activities and television programs, their fears, their opinions on issues related to current events, and so on) can emphasize the ways in which regular and special students are similar yet unique.

Another way to help students understand handicapping conditions is through class visits by handicapped adults to discuss the nature of their handicaps and the feelings associated with them. This approach allows students to receive first-hand information about the day-to-day reality of being handicapped and the kinds of coping and adaptation skills used by handicapped persons for survival. Handicapped adults can also discuss their interests, talents, and career responsibilities.

Instructional units about handicapping conditions can be developed and used effectively in classrooms and expanded to include information relevant to specific academic areas. They also can be enhanced through the use of learning-center materials, books, films, and videotapes about handicapped people. For example, a learning-center activity might include newspaper articles about handicapped individuals in the workforce, comprehension questions that students answer after reading the articles, a list of related vocabulary terms that students can define in their own words, and blank paper on which students can write short essays describing their reactions to the articles or list questions evoked by the articles. Teachers should choose instructional materials carefully to avoid those with stereotypic perspectives.

Simulation activities, designed so that learners experience a handicap through the use of special equipment and specific instructions, can be effective in increasing regular students' understanding of special students. These activities must be planned carefully. Simulations should not be used as introductory activities; rather, they can be applied successfully after students are instructed in the use of coping skills as responses to various handicapping conditions. Wright (1979) has cautioned that simulations can produce negative emotions such as fear, frustration, and helplessness when teachers have not provided prior instruction in the use of successful coping responses. When used carefully, simulation experiences can provide greater insight into the nature of handicaps as well as better understanding of the possibilities for adaptation.

Structured interaction strategies provide opportunities for regular students to work or interact socially with special students. Anderson and Milliren (1983), in *Structured Experiences for Integration of Handicapped Children,* describe over one hundred activities specifically designed to meet the challenges of mainstreaming. Each chapter of the book introduces an element important in the operation of a mainstreamed classroom and supports the theme with activities, exercises, and experiences that involve group participants. Reproducible diagrams and worksheets also accompany some of the activities. The ideas have been field tested in workshops and classes and can be used with children as well as adults. Peer tutoring is an instructional method that allows regular students to tutor special students in the various curriculum areas. It also elicits structured interaction between regular and special students, through which friendships can develop.

Special Students. Although numerous strategies have been reported for preparing regular students to accept special students into the mainstreamed setting, few strategies have been reported for preparing special students to enter regular classrooms. According to Slade (1984), teachers can better prepare learning disabled students for the transition from the special to the regular classroom by:

1. Identifying the new situations or environments to which the students will be exposed (cafeteria, gym, and so forth).
2. Listing the activities that will be required of the students in each of the new environments (e.g., unlocking lockers, changing into gym clothing, and so on).
3. Specifying the skills that students will need to function properly (e.g., memorizing a lock combination).
4. Identifying those skills the child has already mastered.

Further, Slade suggests activities to help learning disabled students develop the skills needed to cope with changes in their physical surroundings, organizational problems, time-management problems, interpersonal relationships, personality differences, and rule changes.

Special students also should receive specific training in the social skills needed to function successfully in mainstreamed classrooms. Barclay and Kehle (1979) found that

> Mainstreaming of EMR children without a very careful assessment of their social skill support system and aptitude for making friends results in generally adverse social-affective consequences particularly if the transition is abrupt and without provision for considerable social support and attention from teachers. (p. 91)

Recent studies have emphasized the importance of teaching general social skills to special students before placing them in the mainstreamed classroom (Hall & Richmond, 1985; Richmond & Blagg, 1985; Van Bourgondien, 1987). Special students, especially learning disabled students, also may benefit from training in nonverbal communication. A deficit ability to accurately perceive and respond to nonverbal cues plays "a significant role in the social interactions of these children, influencing how they are perceived by both peers and significant adults and how they approach others in social situations" (Hall & Richmond, 1985, p. 90).

Dardig (1981) has described several suggestions for making the mainstream a more beneficial educational setting for the handicapped student, including making students more aware of the rules and routines of the regular classroom, which may be quite different than those of the special class. Handicapped students should learn how to follow any oral and written directions different than those they are accustomed to following. Also, the special class teacher must be aware of the length of time that the handicapped student will be required to stay on-task and in-seat in the mainstreamed class and to train the student accordingly. The student's desire to participate in the regular classroom should be encouraged through praise and other social reinforcers as well as initial placements of short duration. Further, regular class teachers can encourage mainstreamed students to make positive responses by, for instance, initially asking them questions they can answer. Regular class teachers also can teach handicapped students how to react to teasing, if necessary, by describing inappropriate behaviors and how to ignore them. Finally, mainstreamed students must have adequate prerequisite skills to function in the regular classroom.

Facilitating the Development of Peer Relationships

Special students' placement in regular classrooms does not guarantee their social acceptance. A goal of mainstreaming is to influence special students' self-concepts positively, by providing more opportunities for social learning than can special classes. To facilitate the development of peer relationships students need to view the teacher as a model of acceptance. The regular teacher can serve as a model and facilitate peer relationships by teaching social skills, initiating peer interaction, and evaluating the classroom climate on a regular basis.

Modeling Acceptance. Teachers exert a powerful and influential force on students' lives. They serve as models for a wide range of social behaviors and constantly communicate important attitudinal messages to students about individual differences. Teachers' likes and dislikes are readily apparent to students and can inadvertently serve as models for students. Establishment of a warm and accepting classroom atmosphere is the first of ten steps identified by Baker et al. (1982) in ensuring successful mainstreaming (see Figure 1.5). In addition

Successful teachers are honest, realistic, and open with handicapped students about learning difficulties, but at the same time, they present a friendly, positive attitude. Essentially they are saying to these students, "I know you can learn and I'm glad you're in my class." The following are subtle ways to build this kind of atmosphere.

1. Collect personal information on a card about each child. For example, ask each of them to write or tell you about his or her greatest accomplishment or a hobby he or she enjoys. This gives you an entry into the child's life. Use this information to start quick, verbal exchanges from time to time.
2. Use body language to show warmth and acceptance, such as extending palms of hands outward when greeting students, standing in close proximity, lecturing in front of the desk rather than being behind it, and making eye contact during a discussion.
3. Let the students get to know you as a person, not just as a teacher.
4. Try to spend time every day with each student. A minute of individual attention from you can make a child's day.
5. Give handicapped students honest praise. Many have suffered much failure in school. They need to know that they are capable of success.
6. And don't be afraid to tell students you love them. This may be the only time some will ever hear those words.
7. Take the pressure of grades off the students by marking them according to their own level, not the class level.
8. When a child is asked a question, give him or her at least five seconds to answer. The average time a teacher waits is .9 seconds, which is much too short.

FIGURE 1.5

Suggestions for Establishing a Warm and Accepting Classroom Atmosphere (*Source:* T. Baker, N. P. Dixon, B. Englebert, M. Kahn, B. L. Siegel, & J. W. Wood [1982]. "Mainstreaming Minimanual: Ten Steps to Success," *Instructor, 91,* 63–66. Reprinted by permission of *Instructor,* March 1982. Copyright © 1982 by The Instructor Publications Inc.)

to behaviors of acceptance modeled by the regular teacher, systematic use of modeling tactics such as role playing and behavior rehearsing can be used (see Figure 1.6). It is important for teachers to reward and reinforce positive social interaction among all students but especially between special and regular students. Praise, attention, use of privileges, tokens, and recognition can be used for reinforcement.

Teaching Social Skills. Although special students should have received some instruction in interpersonal skills before placement in a mainstreamed program, it is unlikely that they acquired all of the skills needed to interact positively

Role Playing

Technically, role playing differs from behavior rehearsing in one major respect. In *role playing,* students assume roles that are not necessarily similar to their own. Through acting, students are helped to anticipate social situations and are encouraged to use strategies for coping with those circumstances.

Behavior Rehearsing

Behavior rehearsing provides students with opportunities to learn and practice responses that they need to use immediately. When teaching appropriate behavior through social modeling, teachers should follow these steps:

1. Set up the act to be observed.
2. Give students instructions to observe specific behaviors. Inform them of which behaviors they are to observe.
3. When possible, have students record or tally responses.
4. Enact the behavior.
5. Discuss the enactment, having students report their observations.
6. Repeat these procedures when necessary.

  With older students it is usually necessary to move them into such activities gradually. Initially, it may be necessary to begin with pantomime, where students simply act out a word or situation without speaking. Other students try to determine what the pantomimist is trying to communicate. After a few sessions of this game, teachers gradually move toward verbalizations and into rehearsing. Steps for shaping reluctant students toward social modeling are:

1. Devote a few minutes to pantomime relating to the subject matter under study. Do this two or three consecutive days at the same time each day.
2. Using the same slot, indicate that in pantomiming students may now give verbal clues, such as the first letter that a word begins with, initials of a person's name, and a verbal description of the act that is being performed.
3. Gradually change the subject matter. In step 1, select topics that relate to academic subjects. Then in each successive session, select a topic that is more related to the personal interests of students until topics are central to students' social behavior.

FIGURE 1.6

Modeling Tactics (Source: From *Teaching Mainstreamed Students, 2nd Edition* by Thomas M. Stephens, A. Edward Blackhurst and Larry A. Magliocca. New York: Pergamon Press, 1988, pp. 192–193. Adapted with permission.)

with their peers. Some of the social skills that may require direct teaching include appropriate ways of

  Giving and receiving compliments.

  Communicating a desire to be included in a group's activities.

Saying "no" when appropriate.

Expressing disagreement with an individual or group.

Giving and receiving affection.

Displaying anger and disappointment.

Special students may not be sensitive to nonverbal cues in social situations, so direct teaching of nonverbal communication skills may be required. Decoding of nonverbal communication involves skills in sensitivity, attention, comprehension, and responsiveness, all of which can be learned through direct teaching (Hall & Richmond, 1985).

Initiating Peer Interaction.   Since interaction among special and regular students usually does not occur spontaneously in mainstreamed classrooms, structured interactions should be planned and implemented. Schulz and Turnbull (1984) have described strategies to increase communication, peer tutoring, cooperative instruction, and friendship skills.

Planned activities to increase student communication are usually informal, teacher-created activities that emphasize communication skills. During regularly scheduled activities students share their experiences, feelings, and ideas. Consider the following example of a teacher-made activity designed to encourage student interaction:

> Sometimes we get a ball of yarn and throw it from one person to another. The person who catches the yarn has to say something good about the person who threw it. Another time we used the yarn, the person catching it had to say something nice about themselves. I have seen some really good results in class morale and closeness. (Schulz & Turnbull, 1984, p. 382)

Many of the activities and experiences described in *Structured Experiences for Integration of Handicapped Children* (Anderson & Millirin, 1983) are designed to increase communication between regular and special students. Although *peer tutoring* and *cooperative instruction* can be used to structure interaction between regular and special students, both strategies are designed primarily as instructional procedures.

Teaching friendship skills involves helping students acquire a range of behaviors, such as "sharing, cooperation, communication, verbal complimenting, nonaggressiveness, and participation" (Schulz & Turnbull, 1984, p. 384). Most special students have had limited opportunities to develop these skills. The skills can be developed naturally in regular classrooms through behavior-management techniques, such as establishing clear behavioral standards, reinforcing desirable behaviors and responses, identifying the expectations of individuals and groups, and creating work assignments appropriate to learners' capabilities.

Evaluating the Classroom Climate.   Since the social-emotional climate of the classroom is crucial to the social, psychological, and cognitive development of students, teachers need to evaluate it periodically. Information about the social climate can be collected informally as well as formally. Regular and special education teachers can construct data collection checklists for use with individual students and the class as a group. Sociometric measures, which reveal the attitudes of group members toward one another, can also be used to assess students' social interaction patterns.

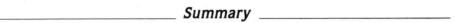

Summary

Mainstreaming, designed to provide instruction for handicapped children in a setting as close to that of their normal peers as possible, is a reality of today's educational system. The responsibility of providing an appropriate education for handicapped students within regular education is shared by both special and regular educators. As students and teachers work together, learn from each other, and share resources, the educational experiences of handicapped students will help them lead normal lives.

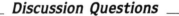

Discussion Questions

1. In what ways does the federal government support the mainstreaming effort?
2. Explain how attitudes can have an impact on mainstreaming and what can be done to facilitate positive attitudes.
3. Discuss ways in which the student and teacher can prepare for mainstreaming.

Chapter 2

The Multidisciplinary Team

ALICE V. WATKINS
California State University,
Los Angeles

JUDY W. WOOD

Chapter Objectives

After reading Chapter 2 the student will
be able to

- Analyze the role, responsibility, and
  functions of consulting professional
  teams
- Outline the process for using
  consulting professional teams in their
  local schools
- Differentiate between the function of
  the IEP team and the consulting
  mainstream team

T he establishment of a multidisciplinary team to determine the identification, eligibility, and placement of a special student was established as a mandate of Public Law 94–142. *Teaming*, defined as assisting with planning instructional interventions for special pupils in mainstreamed settings, has received new attention and considerable support during recent years. However, the use of multidisciplinary teams has been utilized by other professions for numerous years. It has been suggested that the "team" approach provides greater accuracy in the decision-making process by allowing different values and points of views to converge (Pfeiffer, 1980). This chapter looks at the purpose of the team, its members and roles, and the referral-to-placement process.

Multidisciplinary teams have been referred to by numerous names, including child-study teams, mainstreaming teams, pupil-assessment teams, problem-solving teams, teacher-assistance teams, and eligibility teams. For the purpose of clarity, this text uses the term *multidisciplinary team* to refer to the team responsible for deciding the educational future of the special student. Membership on the multidisciplinary team may vary based on the specific handicapping condition of the student. However, those persons who have expertise in assessing the student and who have a personal and educational interest in the student serve as the members of the multidisciplinary team. Regardless of its title, the team can be utilized to assist the mainstream teacher with the task of organizing appropriate instruction for the child who has educational needs.

The primary purposes of the multidisciplinary team are (1) to assist in developing a plan of action that will help meet the educational goals of students without placing them in special education and (2) to plan and evaluate the educational experience for those students who have been identified as in need of special education services. That is, it is as important to keep students in regular classes, when possible, as it is to provide an appropriate special education placement. The team meets these goals by:

1. Receiving and evaluating initial referrals of students who are experiencing difficulty in the regular class or who are in need of placements within special education on entering the educational system.
2. Developing intervention strategies that may be used in the regular class when it is believed the student will benefit most from regular education with provided modifications.
3. Initiating the assessment process for students who are suspected to have a handicapping condition.
4. Evaluating the assessment data and deciding on the appropriate special education placement for the student.
5. Developing the individualized educational program (IEP) for the student.
6. Acting as a support system for the educators who serve the special students.

The exact purposes of the multidisciplinary team may vary from state to state. Some teams may only work with the referral during the prereferral stage (i.e., the stage prior to the formal assessment). During this stage, the team assists the teacher in developing, implementing, and evaluating strategies for keeping the student in the regular classroom. When it is agreed that these intervention strategies do not work, the student is referred to another team for a formal assessment. In some states, the teams for prereferral (informal assessment) and referral (formal assessment) are the same. In other states, the team's composition may change. Some teams work as a unit in the assessment process and also develop the IEP. The educators on the team, in turn, implement the plan. In some areas, the team is responsible for the assessment process and a separate team develops the IEP. Regardless of the specific organization of the team, a unit is formed whose purpose is to plan educationally for special students and students in need of educational support.

Roles of Multidisciplinary Team Members

Membership on a multidisciplinary team requires shared responsibility and open communication. Each member serves as a vital component in the process of seeking appropriate education by way of planning for students who are experiencing difficulty in school. With these roles come unique responsibilities for

The multidisciplinary team members work together to ensure appropriate placement and educational services.

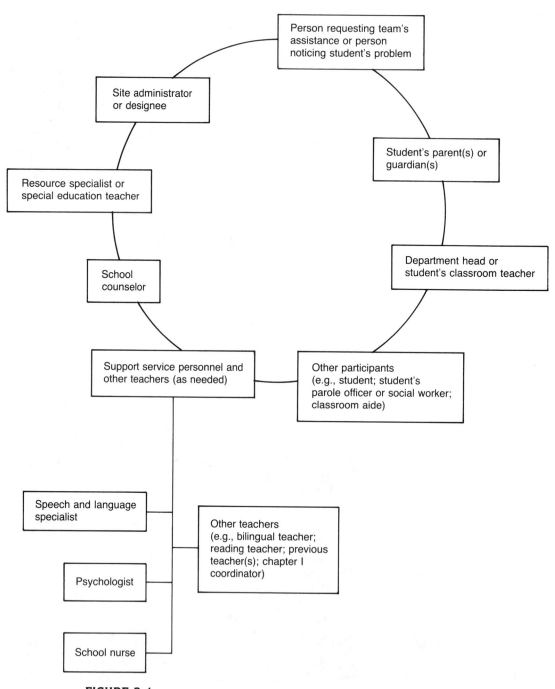

FIGURE 2.1
Multidisciplinary Team Members

36

implementation. The team membership may vary. However, regular and special education are represented by teachers, administrators, and appropriate specialists serving selected roles. Parents and students may serve on the team as well, providing valuable information that can add to the educational plan for the student. For culturally diverse pupils, bilingual specialists and chapter I resource teachers may also provide valuable input. Given the diversity of learning problems, range of ability levels, and age range of the handicapped population nationwide, it is not possible to describe an ideal, "generic" professional team with clearly delineated membership. Instead, teams should be school-based with some freedom to adjust membership in response to the perceived needs of referred pupils. There must be some continuity of membership to ensure that the team develops credibility among both professional colleagues and parents. Team membership will vary as individual experts are needed to address child-specific needs. Figure 2.1 outlines the prospective members of the multidisciplinary team.

Administrators

The site administrator, principal, or assistant principal is an essential member of the team. It is often necessary, when reviewing a handicapped pupil, to include an additional district or regional level special education administrator to ensure that due-process procedures are followed. Membership of the school site administrator, however, is critical.

The site administrator must also ensure that there are adequate resources available to support the team and its recommendations. In order for regular class teachers to participate actively on teams, adequate time must be allotted for such activities as consultation with specialists, attendance at team meetings, and preparation of modified instructional materials. Further, the modification of instruction may require additional curriculum resources and fiscal support. Site-based administrators can arrange flexible schedules, provide substitutes for classroom personnel, and provide leadership for the team.

Of extreme importance is the attitude of the school administrator. As the instructional leader of the school, the principal, or designee, sets educational standards as well as the emotional climate. Without the support of the school principal's positive attitude, mainstreaming becomes a difficult, if not impossible, task.

The roles and responsibilities of the administrator may include:

Completing administrative arrangements for team meetings, such as scheduling the date, time, and place for meetings.

Preparing an organized agenda for the meeting.

Identifying critical personnel and invite them to the meeting.

Inviting parents to the meeting.

Chairing the meeting, or appointing a designee.

Encouraging each team member to participate actively during the meeting.

Ensuring that each person knows what action the team recommends, who is responsible for implementation, and what resources are needed to support implementation adequately.

Communicating administrative support of the team to all members of the school community.

Promoting and committing resources to make consultation viable.

Mainstreaming Teachers

Each educator has a specific role in assisting in the development of mainstreaming. The special educator's role is that of individualizing, diagnosing, and modifying curriculum. The regular education teacher's role is more devoted to specializing the presentation of subject matter in the classroom (Goodman & Miller, 1980). However, the regular education teacher and the special education teacher must develop a working and supporting relationship. Goodman and Miller (1980) suggest that this relationship is based on shared responsibilities for handicapped children, including social integration, academic integration, using existing curriculum materials, and modifying curricular materials as needed.

While the regular education teacher must share new responsibilities with the special education teacher, the regular educator's role changes. As traditional roles remain in place, new roles for the regular teacher develop. The planning of the IEP, using special materials and apparatus, and working with specialized personnel and adapting curriculum have become a part of regular education. The regular educator now expects pressures added to an already overloaded job. In addition to the new school roles, the mainstream teacher has a responsibility to the team, the special teacher, the parents, and the special student.

Responsibility to the Team.   Typically, the regular class teacher is required to implement most of the instructional interventions suggested for the mainstreamed child. Thus, it is critical that the regular educator contribute to the team's discussion of the special pupil. Ysseldyke (1983) found that unless regular class teachers are actively involved in the team process and participate in the team's decision making, they may not embrace team recommendations and implement suggested interventions. This information is valuable for the student referral. The referral for assistance from the team is often initiated by the mainstream teacher. Prior to requesting team assistance, regular class teachers should collect as much information as possible relative to the problems encountered by the child. The referral to the team should include:

1. A clear statement of the child's problem.
2. A clear and concise description of the child's present level of functioning.

3. A brief summary of the child's learning strengths.
4. A prioritized list of the child's learning needs.
5. Identification of the major problem, the primary purpose of the request for assistance.
6. A summary of the interventions that have been tried.

With this information available, the team can approach the process of discovering new solutions with greater clarity and efficiency.

During team meetings, the mainstream teacher can share the accumulation of information gained as a result of extensive observations of and interactions with the child. This facilitates open communication between the regular educator and other members of the team.

Responsibility to the Special Teacher.   Historically it has been assumed that the primary responsibilities of mainstreaming belong to the special education teacher. However, the special educator and regular educator are equally responsible to the mainstreamed child and to the program itself. At the IEP meeting, the regular educator can provide input into the child's educational program that would not be possible if the regular class teacher did not attend. The child's progress should be reported regularly to the special education teacher. If the child begins to slip in the educational mainstream, prompt notice can correct the problem. The regular class teacher is responsible for seeking advice from the special educator about the teaching techniques that have proved successful to the mainstreamed student. Specific methods for adapting instruction can be shared by the special education teacher. Special educators have many special resources that are readily available to the regular educator. The regular class teacher should maintain the objectives established for the handicapped student in the special class and should commit time to the special educator for consultations. Without appropriate regular and special educator communication, the goals of the mainstream program are difficult to implement.

Responsibility to the Parents.   The regular education teacher has an obligation to the parent to maintain communication between the school and home. The teacher should keep the parent informed as to the child's progress in obtaining educational objectives. If behavioral problems exist, parents must be informed of them. Generally, the parent should be kept abreast of any educational development of their child. This communication can be established by written notes or phone calls.

Another aspect of working with parents is that of reporting grades and explaining the educational program. Parents should be made aware of the type grading system being used and of how the educational program has been planned. Because parents of handicapped children often are extremely concerned about social and academic adjustment, teacher should listen attentively to their concerns, provide them with the necessary resources, and be honest in answering their questions.

Responsibility to the Special Student.   Regarding regular educators' responsibility to special students, Larrivee and Algina (1983) recommend that

> teachers be trained to provide positive feedback to students responding to questions, give sustaining feedback when students answer incorrectly, ask questions during instruction which are answered correctly by students, refrain from criticizing student responses, and provide instructional materials and tasks which students appropriately engage in at a low error rate. Furthermore, it is recommended that teachers working with mainstreamed students provide a supportive classroom environment in which there is little student transitional or non-instructional wait-time, need for discipline as well as actual intervention rate is low, and use of punitive interventions is minimal. (pp. 13–14)

The regular class teacher has the responsibility of promoting the integration of mainstreamed handicapped students with nonhandicapped peers. Johnson and Johnson (1980) present the following practical strategies for producing cooperative learning activities for the mainstream.

1. Specify the lesson's instructional goals.
2. Select a group size that is the most appropriate for the child and the lesson.
3. Assign the student to groups so as to maximize learning for the child from the lesson.
4. Physically arrange the classroom so that group members face each other and can see the materials clearly.
5. Provide appropriate materials and utilize group reports when different assignments are given for different levels.
6. Clearly explain to students the task and goal of the lesson.
7. Observe student interactions to ensure that the learning situation is running smoothly.
8. Assist the groups in working out problems.
9. Evaluate the group products and give feedback to group members as well as to the group.

The regular education teacher has an increasing responsibility to the mainstreamed student. With the emphasis to maintain the handicapped student in the regular class setting, either without formal assessment or after formal assessment, the regular education teacher's responsibilities increase. An awareness of this new role and ideas on how better to serve the mainstream student are vital components of the regular educator's training.

Special Education Teachers

At one period in our history, the special education teacher mainly taught handicapped children in self-contained classes. With the mainstreaming effort, the special educator is now being called on to assist the regular education teacher with the educational planning of the mainstreamed student. Roles have expanded to those of (1) providing assessment and instructional planning for the mainstreamed student, (2) conducting remedial and tutorial instruction, (3) providing consultation to the regular class teacher, and (4) participating on the school's assessment and eligibility teams (Pasanella & Volkmor, 1981). The role has expanded beyond the school. With the mandate of the IEP, extra demands on the special teacher's time have developed.

Responsibility to the Team. Mainstreaming handicapped children requires that regular and special educators collaborate and share the responsibility of providing services to special students. Highly trained specialists have developed the skills needed to modify curriculum and instructional interventions based on a comprehensive evaluation of the child's educational needs. As a member of the mainstream team, the special teacher can offer suggestions for modifying instruction, consulting with regular class teachers, and perhaps more importantly, identifying resources, alternative learning materials, and assistive devices that may be appropriate to the needs of the special student.

Responsibility to the Mainstream Teacher. Working with regular educators includes many roles. One such role is that of assisting in the transition to the mainstream. Preparing the regular class teacher and the mainstreamed student for the mainstream is an essential part of providing support. Suggestions for how the special education teacher may assist in the transition into the mainstream include:

1. Assisting the regular education teacher in assessing the characteristics of the mainstream setting. These might include the classroom's physical variables (e.g., grouping, sound, or seating arrangements) or the classroom's instructional variables (e.g., teaching techniques, media, materials, course content, evaluation, classroom management system, and classroom rules).
2. Assisting the regular education teacher in assessing the characteristics of related environments (e.g., cafeteria, physical education/gym, music/art settings, assemblies/school programs, and between-class activities).
3. Assisting the regular education teacher in assessing the characteristics of the interpersonal/social relations in the regular class setting (i.e., student interactions, regular student's attitudes, dress codes, and method of teacher assistance).
4. Providing suggestions to the regular class teacher in making the necessary modifications as needed for items 1–3.
5. Explaining to the regular class teacher what the mainstreamed student can and cannot do as related to items 1–3.
6. Providing the regular educator with vital information relating to the learning characteristics of the mainstreamed student.
7. Providing the regular educator with necessary medical information about the student.

8. Helping the regular educator to become aware of all available resources.
9. Giving the regular education teacher a list of the services provided by the special education teacher.
10. Keeping the channels of communication open between regular and special education.
11. Being available to the regular class teacher.
12. Being familiar with the general education curriculum and its implications for the mainstreamed student's transition.

An important element to be shared by regular educators, special educators, and administrators—one that is perceived as crucial to successful mainstreaming—is *communication* (Schubert & Glick, 1981; Wood & Carmean, 1982). Communication between resource and regular classroom teachers is vital to the success or failure of a mainstreaming approach for exceptional students. Before a handicapped student is mainstreamed into a regular class, the communication role of the special educator in preparing the regular class teacher becomes of paramount importance. The special educator should provide the regular class teacher with background information on the child. An invitation to the IEP meeting should be extended to the regular educator. Measuring goals, providing behavioral-management programs, and assisting in the development of instructional techniques are some of the responsibilities of the special educator.

Hauptman (1983) investigated the factors that can influence the regular classroom teacher's perception of the handicapped child in the classroom. Possible communication links were explored. For example, forms of written communication developed included weekly lesson plan sheets, an information sheet for the student, a teacher checklist, an instructional adjustment summary sheet, and a checklist for behavioral characteristics. Flow charts for the IEP were developed so that the IEP could be read by all mainstreaming teachers. Hauptman found that communication does lead to successful mainstreaming programs.

Loftus and Walter (1981) developed the following ideas to assist the special educator in communicating with regular educators.

1. Be accessible to teachers. If teachers are to be able to discuss problems with you, you should be approachable, available, and able to give them time and attention.
2. Show an interest in the work and opinions of teachers. Initiate informal discussions about their activities in the classroom, views about teaching and the like. These discussions may be conducted in informal settings such as the lunchroom, playground, and around the ditto machine. You may want to observe each teacher's classroom environment. If problems arise concerning a handicapped student's placement, it helps if you know what the classroom climate is like.
3. Make your role known to the teachers. In your conversations with teachers, you may want to talk about the nature of your work, your activities, what

you would like to do, and the kinds of problems you have been involved with (remembering to keep identifiable information about a client confidential). If it is appropriate in your school system, the more formal approach of an in-service workshop could deal with such information.

4. When a teacher has a problem or needs assistance in implementing a program, work with that teacher. Make efforts to help start the implementation of a new program, show (not just tell) the teacher what to do in the classroom, if possible. Be sure to follow-up on the progress of any implementation.

5. Establish an environment conducive to open communication. While crowded lunchrooms and playgrounds are fine for informal greetings, a serious discussion should be allotted sufficient time and distractions minimized (e.g., no children in the room).

6. Express your thoughts clearly and concisely. Think about what you will say (e.g., the issues you want to raise, the opinions you want to express). When talking with colleagues, lead them to rephrase your comments so that you can see if they understand.

7. Listen to the views of others. While it is important that you give your colleagues time to talk, it is equally important that you listen to and understand what is being said. Try to rephrase your colleagues' comments to clarify issues and make sure you understand.

8. At the end of your meetings, clarify points made and activities agreed upon. It may be helpful to put some of the suggestions in writing for future reference (pp. 3–4).

Responsibility to the Parents.   Because of demands put on educators by parents, parents now play a more significant role in the education of their children than ever before. Parents have the greater investment in these children (Gargiulo, 1985). The ability to work successfully with parents places new roles on the special educator. Educators need to be aware of the needs of parents of handicapped children.

One role of the special educators in assisting parents is that of *providing information.* Beginning with the initial screening of the special child, the special education teacher can provide information regarding the characteristics of the specific handicapping condition. Frequently, parents know little, if anything, about how the handicapped child is educated in the mainstream. It may be helpful for parents to know that it is common to experience negative feelings when first finding out that their child is handicapped. Special teachers can provide information as to the process and terms of the eligibility and IEP meetings. A handout explaining the terms to be used can be helpful to parents. The reason for the IEP may need explanation. Rights of parents should not only be given in writing but also explained to parents. Kroth (1985) suggests that special educators prepare a handbook for parents that identifies such information as special personnel, classroom procedures, classroom materials and supplies, transportation, and conference and reporting systems. As the student begins the instructional process, student progress should be reported to parents. Studies show that parents can assist their handicapped child with improvements in a variety of academic and social skills (Hoskisson, 1974; Johnson & Katz, 1973). In addition to student progress information, parents need information on ways to assist the child at home. This could include summer activities, ideas for toys, or ways to assist with school activities. Specific ideas for managing behaviors are useful to parents as well. Frequently, parents have difficulty dealing with inappropriate behaviors at home. Techniques used at school may be carried over into the home. One major concern of parents is that of the future for their child. The special teacher can provide information on available resources for after high school and on into adult life. The handicapped child is a lifelong venture for the parent. The provision of information to make life as easy as possible is a helpful role for the special educator.

One of the most important roles of the special educator is that of the *advocate* for the parent and child. Wolfensberger and Zanka (1973) identify the following as the most desirable characteristics of the special educator in the advocate role.

1. The advocate must have a type of community stability which can sustain its relationship to the protege.
2. The advocate must be willing to undergo training.
3. The advocate must understand the specific advocacy mission.
4. The advocate must have competence in whatever advocacy role or task he or she assumes.
5. The advocate needs to make a commitment to the mission.
6. The advocate should display "good moral character" as judged by the community after selecting his/her advocacy mission.

Another major role of the special educator is that of *helping the parent in the IEP process.* Bronicki and Turnbull (1987) suggest that the mainstreaming process benefits from involving parents in the educational program of their child. Involving parents requires that the special educator provides them with the information necessary to be active participants. During the IEP meeting, the special educator can assist the parent in seeing that their child receives the most appropriate education possible. Parents may need assistance when they are asked if they have anything to include on the IEP. Special and related services need to be clearly explained to parents (e.g., an explanation of the short-term objectives as they relate to the annual goals would be appropriate). Assisting the parent during the IEP meeting provides for a more secure feeling on behalf of the parent.

Special Education Parent and Pupil Rights

State and District regulations provide that certain procedures must be followed in the assessment, program planning, and placement of special education pupils and in the provision of appropriate services to special education pupils.

As parents or guardians of a special education pupil or a pupil being considered for special education services, you have the right to:

1. Receive a written description of the contents of an assessment plan within fifteen (15) school days from the day of referral, and to have up to ten (10) school days in which to consider the assessment plan.

2. Give written consent for the assessment.

3. The completion (within thirty-five (35) school days) of an assessment of your child, the determination of the need and eligibility for a special education program and related services, and the development of an Individualized Education Program (IEP).

4. Have an independent educational assessment by a certificated or licensed professional examiner. The cost of this independent assessment will be paid by the parent or guardian unless the District is not able to demonstrate that its assessment is appropriate.

5. Be invited to the District Eligibility and Planning Committee meeting devoted to a discussion of the assessment findings and program placement recommendations, and
   a. present information at the meeting in person, in writing, or through a representative.
   b. participate in the development of an IEP for your child.
   c. give written consent for any special education placement for your child.
   d. be informed in writing of the District Eligibility and Planning Committee's recommendations, which include a copy of the written IEP for that pupil.

6. A free, appropriate education for your child in accordance with his/her IEP. Whenever possible, this education shall be through the public schools, but in the event that there is not an appropriate educational placement available for your child, the District will assist you in locating an appropriate placement in another district or an approved non-public school.

7. An education for your child with pupils who are not handicapped, to the maximum extent possible. Special day classes, separate special schools or other removal of individuals with exceptional needs shall occur only when the nature or severity of the handicap indicated in the IEP is such that education in regular classes cannot be achieved satisfactorily.

8. Examine all school records of your child and to have such records made available to you for review within five (5) days of the District's receipt of your written request. To have a copy of all school records pertaining to your child, however, the District reserves the right to charge you for the actual cost of reproduction. You may also, within certain guidelines, request to amend the records.

9. Be fully informed in your native language when receiving notices or when you are attending school conferences designed to plan your child's IEP. Please call the school office if there is a need for an interpreter to be present. This includes an interpreter for the deaf. If you prefer, the District will translate any and all notices in Braille, given the availability of a qualified person to assist.

10. Submit a written appeal of any District decision regarding pupil placement, identification, or evaluation.

11. File a written complaint alleging any matter that if true would be considered a violation of federal or state law or regulations governing special education or related services.

12. Be informed when personally identifiable pupil records are no longer needed to provide educational services for your child, and to request that such records be destroyed. All but the permanent record will be destroyed within three (3) years after the child leaves the district. (NOTE: Before making the decision to have records destroyed, parents should keep in mind that the records may be needed by the child or parent for social security benefits or other purposes.)

Source: Downey Unified School District, CA (1980), *The Handbook on Special Education.* Prepared by Instructional Services Division, Special Education, Downey Unified School District, Downey, CA.

Another major role of the special educator is that of *conducting the parent-teacher conference.* There are three aspects to the parent-teacher conference: preconference, conference, and postconference. During the *preconference* phase, Kroth (1985) suggests that for a smooth conference during the planning stage the parent should be notified of the conference time and date, and allowed a choice of times in order to set the meeting at a mutually agreed time. Also, the special educator should prepare for the conference by checking the child's records and gathering work samples that demonstrate the child's weaknesses and strengths for the parents' review. A detailed agenda for the meeting should be planned and the environment arranged so that all parties will be comfortable (i.e., the conference may be conducted at school or in the home). When the meeting is held at the school, the special educator should consider these suggestions:

1. Greet the parents by name at the door as they enter the room.
2. Arrange a comfortable place for them to sit. Do not sit behind a desk and talk across it. This can be threatening and too much like a doctor's office or a judge's chambers.
3. If you plan to show examples of their child's work, do not greet them with a large stack of papers. This may also seem somewhat threatening.
4. When posssible, provide coffee and ashtrays to help them feel more at ease.
5. If the parents need to bring other children, arrange for someone to watch them while you talk (Evans, undated, p.p. 19–20).

When holding meetings at home, the special educator should consider the following suggestions:

1. Be informal, but avoid being too casual in speech. The parents know you are a teacher, not their next door neighbor.
2. Spend some time visiting with the child [and the child's siblings and] parents. Children, especially young children, usually feel the teacher is their "special friend," and they want to feel they are just as important to the teacher as [they are to] their parents.
3. Compliment the home. Notice and sincerely praise family pictures, pets, [a] garden, or whatever is appropriate.
4. If this is your first visit, try to avoid filling out forms. Use the time to learn about the child and [the child's] family, their interests and goals, in an informal manner. If forms are necessary, however, explain why the information is needed.
5. Do not smoke in the child's home unless the parents invite you to smoke. Smoking is extremely irritating to many people and can set a bad tone for your meeting (Evans, undated, p. 20).

During the *conference*, four major activities take place (Stephens & Wolf, 1980). First, much of the initial parent conference usually is devoted to rapport building. Second, because parents have a wealth of information on the child that may not be reflected in the school's records, the special educator should seek to obtain as much information from parents as possible. Third, the special educator should provide information to parents by beginning on a strong positive note and providing specific examples of the student's work. Fourth, the special educator should summarize the information discussed at the conference and reconfirm the follow-up activities as well as the person responsible for each activity.

The *postconference* includes sharing the information from the conference with the student and other professionals. Recording the proceedings of the conference is another important postconference activity (Turnbull & Turnbull, 1986).

Assisting parents in becoming more actively involved with their child's educational future is another role of the special educator. One of the six major components of P.L. 94–142 deals with the participation of parents (Turnbull, 1983). According to the law, parents must be given access to records and information regarding their child, their due process rights, and the policy of the school in regard to the treatment of personally identifiable information. The inclusion of parents at the IEP meeting and their participation on other panels, advocacy groups, and in hearings should be encouraged (Cone, Delawyer, & Wolfe, 1985). Researchers Wiegerink, Posante-Loro, and Bristol (1978) and Cone, Delawyer, and Wolfe (1985), have categorized twelve types of parental involvement:

1. Contact with teachers.
2. Participation in the special education process.
3. Transportation.
4. Observations at school.
5. Educational activities at home.
6. Attending parent education/consultation meetings.
7. Classroom volunteering.
8. Parent-parent contact and support.
9. Involvement with administration.
10. Involvement in fund-raising activities.
11. Involvement in advocacy groups.
12. Disseminating information.

Responsibility to the Special Student.   When preparing the handicapped student for the mainstream, Gresham and Hunbert (1982) suggest that teachers should pay special attention to the behavioral and academic demands of the regular classroom. Salend (1984) suggests that the transition from special to regular education can be made by approximating the new environment prior to mainstreaming. For example, the special education teacher can inventory the regular class' critical features (Salend & Viglianti, 1982). For example, if notetaking is a practice in the regular classroom, this exercise should be practiced in the special class before mainstreaming.

Frequently, handicapped students lack the social skills needed to fully benefit from mainstreaming (Gresham, 1982). Social-skills training is a necessary part of mainstream preparation. The special education teacher has an obligation to identify the social skills that the student inappropriately exhibits and to implement a plan for remediation. Many times the handicapped student is accepted even though there is evidence of an academic difference, but is not accepted when a difference in social skills exists.

Parents

Parents may be the most underutilized resource available to assist professionals attempting to serve a child who has educational and/or behavioral problems.

Frequently, the parent's initial contact with the school is a negative experience. Many times, parents feel unqualified to provide input into the educational planning for the student. However, parents can provide valuable information to the team that cannot be obtained from any other source.

Parents should be invited to be active members of the multidisciplinary team. They can be trained to collect observational data at home and in the community. The child's behavior outside of school may provide significant clues relative to his or her learning style and adaptive behavior skills. This information cannot be provided as readily by professional team members. Parent also can provide day-to-day information while living with the child as well as developmental information gathered from birth.

Pfeiffer (1980) identifies "minimal parental involvement" as one of four problems that frequently interfere with effective team functioning. Ysseldyke (1983) also found that parents often were not active team participants and that they were rarely asked to share their perceptions of their child. A number of researchers have found a positive relationship between parent-school communication and improved student performance in school (Bittle, 1975; Heron & Harris, 1982; Kroth, Whelan, & Stables, 1970). Team leaders should enthusiastically encourage parent participation and solicit their input during team meetings.

Students

Special students may be invited to participate on the multidisciplinary team. Student participation occurs most often during the junior high and senior high school levels. By having students serve on the team, we invite them to become actively involved in planning for their own futures and give them the opportunity to express the goals and objectives that they would like to reach in later life.

School Psychologists

Psychologists have assumed a prominent role in the process of assessing handicapped children. In many school districts, psychologists are given the primary responsibility of determining the child's level of functioning. When appropriate, the school psychologist may assume the following responsibilities for the team.

1. Complete a thorough assessment of the child to determine eligibility for special programs and services
2. Analyze and interpret assessment data for parents and other team members
3. Participate in identification of curricula modifications and instructional interventions appropriate to the identified needs of the pupil

School psychologists are often viewed as influential team members. It is therefore critical that they have the necessary skills to collaborate and communicate effectively with other members of the team.

Related Support Personnel

A cadre of support personnel are available to assist both regular and special educators with programs for handicapped children. Among the individuals who may be invited are:

1. Speech and language specialists.
2. Occupational and physical therapists.
3. Medical personnel.
4. Social workers.
5. Counselors and mental health personnel.

Functions of the Team

The primary function of the team is to assist regular educators in organizing and implementing appropriate interventions for handicapped students encountering problems in mainstreamed environments. The team provides an open forum for discussion of those problems and possible solutions.

In California, the mainstream consulting teams are referred to as *student-study teams.* Moger (1986) investigated student-study teams at thirty California schools. In response to the question, "What is the purpose of student-study teams?" respondents identified the twenty-six items or activities listed in Figure 2.2. The role of the team varies according to the requests of referring teachers, the needs of the pupils, and the nature and severity of the problems presented. It is therefore critical that each team clearly define its goals and purpose. Each member must understand the goals and agree on the stated role of the group (Abelson & Woodman, 1983; Pfeiffer, 1980).

A few of the factors that can contribute to an effective team process include the following.

1. Clear and consistent leadership is provided for the team.
2. All persons involved with the student attend and participate in team meetings.
3. Everyone accepts the responsibilities assigned for completion before or after the meeting.

1. Coordinate the delivery of services and interventions
2. Serve regular education students with learning problems
3. Refer students to other programs, if necessary
4. Ensure correct academic placement
5. Provide the team approach to work on students' problems
6. Act as a resource in developing interventions
7. Make recommendations for modifications/interventions
8. Develop interventions to enable students to function in the regular education program
9. Provide a quick approach to maximize each student's education
10. Plan regular education strategies *before* deciding on special education referrals
11. Provide assistance to classroom teachers
12. Provide specialists to assist with students' problems
13. Review difficult cases
14. Discuss student problems *rather than* eligibility for special education
15. Serve regular education students with behavioral problems
16. Coordinate the delivery of services to students
17. Develop creative ways of dealing with students
18. Provide immediate support for classroom teachers
19. Serve regular education students with behavioral problems
20. Monitor the progress of modifications and interventions
21. Encourage staff and parent participation in student strategies
22. Provide psychologists with good skills to assist assessment tool selection
23. Provide regular education teachers a chance to brainstorm ideas and techniques to use with students
24. Make remediation to total school (versus special education) program
25. Eliminate unnecessary assessment
26. Provide secondary resource specialist program referrals

FIGURE 2.2
Purposes of Student-Study Teams (Rank Ordered) (*Source:* R. L. Moger [1986], *For the Final Report of a State Educational Agency Federal Evaluation Study* [conducted by the Program Evaluation & Research Division, California State Department of Education—Contract no. G0084C 3505] [Washington, DC: U.S. Department of Education]. Adapted with permission.)

4. Regular class teachers are provided time to attend meetings and participate in team decision making.

In summary, teams function ideally when their members view themselves as collaborators with classroom teachers. When functioning effectively, they can become active participating partners in the process of identifying innovative methods of assisting students in mainstream settings.

_____ *Case Study* _____

THE MULTIDISCIPLINARY TEAM

Marie Kennedy teaches third grade in a large metropolitan school district. Rosa entered her class in late October. She is a good student, friendly and outgoing, and highly motivated. Marie noted that Rosa "never stops trying." Rosa appeared to speak little or no English in November. Marie had to rely on other children to serve as interpreters for her during the first few months.

Rosa did not appear to read either English or Spanish. She could count, and once she understood the English words for the numerical symbols, could complete simple computational problems in arithmetic.

In addition to generally low academic achievement, Rosa had very poor coordination. This was evident during PE and art periods. She was less skilled at ball games than the other students in her class. She did not catch or kick the ball as well, was slower when running, and could not master the jump rope as well as younger children on the playground. During art, she had difficulty cutting, coloring, and painting pictures neatly.

Marie began to suspect that Rosa also had difficulty remembering the names of the letters of the alphabet, numbers, names of objects, and frequently, directions for completing assigned tasks.

In January, following two months of observation and trying alternative approaches to teaching, Marie contacted her principal and requested assistance from the school teacher-assistance team. A written referral was submitted following a brief consultation with the principal. A meeting of the team was scheduled for the following week.

The team met for one hour and, following a brief discussion to clarify the problem, recommended several intervention strategies. The bilingual coordinator was asked to observe Rosa and suggest specific curricular modifications for Marie. The coordinator was also asked to find a bilingual tutor for Rosa while the team determined her eligibility for a bilingual class placement. The team also recommended a comprehensive assessment by a qualified bilingual psychologist to determine Rosa's eligibility for special education services. During the interim between additional assessments by special education and bilingual education personnel, the team suggested modifications for Rosa's classroom teacher.

The team agreed to review Rosa's progress in two weeks. The principal agreed that Rosa's case was a priority. He therefore agreed to expedite the referral to other special services as quickly as possible.

The Referral Process

The referral process begins when it is noticed that the student is experiencing learning and behavioral problems. The process is completed when the student is either assisted in the regular classroom with necessary program modifications or when the student is placed in the appropriate special education setting. Even though the process may end with the support, for the student and for the educators who will be working with the student, it is a continuous process.

Phase I: Initial Referral

The *initiating referral* for a student may come from various sources: classroom teachers, parents or guardians, the student, or other professionals as appropriate. This initial referral is made to the principal of the school where the student attends. The vast majority of referrals are made by the regular classroom teacher. Phase I of the referral process is outlined in Figure 2.3.

Mainstream teachers can play a critical role in the referral process, as they have many opportunities to observe and record systematically a student's behavior in the learning environment. Based on recorded observations, teachers can describe:

1. The student's present level of functioning.
2. The student's learning strengths.
3. The specific problem that is interfering with school success.
4. The specific attempts that have been made to ameliorate the problem.

Prior to initiating a formal request for assistance, classroom teachers should confer with their school principal or an appropriate site administrator, school counselor, or school psychologist to discuss the specific problem and their prior attempts to develop successful solutions. During that discussion, a decision should be made to try another instructional approach or to refer the student to the team for review. If a decision to delay the referral is made, the mainstream teacher should carefully document successive efforts to meet the child's needs. If the student continues to experience difficulty, a written referral for assistance should be sent as quickly as possible to the school-based team.

A *formal written referral* to the multidisciplinary team may be initiated by classroom teachers, educational specialists, parents, and in some instances the student needing assistance. The process for requesting assistance should be simple and require a minimum of paperwork, and should allow equal access for any individual requesting a team review. The written referral to the team triggers the beginning of the formal process. A sample of a team assistance request form is shown in Table 2.1.

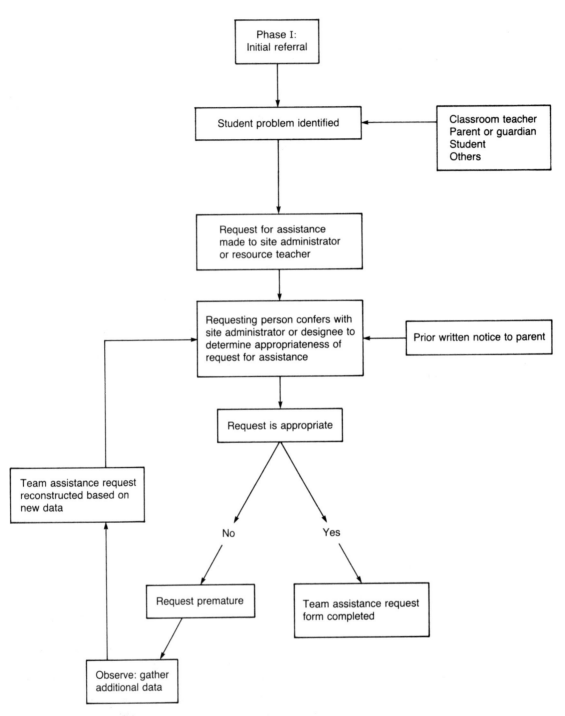

FIGURE 2.3

The Referral Process: Phase I—Initial Referral

TABLE 2.1
Request Form for Team Assistance

Student's Name _____   Grade Level _____

Referring Teacher _____   Date _____

Describe the student's problem:

How often does this problem occur?

_____ Several times a day   Comments:
_____ Daily
_____ More than once a week
_____ Weekly
_____ Occasionally

Describe the modifications that have been attempted to solve this problem (e.g., assignments, instruction, curriculum, counseling, environment):

Have the parents been contacted about this problem? ____ yes ____ no ____ don't know

Summary of consultation with parents:

Describe the student's learning strengths, special interests, or skills:

Additional information, other concerns about the student, general comments, and so forth:

At this point, the mainstream teacher should continue to observe the student in a variety of learning situations. These observations may provide valuable information that is not readily available to other individuals and impossible to attain during formal testing. For example, teachers can best provide a history of the student's problem by describing the frequency with which the behavior occurs and under what conditions. They can also provide a more comprehensive picture of the student's performance in comparison to other children in the class. Further, it is recommended that teachers collect representative samples of the student's work, particularly if the presenting problem is poor academic achievement.

Phase II: Team Meeting

Although variations exist among states, a team or another appointed person generally assumes the responsibilities of calling the team meeting, arranging for physical space for the meeting, setting the team agenda, and notifying all prospective participants. This team or person should also ensure that each member is prepared to present any additional information that the team can utilize during the meeting. The team meets primarily to review the referral, clarify the problem, and develop a plan of action (see Figure 2.4).

At this point, the team may elect to provide suggestions to the classroom teacher for making adaptations to the instructional program, or it may feel,

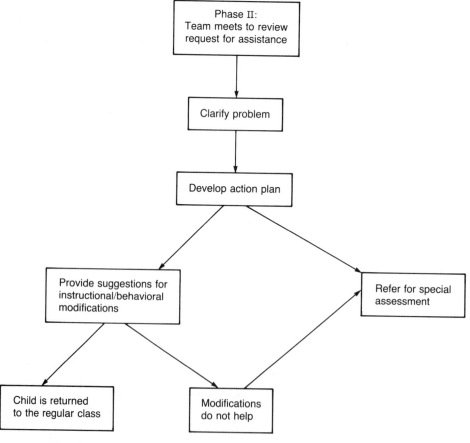

FIGURE 2.4

The Referral Process: Phase II—Team Meeting

based on the data presented, that the assessment process should begin immediately. Frequently, the modifications provided make it possible for the student to continue in the regular class without continuing the referral process. Based on their review of the student's problem, team members often find, collectively, that they have many possibilities for modifying instruction. Team members generally have a repertoire of possible interventions and combinations of modifications from which to draw their recommendations. Typical suggestions for assisting mainstream teachers with handicapped students can be grouped into several broad categories, including modification of the learning environment, instructional approach, instructional materials, the instructional day, and the learner's tasks. The balance of this text expands on these categories in relation to specific academic areas.

Phase III: Assessment

When modifications of the program fail to result in improved student performance and achievement (the prereferral process), the team may refer the student to be evaluated for special educational services (the referral process). In this instance, the legally mandated procedure as prescribed by Public Law 94–142 is initiated.

It should be noted that a written notice must be given to all parents before the agency proposes to initiate or change the identification, evaluation, or educational placement of a child or if the agency refuses to take such an action. In addition, parents must give written permission to the team to evaluate and place their child. The legally prescribed guidelines for completing a comprehensive assessment are outlined in Figure 2.5.

Evaluations must be made by a multidisciplinary team or group and at least one expert in the area of suspected disability. Federal law requires that:

1. The child is assessed in all areas related to the suspected disability.
2. No single procedure is the sole criterion for determining an appropriate educational program.
3. Tests and other evaluation materials are provided and administered in the child's native language or other mode of communication unless clearly not feasible.
4. Evaluation materials are validated for the purpose for which they are used.
5. Evaluation materials are administered by trained personnel in conformance with instructions provided by their producer.
6. Tests and other evaluation materials include those tailored to assess specific areas of educational need and not merely a single general IQ.
7. Evaluation materials selected and administered to a child with impaired sensory, manual, or speaking skills must yield results that accurately reflect the child's aptitude or achievement level or other factors they purport to measure.

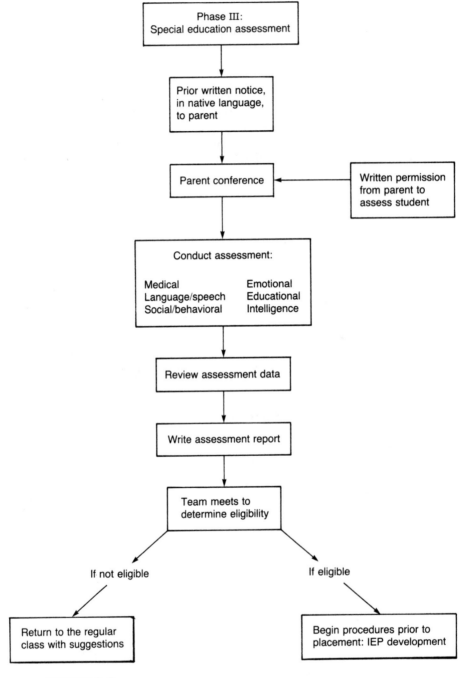

FIGURE 2.5
The Referral Process: Phase III—Assessment

Phase IV: IEP Development and Placement

At the time that a student is determined to be eligible for special education services, the team, or an appointed IEP team, develops an individual educational plan (IEP) for the student. Team members must include a representative of the agency other than the child's teacher, one or both of the child's parents, the child (when appropriate), and other individuals as selected by the parent or agency. When the child is being evaluated for the first time, a member of the evaluation team or someone who is knowledgeable about the evaluation procedures and results must attend the meeting. (Phase IV of the referral process is outlined in Figure 2.6.)

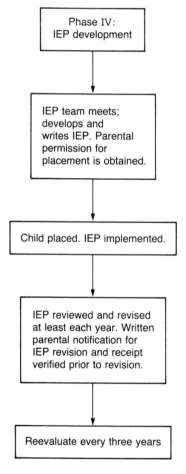

FIGURE 2.6

The Referral Process: Phase IV—IEP Development and Placement

The IEP, a communication tool used by parents and the school, is a written agreement of resources, special education, and related services to be provided. It is also a vehicle for determining if a child is progressing toward the stated educational outcomes. The format of an IEP may vary from state to state. However, the required components appear on all IEPs. Table 2.2 presents examples of the components of an IEP. The development of the IEP is a team effort and not just the responsibility of special educators.

When formally placing in special education programs, local education agencies must ensure that a continuum of placement options is available to meet

TABLE 2.2
Components of the IEP

Component	Description	Example
Present level of educational functioning	Information obtained from norm- or criterion-referenced tests. Gives actual level and skill at which a child is functioning.	Student can add number facts from 1 to 20 with 100% accuracy.
Annual or long-range goals	Projection of how far teachers think the child can progress during the school year. Each present level of educational functioning has a projected annual goal.	Student can add two digits, one addend without regrouping with 95% accuracy.
Short-term instructional objectives	An objective, written in behavioral terms, listing the intermediate steps between the present level of performance and the annual goals.	Student can add zero as addends with 95% accuracy. Student can add three or more digits in a column with 95% accuracy.
Beginning and ending dates	Projected dates for initiation of services and anticipated duration of services.	September 1990, to May 1990. Student will be evaluated each six weeks.
Objective criteria and evaluation procedures for short-term objectives	Statement of criteria and evaluation procedures for completion of short-term objectives.	Criterion checklists, teacher-made tests, work samples.

the needs of handicapped students. Placement options for the public school set-ting are discussed in Chapter 1. In review, the IEP team may recommend one of the following placements:

1. A regular class with assistance from specialists.
2. A resource room (part-time) and a regular class.
3. A special education class (full-time).
4. Other nonpublic school placements.

TABLE 2.2
(continued)

Component	Description	Example
Special education services	Type of specific service child is receiv-ing.	Educably mentally retarded (EMR) resource.
Related services	Any service outside of special education re-quired for appropriate education.	Speech therapy.
Regular classroom par-ticipation	Curriculum areas and amount of time each day the handicapped child will spend in the regular classroom.	Art, 30 minutes twice a week; physical educa-tion, 30 minutes each day; music, 30 minutes a week.
Projected dates for assessment	IEP must be reviewed at least annually by the IEP committee to determine whether short-term instruc-tional objectives are being achieved.	May 1990.
Committee members present	The IEP must be signed by all commit-tee members.	
Parental signature	Parents present at the IEP meeting are asked to sign the IEP.	

Source: J. W. Wood, (1984), *Adapting instruction for the mainstream: A sequential approach to teaching* (Columbus, OH: Merrill), p. 10. Adapted with permission.

Moving the student from one placement to another placement also must be decided by the team and should be based on many factors. The student's academic and social levels of functioning should be considered. When moving a student from a more restrictive environment to a mainstreamed environment, careful consideration should be given to class size, teacher selection, specific subjects that the student will study, and the match between the handicapped student's present level of functioning and the regular class curriculum. Attention should be given as well to assessing the handicapped student's abilities and to making the appropriate modifications within the regular class. Simply moving a student into the mainstream to meet the mandate of the law does not meet the student's needs nor the spirit of the law.

The actual placement in special education must begin on the date specified in the IEP. The team should assume the responsibility of monitoring the pupil's progress. They must also review the program annually. Any member of the team may request a meeting to review, revise, or modify the program during the year. Public Law 94–142 mandates the placement of handicapped pupils in settings with nonhandicapped peers to the maximum extent possible. It is therefore essential that the IEP team closely monitor the pupil's progress once the special education begins. The pupil should be placed in environments that facilitate interaction with nonhandicapped pupils. It is important to note, however, that the IEP team has the legally mandated responsibility to monitor the special education pupil's placement progress.

Summary

Multidisciplinary teams are variously described as problem-solving teams, teacher-assistance teams, and student- or child-study teams. To some extent, they are all of these things. They provide critically needed support and assistance for mainstream teachers attempting, without success, to serve the student with special needs in the regular class. Collectively, the team can help educators and families identify the most appropriate educational programs for a handicapped child. They can also, in collaboration with the mainstream teacher, dramatically modify the instructional program, environment, and approach utilized to support the pupil in the mainstream.

Discussion Questions

1. Suggest procedures or criteria that could be used to measure the degree to which the professional team is functioning effectively.
2. Discuss the primary advantages of using consulting professional teams. What critical variables should be considered prior to a team meeting? By whom?

3. Describe the problems that you, as a teacher, would most likely refer to the professional team. What outcomes would you anticipate as a result of your referral?
4. Describe procedures that you, as a teacher, would use to encourage parents to participate as team members.
5. What is the role of the school psychologist on the team? How can the psychologist best assist you?

Chapter 3

Educational Characteristics and Implications

JUDY W. WOOD

With contributions by:

CAROLYN K. REEVES
University of Southern Mississippi

JENNIFER W. MIEDERHOFF
Virginia Commonwealth University

Chapter Objectives

After reading Chapter 3 the student will be able to
- Define the various handicapping categories
- List the educational characteristics of handicapped students
- Identify and discuss ways of working with each type of handicapped student

C lassroom teachers encounter children with a variety of strengths and weaknesses. It is not uncommon to hear a teacher express concern over a child's inability to learn material presented in the classroom. However, each child is unique, and teachers assume the responsibility of helping each student to develop to his or her maximum potential. As Dr. E. H. Barton states:

> As a person I fit no preconceived mold. I come to you with my unique fears and hopes, uncertainties and convictions, weaknesses and strengths. I come also with unrealized potentials. Potentials with fewer fixed limits than I am aware of or you should set for me until together we can more fully explore what I may become.

This chapter provides an overview of the educational characteristics of handicapped students and the implications for teachers helping them explore what they may become. The information presented here is somewhat general and offered as introductory material. Additional information can be obtained from the sources listed in the References section near the end of this book.

The following exceptionalities are discussed in this chapter:

- Mild handicaps, including mental retardation, emotional disturbances, and learning disabilities
- Speech impairments
- Sensory handicaps, including visual handicaps and hearing impairments
- Physical and health impairments

Obtaining knowledge about specific handicapping conditions is helpful to teachers as they prepare to teach special students. Here we discuss the preceding types of handicapping conditions by defining each category, presenting the characteristics of each exceptionality, and sharing tips for working with the students in the mainstream.

Students may have handicaps that range from mild to severe. Because many severely handicapped students are served in environments other than the regular classroom, this text addresses only those with mild conditions in the areas of mentally retarded, emotionally disturbed, learning disabled, speech impaired, visually impaired, hearing impaired, and physically handicapped.

Mild Handicaps

Frequently, students with mild educational handicaps are served in regular class settings. Depending on the type of handicapping condition, the student is seen by the regular teacher from part of the school day to, in some cases, all of the school day. The three handicapping areas covered here include mental retardation, emotional disturbances, and learning disabilities. These categories comprise the largest group of students served in mainstreamed settings.

Mental Retardation (MR)

The most widely recognized definition of *mental retardation,* found in the *Manual on Terminology and Classification in Mental Retardation* (Grossman, 1977), is as follows:

> Mental Retardation refers to significantly subaverage general intellectual functioning existing concurrently with deficits in adaptive behavior, and manifested during the developmental period. (p. 11)

Within this definition there are three major components: (1) subaverage general intellectual functioning, (2) deficits in adaptive behavior, and (3) manifestation during the developmental period. *Subaverage general intellectual functioning* refers to an IQ score obtained on an individual intelligence test of more than two standard deviations below the mean for that test. *Adaptive behavior* refers to the measure or degree to which one "meets the standards of personal independence and social responsibility expected of [one's] age and cultural group" (Grossman, 1977, p. 122). The *developmental period* is considered to be the period of a child's life extending from conception to age 18. For a student to be categorized as mentally retarded, he or she must meet each of the above three criteria.

The preceding definition includes all degrees of retardation, including the severely and profoundly retarded child who would not be placed in regular classrooms. Only students experiencing mild degrees of mental retardation can, depending on the ability of the student, be placed in regular class settings. Generally, these students spend more of their instructional time within the special education classroom.

Characteristics of Educable Mentally Retarded Students. Numerous characteristics contribute to the educable mentally retarded student. However, no single child exhibits all of the characteristics reported. Some are peculiar to only certain children. Basically, the characteristics of this population fall into four major groups: social/emotional, learning, academic, and physical and health characteristics.

Socially/emotionally, the mentally retarded student has a low self-image and is not well accepted by nonhandicapped peers. Frequently, mentally retarded students develop a failure set, establishing goals that are too low for their abilities. Their locus of control is extrinsic rather than intrinsic. Thus, they see outside elements as in control. When the mentally retarded student fails vocationally, it is usually due to social/emotional factors rather than to the ability to complete the required tasks.

Mentally retarded students exhibit *learning characteristics* common to many. They work better with concrete concepts rather than with abstractions, have difficulty with short-term memory and in organizing information for later recall, and find it difficult to transfer learned information.

Academically, mentally retarded students do not achieve expected levels. They frequently function 3 to 4 years behind their normal peers and reach from a second- to a sixth-grade level of achievement after formal education is completed. They are not ready for basic academic skills on entering school and frequently benefit from a functional curriculum.

Physically, the mentally retarded student is below average in height, weight, and skeletal maturity. Many of these students display concomitant physical problems.

Students who are mildly retarded are usually identified as such during the early school years when they fail to meet age expectations in cognitive and developmental areas. Mildly mentally retarded students may be slow in learning and have difficulty paying attention, remembering what they learn, and generalizing incidental learning. All instruction should be in small steps and carefully sequenced.

Capabilities of Educable Mentally Retarded Students.   The long-range goals for mildly retarded students should include the areas of behavior, appearance, and self-sufficiency. With appropriate educational experiences, mildly retarded students can become independent, self-supporting citizens by the time they reach adulthood (Cartwright, Cartwright, & Ward, 1984). Mildly retarded students can reach academic goals, even though it takes them longer than regular students to do so (MacMillan, 1982).

Basic communication skills, both oral and written, can be acquired by the educable mentally retarded student. During instruction, ambiguities should be kept to a minimum. Teachers should place maximum emphasis on *functional* achievement in those areas that will help the student become financially and socially independent adults. For example, once basic reading skills have been acquired, teachers should stress reading for information, following directions, filling out application forms, locating information in newspapers, and reading for pleasure. Similarly, mathematics instruction should emphasize functional skills. Mildly retarded students can be taught basic mathematics skills needed for survival. It is important for teachers to provide mildly retarded students with direct experiences designed to help them see relationships, apply knowledge, and generalize.

Mildly mentally retarded students, if given intermittent practice, will retain and remember information once they have learned it. They can acquire problem-solving techniques after a number of successful experiences with the same general series of steps. Mildly retarded students can learn appropriate responses to social situations as well. Carefully planned training, with frequent practice and reinforcement, can help students acquire appropriate response repertoire.

Emotionally Disturbed (ED)

Emotionally disturbed children exhibit one or more of the following characteristics over an extended period and, as a result, their educational performance begins to be adversely affected.

- An inability to learn, which cannot be explained by intellectual, sensory, or health factors
- An inability to build or maintain satisfactory interpersonal relationships with peers and teachers
- Inappropriate types of behavior or feelings under normal circumstances
- A general pervasive mood of unhappiness or depression
- A tendency to develop physical symptoms or fears associated with personal or school problems

The term *emotionally disturbed* includes children who are schizophrenic or autistic. However, it does not include children who are socially maladjusted, unless it is determined that they are seriously emotionally disturbed (*Federal Register*, 1977, p. 42478).

Emotionally disturbed students (also referred to as the *behaviorally disordered*) make up approximately 3% of the school-aged population (U.S. Department of Education, 1984) and can be classified from mild to moderate to severe. In general:

> mildly and moderately disturbed children can be managed by parents and teachers, with some special services provided by a mental health specialist, such as a clinical psychologist, a counselor, or a therapist. There is usually no need to remove these children from their normal pattern of living at home and attending school during the day. (Cartwright, Cartwright, & Ward, 1984, p. 226)

As a group, emotionally disturbed children do not do as well in schools as normal children. This most likely occurs because (1) they frequently do not respond to the opportunity to learn what is being presented, and (2) the pattern of failure in academic situations is cumulative so they do not have the skills, or prerequisite concepts, needed to handle progressive academic content.

Characteristics of Emotionally Disturbed Students. In terms of their visibility in the classroom, emotionally disturbed children are frequently noticed by the teacher. Cullinan and Epstein (1986) summarize the major characteristics of children and youth who are emotionally disturbed in three categories: environmental conflicts, personal disturbances, and learning disorders.

Students who are experiencing *environmental conflicts* often display aggressive disruptive characteristics such as fighting, bullying, violating rules, and the like. These students may be hyperactive (overactive, impulsive) or socially maladjusted (stealing, fighting, truancy). *Personal disturbances* include anxiety disorders such as crying and statements of worry. The student may socially withdraw. Lastly, the emotionally disturbed student may display *learning disorders*, which may result in deficits in basic academic skills and overall educational achievement.

Emotionally disturbed students tend to exhibit either "too much" or "too little" behavior. Students exhibiting too much behavior may be defiant, disruptive, and/or destructive, whereas students exhibiting too little behavior may be shy, hypersensitive, moody, and/or withdrawn. Cognitive, social and emotional, communication, and motor development are the areas most affected in students who are mildly emotionally disturbed.

Capabilities of Emotionally Disturbed Students.   Emotionally disturbed students need educational programs that stress behavior management and the development of skills in personal relationships. These students need and can acquire such basic skills as sitting in a seat, concentrating on a task, and completing short assignments. Teachers must "concentrate on getting disruptive behavior under control *before* any academic work can be presented" (Cartwright, Cartwright, & Ward, 1984, p. 228). Emotionally disturbed students can master academic tasks when they are appropriately sequenced and presented and when attention is given to getting deviant behavior under control. They need to know which behaviors the teacher will not tolerate and the consequences for engaging in those behaviors (e.g., knowing "time out" will be the result, if a student has a tantrum). Emotionally disturbed students usually respond to positive, corrective feedback when they make an error. Teachers need to communicate care and concern rather than a desire to punish when reacting to inappropriate behaviors. Students who withdraw from interpersonal relationships can be helped by contact with adults who are warm and accepting, but who are consistent in their responses to inappropriate behaviors.

Behavior modification procedures are effective with emotionally disturbed students. Providing appropriate models, allowing students to rehearse acceptable behaviors, and reinforcing such behaviors have been shown to be effective with emotionally disturbed students (Wallace & Kauffman, 1978).

Learning Disabled (LD)

Experts estimate that 1–3% of our school-aged population is learning disabled. However, in reality, schools serve a greater number. A current definition of *learning disabled* is as follows:

> "Specific learning disability" means a disorder in one or more of the basic psychological processes involved in understanding or in using language, spoken or written, which may manifest itself in an imperfect ability to listen, think, speak, read, write, spell, or to do mathematical calculations. The term includes such conditions as perceptual handicaps, brain injury, minimal brain dysfunction, dyslexia, and developmental aphasia. The term does not include children who have learning problems which are primarily the result of visual, hearing, or motor handicaps, of mental retardation, of emotional disturbance, or of environmental, cultural, or economic disadvantages. (*Federal Register,* 1977, p. 42478)

The National Joint Committee on Learning Disabilities (NJCLD) has proposed a new definition of LD. This organization, moved by displeasure over the present definition in P.L. 94–142, defines *LD* as follows:

Learning disabilities is a generic term that refers to a heterogeneous group of disorders manifested by significant difficulties in the acquisition and use of listening, speaking, reading, writing, or mathematical abilities. These disorders are intrinsic to the individual and presumed to be due to central nervous system dysfunction. Even though a learning disability may occur concomitantly with other handicapping conditions (e.g., sensory impairment, mental retardation, social and emotional disturbances) or environmental influences (e.g., cultural differences, insufficient/inappropriate instruction, psychogenic factors), it is not the direct result of those conditions or influences. (Cited in Hammill, Leigh, McNutt, & Larsen, 1981, p. 336).

Characteristics of Learning Disabled Students.   Children who are eligible to be placed in a class for the learning disabled must have an average or above-average IQ. Learning disabled students have specific characteristics that interfere with behavior, performance, and learning abilities. These characteristics may exist singly or in any combination. No one set of characteristics or behaviors will be found in *all* children who are categorized as learning disabled.

Mercer (1979) has identified six areas within the domain of problems faced by learning disabled children—academic learning difficulties, language disorders, motor disorders, social/emotional problems, perceptual disorders, and memory problems. Academically, the learning disabled student may read below grade level and exhibit problems in spelling, writing, punctuation, grammar, or arithmetic. The learning disabled student may have problems in oral expression or receptive (understanding) language. Poor general coordination, hyperactivity (excessive movement), or hypoactivity (lack of activity) are characteristics of motor disorders. Socially, the learning disabled student may be withdrawn, lack organizational skills, have difficulty beginning or completing tasks, not be able to complete tasks done on previous days, have a low level of frustration, and exhibit poor self-esteem. Perceptually, the learning disabled student may have visual and auditory problems with perception, discrimination, and memory. The learning disabled student also has problems remembering facts, figures, abstractions, and the like.

Capabilities of Learning Disabled Students.   No two learning disabled students have the same set of problems; therefore, the capabilities of learning disabled students vary. However, all learning disabled students are capable of learning academic content in their problem area(s) when effective instructional procedures are identified and implemented. The key is identifying the combination of instructional procedures that will be effective with each student.

Learning disabled students can learn to compensate for learning problems by making lists, rehearsing steps in completing a task, organizing thoughts, using cues, and so forth. They can be taught to "shut out" interfering sights and sound and to cope with distractions (Morsink, 1984).

Implications for the Teacher

Listed here are several ways in which the teacher can be of help to the mildly handicapped student who is experiencing difficulty in the learning situation.

Have the child work at his or her own ability level in each academic area. This may vary in reading, spelling, language, and math with one or more areas being lower than the others.

Plan and provide a number of successful experiences, as tolerance for failure is low.

Provide clear instructions, and recognize that while the child may appear to understand, in fact, he or she may be confused. Avoid instructions involving more than two steps at a time.

Consider special physical arrangements in the classroom to decrease over-stimulation and distractability. A "cubicle" or desk set away from distractions may be necessary to maintain attention to learning tasks. However, if this approach is used, it should be made clear to the child that this is not a punitive arrangement.

Be alert to possible signs of emotional disturbance or behavior problems. If problems seem to exist, the recommendations given earlier for emotionally handicapped children are applicable.

Utilize multisensory [auditory, visual, tactile (touch), and kinesthetic (movement)] approaches to instruction whenever possible.

Communicate with the resource teacher to discuss which methods being employed seem to be most successful.

Sequence learning tasks into steps that can be successfully achieved by the child. Reinforce successful achievement of each step.

Use short assignments. If an entire worksheet (e.g., math problems) appears frustrating, cut the worksheet into strips, allowing the child to complete one strip at a time (applies to the lower elementary level only).

In reading, the child may frequently confuse similar words (e.g., *can* and *ran*, *talk* and *walk*, *was* and *saw*). Ask the child to spell the word orally and repronounce it.

Record the child's progress in graph or chart form. Share this with the child so that he or she may *see* the progress.

Design teacher-made games for use as individual or small-group activities to reinforce the skills being developed.

Structure and consistency in the classroom environment, as well as a daily routine, are extremely important. If changes in schedule are to occur, prepare the child ahead of time and reemphasize the change periodically.

Utilize cross-age, peer, and volunteer tutors.

MILDLY HANDICAPPED

Learning Disabilities—
The Special Teacher's View

Ms. King has been teaching for 10 years. She has the primary self-contained class for children with learning disabilities (LD). Her eight students range in age from 5 to 8 years. They are attractive, bright, normal appearing children who enter class eagerly, full of chatter. Ms. King explains that the children are with her for most of the day but all are with regular classmates for music, art, library, lunch, and physical education. In addition, one student is mainstreamed for math and one student for math and science. Most of the students have reading problems and auditory processing difficulties. Some also have perceptual-motor delays, which makes writing and drawing difficult. The biggest problems for the learning disabled students in the regular classroom are reading, following directions, paying attention, and completing written assignments on time.

Ms. King has developed excellent rapport with the regular teachers who accept special students in their classrooms. Ms. King splits the children into groups to avoid overloading any one teacher. She has also observed that some teachers are simply unable to work with special students and suggests that they should not be forced to do so. Ms. King's role is as the primary teacher for reading, language arts, and math. She also teaches science and social studies to those students who are not mainstreamed for these subjects. To aid the regular teacher, Ms. King offers to read tests to the students individually, help with homework, and adapt assignments. She also serves as a consultant whenever the regular teachers have questions about the LD children.

Mainstreaming works! This is the message Ms. King has for teachers and parents. With planning and cooperation between special and regular teachers, school and home, teacher and children, mainstreaming can help the LD child feel accepted by peers and can speed the child's return to the school's regular program.

Hints for Regular Teachers
1. Assign a regular student to be the "special friend" of the mainstreamed child. Even very young children enjoy the responsibility of going to get their friend for classes, special activities, and lunch. Because the children take their job seriously, the teachers do not have to remember to include the mainstreamed child.
2. Send a copy of your weekly lesson plan to the special teacher. This

way the teacher can relate the lessons to your topics and make the child's program more integrated.

3. Talk to your students before the mainstreamed children arrive and allow the special teacher to speak to them as well. It can be explained that LD children are not really different from themselves. Explain that LD means "learns differently," and that the mainstreamed child can learn just as much as they can, but may need a different approach.
4. Treat the mainstreamed child as normally as possible but do make adaptations when necessary.
5. Keep directions short and simple. Check on the LD child as he or she begins the assignment to see that the child is on the right track.
6. Seat the LD child near the teacher. This makes checking on the child easy and unnoticeable.
7. Ask the resource teacher to give the student a test orally in a one-to-one setting if needed.
8. Let the special teacher grade essay questions if the child's spelling, handwriting, or writing style is confusing.
9. Give only one assignment at a time. "Do page 17 in math, then copy these sentences from the board, then read 'Johnny's Big Day' in your reader," is confusing to a child with auditory processing problems.
10. Verbal (not written) directions are usually best for the younger child. Pair verbal and written directions for the older child.
11. Some LD children *must* finger count in math; place them in the rear of the room if this is not allowed for others.
12. Cut timed tests in half for the LD child.
13. Avoid purple dittoes for the LD child as they are often hard to read. Make a black copy for them instead.
14. If you hand-write worksheets, you may need to read them to the child or let the special teacher read or type them.
15. Use color coding as a learning device. For example, vocabulary words may be on green cards one week, blue the next. Parents and resource people can be told to study "green words."

Learning Disabilities—
The Regular Teacher's View

Mr. Johnson teaches a regular fourth-grade class in a rural elementary school. He has 26 students in his class; six of them are learning disabled. Two of the six are from the self-contained LD class and are with Mr. Johnson for 1 to 2 hours daily. The other four children are from the resource LD class and are with him all day, except for the language arts period, which they spend with the LD teacher.

Mr. Johnson says that learning disabled students are not very different from his regular students. They are not brighter nor slower, better nor worse behaved. But they do learn in different ways and each one is an individual with different needs.

Most of the learning disabled students that Mr. Johnson has have difficulty reading. For this reason, they have problems following written directions and working on silent reading assignments. Some of the children also have auditory discrimination problems that make it difficult for them to concentrate on the important noise (primarily speech) in the classroom. The learning disabled students are also sometimes lacking in self-esteem, probably because of their difficulty with some academic tasks such as reading.

Mr. Johnson learned to make adjustments for learning disabled children through experience, since his formal education did not include any training in special education. He feels that an introductory course in special children should be offered to all regular class teachers. County-wide workshops would also help fill a need for teachers who have mainstreamed children in their class. Mr. Johnson also feels that the school principal is a primary factor in the acceptance or rejection of mainstreamed chidren, and should be included in classes and workshops along with the teachers. In his case, Mr. Johnson feels that the principal has done an excellent job in preparing the regular teachers to accept special children.

Mr. Johnson feels that his regular students are accepting of the LD children in their classroom primarily because the children are identified early in their school years and have "always been there." The children are so used to being in class with children who "go out" for resource, speech, adaptive physical education, and so on, that they do not see it as unusual. The LD children are treated normally and they react in kind.

Mr. Johnson stresses the importance of keeping the parents of the mainstreamed children informed and involved with their child's progress. He has observed that the children who make the most progress in the mainstreaming program are those whose parents are the most actively involved in school life. The parents who work at home with children, reinforcing what the school has begun, see the biggest gains.

Finally, Mr. Johnson offers the following tips for parents and for other regular teachers who are asked to accept special children in their class.

For Parents
1. Talk to the teacher regularly and always try to attend IEP conferences, reevaluations, Open House, and other "open school" days.
2. Volunteer to help in your child's school. He or she will be proud to see you there! It will also tell your child that you find school important enough to give your time to.
3. Make sure the child completes assigned homework. Check it to see if your child did the work correctly.

For Other Regular Class Teachers

1. The biggest key to working with mainstreamed children is flexibility. Be willing to juggle your schedule and make small changes that will facilitate the special child.
2. Work closely with the special education teachers. Mr. Johnson feels that socializing with each other helps to develop a good working relationship.
3. Ask the special teacher what you can do to help when a problem arises in your class. Reinforce each others' programs.
4. For LD children with auditory discrimination problems, provide seating in the quietest area of the room.
5. To help in following directions, verbally reinforce all directions for the LD child. Check on the child to see that he or she understands without making the child feel conspicuously different. Some LD children do not want to be isolated for special work; respect this, and include them in a group designed to meet their needs.
6. LD children who are easily distracted love using earphones to listen to tapes in the listening center. Use this device for reading comprehension development.
7. If the child has difficulty completing written tests, allow the child to take them to the special teacher to read orally. Mr. Johnson reads the test to all of his students.

Learning Disabilities— The Parent's View

Brenda Carson is a 9-year-old learning disabled child. She has been professionally diagnosed as having a cerebral dominance problem and minimum brain dysfunction. Psychological testing also revealed perceptual-motor difficulties. When Brenda was a preschooler, she was thought to be emotionally disturbed. Because Brenda constantly bothered the other children, would not do her schoolwork, and was generally poorly behaved, her teachers believed she was disturbed. After years of failure in school, Brenda did develop emotional problems and often talked of dying. Ms. Carson, Brenda's mother, suspected that Brenda had a learning disability but could not get confirmation from the professionals. Since Ms. Carson has both a brother and a sister who are severely learning disabled, she recognized the same characteristics in Brenda.

Ms. Carson persisted for 4 years in seeking help for Brenda. Brenda was finally evaluated at age 8 and labeled learning disabled. She is now in the primary learning disabilities classroom and is making good progress. Her teacher says Brenda is bright and is particularly adept in math. She is also very verbal and uses expressive language well. Her weaknesses are in reading, writing, and following directions. Brenda is mainstreamed for math, physical education, and music. She gets along well with the regular students and has many friends. She is an outgoing, friendly child and other children are attracted to her. She is always with other children at school and at home.

Ms. Carson feels that the school did not recognize Brenda's problem early enough and that the school system should evaluate children at an earlier age so that the children can receive help before their self-esteem suffers. Ms. Carson also believes parents must actively pursue help for their children when they believe there is a learning problem. She suggests that parents document everything pertaining to the child's problem, including meetings with teachers, doctors' appointments, professional evaluations, and important aspects of the child's development. This is beneficial when the child is being tested and considered for special class placement.

Suggestions for the School
1. Refer learning disabled children to the school guidance counselor as needed to work on low self-esteem and other emotional problems.
2. Provide a support group for parents in the school. Alternate meetings with and without the child's teachers.
3. Allow LD children to have their own section in the school newspaper.
4. Teachers should be more aware of LD characteristics and trained to detect problems at an early age.
5. LD children have wide mood swings. Teachers should make allowances for a child who is having a bad day.
6. Use a language-experience approach to reading.
7. Give homework each school night with directions for parents if necessary. Provide work for summer vacation so that regression does not take place.
8. Use behavior modification to eliminate undesirable behavior.
9. Tell parents specific skills and activities to work on to reinforce the educational program.

Suggestions for Parents
1. Keep your pediatrician involved in the academic progress of your child and aware of the special needs of the LD child.
2. Form a parent support group at your school and get actively involved in your child's education.
3. Set aside a few minutes each night for a "reading hour" and let your child read to you. After he or she reads, ask questions to check comprehension. If the child does not know a word, say it. If the child stops to decode every unknown word, he or she will not remember what is being read.
4. Avoid picture books for the child to read aloud. Learning disabled children are good at "bluffing" from the pictures. Take the book to a copier and block out the pictures so that the child must concentrate on the words.

5. Let the child make up a story that you print on paper. Wait a week and then have the child read it to you.
6. Designate a certain time each night for homework. Post the starting time on the refrigerator.
7. Take advantage of tutoring programs at local universities. For a small fee, your child can receive reading and other instruction from the experts.
8. Volunteer to be your child's room parent if you can. This tells the child that you consider school to be important. It also allows you to be aware of what is happening in the classroom.
9. When your child is learning the alphabet, cut letters out of sandpaper. Place them one at a time on the refrigerator and have the child touch them often and say the letters.
10. Both parents should work with the child as well as spend time doing "fun" things.

Speech and Language Disorders

According to the *Federal Register* (1977), *speech-impaired* is defined as "a communication disorder, such as stuttering, impaired articulation, a language impairment, or a voice impairment, which adversely affects a child's educational performance" (pp. 42478–42479). Approximately 5% of school-aged children are estimated to have speech and language disorders. It is not uncommon for students to have a speech or language impairment as well as another handicap.

For study purposes, we discuss communication disorders of the following categories:

A. Speech disorders
   1. Articulation disorders
      a. Omissions
      b. Substitutions
      c. Distortions
      d. Additions
   2. Voice disorders
      a. Pitch disorders
      b. Intensity disorders
      c. Quality disorders
   3. Disorders of fluency (stuttering)
B. Language disorders

Speech Disorders

Most authorities in the field classify speech disorders into three major sections: articulation disorders, voice disorders, and disorders of fluency. Language disorders may be viewed as one type of speech disorder. However, the American Speech and Hearing Association views speech and language disorders as major categories.

Articulation Disorders. Speech problems associated with poor speech and sound production are called *articulation disorders*. This group may be further divided into disorders of omissions, substitutions, distortions, and additions as follows.

Omissions—Errors where the child omits a sound normally found in a word (e.g., *I uv u* for *I love you*). These errors are quite common in young children and are usually outgrown even without therapy.

Substitutions—Errors when a child substitutes one sound for another, also referred to as *baby talk* (e.g., *wed* for *red*; *fank you* for *thank you*).

Distortions—Errors where sounds are somewhat close to the intended sound; however, not completely correct (e.g., lisps are errors of distortions).

Additions—Errors where a sound is added to a word. At times these are usually characteristic of geographic regions and speech patterns of select groups.

Children with articulation problems may experience difficulty with one or more sounds. Errors of distortion are more easily corrected than those of omissions and substitutions.

Voice Disorders. Voice disorders frequently result from vocal abuse and require medical attention in addition to speech therapy. Voice disorders may be of pitch, intensity, or quality. The speech may be hoarse, harsh, nasal, breathy, or inappropriate for the pupil's age and sex. Frequently, voice disorders are combined with other speech disorders, forming a complex communication disorder.

Pitch—The voice is too high or too low and may have a break in flow. Effective communication may be reduced.

Intensity—Refers to "loudness" of voice. The voice is "too loud" or "too soft."

Quality—Voice is too nasal, hoarse, breathy, harsh. Frequently requires medical treatment.

Stuttering. Stuttering is a disorder of rhythm in which the child's flow of speech is interrupted. Although this disorder has been a source of fascination for many years to those who study speech disorders, experts do not agree on its cause. Stuttering usually begins between the ages of 3 and 5 years and involves the following forms of disfluency: repetitions, prolongations, hesitations, and interjections. Although little is known about stuttering, Gearheart and Weishahn (1980) have identified several characteristics of the disorder.

1. Those who stutter rarely or never do so while singing.
2. Those who stutter rarely stutter while speaking in unison, in synchronization to a rhythmic beat, while alone, or while swearing (these are somewhat less absolute than item 1, but nevertheless usually true).
3. Even for those who stutter regularly, there is no situation that absolutely ensures stuttering; that is, it cannot always be induced.
4. Stutterers tend to stutter on the same words when reading and rereading the same passage but may not stutter on these same words in other sentences.
5. As a group, stutterers tend to be able to predict their stuttering.
6. Time pressure is a factor that appears to lead to an increase in stuttering.
7. Stutterers cannot be shown to be biologically different from nonstutterers.
8. Stuttering has been eliminated or significantly reduced by totally different procedures in cases that seemed to be very similar (i.e., there is not a readily demonstrable, significant correlation between type of stuttering and any particular remedial technique).
9. Stutterers can hear how their speech flows, and although they understand what normal fluency is, they cannot attain it.
10. In many cases (more than 75% by some estimates), stuttering ceases without reason.

Language Disorders

"Language disorders refer to any consistent difficulty in understanding or expressing language" (Morsink, 1984, p. 33). Of all of the communication disorders, language disorders are the most serious. Generally, language disorders may be placed into three major categories—receptive language disorders, expressive language problems, and mixed receptive/expressive disorders.

Receptive language disorder—The inability to comprehend questions and follow commands expected for one's mental age (Blackhurst & Berdine, 1981).

Expressive language disorder—"When a child's ability to send messages is significantly below his ability to receive them" (Blackhurst & Berdine, 1981, p. 123).

Mixed receptive/expressive disorder—When a child has both a receptive and expressive disorder.

Characteristics of Students with Speech and Language Disorders

Children who are communicatively handicapped are said to have defective speech. This defective speech interferes with communication, causes the possessor to be maladjusted, and/or calls unfavorable attention to itself. But, more than just speech, language may also be affected. This communication handicap interferes with or limits to varying degrees the youngster's ability to formulate, express, receive, or interpret oral language. Communication problems may vary in degree from mild, when the child is understandable but errors are noted in his or her speech, to severe, when the pupil is completely unintelligible. Educators must be aware when children exhibit any of these characteristics. Determining whether a person has a speech problem can be accomplished by answering the following questions:

1. *Can I understand this person?* This is the simplest judgment you will have to make. If you cannot understand or can understand only with difficulty what a person is saying, he or she has a communication disorder.
2. *Does this person sound strange?* If you can understand someone, but the person does not sound as he or she should, a problem exists. An adult who sounds like Elmer Fudd—a 200-pound adult male who sounds like a 9-year-old female—and a person who has a flat, expressionless manner of speaking have communication problems.
3. *Does this person have any peculiar physical characteristics when speaking?* A person who has distracting mannerisms that interfere with the message has a problem. These mannerisms might include unnecessary or unexpected movements of the lips, tongue, nostrils, arms, legs, or posture.
4. *Is the communication in a style inappropriate to the situation?* We do not expect the president of the United States to greet Congress before the annual State of the Union Address by saying, "Hey, what's happenin'? It's cool at my pad, what's goin' down here?" Our point is that we normally shift our style of communication to fit a given situation. A speaker unable to do this may have a problem.
5. *Do I enjoy listening to this speaker?* This is a judgment we all feel uncomfortable making. If the reason we do not enjoy a speaker is that we do not like the message being conveyed, the speaker does not have a problem. If, on the other hand, we do not enjoy a speaker for one of the reasons mentioned here, the person probably does have a problem. Speakers who can alienate people merely by introducing themselves need help.
6. *Is the speaker damaging his or her communication mechanisms?* Like most other parts of the body, the organs used in communication can be misused. Although diagnoses of physiological abuse can only be made by specialists, listeners can often detect signs of strain in a speaker's voice. Teachers should

always refer to professionals when they suspect that children may be in-
juring their voices while speaking. An unnecessary referral hurts no one, but
overlooking a symptom can have disastrous consequences.

7. *Does the speaker suffer when attempting to communicate?* This is difficult
   to judge in that a listener usually cannot determine how a speaker feels about
   his or her efforts to communicate. Many people considered normal com-
   municators by their peers suffer emotionally as a result of shortcomings they
   imagine. Communication problems such as these without obvious symptoms
   are among the most difficult to treat. (Culatta & Culatta, 1985).

Implications for the Teacher

The influence of the classroom teacher is invaluable to the speech pathologist
in motivating pupils with a speech and language deficit to improve their speech
and in preventing them from feeling resentful, different, or penalized because
of their problem. In addition to the evaluative and therapeutic services provided
by the speech pathologist, the classroom teacher must provide an environment
that enhances the use of correct speech and language patterns learned during
the therapy sessions. An effective classroom teacher can aid the speech
pathologist by:

1. Becoming acquainted with the aims and objectives of the therapy program.
2. Helping to develop an attitude of acceptance on the part of other children
   toward the communicatively handicapped child.
3. Reinforcing good speech and language performance during classroom activities so to establish the importance of using what is learned during the
   therapy sessions.
4. Helping the speech pathologist to evaluate progress at different stages of
   the therapy program.
5. Assisting disfluent or stuttering children by letting them talk without inter-
   ruption and without making suggestions as to how they should talk. In other
   words, do not ask the student to hurry up, speak more slowly, stop and
   start over, or take a deep breath before speaking. These "suggestions" place
   more attention on "how" the child is speaking rather than "what" the child
   is saying.
6. Accepting the child's disfluencies as his or her way of talking without showing disapproval, fear, embarrassment, irritation, or surprise.
7. Helping pupils receiving medical attention and speech therapy for a voice
   problem to follow their treatment programs, especially if they should avoid
   abusing their voices or be on vocal rest.
8. Realizing that children with a cleft palate or lip may require special academic help for those extended periods of time that they must miss school
   due to surgery and visits to a specialist.

9. Becoming aware of the cerebral palsied child's strengths and weaknesses in all areas and helping to develop these strengths to their fullest capacities.
10. Remembering that, for speech and language handicapped youngsters to improve, they must be seen by the speech pathologist. Thus, the teacher should refer any youngsters suspected of having a speech, language, hearing, or voice problem to a speech pathologist for evaluation.

Case Study

SPEECH IMPAIRED

The Special Teacher's View

Ms. Hunter teaches speech to children with speech, language, and listening difficulties. At the beginning of each school year, she screens all kindergarten, third, and fifth graders to determine which children need her services. Her primary rule is that a child needs speech class if his or her speech is affecting performance in the regular class. There are basically eight categories of speech disorder: articulation, voice, stuttering, language, cleft palate, cerebral palsy, hearing-impaired and deaf, and mentally retarded.

Two of Ms. Hunter's students are Joey and Michelle. They are in the same kindergarten class and come to speech for 30 minutes twice a week. Ms. Hunter likes for children from the same class to come together to speech because she feels that the carry-over to the regular class is greater. Joey has serious language delays and did almost no talking when he first arrived. Ms. Hunter used behavior modification to reward Joey every time he talked. This was also done in the regular class. Now, after five months in speech, Joey says "hello" first and is using speech more all the time. Michelle has a moderate stuttering problem. She does not let her disfluency keep her from talking and, in fact, does not seem to notice she has a problem. She too has made progress and her speech is improving.

Ms. Hunter has found the regular teachers very receptive to speech impaired children. They often seek Ms. Hunter's advice on ways to help the children and are eager to make adaptations in class. Ms. Hunter does several things to help the mainstreamed speech impaired children. First, she talks with the parents. Parents often feel there is a stigma in having a child in speech class and some are afraid placement there may result in other special education classes. Ms. Hunter reassures them that these things are untrue and explains her program in detail. Ms. Hunter then regularly sends home suggestions for the parents to help their child's speech. For example, she encourages parents to use open-ended questions rather than those requiring just yes or no. She also stresses the importance of practicing conversation at home.

For the regular classroom, Ms. Hunter makes a copy of rules for good speech and posts it in a conspicuous spot. She asks the teacher to refer to it often to reinforce concepts introduced in speech class. This is not only helpful for the speech impaired children but for the other children as well. She asks the regular teacher to send her a copy of the lesson plans and course objectives so that Ms. Hunter can coordinate the sessions. For example, if the class is studying Indians, Ms. Hunter will get a book from the library on Indians. Her group will then read aloud from the book and discuss the topics. Because of the focus on production of letter sounds, carry over is great when the children begin phonic sounds in class. Ms. Hunter provides the primary teachers with a list of sounds and developmental ages when those sounds should be produced correctly. This helps teachers to informally screen for articulation problems.

The Regular Teacher's View

Mr. Pierson has 12 years' teaching experience and is an "old hand" at working with mainstreamed children. He had no special education courses in college but has educated himself through experience.

Working with special children is not much different from working with regular children, Mr. Pierson believes. "At first you do feel a little intimidated and wonder if you will be expected to reorganize your entire curriculum for one child. You find this is not true at all, that you must merely assume that *all* children have different styles of learning and different needs. This is probably easiest at the kindergarten level, where course objectives run throughout the year and everyone is on their own level developmentally."

This year, Mr. Pierson has two students who are speech impaired. His primary adaptation for these children, who have both speech and language difficulties, is to lessen the difficulty of the academic tasks. He also attempts to give the two children as much individual attention as possible without sacrificing the needs of the rest of the class. This balance is the main skill that the teacher with mainstreamed children must master.

Mr. Pierson does not see that the speech impaired children are very different from the other children. Because of their expressive language problems, however, they do not volunteer to answer questions often and are not as verbal as the other children. They do leave the classroom to work with the speech therapist, and the other children are curious about where they are going. But it is not a stigma, it is a privilege to be able to leave the classroom.

The most helpful advice Mr. Pierson can offer to other regular classroom teachers is to rely on the special education teachers for aid in working with children with special needs. He has found that the special personnel (i.e., the speech and language therapist, the learning disabilities teacher, and so on) are invaluable as partners. Together problems can be examined and solutions obtained. Also, Mr. Pierson stresses the importance of giving parents specific instructions for reinforcing the curriculum at home. He has learned that parents are usually willing to work with the child if they know exactly what they should do.

Hints for Teachers
1. Pair auditory and visual instruction. Pair different methods of presentation (auditory, visual, kinesthetic, and so on) until you find the one with which the child learns best.
2. In upper grades, teachers should try to focus on overall objectives rather than keeping everyone on the same page in the book. This makes adapting the curriculum easier.
3. Provide in-service training for teachers.
4. Learn to budget time wisely so to work with special children.
5. Be consistent in working with the special needs children.
6. Reinforce the resource and special teachers.

The Parent's View

John Newfield is an 11-year-old student at a large suburban middle school. He has both speech articulation and disfluency problems and is also learning disabled. John is mainstreamed into all regular classes. He received speech therapy two or three times a week for five years until he was dismissed last year.

Mr. Newfield, John's father, reports that John's speech problems were first apparent when he was 4 years old. Since he was a special education teacher, Mr. Newfield was aware that the disfluency among young children was not uncommon. John was assessed by a speech therapist at age 5 and began therapy at that time.

John's speech therapist helped to diminish greatly the frequency and severity of his articulation and disfluency problems. His speech therapy program consisted primarily of articulation training. Additionally, the speech teacher assisted the regular class teachers in reinforcing good speech habits in the regular classroom. The special teacher emphasized that the regular teacher should not ask John to take a deep breath, slow down, start over, use unusual facial gestures, or in any other way indicate concern over John's disfluencies. To do so, would reinforce the speech difficulties John was experiencing.

The Newfield family also has had a significant positive influence on the remediation of John's speech. John's problems were discussed carefully with his older brothers years ago, and Mr. Newfield outlined ways the brothers could help John. These suggestions included giving John direct eye contact when he spoke, as it appeared that if eye contact was not made it increased the severity of the disfluencies. Also, he stressed a few significant things that were *not* to be done, including interrupting when John was talking; using facial expressions to indicate impatience or sympathy; telling John to stop, slow down or start over; or trying to talk at the same time. Mr. Newfield always maintained a positive attitude about John's problems. He remembers telling John often that he would outgrow the speech problems and that they would eventually go away. Additionally, Mr. Newfield identified situations that were stressful for John and where speech symptoms appeared to worsen. These are referred to as *hard-speech* situations. An example of a hard-speech situation at home is at the dinner table where everyone attempts to speak at once. Mr. Newfield consistently reminded all of his children to take turns speaking until they did this automatically. With other hard-speech situations outside of the home, such as when John was asked to read aloud in Sunday school or to speak to a large group of Cub Scouts, Mr. Newfield privately talked to the leaders and explained John's problems. He asked them not to place pressure on John in situations that emphasized speech and he also outlined positive things that the leaders could do to help John.

During the early years of John's schooling, he experienced a great deal of academic failure due to his learning disabilities. It appeared to Mr. Newfield that there was a correlation between the pressure John experienced academically and the severity of his speech problems. Currently, John is experiencing almost no academic problems, and his articulation difficulties have completely disappeared. He is disfluent very rarely now, and only in stressful situations or when he is very excited. Mr. Newfield feels confident that these last traces of John's problem will eventually go away.

Mainstreaming, for the most part, has been a positive experience for John. One of his primary teachers allowed his classmates to tease and mimic him, but now John is well accepted and regarded positively by the other children. Mr. Newfield feels that it is important that teachers have a positive attitude toward handicapped children and that they encourage good attitudes and conduct toward the handicapped among their students. He also stresses the need for teachers to communicate to parents often about their child's progress.

In the end, Mr. Newfield feels that most of the credit for John's dramatic recovery in speech should be given to John. Despite his significant problems, John remains optimistic and persistent. He works hard in school and never gives up. He has always refused to get discouraged by his early failures and even now struggles daily to make good grades and to succeed. John's learning disabilities are in reading, while math has always come easily to him. He told his parents recently how much he likes math. When asked why, he replied, "Because when I go to math class, my mind can rest." That should remind all of us who live and work with mildly handicapped children how much work it is for some of them to cope with the demands of school. Often, all children, and particularly our "special" ones, need time for their minds and bodies to rest.

Visual Impairments

A *visual handicap*, or legal blindness, refers to a central visual acuity for a distance of 20/200 or less in the better eye with correction or, if greater than 20/200, a field of vision no greater than 20 degrees at the widest diameter (Hartfield, 1975).

Visual acuity is a measure of the sharpness of vision. Recorded normal visual acuity is 20/20. On the Snellen eye chart (see Figure 3.1), the large E indicates the 20/200 line. In other words, what the legally blind person can see at 20 feet the normal person can see at 200 feet.

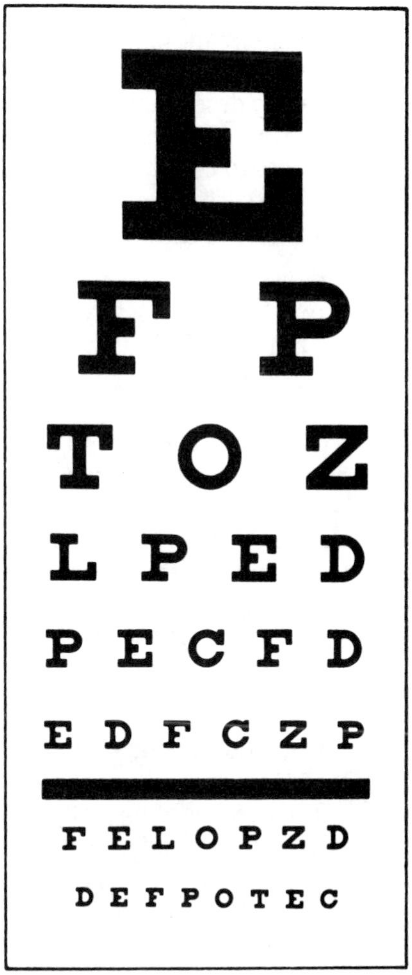

FIGURE 3.1
The Snellen Eye Chart (Reprinted with permission from the National Society to Prevent Blindness. Prevent Blindness, a non-profit organization established in 1908, provides sight-saving programs and services through twenty-seven affiliates/divisions.)

The *better eye* means that if a person is legally blind in one eye but has good vision in the other eye, the person cannot be classified as visually impaired.

With best correction refers to the use of glasses or contact lenses. That is, a person is visually impaired if he or she still has an impairment of 20/200 while wearing glasses or contact lenses.

The *visual field* is the peripheral vision, or the total area we can see at one time without moving our gaze. For example, if you drew a straight line to an object at which you were looking and you could not see more than 20 degrees from either side of the object, you would have a deficit in your visual field and be classified as legally blind.

According to the *Federal Register* (1977), the definition of *visual handicapped* means "a visual impairment which, even with correction, adversely affects a child's educational performance. The term includes both partially seeing and blind children" (p. 42479). Definitions for visually handicapped divide this category into two specific sections: the blind and the partially seeing. The term *partially seeing* describes those students who have serious visual limitations, after correction, but who are able to use vision as a major avenue of learning. The term refers to those individuals who have visual acuity between 20/70 and 20/200 in the better eye after proper correction. Partially seeing persons may need varying levels of support, depending on the efficiency with which they use their sight.

Characteristics of the Visually Handicapped Student

Of major importance to the classroom teacher is the ability to identify a child who has a visual impairment. The more severe the impairment, the more likely that the handicap was identified in early years. However, many times the visual impairment has gone unnoticed until the early school years. One of the most effective means of identifying a visually impaired student is to be aware of the characteristics that signal a visual problem. Table 3.1 provides the educator with a checklist of observable clues to vision problems.

Common Types of Visual Impairment

The number of partially seeing people greatly exceeds the number of those who are legally blind. Approximately 2 out of every 1,000 children can be classified as legally blind or partially seeing, and a total of 25% of the general school-aged population may have some type of visual impairment, most of which can be corrected (Gear, 1979). Although there are numerous types of visual defects,

TABLE 3.1
Checklist of Observable Clues to Vision Problems

Student's Name _____ Date _____

1. Appearance of Eyes:

   One eye turns in or out at any time _____
   Reddened eyes or lids _____
   Eyes tear excessively _____
   Encrusted eyelids _____
   Frequent styes on lids _____

2. Complaints When Using Eyes at Desk:

   Headaches in forehead or temples _____
   Burning or itching after reading or desk work _____
   Nausea or dizziness _____
   Print blurs after reading a short time _____

3. Behavioral Signs of Visual Problems:

   a. *Eye-movement abilities (ocular motility)*

      Head turns as reads across page _____
      Loses place often during reading _____
      Needs finger or marker to keep place _____
      Displays short attention span in reading
      or copying _____
      Too frequently omits words _____
      Repeatedly omits "small" words _____
      Writes up or down hill on paper _____
      Rereads or skips lines unknowingly _____
      Orients drawings poorly on page _____

   b. *Eye-teaming abilities (binocularity)*

      Complains of seeing double (diplopia) _____
      Repeats letters within words _____
      Omits letters, numbers, or phrases _____
      Misaligns digits in number columns _____
      Squints, closes, or covers one eye _____
      Tilts head extremely while working at desk _____
      Consistently shows gross postural deviations
      at all desk activities _____

   c. *Eye-hand coordination abilities*

      Must feel things to assist in any interpretation
      required _____
      Eyes not used to "steer" hand movements (ex-
      treme lack of orientation, placement of words
      or drawings on page) _____

(continued)

TABLE 3.1 *(continued)*

Writes crookedly, poorly spaced; cannot stay
on ruled lines   _____
Misaligns both horizontal and vertical series of
numbers   _____
Uses other hand as "spacer" to control spacing
and alignment on page   _____
Repeatedly confuses left-right directions   _____

   d. *Visual form perception (visual comparison,
      visual imagery, visualization)*

Mistakes words with same or similar
beginnings   _____
Fails to recognize the same word in next
sentence   _____
Reverses letters and/or words in writing and
copying   _____
Confuses likenesses and minor differences   _____
Confuses same word in same sentence   _____
Repeatedly confuses similar beginnings and
endings of words   _____
Fails to visualize what is read either silently or
orally   _____
Whispers to self for reinforcement while
reading silently   _____
Returns to "drawing with fingers" to decide
likes and differences   _____

   e. *Refractive status (nearsightedness, farsighted-
      ness, focus problems, etc.)*

Comprehension reduces as reading continues;
loses interest too quickly   _____
Mispronounces similar words as continues
reading   _____
Blinks excessively at desk tasks and/or
reading; not elsewhere   _____
Holds books too closely; face too close to desk
surface   _____
Avoids all possible near-centered tasks   _____
Complains of discomfort in tasks that demand
visual interpretation   _____
Closes or covers one eye when reading or doing
desk work   _____
Makes errors in copying from reference book
to notebook   _____
Squints to see chalkboard, or requests to move
nearer   _____

TABLE 3.1 *(continued)*

Rubs eyes during or after short periods of visual activity	_____
Fatigues easily; blinks to make chalkboard clear up after desk task	_____

4. Observer's Suggestions:

Source: Copyright © 1968, Optometric Extension Program Foundation, Inc. Reproduced by special permission. The Foundation suggests that the entire guide, "Educator's Guide to Classroom Vision Problems," be read before the Checklist is administered. Information and copies of the Guide and Checklist or Checklist only may be obtained by writing to the Optometric Extension Program Foundation, Inc., Duncan, OK 73533.

we need only to be familiar with the four types most commonly found in schools—myopia, hyperopia, astigmatism, and strabismus. Table 3.2 describes each of these defects in detail.

Implications for the Teachers

In working with the visually impaired student, many of the ideas for working with the partially sighted are applicable. A few basic suggestions that the teacher can use are as follows:

1. Do not grab the blind person in an attempt to assist; instead let the blind person place his or her hand through your arm or place it lightly on your shoulder.
2. When coming to an obstruction (e.g., a step or tree limb), simply step down or duck your body. Your body language indicates what is ahead for the blind person.
3. When entering a new room, explain the layout of the room to the blind person. Be sure that furniture, suitcases, books, and so on are not positioned in the center of the walking floor space.
4. Assign a friend to a blind student until the student becomes oriented to the physical design of the classroom.
5. In the school cafeteria, describe to the blind person the food being served and where the food is being placed on the plate.
6. Let blind persons speak for themselves—they are not helpless, only blind.

TABLE 3.2
Common Visual Defects

Defect	Description	Results	Improvements
Myopia (nearsightedness)	Eyeball too long; focus in front of retina.	Child cannot see distance clearly; no difficulty with close work, but strains and squints to see at a distance.	Glasses with concave lenses.
Hyperopia (farsightedness)	Eyeball too short; focus falls behind the retina rather than on the retina.	Child must shift the focus of the eye to see clearly at a distance, and shift again for close vision. The child will be distracted easily, tire quickly, and may look glassy-eyed.	Glasses with convex lenses.
Astigmatism (blurred vision)	Distortion in the shape of the lens or cornea. Some light rays focus on the retina, but others focus in front, or would fall in back of the retina.	Eye strain and blurred vision for both distant and near objects.	Hard contact lenses (make the cornea spherical as it should be).
Strabismus ("lazy eye")	Visual axes are not straight and one eye turns out (exotropia) or one eye turns in (esotropia).	May cause double vision, the brain suppresses the image in the deviating eye; this can lead to dimness of vision because of disuse. Child may suffer from nausea and fatigue.	Specific medical treatment, which should be done before the age of 5 or 6.

Source: G. Gear, Peat, I., Sprain, T., Donaldson, C., & Butler, K. (1979), *Billy: The visually impaired child in your classroom* (Birmingham: Alabama University, School of Education, Bureau of Education for the Handicapped (HEW/OE); Washington, DC: Division of Personnel Preparation) (ERIC Document No. ED 176 456), p. 6. Adapted with permission.

Most importantly, treat the blind person just as you would any other child. Do not be overly concerned with using words such as *see* rather than *look*. Blind persons know their limitations and are not sensitive to the seeing world. When you are unsure of yourself in trying to help blind students, ask them for advice.

Arranging the Classroom. Leslie (1980) suggests several ways in which the teacher can effectively arrange the physical setting of the classroom.

- Provide more space for the students who use braille.
- Tables twice as long as the traditional desk are needed to accommodate special materials.
- Provide the student with a long desk and a bookcase, both placed in an L-shaped position for easy access.
- Feel free to change the blind child's seating arrangement but do so with his or her help.
- Students who are partially sighted require less space than the blind child; however, they do need space in which to store materials.
- Provide proper lighting and avoid glare.
- Seek the advice of the teacher for the visually impaired in regard to proper seating.

Orientation to the Classroom. When you receive a child who is blind or partially sighted, it is important that you provide an orientation to the classroom. Leslie (1980) provides the following suggestions.

- Most blind or visually impaired students have had mobility training and thus know how to move safely within the classroom.
- Do not leave classroom doors half open—they should remain shut or open completely.
- Have the student come to school before the rest of the class to explore the new environment.
- If children hesitate about exploring the classroom, assist them by walking them around, explaining the major stationary items such as the door, windows, sink, closet, chalkboard, and the storage areas.
- Clearly define the parameters of the work space so the student does not interfere with a classmate's space.
- Orientate the student to major areas of the school such as the bathroom, cafeteria, gym, and exits and entranceways.
- In the cafeteria, the noise makes it more difficult for visually impaired students to function. Assist them several times in moving through the line and finding the tray, tools, and so on. Have another student carry the tray until you are sure that the student can carry the tray and find the table.
- Acquaint the child with the playground equipment.
- During the orientation process, point out special sounds that help in orientation (e.g., the ticking of a clock or noise from cars).

Classroom Guidelines.   Several guidelines that prove successful in helping the classroom teacher to work with the visually impaired student are listed in Table 3.3.

TABLE 3.3
Classroom Guidelines for the Visually Impaired

Grouping and Peer Relations

Establish a warm and accepting environment.

After the initial orientation, encourage children to let visually impaired students try it on their own.

Role-play the class feelings toward the teacher having to give extra time to the visually impaired child.

Help the visually impaired child feel like one of the group and not as a special student.

Share some special equipment with all students.

Written Work

Use bold-line, nonglare paper when needed.

Use colored pencils or felt-tip markers when helpful.

For the visually impaired student using braille, let the resource teacher interline the braille materials in script so the assignment can be evaluated.

Let the child who can type, type his or her assignments. A friend may be assigned for proofreading.

Use a nonglare chalkboard. Keep the surface clean. Black on white or white on black are the best combinations of color.

Read notes aloud from the board as you write them. Carbon copy or Xerox another student's class notes. Tape record notes.

Some visually impaired students can see work done on the overhead projector.

For testing, let the resource teacher copy in braille or have an older student read the test aloud.

Audiovisual Materials

Use narrated films followed by a class discussion.

Find the most suitable seating arrangement for the student.

Small filmstrip viewers can be used by children with some sight.

Television with adequate narration or dialogue can be used.

Models

Use models that are as realistic as possible.

Many museums loan useful models of animals, birds, snakes, and so on.

TABLE 3.3 (*continued*)

Field Trips

Focus on a few items instead of several.

Point out the sounds or odors when items cannot be touched.

Allow the student to experience sounds and odors. Do not overdo the verbalization.

Provide an orientation to the class regarding where they are going, what they will see and hear, and what you expect them to do on the trip.

Source: M. Leslie (1980). *Teaching the visually impaired child in the classroom.* MAVIS Sourcebook 3 (Washington, DC: Bureau of Education for the Handicapped ERIC Document No. ED 195465), p. 1–29. Adapted with permission.

Assisting the Blind

Childhood blindness has declined in recent years due to a decline in the visual disorder *retrolental fibroplasia*, often caused by giving too much oxygen to premature babies. In the early 1950s, it was discovered that the oxygen given in large amounts to premature infants was resulting in a large number of blind babies. Oxygen levels were then reduced. Presently, a leading cause of blindness in infants results from prenatal maternal rubella. However, with scientific advancements, fewer cases of infant blindness are being recorded.

The blind children of today function effectively within regular classes. They use special reading devices, large-print books, braille books, or talking books. A blind child moves through the day more slowly than the normal child. However, there are several things a classroom teacher should know in order to make the day flow smoothly.

Mobility and the Blind Student. Mobility training for the blind begins in the early years. It is essential that blind students learn how to move and be in control of their environment. According to Morsink (1984), "mobility training begins with a sighted guide, who walks one-half step ahead, while the student holds the guide's arm with fingers inside and thumb out. . . . The guide may pause at doorways and stairs, or near a chair, indicating through body language what is present" (p. 44). There are numerous travel aids available to the blind person, including guide dogs, canes, and electronic devices. However, orientation is a basic skill of mobility that all blind persons should possess (Cartwright, Cartwright, & Ward, 1984).

Braille for the Blind. Braille, a complicated method of communication, is a system of reading and writing that is taught to blind persons by highly skilled specialists. Braille, developed in the 1800s by Louis Braille, consists of a combination of dots within a cell (see Figure 3.2). Presently, there are braille codes for numerous subjects including music, science, and mathematics. Braille can be embossed with a slate and stylus or a braillewriter.

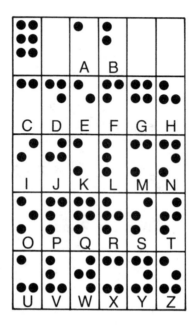

FIGURE 3.2
The Braille Alphabet

Hearing Impairments

Educationally, individuals with hearing impairments may be classified as either deaf or hard of hearing. According to the *Federal Register* (1977), *deafness* is defined as "a hearing impairment which is so severe that the child is impaired in processing linguistic information through hearing, with or without amplification, [and which] adversely affects educational performance" (p. 418). *Hard of hearing* is defined as a hearing impairment, whether permanent or fluctuating, that adversely affects a child's educational performance, but that is not included under the definition of "deaf" (pp. 41, 418).

It is estimated that sixteen million Americans have some degree of hearing loss. Of this number, only two million are considered deaf. The majority of children with hearing disabilities are born with them. Therefore, early detection of a hearing impairment is of great importance. Even though most hearing impaired children are identified prior to the early school years, it is important for educators to be aware of the characteristics of hearing impaired children for early identification.

Characteristics of Hearing Impaired Students

Gearheart and Weishahn (1980) provide a list of behaviors that can indicate a severe or mild hearing loss. When the classroom teacher observes these behaviors in a child, referral for an evaluation may be in order.

Communication opens the doors for learning.

1. The student shows a lack of attention.
2. The student turns or cocks his or her head an unusual amount of the time.
3. The student has little difficulty following written directions but difficulty following oral directions.
4. The student exhibits behaviors such as shyness, acting out, stubborness, or is withdrawn.
5. The student is reluctant to participate in oral activities.
6. The student looks to the class for clues for instructions.
7. The student's best achievement is in small groups.
8. The student exhibits a speech defect.
9. There is a difference between the student's expected and actual achievement.
10. Medical indications such as frequent earaches, sore throats, or fluid from the ears may indicate a hearing loss.

Implications for the Teacher

Today, more than ever before, we are seeing more and more hearing impaired children in the regular classroom. The following list provides the regular class teacher with suggestions for making the classroom more appropriate for hearing impaired children.

1. Accept the hard-of-hearing child as an individual. An awareness of the child's assets and limitations is needed. Capitalize on the assets and help the child feel that he or she belongs. Do not pamper or overprotect the child.
2. Remember that most hard-of-hearing children are just as intelligent as their normally hearing friends.
3. Encourage the child's special capabilities and help the child to experience success and achievement in some special task.
4. Remember that the hard-of-hearing child cannot understand everything all of the time regardless of the child's level of intelligence or degree of effort.
5. Use as many visual aids as possible. Demonstrate and describe what you want the child to understand. Use gestures.
6. Use the blackboard as much as possible. Do not talk while writing on the board, as the child cannot see your lips.
7. Use a natural tone of voice. Use a normal rate of speech, not too fast or too slow. Use a natural loudness of voice; do not yell.
8. Speak clearly and distinctly but do not exaggerate lip movements. Project your speech. Guard against talking with your lips closed or having your hand or book in front of your face while speaking.
9. Speak with the light on your face. Allow the light to be behind the child.
10. Rephrase questions and use repetition of key words. Try to avoid walking around while dictating problems or pronouncing spelling words.
11. Seat the child where he or she can see your face clearly. Allow the child to change seats if your face cannot be seen easily. Seat the child in the second or third row, if possible. Try to direct the child's better ear toward you and the class.
12. Write key words, new words, new topics, and so forth on the board. Say them to the class so that the hard-of-hearing child may see them on your lips as well as on the blackboard.
13. Whenever possible, preview new work with parents so they can review the topics at home.
14. Do not assume that a hearing aid makes the hard-of-hearing child's hearing "normal." No aid is free of distortion and many aids do not help discrimination of sounds.
15. Never shout, especially if a child is wearing an aid.
16. Discuss with the class members the problems of the hard-of-hearing child and of wearing an aid.
17. Encourage the hard-of-hearing child to ask for repetition. Do not become impatient if the child wants to "make sure" he or she understands.
18. Remember that all noise is made louder by a hearing aid and the child may have difficulty understanding when there is excessive noise in the room.
19. Remember that soft or voiceless sounds such as the *f, s, th, k,* and *sh* sounds may not be heard by the hard-of-hearing child. If the child does hear them, they may be greatly distorted. The child may also distort those sounds in his or her speech.

20. Remember that a child repeats what is heard or what he or she thinks is heard. Many speech defects are really caused by defective hearing. Distorted speech is often caused by distorted hearing.
21. Remember that a hearing loss can occur or reoccur at any time, especially if the child has a cold, allergy, sore throat, or earache.
22. A hard-of-hearing child often "daydreams" because he or she does not hear you. Always get the child's attention, then make your statement.
23. The hard-of-hearing child fatigues easily because he or she is straining to perceive with the eyes what is written and what is being said.
24. Teach hard-of-hearing children to use the dictionary pronunciation key so that they can help themselves.
25. Encourage children to participate in musical activities, which can stimulate their residual hearing and add rhythm to their speech.
26. Encourage and promote active participation in school and social functions.
27. Seek professional help and advice from qualified persons and agencies who are recommended by your physician; ear, nose, and throat (ENT) specialist; nurse; educator; or speech and hearing center.
28. Do not "talk over the child's head." Phrase your thoughts in simple, easy-to-understand language, but always speak in complete sentences.
29. Because of the additional movements involved and the consequently greater opportunity for the child to observe, longer words or phrases are sometimes better than short ones.
30. Do not be overcritical if the hearing impaired child talks to classmates. Since it is difficult for the child to understand what is being said, he or she may look to or ask another student to confirm understanding.
31. Remember that even two children with almost identical hearing losses may function differently and hence cannot be effectively lumped into one generalized category for teaching purposes.
32. Institute a friendship system whereby one or more classmates help the hearing impaired child with directions, assignments, or notes that were missed.
33. Try to stand in one place when lecturing so it is easier for the child to speech-read.
34. Do not cause the child to feel inferior by exclusion from speaking assignments; rather, try to maneuver the child's presentation so that it is shorter and within his or her range.

Physical Handicaps

According to the *Federal Register* (1977), *physically handicapped* refers to

a severe orthopedic impairment which adversely affects a child's educational performances. The term includes impairments caused by cogenital anomaly

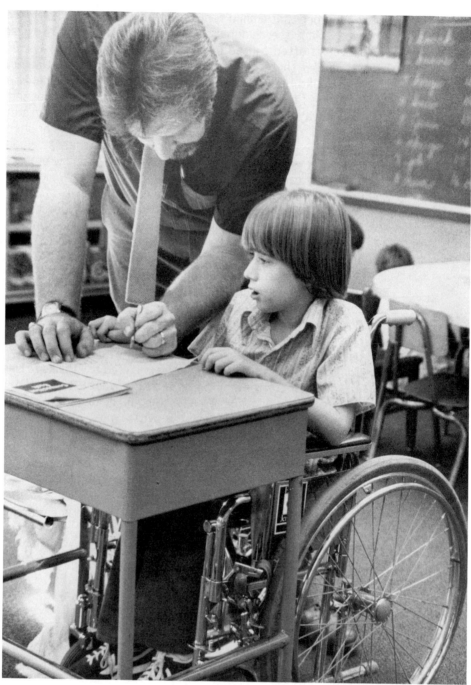

Individualizing makes education special.

(e.g., clubfoot, absence of some member, etc.), impairments caused by disease (e.g., polio myelitis, bone tuberculosis, etc.) and impairments from other causes (e.g., cerebral palsy, amputations and fractures or burns which cause contractures). (p. 42468)

The term *health impairment*, as included in the *Federal Register* (1977) means

> Limited strength, vitality or alertness due to chronic or acute health problems such as a heart condition, tuberculosis, rheumatic fever, nephritis, asthma, sickle cell anemia, hemophelia, epilepsy, lead poisoning, leukemia or diabetes which adversely affect a child's educational performances. (p. 42478)

Within these definitions there are numerous types of physical and health conditions. The main intent of this text is to provide teachers with information on how to work with the special needs student in the classroom. Thus, an in-depth study of the specific conditions is not undertaken here; rather, we focus on some general characteristics of physically handicapped children and some implications for teachers.

Characteristics of Physically Handicapped Students

Characteristics of the physically handicapped child may vary with each of the various handicapping conditions. A classroom teacher should have a basic knowledge of each of the conditions so to better understand each particular child. The following is a list of characteristics that may assist the teacher with general considerations for the physically handicapped child.

1. Tires more quickly than others in the class
2. Excessive absences due to medical appointments
3. Difficulty in performing gross motor tasks
4. Inability or difficulty completing manipulative activities (e.g., holding a pencil, cutting, drawing, stringing beads)
5. Difficulty distinguishing differences in size, depth, and spatial relationships (common among children with cerebral palsy)
6. May be socially delayed due to a lack of interaction with other children.

Implications for the Teacher

There are many suggestions for the classroom teacher in working with the student who has a physical handicap. Some of these include:

1. Being aware of all associated handicaps of the student.
2. Allowing adequate time for the student to travel from room to room and to get positioned in the classroom.
3. Being aware of the procedures by which to treat a seizure.
4. Preplanning all emergency situations.
5. Working closely with all therapists involved in the education of the student.
6. Stabilizing all structures such as chairs when sitting, wheelchairs, and so on.
7. Preplanning for any barriers that the school may have. (A good suggestion here is for the teacher to role play the student while moving around the school (e.g., in a wheelchair, with braces or crutches).
8. Remembering that the student may exhibit low vitality and have poor stamina.

What You Can Do

The following suggestions will be helpful to teachers in treating a seizure:

1. Be sure to obtain and read current literature on epilepsy.

2. Remember that epilepsy is a very common condition, and is no disgrace.

3. Most persons with epilepsy can become seizure-free if they take medication as prescribed by their doctors.

4. If a grand mal seizure should happen in class, it is vital that the teacher remain calm. Students will assume the same emotional reaction that the teacher does.
   a. Try to prevent the patient from striking his head or body against any hard, sharp, or hot object.
   b. Do not try to revive the patient. Let the convulsion run its course.
   c. Do not try to restrain the patient's movements or to put anything in the teeth.
   d. Turn the child gently on his side and make sure his breathing is not obstructed.
   e. Carefully observe the details of the attack for a subsequent report to medical personnel.
   f. On the very rare occasions when an actual attack continues for more than five minutes, the child's doctor should be called for special instructions.
   g. Do not be frightened if the person in a seizure may appear not to be breathing momentarily.
   h. Remember a seizure cannot hurt the onlookers.

i. When the patient regains consciousness, he may be incoherent or very sleepy. He should have the opportunity to rest.
j. Proper persons must, of course, be notified.
k. If the child has two successive seizures within a short period of time, contact the child's doctor immediately.

5. Turn a grand mal seizure in a class into a learning experience, where accurate information, wholesome attitudes, and understanding (not pity), are end results. Such an experience need not be frightening.

6. Remember that "with proper treatment, most children with epilepsy are able to live like any other children."

7. Do not pamper a child with epilepsy for fear he may have a seizure. Do not let him "rule the roost."

8. Remember that sometimes you or a member of your family may have a seizure.

9. Treat seizure patients as you would have others treat you or your child under similar circumstances.

Copyright Epilepsy Foundation of America, successor in interests to the Epilepsy Association of America, 1968.

Summary

All students are different and many may require special adaptations in order to experience success in the regular classroom. Having a better understanding of the characteristics of special needs students helps the educator to plan for a more positive educational experience.

Discussion Questions

1. List the educational characteristics of students who are mentally retarded, learning disabled, and emotionally disturbed.
2. List some suggestions for teaching students with mild handicaps.
3. List and discuss the three areas of communication problems.
4. Discuss techniques for working with a child who stutters.
5. Discuss why it is important to have knowledge of the characteristics of handicapped students.

Chapter 4

The Culturally Diverse Student Population

ALICE V. WATKINS
California State University,
Los Angeles

Chapter Objectives

After reading Chapter 4 the student will
be able to

- Describe the value of incorporating
  multicultural education into the
  mainstreamed curricula
- Develop a plan for teaching handicapped culturally diverse students in
  mainstream settings

D uring the last decade, the United States has seen a dramatic increase in the enrollment of minority children in public schools. As the number of minority students continues to rise, educators of this student population face greater challenges at every level of public education. This chapter discusses the needs of culturally diverse children who are also handicapped and offers suggestions for providing the support needed to meet their needs in mainstreamed classroom settings.

Special Class Placement of Culturally Diverse Students

Education is more than reading, writing, and arithmetic; education is preparation for life. Students need more than facts and problem-solving skills; they need to know how to lead full and useful lives in a complex world. In a nation made up of a variety of races and nationalities, that means learning how to live and work with people of different skin colors and cultural backgrounds. If one accepts this broad view of education, one cannot imagine a worse way of undertaking it than in a classroom segregated by race, national origin or handicappedness. Segregated classrooms deny millions of Americans the opportunity to become acquainted with the minority child whose future they share. (Oden, 1976, p. 56)

Historically, the special class has been the primary placement option used for culturally diverse, handicapped children. The National Coalition of Advocates for Students (1985) reported that large numbers of poor and minority students have been misclassified, excluded from the mainstream, and stigmatized by placement in classes for the mildly retarded. The Coalition also reported that black students, most of them males, have been placed in classes for the mildly mentally retarded at a rate more than three times that of white students. In 1987, Chinn and Hughes found that blacks were still overrepresented in classes for the educable mentally retarded, trainable mentally retarded, and emotionally disturbed.

For two decades, parents of ethnic minority groups challenged the segregation of culturally diverse children in self-contained special education classes. In the absence of clear evidence that special class placement resulted in superior achievement by their children, parents fought for significant changes in the policies and procedures used to refer, assess, and place children in programs for the handicapped (Abeson, 1976). Parents also sought to force policymakers to address the problem of overrepresentation of culturally diverse children in special education programs.

However, despite their parents' efforts and landmark litigation, culturally diverse children continue to be at risk for identification and referral to special education. The problem appears to be of particular concern to educators in heavily populated states with large metropolitan centers. During 1982 to 1983, more

106

than 25% of all the handicapped children served under Public Law 94–142 resided in California, Illinois, New York, and Texas (*Education Week*, 1986). California, New York, and Texas are also among the states serving the largest number of nonwhite students. According to recent enrollment statistics, California has more nonwhite than white students in elementary school, 46% of the students in Texas are Hispanic, and twenty-five of the nation's largest school districts serve more children from culturally diverse backgrounds than majority group homes (*Education Week*, 1986). A closer examination of the data available for California in 1983 reveals that 154,156 of the children enrolled in public schools were identified as "ethnic minority group members" and handicapped—more than 42% of California's handicapped school-aged children. No single ethnic group was significantly disproportionally placed, based upon their incidence in the general population. However, the demography of special education in California graphically illustrates both the size and the diversity of the population of handicapped, culturally diverse children. It should be noted that California's school population is clearly impacted by a disproportionately high immigration population. It is estimated that 17.4% of all legal immigrants and more than 30% of all of illegal immigrants in this country live in California (*Education Week*, 1986).

Thus, given the dramatic growth of the culturally diverse student population and the opposition of parent activists toward segregated special classes, educators must explore new approaches to teaching minority children with special needs. The movement of handicapped children of diverse cultural backgrounds from segregated special education classes to mainstreamed environments clearly reflects a broader view of public education.

Characteristics of Culturally Diverse Students

The culturally diverse population includes, but is not limited to, individuals who may be grouped into one of the following broad categories:

1. *Asian or Pacific Islander*, or persons having origins in the Far East or Southeast Asia.
2. *Black Americans*, or persons having origins in one of the black racial groups of Africa.
3. *Hispanic*, or persons having origins in Mexico, Puerto Rico, Cuba, or Central or South America.
4. *Native Americans*, or persons having origins from North American peoples or Alaska.

It is estimated that 21% of America's population today (about 50 million people) are nonwhite (*Education Week*, 1986).

Given the size and diversity of our minority population, it is not possible to generalize across ethnic groups in order to describe the educational characteristics of the culturally diverse child with special educational needs. It is, however, imperative that teachers recognize the degree to which the handicapped, culturally diverse child may face double jeopardy. The barriers to school success encountered by children of ethnic groups have not disappeared. The rising drop-out rate among cuturally diverse groups, the decline in the numbers entering college, and the continuing discrepancy in achievement, as measured by standardized tests, between white and nonwhite students are compelling evidences of their inability to achieve equity in public education. If the child is also mentally, physically, or behaviorally disabled, success in the mainstream may prove to be even more elusive.

It is imperative that educators recognize the diversity and impact of the child's cultural background on school behavior. Nazzaro (1981) has suggested that there are behavioral characteristics typical of the four major cultural groups (see Tables 4.1 through 4.4), but cautioned educators to consider each child as an individual learner. She has proposed that the interface between cultural values and exceptionality can provide clues for interpreting the behavior and level of responsiveness to authority that children of various ethnic groups exhibit.

Much of the literature regarding the learning characteristics of nonwhite children lacks empirical research support. At best, educators can only assume that there is a relationship among the cultural values of the child's home and his or her approach to learning, school achievement, and school personnel. The degree to which the background of the minority child may negatively affect school achievement is highly speculative. Although one child may exhibit behaviors that appear to be related to cultural values and experiences, rarely is it possible to generalize those behaviors to all or most members of the child's cultural group. It is impossible to attribute a specific behavior to all handicapped white children; culturally diverse children are no less heterogenous. Each child must be evaluated individually to determine how and under what conditions learning may best occur.

Accepting Cultural Diversity

Much has been written about the acceptance of handicapped pupils in mainstreamed settings. In general, however, the studies have not focused specifically on attitudes of nonhandicapped children toward handicapped, culturally diverse children. However, a large body of research does address issues relative to the adjustment and acceptance of mainstreamed children identified as mentally retarded. A review of the findings suggests that children with cognitive or behavioral handicaps do not achieve greater social acceptance by their nonhandicapped peers as a consequence of placement in mainstream settings (Corman & Gottlieb, 1979; Gottlieb, 1981; MacMillan, Keogh, & Jones, 1986;

TABLE 4.1
Exceptional Asian Students

Exceptionality	Relevant Characteristics of Condition	Relevant Characteristics of Culture	Possible Implications
Visually impaired/blind	Passive learning style, especially in early childhood	Passive learning style	May need extra encouragement in developing independence
	Dependent on authority for direction	Dependent on authority for direction	
Communication disordered	Nonverbal	Inconspicuous, nonverbal	Others may not realize problem exists
	Gives the impression of understanding directions and questions but does not	Skilled at watching and imitating	Others may think child understands when he or she does not
	Fails to hear some sounds	Non-English-speaking child fails to hear sounds not in native language	May confuse communication problems stemming from a handicap with problems caused by a lack of familiarity with English
	Unable to answer general information items because of different acculturation patterns related to deafness	Unable to answer general information items because of different cultural experiences	May wrongly assume that inability to answer questions is due to one of these reasons when it is really because of the other or a combination of both
	Uses other senses for communication (e.g., sign language)	Facility for rote visual learning (e.g., complex written language)	
Emotionally disturbed/ behavior disordered	Anxiety, psychosomatic complaints, hysteric blind and deaf reactions; school phobia resulting from not being able to satisfy achievement demands of home and school	Traditionally, child inhibited, conventional, subservient to authority	Requires special understanding by educators of traditional cultural expectations
	Suicide	Suicide	Japanese culture once reinforced this alternative as a way of

(continued)

TABLE 4.1 *(continued)*

Exceptionality	Relevant Characteristics of Condition	Relevant Characteristics of Culture	Possible Implications
			ending a shameful situation
	Delinquency	Youths refuse to give unquestioning obedience to parental views	Less traditional youths may use crime as a statement of rebellion
	Anxiety, depressive reactions	Youths may become angry at racial barriers then feel guilty for denying their own ethnicity	Requires special effort to reduce racial barriers so youth will not desire to deny ethnicity
	Aggressive, acting out, challenging, militant	Desire to assert ethnic identity	May be particularly shame-producing for more traditional parents
Mental retardation	Limited level of educational achievement	Social class and self-esteem determined by level of identity	May have poor self-esteem; family may feel shame
Learning disabled	Achievement below ability	Value placed on high academic achievement, industriousness	Child may try to compensate for disability by working extra hard, memorizing material, etc., so as not to bring shame on family
	Faulty perception of sounds, words, and so on	Failure to perceive unfamiliar sounds; or remember words out of context for non-English-speaking children	May lead to confusion in diagnosing problem
	Hyperactive	Self controlled	Behavior may be a source of shame to parents and self
Gifted	High academic achievement	Expectation of high academic achievement	Risk that gifted child may be taken for granted and not identified as special

Source: J. N. Nazzaro (1981). Special problems of exceptional minority children, in *Culturally diverse exceptional children in school* (Washington, DC: National Institute of Education, ERIC Document Reproduction Services No. 199 993).

TABLE 4.2
Exceptional Black Students

Exceptionality	Relevant Characteristics of Condition	Relevant Characteristics of Culture	Possible Implications
Visually handicapped	Dependent on others for stimulation in infancy	Early independence encouraged; dependence on siblings for child care	Adequate stimulation may not occur
	Dependent on oral modes of communication	Sensitive to verbal tone and inflection	May be sensitive to subtle implications of language
Communication disordered	Nonverbal	When there are many children in the home, children often speak for each other	Others may not notice child's poor communication skills
	Poor use of language	Language is a valued and specialized part of the culture	May be rejected, ignored, isolated by other group members
	Gives impression of understanding but does not	Skilled at interpreting body language	Others may think the child understands when he or she does not
	Fails to hear some sounds	Dialects and black English do not use some sounds	May confuse communication problems stemming from a handicap with problems stemming from use of dialect
	Unable to answer general information items because of different acculturation patterns related to deafness	Unable to answer general information items because of different cultural experiences	May wrongly assume that inability to answer questions is due to one of these reasons when it is really because of the other or a combination of both
	Uses other modes of communication	Uses posture and gesture in communicating	
Emotionally disturbed/ behavior disordered	Delinquency	Youths may rebel against system when they believe they have little hope for success	Antisocial behavior may be used to achieve status when it cannot be achieved within the system

(continued)

TABLE 4.2 *(continued)*

Exceptionality	Relevant Characteristics of Condition	Relevant Characteristics of Culture	Possible Implications
	Drug and alcohol abuse	Youths may become drug or alcohol dependent in environment where narcotics are commonly used as an escape	
	Aggressive, acting out, challenging, militant	Desire to assert racial identity	Needs to be directed into positive channels
Mental retardation	Limited level of educational achievement	Historically, received little or no schooling	Family may give up on schooling
	Slow thinking	Tolerance for broad range of abilities	May not be perceived as disabled except related to academics
	Poor performance on tests of intelligence	Poor performance on tests normed on non-black populations	Misdiagnosis: parental hostility and defensiveness
Learning disabled	Achievement below ability	Ability often misjudged because of test bias	Students with learning disabilities misdiagnosed as mentally retarded
	Faulty perception of sounds, words, and so on	Words not spoken with familiar intonation not paid attention to	Child believed to have auditory perceptual problems when there is simply a failure to recognize meaning without the cues of dialect
	Hyperactive	Interactive style	Child engaged in interactive process may be viewed as hyperactive
Gifted	Creative thinking	Good at problem solving	May be an area of excellence
	High academic achievement	Does poorly on tests	May be overlooked if selection is based on test performance

TABLE 4.2 *(continued)*

Exceptionality	Relevant Characteristics of Condition	Relevant Characteristics of Culture	Possible Implications
	Special talents/gifts	Culture supports athletic excellence	May neglect one dimension (e.g., intellectual) because another (e.g., athletic) appears to have greater payoff
	Leadership	Socially organized around leaders	Identification of gifted leaders may be better accomplished outside school setting

Source: J. N. Nazzaro (1981), Special problems of exceptional minority children, in *Culturally diverse exceptional children in school* (Washington, DC: National Institute of Education, ERIC Document Reproduction Services No. 199 993).

Students from all cultures have similar interests and needs.

TABLE 4.3
Exceptional Hispanic Students

Exceptionality	Relevant Characteristics of Condition	Relevant Characteristics of Culture	Possible Implications
Visually impaired/blind	Dependent on others for stimulation in infancy	Many supportive people around to stimulate infant and young child	
Communication disordered	Nonverbal	Highly verbal	Early recognition of communication problem
	Poor use of language	Bilingual child may have poor language skills	Bilingual situation may mask true communication disorder
	Gives the impression of understanding but does not	Skilled at understanding needs and feelings from nonverbal cues	Sensitivity may substitute for hearing and problem may be masked
	Fails to hear some sounds	Hispanic does not hear all English sounds because some do not exist in the Spanish language	May misdiagnose communication problem stemming from handicap with problems associated with bilingualism
	Unable to answer general information items because of different acculturation patterns related to deafness	Unable to answer general information items because of different cultural experiences	May attribute failures to wrong cause
	Uses other modes of communication	Uses gestures in conjunction with language	Many gestures are integral parts of language
Emotionally disturbed/ behavior disordered	Depressed, anxious, withdrawn	Conflicted when forced into a role that contradicts values	May not be able to cope; may drop out if situation is too uncomfortable
	Drug and alcohol abuse	Youths may turn to drugs or alcohol in situations where family roles and responsibilities have broken down	Requires special extended family and community effort to combat abuse

TABLE 4.3
(continued)

Exceptionality	Relevant Characteristics of Condition	Relevant Characteristics of Culture	Possible Implications
	Aggressive, acting out, challenging, militant	Desire to assert cultural identity	Needs to be directed into positive channels
Mental retardation	Limited level of educational achievement	Historically, received little or no schooling	Drop-out rate high, even among nonhandicapped
	Slow thinking	Adapts roles and expectations to abilities	Person assured of place in community in spite of limitations
	Poor performance on tests	Most tests not appropriate, especially timed tests	Frequent misdiagnosis
	Noncompetitive	Noncompetitive	Best to use team or cooperative approach to learning
Learning disabled	Achievement below ability	Weak skills in both English and Spanish	Problem determining nature of learning problem
	Faulty perception of sounds, words, and so on	Many English words sound alike to Spanish speaker	Problem determining cause of misperceptions
Gifted	High achievement	Reluctant to set self apart from peers; willing to achieve for the family	May be reluctant to show ability
	Leadership	Those who are capable are expected to help	May not be recognized as special

Source: J. N. Nazzaro (1981), Special problems of exceptional minority children, in *Culturally diverse exceptional children in school* (Washington, DC: National Institute of Education, ERIC Document Reproduction Services No. 199 993).

Semmel, Gottlieb, & Robinson, 1979). Semmel, et al. (1979), in their review of research on mainstreaming, could not find conclusive evidence that handicapped children experience a high level of social acceptance in regular education settings. This is consistent with the history of integrating black children in previously all-white schools. Change of placement, as a function of legally mandated policy, will not assure acceptance of culturally diverse children. However,

TABLE 4.4
Exceptional Native American Students

Exceptionality	Relevant Characteristics of Condition	Relevant Characteristics of Culture	Possible Implications
Visually impaired/blind	Passive learning style	Passive learning style	
	Dependent on others for stimulation in infancy	Culture dependent on visual learning	May have added difficulties adjusting to disability
	May be corrected or improved with lenses	Tendency to ridicule use of eyeglasses	Poor vision may not be corrected
Communication disordered	Nonverbal	Children expected to be quiet and observant	Condition may be masked
	Poor use of language	Bilingual child may have poor language skills	Bilingual situation may mask true communication disorder
	Gives the impression of understanding but does not	Much communication occurs at a nonverbal level	Hearing problems may not be recognized
	Fails to hear some sounds	High incidence of *Otitus Media* causing hearing loss	People accustomed to hearing loss and may tend to ignore problem
	May be corrected or improved with hearing aid	Tendency to ridicule use of hearing aid	Poor hearing may not be corrected
	Unable to answer general information items because of different acculturation patterns related to deafness	Unable to answer general information because of different cultural experiences	May attribute failures to wrong cause
	Uses other modes of communication	May use gestures to supplement language	May not be motivated to develop verbal skills
	Tends to associate with deaf subcommunity	Community accepts wide range of disabilities and accommodates them within work hierarchy	Disability may not be perceived as tremendous handicap
Emotionally disturbed	Depressed, anxious, withdrawn, suicidal	Feelings of unworthiness, due to conflict of values	Common syndrome; may not receive attention

TABLE 4.4
(continued)

Exceptionality	Relevant Characteristics of Condition	Relevant Characteristics of Culture	Possible Implications
	Delinquency	Inability to succeed may lead to rebellion	Ridicule may be more effective deterrent than other punishments
	Alcohol abuse	Alcohol abuse	Requires special extended family and community effort
	Militant	Desire to assert cultural identity	Need to be directed to productive channels
Mental retardation	Limited level of educational achievement	High drop-out rate, social promotions	Academic achievement not a primary value—high drop-out rate
	Slow thinking	Community adjusts to wide range of ability	Person assured role in community in spite of limitations
	Poor performance on tests	Most tests not appropriate, especially timed tests	Frequent misdiagnosis
	Noncompetitive	Noncompetitive	Best to use cooperative approaches to learning
Learning disabled	Achievement below ability	Weak skills in both native language and English	Problems determining nature of learning problem
	Faulty perception of sounds, words, and so on	Auditory loss from ear infections	Needs careful diagnosis to separate hearing loss from other perceptual problems
Orthopedically impaired	May have deformity or loss of limbs	Importance of body. Tendency to scapegoat on individuals with this type of handicap. Culture 'takes care of its own'	Adjustment may be difficult or assimilated with no problem
Epilepsy/ brain damage	Seizures	Some groups fear and are disgusted by seizures. Others accept this as quirk of nature	Individual ostracized; normal social adjustment is dependent on view of tribe

(continued)

TABLE 4.4 *(continued)*

Exceptionality	Relevant Characteristics of Condition	Relevant Characteristics of Culture	Possible Implications
Gifted	High achievement	Anonymity, passive learning style	Individual may mask ability so as not to be singled out
	Leadership/talent	Display of leadership ability in youth may not be sanctioned in tribe except in arts and sports	May have few opportunities to develop abilities. Talent may be ridiculed or promoted depending on tribe

Source: J. N. Nazzaro (1981), Special problems of exceptional minority children, in *Culturally diverse exceptional children in school* (Washington, DC: National Institute of Education, ERIC Document Reproduction Services No. 199 993).

teachers and nonhandicapped children can learn to accept and appreciate the cultural diversity of individuals from differing backgrounds. Rodriguez (1982) suggests that multicultural education is a way of learning to accept individuals of differing backgrounds. He further suggests that an effective multicultural approach allows both teachers and students to benefit from continued exposure to people and things to which they are not accustomed. Most regular class teachers cannot possibly become thoroughly knowledgeable about each of the major cultural groups. However, it is possible for teachers to create opportunities for children and their families to share the richness of their cultural heritage during learning experiences organized throughout the curriculum. In addition to promoting a sharing of diverse cultures in the classroom, teachers also can introduce and teach the values that lead to acceptance and appreciation of cultural diversity.

Dillard, Kinneson, and Peel (1980) identify the classroom teacher's attitude as a critical factor when mainstreaming culturally diverse children.

> Often, classroom teachers know which students they will promote and which retain. Students, too, are characterized as slow, average, or fast learners. Some students may even be judged as bright with much potential while others are viewed as having limited ability. Aside from the horrors of test results professionals use for ability grouping, teachers' anticipated notions (mind sets) of students' ability or potential at the outset of a school year correlate highly with the end-of-the-year grades. Positive mind sets seem strongly related to high teacher expectations of students and high performance results. (p. 78)

Dillard et al. conclude that teachers' anticipated notions, mind sets, attitudes, and expectations influence handicapped student's achievement in regular classroom settings.

Mainstream teachers can promote cultural diversity in the classroom by including instruction that focuses on multicultural education. For example, the social studies curriculum should stress information about various ethnic groups, their cultural heritage, and their contributions to the development of our nation. The classroom environment should become a show place for the contributions of individuals from various ethnic groups in the surrounding community. Multicultural materials and activities should be a part of the daily curriculum and presented as an essential component to becoming a member of the community.

Finally, acceptance of cultural diversity demands a commitment by adults to a classroom climate that is psychologically supportive of all children. There is little question that teachers who view all children as important, valuable, and capable of learning generally enjoy greater success in the classroom. Full acceptance of diversity can foster the development of an exciting, richly colorful environment in which the teacher, pupils, and community participate in sharing and growing.

Assessment of Culturally Diverse Students

The challenge of providing appropriate instruction to handicapped children of diverse backgrounds is confounded by the difficulty of determining their specific learning needs. The process is particularly complex if the child also has limited English proficiency. Guerin and Maier (1983) consider the assessment of minority students to be the most serious challenge facing educators. School personnel are required to assess each child referred for possible identification as a handicapped individual. If the child is nonwhite, the procedural guidelines used must also protect against possible racial or cultural bias. The child must be assessed in his or her native language and care must be exercised in the selection of the tests. A comprehensive assessment is required by Public Law 94-142 for any child referred for services for handicapped pupils. It is important that regular educators be aware of the regulations governing the assessment of students from culturally diverse groups.

The legal requirements for assessment of minority children are clear, yet problematic for educators. Initial attempts to develop nondiscriminatory and nonbiased tests have not been successful (Drew, 1973; Guerin & Maier, 1983; Heller, Holtzman, & Messick, 1982). The problem of testing children who are not proficient in English continues to challenge educators. Frequently, educators turn to the most available solution—bilingual translators. Guerin and Maier (1983) note that words, problems, and tasks seldom translate well from one language to another. They suggest that translations of experiences relevant to one culture are often not language appropriate for a different language or culture. Nationally, there is a critical shortage of bilingual personnel sensitive to the cultural diversity of students and capable of administering assessment instruments in the language in which the bilingual or limited English-speaking child is most proficient.

Baca and Cervantes (1984) state that, when assessing language among minorities, the comprehensive assessment program must involve a team that includes the parent or guardian, the student's teachers, an administrative representative, and those individuals responsible for actual assessment. The authors further recommend an assessment procedure for bilingual exceptional children that includes gathering the following information:

1. Referral data
2. Primary language data
3. Observational and interview data
4. Other data available, including school records
5. Language proficiency
6. Educational assessment data
7. Perceptual-motor or psycholinguistic assessment data
8. Adaptive behavior data
9. Medical or developmental data
10. Intellectual assessment data

Thus, classroom teachers should be active participants in the assessment process. In addition to initiating the referral for identification as handicapped, the regular class teacher can provide critically needed information regarding the child's educational performance within the classroom environment.

--- *Case Study* ---

THE CULTURALLY DIVERSE POPULATION

Lee Nelson teaches freshman and sophomore classes in United States history, geography, and family studies. In two of his five classes, he has several identified handicapped students, all of whom are black or Hispanic. Lee is also an assistant coach for the varsity football team and head coach for the varsity football and the junior wrestling teams. He became interested in mainstreaming last year as a result of his contact with Reynard, a ninth-grade wrestler and football player.

Reynard is diagnosed as learning disabled and legally blind in one eye. He is an attractive 15-year-old black male. He was previously placed in special education classes for five years (grades 2–7). However, when Reynard's parents moved from a large inner-city school district to a smaller suburban district, they requested placement in a less restrictive program. Reynard was placed in a resource room for 50% of the school day.

Upon entering high school, Reynard persuaded his counselor to program him into only two special education classes. With the enthusiastic support and encouragement of the head coach, he developed the following program for his freshman year:

1. English/Reading (special education).
2. Remedial Math (mainstream).
3. United States History (mainstream)—first semester; Geography (mainstream)—second semester.
4. General Science (mainstream—low ability track).
5. Varsity Sports/Athletics (mainstream).

When evaluated as an entering freshman, Reynard was tested at the sixth-grade level in arithmetic, fourth-grade in reading, and third-grade in spelling. His IQ was listed as 105 (as measured by the Wechsler Intelligence Scale for Children—Revised). Reynard does not regard himself as handicapped. He refused to work with the itinerant teacher for the visually handicapped during his last year of elementary school. He adamantly refused to enroll in more than one special education class in high school. He is persistent, works hard, and is characterized by the football coach as one of the "toughest competitors on the field." Reading is a slow and laborious task for Reynard. He deeply resents the "childish" books used by the resource teacher and has openly reported that he "read that stuff in grade school."

During the third month of his freshman year, Reynard and his family witnessed the bizarre random slaying of his father by a mentally ill man who attacked a group of church-goers. It was following this tragic incident that Lee began to counsel Reynard. He also arranged to have Reynard transferred to his history class and programmed into his geography class for the second semester. Reynard agreed to the program change and admitted that he was struggling in both history and science.

Lee's classes are large, and because of his popularity as a coach, his classes were typically filled with athletes who were successful in sports but relatively low-achieving students. Although Reynard was his first identified handicapped student, he was functioning at an academic level consistent with many of the other athletes in Lee's class. As a consequence, Lee was highly motivated to devise instruction to meet Reynard's learning needs and those with similar learning problems.

Lee consulted with the Chapter I coordinator at the feeder elementary school and learned that there was a state clearinghouse (a depository that would furnish, without cost, large-print editions of all state-approved textbooks). He also learned that they could provide tape recorded editions of textbooks and supplementary readers. He immediately ordered large-print history and geography books and selected tapes that could be utilized for extra reading. Realizing that the young students in his classes would not accept a classroom environment that would suggest that they were "special" or "retarded," Lee moved his class to an empty science lab that was equipped with tables with electrical outlets. He was then able to diversify his delivery of instruction, and as an alternative to large group lectures, he began to:

1. Organize small groups for mini-lectures followed by independent study.
2. Provide taped instruction and reading materials for those students who appeared to benefit from the addition of auditory input.
3. Recruit peer tutors to work with groups of 2–3 students. Sessions led by peer tutors focused on discussions of study questions and specific problem-solving tasks.
4. Use assigned "hypothetical and real problems" to stimulate interest in subject content. A series of practical "problems" were developed. As an alternative to one or more written exam questions, students could select task cards that presented an historical fact, event, person, and so on. The incident was telescoped to twentieth-century America and students were asked, given the realities of today's society, to find "new" solutions to the problem.
5. Develop study guides, including specific and concrete suggestions for organizing time, for each freshman and sophomore class. With assistance for the Chapter I funded, and a reading resource teacher and a bilingual aide in the reading lab, the guides were written at two reading levels and in Spanish (only one Spanish guide for the geography class was completed).
6. Offer special projects in each class as an alternative assignment to completion of a term paper.

Reynard selected to complete a special project that involved tracking his own high school football and basketball teams by reproducing local maps and determining routes and distances traveled. While monitoring his progress on this task, Lee discovered much about Reynard's reading ability, his problem-solving skills, his understanding of spatial relationships, and most critically, his ability to generalize skills acquired in school to practical utilization in the community.

While attempting to adapt instruction in a regular high school class, Lee Nelson not only gained insight relative to the needs of a handicapped adolescent but also found better, more creative ways to assist large numbers of regular students, who were typically disinterested and minimally achieving in history and geography.

Heller, Holtzman, and Messick, (1982) note "that the main purpose of assessment in education is to improve instruction and learning." They further conclude that:

> an ideal assessment process would take place in two phases, beginning with an assessment of the learning environment and proceeding to a comprehensive assessment of the individual child only after it has been established that he or she fails to learn in a variety of classroom settings under a variety of well-conceived instructional strategies. (p. 69)

Mainstream teachers assume the primary responsibility for the curricula and instructional adaptations necessary to serve culturally diverse, handicapped children appropriately in regular classroom settings. Consequently, teachers need to become knowledgeable about the assessment procedures utilized by the local school district, to recognize the limitations of formal testing of minority children, and to gather systematically additional information that can be used to improve instruction. They should also develop the skills needed to relate assessment information to direct instruction.

The parent is another source of valuable information regarding the student's functional skills and abilities that may not be readily apparent to school personnel. Many culturally diverse children function differently, for a variety of reasons, at home and in the community. A child who may appear shy, withdrawn, and noncommunicative in school may be different at home among family and friends who share the same culture and language.

In summary, the assessment of children who are culturally diverse and handicapped must involve regular classroom teachers, specialists, and parents. The child must be observed in a variety of social and educational settings, using a variety of assessment instruments sensitive to the child's native language, cultural values, and experiences that have contributed to his or her growth and development.

Special Services for Culturally Diverse Students

Mainstreamed students identified as culturally diverse and handicapped will spend at least a part of the day in a regular class. They may, however, be eligible for assistance under other programs, including bilingual education, Chapter I, special education and related services, such as speech therapy and adaptive physical education.

Bilingual education may be available as a resource and supportive service for the handicapped, culturally diverse student. In bilingual programs, children receive instruction designed to help them develop the skills and concepts appropriate to their age and grade level in the language they understand. Instruction is designed to promote the cultural backgound of the student while assisting the child to integrate into the mainstream. The bilingual teacher also helps the child to become proficient in the use of English and develops concepts using English as the primary language.

Bilingualism is generally defined as the ability to use, with varying degrees of proficiency, two different languages. Baca and Cervantes (1984) define bilingual education simply as the use of two languages to deliver instruction to the child. Bilingual specialists are sensitive to the fact that linguistically diverse children vary dramatically in the degree to which they are proficient in English. For that reason, language instruction in bilingual programs may occur at three different levels and may vary substantially. At the first level, teachers may use an unilingual approach and present concepts in only one language. The primary goal of instruction is the development of a specific language skill, such as listening, speaking, reading, or writing. At the second level, teachers may use a bilingual approach to the acquisition of English as a second language. Using the primary language of the student to introduce new concepts, the child is taught the English language. The third approach involves the concurrent use of English and the child's native language. The teacher presents a concept in the child's native language and then immediately in English. The concurrent method is used to help students who are limited English speakers develop concepts in academic content areas.

It is difficult to determine the precise number of handicapped children from diverse cultural backgrounds who are also bilingual. However, given the number of Hispanic and Asian children identified as handicapped, it is generally assumed that a significant number are to some degree bilingual and capable of benefitting from bilingual education. In bilingual programs, teachers and aides who are fluent in two or more languages can provide opportunities for children to increase their understanding of English as they also develop fluency and form new concepts.

Mainstream teachers may seek assistance from bilingual specialists to determine the degree to which the child is bilingual; this is essential to the identification of the language service most appropriate to the needs of a specific student. Regular educators must attempt to separate carefully children who have limited English proficiency from those children who are mentally, sensory, or physically disabled. There is growing concern among bilingual and special educators that the handicapped, culturally diverse population includes children who are not proficient in any language. For this group of individuals, a language development program appropriate to the individual needs of the child, rather than bilingual education or English as a second language (ESL) program, may be offered by qualified speech and language specialists. Ortiz (1984) suggests that educators are often unable to determine whether academic problems are related to language differences, a lack of language proficiency, or a handicapping condition. The speech and language specialist can provide valuable assistance to the mainstream teacher attempting to determine the appropriate needs of a child who is not fluent in English.

Culturally diverse children may also qualify for services provided by *Chapter I* resource personnel. Chapter I of the Education Consolidation and Improvement Act of 1981 provides federal funding for support of compensatory education services in reading and math for students in low-income schools. In 1980, over five million children received compensatory education. Culturally diverse children living in economically poor communities may qualify for Chapter I services if there is a discrepancy between their academic achievement and the expected level of achievement for their age group. For the mainstreamed handicapped child, remedial assistance from Chapter I resource personnel is a viable alternative to placement in special education.

However, the culturally diverse child with an authentic handicapping condition may be referred to special education for review, assessment, and possible placement. The individual education program (IEP) team must assume the responsibility for determining the degree of special education support that the child will require to remain in a mainstreamed setting. For children who appear to have limited language proficiency, the team must also determine whether it is the handicapping condition or the child's limited language proficiency that constitutes the greater need.

What You Can Do

- Introduce and teach the values that lead to acceptance and appreciation of cultural diversity.

- Organize instruction with a focus on multicultural education.

- Present to students the contributions of individuals from various ethnic groups from the surrounding community.

- Introduce multicultural materials and activities into the daily curriculum.

- Provide a classroom climate that is psychologically supportive of all children.

- Be an active participant in the assessment process.

- Become acquainted with parents of culturally diverse students.

Role of Special Education Teachers

The special educator is one of several professionals available to assist regular class teachers with the task of adapting instruction for handicapped pupils.

Generally, special educators function in a consulting role when dealing with regular teachers. However, given their knowledge of handicapping conditions, special educators can identify instructional resources appropriate to the needs of the individual learners and monitor the child's progress in the mainstream. The special class teacher can also assist with the adaptation and modification of curriculum materials, organization of instruction, and, when appropriate, demonstrate techniques for providing direct instruction that effectively accommodates the child's handicapping condition.

Adaptations for Mainstreaming

The individualized education program (IEP) for each handicapped student is developed by a team. However, if the individual is placed in the mainstream, the regular class teacher becomes the critical program implementor. The methods selected for teaching each individual student must be appropriate to his or her needs and allow for the development of skills to the maximum extent possible. Accomplishing this goal with children who are also culturally diverse is formidable for many teachers faced with the task of adapting the regular class environment to accommodate their needs.

Social Studies Instruction

Fundamental to adapting instruction for culturally diverse students is acceptance of the rich diversity of various ethnic communities. Lewis and Doorlag (1987) suggest that multicultural education must be the major instructional approach used with culturally diverse students. Baca and Cervantes (1984), Chinn (1982), and Gonzales (1979) also stress the importance of multicultural education for this group of students. Baca and Cervantes (1984) suggest that teachers of bilingual exceptional children develop curriculum materials that are culturally relevant and sensitive to the underlying cultural and linguistic concepts of the child's background and experience. Chinn (1982) calls for a broad definition of multicultural education that includes examining the dynamics of diverse cultures, linguistic variations, and diverse learning styles.

The mainstream environment must allow children to share their cultural heritage in a positive, supportive climate. Social studies instruction can provide a wonderful opportunity for teachers to organize age-appropriate and culturally sensitive issues and topics. Because of the flexibility that most teachers enjoy, the social studies curriculum can be utilized to explore a wide variety of ideas. For example, the simple presentation of a monthly calendar can become a multicultural education lesson with exciting implications for learning. An enterprising teacher can use the calendar to introduce children to people of achievement and historical events representative of numerous ethnic groups in America.

Instructional units that focus on multicultural themes can provide another opportunity to use the diversity of pupils' backgrounds to enhance classroom participation and academic achievement. Topics that focus on the world community, contributions of various ethnic groups, the art, music, and folklore of various groups, and the customs of communities can be used to develop integrated units of study that promote cultural diversity. This can lead to the organization of a richly stimulating continuum of experiences appropriate to the needs of culturally diverse student populations. Teachers must ensure that textbooks, media, and other instructional materials are free of racial and sexual biases and stereotyping. Educators should also involve parents and other members of the community in the class. It is particularly critical to expose culturally diverse, exceptional children to appropriate role models from their own community.

Reading and Language Arts Instruction

Culturally diverse children with handicapping conditions should not be viewed as a homogeneous group. Within ethnic groups, children will differ from each other in terms of learning aptitudes and skills as much as they differ from majority group children. Therefore, it is not possible to identify a specific list of instructional strategies most appropriate to the needs of all culturally diverse exceptional children. However, it is necessary to address a major concern of parents, teachers, and policymakers: the problems related to teaching handicapped culturally diverse children to read. Reading is essential to school success. Low achievement in this subject area continues to be characteristic of economically poor, culturally diverse children, both handicapped and nonhandicapped.

Providing reading instruction for handicapped, culturally diverse children in mainstreamed settings can be extremely difficult. Baca and Cervantes (1984) recommend that teachers provide instruction in all academic areas, throughout the K-6 grades, in the primary language of the child. Beginning readers who are bilingual or monolingual in a language other than English should receive reading instruction from individuals proficient in the child's native language. Harber (1982) found that dialect interference (the result of the difference between the dialect of the child and the dialect taught in the schools) is a factor in the poor reading achievement of urban black children. Nonstandard English dialects may affect the child's understanding of, and ability to reproduce accurately, phonetic sounds. It may also affect oral reading performance and comprehension.

Additional factors affecting the low reading achievement of culturally diverse children include the nature of the handicapping condition and its impact on the individual's ability to learn, lack of familiarity with the culture, values, and experiences portrayed in reading textbooks, and characteristically low cognitive achievement, particularly among the urban poor. Currently, there is a scarcity of definitive research that clearly establishes the efficacy of using a single method teaching culturally diverse children to read. However, given the discrepancy between these students' age and reading achievement levels, it is appropriate to discuss methodological adaptations that allow teachers the flexibility they need to accommodate the needs of each pupil. The adaptations presented in this chapter are suggested for use with English-speaking handicapped pupils. Limited and non-English proficient handicapped pupils should be referred to bilingual teachers for reading instruction.

Instructional Methods and Approaches to Reading

Most teachers utilize a combination of instructional methods and approaches to reading. There is no "one" method that has been demonstrated to be clearly superior. Using an eclectic approach allows the flexibility necessary to accept and accommodate differences in individual life-styles, learning rates, and attitudes toward learning and achievement. Using a single method, at the exclusion of all others, generally excludes the possibility that each child in a given group will enjoy reading success. Teachers can utilize a combination of several approaches, each of which is modified to meet the needs of individual learners. To successfully modify reading instruction for culturally diverse exceptional learners, teachers must be knowledgeable about, and capable of implementing, a wide range of methodological approaches to teaching reading.

Reading and the Culturally Diverse Young Adult

Among the handicapped, culturally diverse student population, adolescent and young adults who are also reading disabled often are extremely difficult to teach. The following essay was dictated by a young black man enrolled in an urban high school class for learning disabled pupils. The essay was written just weeks before he was incarcerated for his participation in a gang-related homicide. The would-be writer was a sullen, angry, and unpleasant young man with a passion to learn to read that drove him to enroll voluntarily in a tutoring program that offered individualized reading instruction. Although he was considered hopelessly incorrigible by school personnel, his behavior during tutoring sessions was exemplary. In his own words, "learning to read was everything." He was habitually truant and had a long history of short-term suspensions. He had attended six inner-city schools during seven years. During his first semester of enrollment in the tutoring lab, he was absent only once.

> We have to learn to read before we can be real. Reading is everything. You can't do nothing unless you can read. We go to school to get an education. Education means communication. If you can read and write you can communicate with

Presidents. You have to read to pass a driving test and read signs. Even if you have good clothes on the outside, you haven't got anything on the inside unless you can read.

The plight of the adolescent described here is shared by 18–24 million young Americans who are functionally illiterate, based on an assessed reading ability below the fifth-grade level. The incidence of illiteracy among culturally diverse youth provides a compelling rationale for developing individualized reading programs that are socially and culturally appropriate. Individual reading programs should be designed to include:

1. Regularly scheduled individual conference time with the pupil.
2. Time for private, daily reading sessions with the teacher.
3. Appropriate practice and drill experiences designed to teach specific skills and approaches to learning.
4. Numerous opportunities to apply the reading skills to functional, socially appropriate experiences at home, at school, and in the community.

Summary

Teaching handicapped, culturally diverse children presents both a challenge and an opportunity for teachers to promote the acceptance of all children. Mainstream teachers are confronted with the task of structuring a learning environment that facilitates the acceptance of diverse populations, their customs, values, and contributions to the larger community.

Beginning with an appropriate and bias-free assessment of the child, the teacher must learn as much as possible about the student by involving parents, utilizing specialists and resource personnel, and observing the child within the mainstream setting. Based on knowledge of the child's needs and the objectives stated in the IEP, the mainstream teacher must develop instruction that is both sensitive and appropriate to the needs of the handicapped, culturally diverse child.

Discussion Questions

1. List your concerns relative to serving handicapped, culturally diverse children in your mainstream classroom. For each problem or concern identified, suggest two strategies that you could possibly employ.
2. Discuss the primary problems relative to the assessment and evaluation of handicapped minority pupils.
3. Simply placing handicapped, culturally diverse children in nonrestrictive mainstream environments does not ensure acceptance by their peers. Outline a program that you could implement to help the culturally diverse pupil gain social acceptance.

Chapter 5

Designing a Mainstreamed Environment

CAROLYN K. REEVES
University of Southern Mississippi

Chapter Objectives

After reading Chapter 5 the student will be able to

- Describe why a systematic approach to designing a mainstreamed environment is necessary
- Explain the relationship between instructional and behavioral management, as components of classroom management
- Determine how the three major components of the instructional process interact

D esigning a mainstreamed environment should be approached as *systematically* as the development of a handicapped student's IEP. A successful mainstreamed environment does not just happen; it is the result of careful planning and preparation prior to implementation. All aspects of the environment—emotional and social, physical and ecological, instructional and behavioral—and the instructional process must be systematically addressed when considering the needs of special students in the mainstreamed classroom.

The emotional/social environment is the foundation of a mainstreamed environment. It is the base on which the physical, instructional, and behavioral management environments are built. In Chapter 1, the stage is set for laying a firm foundation for developing the emotional/social environment within a school. Those factors that contribute to a positive emotional/social environment and a *systematic approach* for increasing acceptance of a mainstreamed program by teachers and students are discussed. Chapter 5 begins with a description of the physical and ecological elements that affect the learning environment, and then identifies those areas that must be assessed prior to implementation of a mainstreamed program. The next section of this chapter, on classroom management, discusses the methods that facilitate the delivery of instruction as well as the behavioral management procedures that can be used to prevent and change student misbehavior. The discussion emphasizes that effective management techniques must be based on careful observation and used with consistency. Finally, the instructional process is addressed; the components of instruction that must be adapted to meet the instructional needs of special students are described.

This chapter demonstrates how all aspects of a successful mainstreamed environment must *interact and combine* in various ways to meet the needs of regular and special students and teachers in mainstreamed settings. In short, it shows why a *systematic approach to designing the mainstreamed environment* is so essential.

The Learning Environment

Aspects of the learning environment that affect the mainstreamed program include its physical facilities; affective climate; instructional materials, equipment, and resources; and scheduling. Assessments of these elements must be made prior to implementation of a mainstreamed program. Classroom schedules that facilitate the mainstreaming process must be established. All of these elements, referred to as *ecological factors* by some authors (Bulgren & Knackendoffel, 1986; Thurman & Widerstrom, 1985), constantly interact and influence the behaviors of students and teachers.

Physical Facilities

Requirements for the physical environment are determined by the needs of the people who will use the facilities. Buildings and classrooms housing mainstreamed students can be altered, if necessary, to accommodate special students. Structural modifications to accommodate physically handicapped students, such as the widening of doorways and the construction of entrance ramps, may be required. Also, students with physical handicaps may need special equipment, such as wheelchairs, walkers, and standing tables, to take full advantage of the learning environment. In short, the physical facilities should provide open access to all students.

Classroom Light, Temperature, and Ventilation.   In general, classrooms need good and appropriately placed lighting, sufficient wall space of a subdued color, and adequate ventilation. Teachers should make sure that all student work areas are well lighted and that glare is not a problem. Classrooms equipped with variable lighting equipment (e.g., brighter lighting for reading and study areas and softer lighting for discussion areas) are desirable.

By occasionally checking with regular and special students about the classroom's temperature, teachers can maintain a moderate and desirable temperature in the room. Also, it is important to make sure that special students' internal temperature maintenance mechanisms are intact, because changes in external temperature can pose significant problems in their ability to maintain body temperature. Although windows are a good source of light and ventilation, students may become distracted by outside events and noises when windows are opened. However, ventilation is necessary to prevent students from becoming sleepy and lethargic.

Classroom Noise Level.   The noise level of a classroom should be kept at a minimum. This is especially important in classrooms where learning disabled or emotionally disturbed students are enrolled, in that they are easily distracted by noise and movement. Carpeting, acoustical ceiling tiles, drapes, well-insulated walls, and careful room arrangement can decrease the noise level within a classroom. Some classroom noise related to learning activities is acceptable, but extraneous outside noise should be kept at a minimum.

Classroom Furniture.   The furniture in the classroom should be comfortable, durable, and functional. The desks, chairs, tables, and standing tables should fit students properly. Special students often have difficulty doing written work neatly, so their desks and chairs must fit them properly. In particular, students should be able to place both feet on the floor with their knees about even with the seat. The desks should be high enough for students to "look down at the desk tops and be able to place their entire arms, from elbow to hands, horizontally on the desks" (Stephens, Blackhurst, & Magliocca, 1982, p. 149).

Classroom Size and Arrangement. The classroom should be large enough to accommodate individual, small-group, and large-group instruction and to allow for barrier-free movement from one work area to another. Classroom crowding must be avoided. McAfee (1987) investigated the relationship between classroom crowding and the behaviors of special students at the elementary and secondary school levels. He found that higher rates of aggressive behavior occurred under crowded conditions. Smith, Neisworth, and Greer (1978) have suggested that the initial success of a mainstreamed program may be the result of adequate space, such that "individuals and groups [can] keep their distance from each other while they are in the process of getting accustomed to each other" (p. 137). In addition to avoiding classroom crowding, school principals must ensure that the teacher-to-pupil ratio is lower in mainstreamed classrooms than is typically found in regular classrooms.

The *seating arrangement* within a classroom can affect the behavior of students. Special students should be seated in the spot most favorable to them. Students who require special equipment, or who have mobility problems, should be seated near the room's entrance as well as close to the group with which they are likely to work. Also, a place should be provided for crutches, walkers, and wheelchairs.

Children with severe vision problems should be seated where it is easiest for them to locate their seats. They should also be able to locate, retrieve, and return equipment they use, so that they do not become dependent on the teacher for obtaining learning materials and equipment. Children with severe hearing problems should be seated near where the teacher stands when giving directions. In this area, the light should fall on the teacher's face; that is, students should not have to face into the light to read the teacher's lips. Children with severe visual or hearing problems should be seated so that they are able to read material that is written on the chalkboard. Further, children who are easily distracted should be seated in quiet areas. They should be placed near children who are self-directed, quiet students. Sometimes it is necessary to seat easily distracted students near the teacher's desk.

The classroom should be arranged so that *student movement* creates the smallest disturbance possible when students move into smaller groups, walk to get supplies, or go to different learning centers. Hart (1981) suggests that teachers first plan room arrangements on paper, marking the pathways that each special student would follow to get to various places in the room. The classroom should be arranged to facilitate students' use of educational media, carrels, chalkboards, and learning centers as well as the teacher's management procedures.

Dividing classroom space into performance areas or zones to accommodate routine tasks and activities has been suggested by many authors (Berdine & Cegelka, 1980; Mercer & Mercer, 1981). When dividing the room into separate areas, space for both large- and small-group instruction must be kept in mind. Some teachers set up small-group instructional areas for specific subjects or

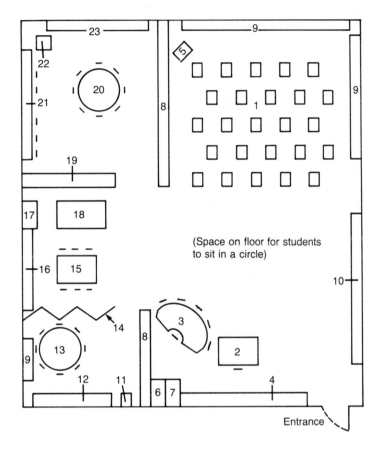

(Space on floor for students to sit in a circle)

Entrance

Legend

1 Individual desks/large-group instruction
2 Teacher's desk
3 Individual/small-group instruction (teacher-directed)
4 Bookshelf for teacher's books/supplies
5 Television
6 File cabinet 1
7 File cabinet 2
8 Low bookshelf (or shelves)
9 Chalkboard
10 Student boxes (cubbies)/lockers, with bulletin boards above

11 Microcomputer
12 Cabinets for supplies
13 Math center table
14 Folding screen
15 Science center table
16 Science equipment/materials
17 Sink with running water
18 Science standing table
19 Library/reference bookshelf (low)
20 Language arts center table
21 Recorders/headsets
22 Typewriter
23 Bulletin/magnetic/peg boards

FIGURE 5.1

Floor Plan for a Self-Contained Elementary Classroom

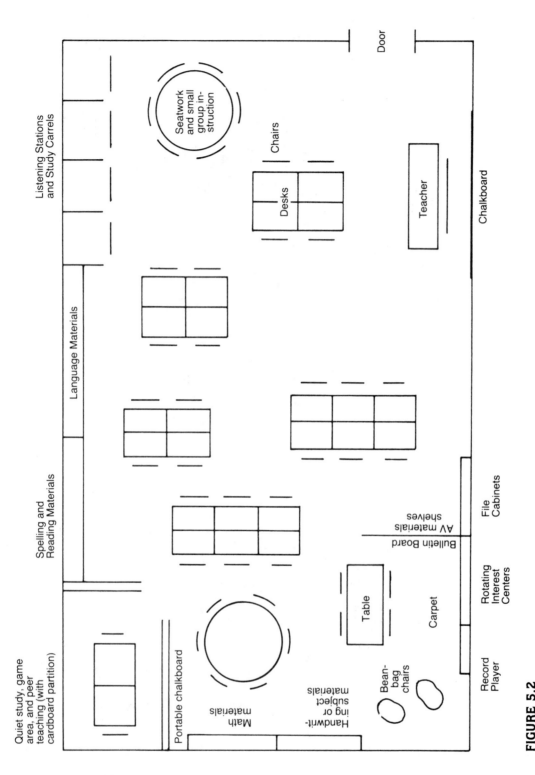

FIGURE 5.2

Classroom Floor Plan (Source: C. D. Mercer & A. R. Mercer [1989]. Teaching students with learning problems. *3rd ed. [Columbus. OH: Merrill]. p. 85. Reproduced by permission.)*

activities. For example, separate learning centers or stations for the different academic areas—math, reading, writing, science, and so on—can be established; these areas can be used by the teacher for direct instruction or by students for self-directing activities (Lewis & Doorlag, 1987). Even at the secondary level, Mercer and Mercer (1981) recommend a separate learning center or station for single subjects in an academic area (e.g., an English classroom could have learning centers for grammar, literature, reading, and listening activities).

In addition to small-group instructional areas, each student needs his or her *individual work space.* Usually the student's desk serves this purpose and is used also during large-group instruction. Easily distracted students may need cubicles, carrels, booths, or partitions as individual work areas (Lewis & Doorlag, 1987). Many *floor plans,* such as those shown in Figures 5.1 and 5.2, can be planned so as to accommodate both small- and large-group instruction.

Affective Climate

Affective elements of a learning environment are just as important as its physical aspects, in that a positive school or classroom atmosphere sets the stage for the development of trust that is necessary for learning to occur efficiently. In general, the teacher determines the atmosphere of a classroom, which, in turn, influences the demeanor of the students. Before implementing a mainstreamed program, the school principal should assess affective elements associated with the classrooms of regular teachers being considered for involvement in the program.

Teacher Behavior. Smith, Neisworth, and Greer (1978) have identified five elements, represented by continuous dimensions, that can be used to evaluate the affective structure of a learning environment. Since these elements describe *critical dimensions of behaviors exhibited by teachers,* they can be used to help determine which classrooms have the potential for providing the most appropriate atmosphere for special students. The five elements are identified and briefly described in the following paragraphs.

The *positive-negative dimension* refers to the attitudes and behaviors displayed by teachers as they interact with students during the teaching-learning process. Positive behaviors by teachers help students develop a sense of security within the classroom setting, and positive teacher expectations about student performance lead to increased achievement. Positive and enthusiastic teacher behaviors are modeled by students and affect learning outcomes.

The *planned-haphazard dimension* refers to the extent to which teachers plan and prepare for learning experiences that will engage students' interests. A planned environment is characterized by consistent schedules, procedures, and teacher behaviors. Carefully planned activities permit students to understand the purpose of the activities and the steps involved in attaining expected outcomes. A planned learning environment promotes the participation of all students by providing opportunities for them to engage in appropriate learning activities.

The *flexibility-rigidity dimension* is especially important in mainstreamed classrooms because of the varying needs and abilities of students. Flexible teachers are willing to try new ideas and techniques in an objective manner and to make adaptations in lesson plans to meet the individual needs of students.

The *consistency-inconsistency dimension* is closely tied to the conditions that characterize a planned learning environment by its emphasis on consistency. A consistent learning environment leads to feelings of trust and security and reduces anxieties sometimes associated with learning situations. Rules and standards are clearly communicated in a consistent learning environment, and students receive consistent consequences for their behavior based on the established rules and standards. Consistency does not connote rigidity, but it does mean that teachers act in accordance with established rules and procedures while recognizing that modification, or renegotiation, of rules may be necessary.

The *understanding-intolerance dimension* refers to the degree to which mutual tolerance and acceptance characterize a learning environment. Teachers who match learning experiences to the characteristics of individual students are demonstrating that they understand and accept them as individuals with varying needs and abilities.

In summary, teachers are likely to be successful in their mainstreaming efforts if they understand and accept their students, have positive attitudes, plan effectively for instruction, are flexible in their thinking, and display consistent expectations and discipline procedures. These dimensions of teacher behavior should be considered carefully by school principals when placing special students in the classrooms of regular teachers.

Student Behavior.   The behaviors and traits of regular students in classrooms where special students may be placed should be considered *prior* to implementation of a mainstreamed program. The teacher needs the support of the regular students to create and maintain a meaningful learning environment for *all* students. In addition to having a positive attitude toward special students, certain traits and behaviors of regular students influence mainstreaming efforts in classrooms. Among the traits needed by regular students are (1) a sense of *maturity* about individual differences and the idea of change; (2) well-developed *social skills*; (3) a degree of *seriousness about learning*; and (4) a *willingness to work with others* to achieve a common goal. Refinement of these traits can be developed through implementation of teacher-directed activities. For example, a suggested activity for developing students' maturity about individual differences is to have each student divide a sheet of paper in half, and list on one half some of the behaviors or traits that the student feels are unique to him- or herself as an individual (e.g., drinking orange juice at the end of the breakfast meal rather than at the beginning). On the other half of the sheet, each student can list some of his or her behaviors or traits that are common among most students (e.g., wanting to sleep late on weekend mornings). These lists can be used to promote class discussion about the ways in which individuals differ and the importance of respecting individual differences. Also, role-playing activities can be used to help students refine their social skills, and short activities that emphasize the benefits of teamwork (e.g., the "Five Square Team-Building Activity," developed by Freiberg, Cooper, & Ryan, 1980) can be used to help students develop a willingness to work with others to achieve a common goal.

In general, students who possess the traits noted earlier more often exhibit classroom behaviors conducive to mainstreaming, such as staying on task, self-directed learning, appropriate self-control, consideration for the rights of others, and the demonstration of personal responsibility when working on group projects. Everyone benefits when special students are placed with the right peer group.

Instructional Materials, Equipment, and Resources

Before implementing a mainstreamed program, assessment of existing instructional materials, equipment, and resources should be made. Together the school principal, regular teacher, and resource teacher should conduct the assessment. Not only does this show the principal's support of the teacher, but it also provides the principal with first-hand knowledge of the instructional materials, equipment, and resources that are needed to implement a mainstreamed program successfully. The resource teacher can offer suggestions for use of materials and ideas for adapting materials.

Since instructional materials and equipment are used by teachers to facilitate and evaluate student performance, the materials should be evaluated based on the needs of the particular special student(s) who will be in the classroom. If possible, the regular teacher should have previously reviewed the IEP for each special student who will be enrolled in the classroom, thereby making the assessment procedure more useful.

Materials and Equipment. Appropriate *instructional materials* match the academic area for which they are selected and meet the needs of the special student(s) who will be working with them. Effective materials *must match the structure of the academic subject* (i.e., illustrate the major concepts in a subject) as well as the objective(s) of the lesson to be taught. Morsink (1984) illustrates the importance of these matches:

> In reading, for example, there is a phonemic structure to the alphabetic code; it is shown in sound-symbol patterns that occur with some regularity (for example, the patterns *ee, oa* are consistent markers for the long vowel 65 percent of the time). A match would occur if the teacher selected materials in which

Computers assist in individualizing instruction for students.

students were given an opportunity to learn and apply these patterns and other predictable patterns in reading unknown words.

A mismatch would occur if materials taught an overgeneralization, such as "When two vowels go walking, the first one does the talking." This generalization applies to less than 45 percent of the structure of the English code; in some cases, such as /ui/, it applies only 6 percent of the time, and in the case of the two-vowel patterns of diphthongs (*ou, oi, eu,* etc.) the overgeneralization can be quite confusing. Similar kinds of structural mismatch would occur in social studies materials showing only nonhandicapped or all-white persons in pictures portraying the American population, since this limited sample is a distortion of reality. (pp. 108–109)

Other factors to consider when selecting instructional materials are the difficulty level, durability, mode of response elicited by the material, and adaptability to individual levels of the students who will be using them. Commercial materials need to be validated (i.e., proven effective) for use with special students.

Teachers should use a *filing system to organize instructional materials* by content area and skill within the content area. Color coding of materials facilitates their organization; color coding can also be used to make materials self-checking so that students can receive immediate feedback to their responses. Manipulative, concrete materials should be used as much as possible because they *teach*; worksheets tend to *assess* learning, although they may not be labeled "tests." Paper-and-pencil activities tend to call for what is *known* about a topic, or when little is known, the results of the paper-and-pencil activity reflect this. A checklist for evaluating instructional materials is shown in Table 5.1.

TABLE 5.1
Checklist for Evaluating Instructional Materials

Instruction
1. Are instruction procedures for each lesson clearly specified?
2. Does the material provide a maximum amount of direct teacher instruction on the skills/concepts presented?
3. Does the direct teacher instruction provide for active student involvement and responses?
4. Are the direct instructional lessons adaptable to small-group/individual instruction?
5. Is a variety of cueing and prompting techniques used to elicit correct child responses?
6. When using verbal instruction, does the instruction proceed in a clear, logical fashion?
7. Does the teacher use modeling and demonstration when appropriate to the skills being taught?
8. Does the material specify correction and feedback procedures for use during instruction?

Practice
1. Does the material contain appropriate practice activities that contribute to mastery of the skills/concepts?
2. Are the practice activities directly related to the desired outcome behaviors?
3. Does the material provide enough practice for the slow learner?
4. Does the material provide for feedback on responses during practice?
5. Can the learner complete practice activities independently?
6. Does the material reduce the probability of error in independent practice activities?

Sequence of instruction
1. Are the scope and sequence of the material clearly specified?
2. Are facts/concepts/skills ordered in a logical manner from simple to complex?
3. Does the sequence proceed in small steps, easily attainable by the handicapped learner?

(continued)

TABLE 5.1 *(continued)*

Content
1. Does the selection of the concepts and skills adequately represent the content area?
2. Is the content consistent with the stated objectives?
3. Is the information presented in the material accurate?
4. Is the information presented in the material current?
5. Are various points of view concerning treatment of minorities and handicapped people, ideologies, social values, sex roles, socioeconomic class, etc., objectively represented?
6. Are the content and topic of the material relevant to the needs of the handicapped students as well as to the other students in the regular classroom?

Behavioral objectives
1. Are objectives clearly stated for the material?
2. Are the objectives consistent with the goals for the whole classroom?
3. Are the objectives stated in behavioral terms including the desired child behavior, the criteria for measurement of the behavior, and the desired standard of performance?

Entry behaviors
1. Does the material specify the prerequisite student skills needed to work with ease in the material?
2. Are the prerequisite student skills compatible with the objectives of the material?

Initial assessment/placement
1. Does the material provide a method to determine initial placement into the material?
2. Does the initial placement tool contain enough items to accurately place the learner into the material?

Ongoing assessment/evaluation
1. Does the material provide evaluation procedures for measuring progress and mastery of objectives?
2. Are there sufficient evaluative items to accurately measure learner progress?
3. Are procedures and/or materials for ongoing record keeping provided?

Review/maintenance
1. Are practice and review of content material provided?
2. Are review and maintenance activities systematically and appropriately spaced?
3. Are adequate review and maintenance activities provided for the slow learner?

Motivation/interest
1. Are reinforcement procedures built in or suggested for use in the program?
2. Are procedures specified for providing feedback to the student on his/her progress?
3. Has the program been designed to motivate and appeal to students?

Adaptability to individual differences
1. Can the pace be adapted to variations in learner rate of mastery?

TABLE 5.1 *(continued)*

2. Can the method of response be adapted to the individual needs of the learner?
3. Can the method of instruction be adapted to the individual needs of the learner?
4. Can the child advance to subsequent tasks when he has demonstrated proficiency?
5. Can the learner be placed in the material at his own level?
6. Does the material offer alternative teaching strategies for students who are failing to master an objective?

Physical characteristics of the material
1. Is the format uncluttered?
2. Is the format grammatically correct and free of typographical errors?
3. Are photographs and illustrations clear, attractive, and consistent with the content?
4. Are the type size and style appropriate to the students?
5. Are auditory components of adequate clarity and amplification?
6. Are the materials durable?
7. Can the materials be easily stored and organized for classroom use?

Teacher considerations
1. Is a teacher's manual or set of teacher guidelines provided?
2. Are teacher instructions clear, complete, and unambiguous?
3. Does the material specify the skills and abilities needed by the instructor to work effectively with the material?

Source: J. W. Affleck, S. Lowenbraun, & A. Archer, [1980], *Teaching the mildly handicapped in the regular classroom* (2nd ed.) (Columbus, OH: Merrill), pp. 125–127. Reprinted by permission.

Instructional *materials centers,* funded by governmental sources, are located in many areas in the United States. On request, these centers lend materials for classroom use. It is a good idea to borrow specialized materials and try them out before purchasing them. The work of Stowitschek, Gable, and Hendrickson (1980) contains suggestions for effective use of a materials budget as well as ideas about selection, management, and adaptation of instructional materials for special students. For each of the academic areas, a variety of instructional materials are needed.

Teachers need *equipment* to teach effectively as well as adequate storage space for the equipment. Equipment should be stored in areas or on shelves where it can be easily retrieved and returned by students. Also, the school principal should arrange for proper maintenance of all equipment. Specialized equipment, such as wheelchairs, hearing aids, and other physical prostheses, may be necessary for physically handicapped students. The regular teacher should consult the proper professional team member about the correct use and maintenance of specialized equipment.

Resources. Locating available resources and planning for their use can provide tremendous support for a mainstreamed program. Materials and information from professional organizations, such as the Council for Exceptional Children and government-funded centers, can reduce the cost and frustration associated with initial mainstreaming efforts. Human resources, such as parents, community volunteers, and members of civic clubs, can be a great source of support.

Parents and other family members can be used as change agents in the learning environment. Many preschool programs for special students use parents as the primary change agents for the children (Thurman & Widerstrom, 1985). The skills and talents of parents can also be used to help prepare and develop materials for classroom use as well as to help implement instructional procedures.

Volunteers can help develop and prepare materials, and they can be trained to assist with the implementation of instructional programs. Appropriate recruitment, training, organization, and recognition of volunteers keeps them actively involved with mainstreamed programs (see pp. 156–158). Also, classroom peers and older students can provide volunteer services to mainstreamed classrooms. Some of the ways in which peers can enhance a mainstreamed program are described later in the chapter (see pp. 158–159).

Scheduling

Even with a supportive emotional/social environment, an adequate learning environment, and an appropriate instructional process, mainstreamed programs cannot be successful without workable scheduling plans. Although the master schedule of a school sets the parameters of classroom schedules, regular teachers do have some flexibility in arranging their classroom schedules.

Classroom Schedules.   Most special students in regular classes receive individual or small-group instruction from the resource teacher. The students may leave the regular classroom to receive instruction in the resource room for a specified period of time daily or weekly, or the resource teacher may come to the student's regular classroom to provide instruction. To ensure maximum educational progress, resource and regular teachers need to coordinate their schedules carefully and maintain close communication relative to the performance of each special student they serve. Regularly scheduled conferences between regular and resource teachers can be used to discuss the special student's progress and to resolve problems, such as scheduling conflicts, grading, peer relationship problems, and so forth.

At the *elementary school level*, regular teachers should work with the resource teacher in planning a schedule that accommodates the needs of both regular and special students. Most special students, as well as young students, need a structured, consistent schedule. Posting of the daily schedule can be helpful to all students.

In general, special students should be scheduled for remedial or special instruction by a resource teacher at the same time the subject is being taught in the regular classroom. For example, if a student is to receive special instruction in math, he or she should go to the resource teacher for math instruction during the regular students' math period (Schulz & Turnbull, 1984). Also, special students should not be scheduled for work in the resource room while regular students are participating in music, art, physical education, or library classes, because special students enjoy and need these classes. Table 5.2 shows a sample regular classroom schedule that serves both regular and special students at the elementary school level.

At the *secondary school level*, regardless of the scheduling approach used (e.g., conventional scheduling, flexible scheduling, flexible modular scheduling, or some other), arrangements must be made to offer secondary students those courses required for high school graduation, college entrance, training in a vocational-technical area, and electives as well as opportunities to participate in meaningful extracurricular activities. Although special students frequently participate in secondary prevocational training, some special students are able to complete college-preparatory courses successfully. When preparing the master schedule of a secondary school, principals should consult with the regular classroom teachers who teach special students and the special education teacher(s) or resource teacher(s) to determine the scheduling needs of special students.

Wood (1984) lists the following suggestions for effective scheduling of special students in secondary schools.

1. Having small classes—4 to 5 students per resource class
2. Allowing students in each resource class to have the same mainstream teachers when taking the same courses
3. Grouping students in each resource class by grade or ability level—for example, four students who read poorly and need extra help, but are scattered among three eighth-grade classes, should be in the same resource class
4. Including special education teachers in preparation of the school's master schedule so that they can prevent future scheduling problems and represent special students' needs
5. Scheduling special education teachers' off-periods around special students' resource schedules
6. Not scheduling the school's one-period elective offerings concurrently
7. Using special education teachers to select effective mainstream teachers for the students
8. Notifying the mainstream teacher when schedules are complete so that the teacher has time to select materials and prepare individual assignments
9. Balancing sections throughout the day. (If courses are taught on different levels, sections should be available in the morning as well as in the afternoon.)
10. Planning morning sections for vocational students, co-op students, and athletes
11. Alternating academic courses with basic and college preparatory sections. (pp. 64–65)

TABLE 5.2
Sample Elementary Classroom Schedule[a]

8:00 A.M.	Students arrive at school
8:05	Attendance check; collection of lunch money R students begin workbook assignment listed on board (self-directing) S students begin work on individual assignments from learning contracts, learning activity packets, or programmed materials (self-directing)
8:15	Opening exercises; announcements; all students encouraged to participate in 5–10 minute whole-group discussion of some topic (e.g., local current event, an upcoming holiday); establish instructional goals for the day
8:30	Language arts instructional block begins R students receive teacher-directed reading instruction in reading groups and then rotate through spelling/writing and punctuation/grammar learning centers S students go to resource room for reading instruction during a designated 30–35-minute period, and participate in regular class learning centers the remainder of the day
10:00	Recess and restrooms
10:15	Mathematics instructional block begins R students receive whole-group, teacher-directed lesson followed by workbook and math learning center assignments S students go to resource room for 1 hour for math instruction; on return to regular class continue with language arts learning center assignments that may not have been completed before recess
11:30	Teacher gives one-to-one assistance where needed for *all* students to complete morning assignments; students who have finished all assignments and who have earned "free time" because of good behavior

[a]R = regular students; S = special students.

Since all students at the secondary level construct their own daily schedules by selecting certain courses, administrators may need to assist special students in scheduling special education classes or other special services that they may need. Arrangements should also be made to facilitate special students' movement from class to class. Regular teachers and resource teachers at the elementary and secondary levels should exchange copies of their typical daily schedules to ensure coordination of routines and classroom procedures used with special students. Teaching strategies effective with special students at the secondary level are described later in the chapter.

Resource Room Scheduling.   A vital part of mainstreamed students' educational experience is their participation in resource room activities. Not only does the

TABLE 5.2
(continued)

	may select any activity (time is also used to let students go wash hands for lunch, in groups of three)
12:00 P.M.	Lunch
12:25	Relaxation time: teacher reads to students or plays records for their listening enjoyment (soft music)
12:35	Science instructional block begins *All* students receive short teacher-directed lesson, followed by: R students working in science learning center on various activities S students working on activities specified in learning contracts (which are related to the topic being studied by the whole class)
1:10	Recess and restrooms
1:25	Social studies instructional block begins *All* students watch 20-minute ETV program on "Ways People Communicate," followed by whole-group discussion of the program
2:00	Art class on Mon. and Wed.; music class on Thurs.; physical education class on Tues. and Fri. S students go to speech therapist on Wed.
2:30	Students prepare to go home: clean up around desks, put away all materials and supplies in classroom, collect things to take home, and, when time permits: *All* students take turns sharing orally their personal experiences (something new in their lives, what they plan to do the rest of the day, and so on) with the rest of the class (teacher uses this opportunity to remind students of speaking and listening skills required for effective communication)
2:45	Students depart for home

resource teacher provide instruction in academic areas from a special educator's perspective, the resource teacher can also teach special students "social survival skills," encourage special students to develop a sense of self-worth, and assist them in the development of independence. Wood (1984) points out that

> the resource room provides the mainstreamed student with additional time for completing class work, homework, or tests, with an environment free of anxiety, with alternative materials, learning stations, and equipment not available in the regular classroom, and with an environment more easily adaptable to special behaviors such as distractibility, short attention spans, hyperactivity, and so on. (p. 66)

Resource room scheduling includes both inter-resource scheduling and intra-resource scheduling. *Inter-resource scheduling* (i.e., scheduling between resource room and regular class) can sometimes be difficult because of conflicts with other schedules. Special students should not be held accountable for missing regular class content while working in the resource room. To avoid this problem, schedules for special students should be such that the students do not miss subjects that they will be responsible for later, or the resource teacher can plan with the regular teacher so that special students are not behind when they return to the regular classroom. Also, special students should not miss subjects or activities they enjoy, such as art, physical education, and assembly programs, because of their resource room schedule; on days when special subjects or activities are offered, the resource teacher can arrange for the student to come to the resource room at a different time. With effective communication between the regular teacher and the resource teacher, and mutual concern for special students' educational needs, scheduling conflicts can be resolved.

Intra-resource scheduling (i.e., scheduling within the resource room) should be coordinated with the schedules of the regular class as much as possible. For example, when language arts instruction is scheduled as the first instructional block of time in the regular classroom, followed by the mathematics block of time, the resource room should have a similar schedule. By coordinating resource room and regular room instructional blocks, it is easier to arrange special students' resource room work so that those regular class subjects they are capable of doing are not missed. Also, scheduling within the resource room should follow a consistent routine so that students do not become dependent on the resource teacher for beginning and completing assignments. Following a set of procedures for working through each lesson helps the student feel a sense of control over his or her own learning. For example, a set of procedures for mathematic lessons might be the following. The procedures should be posted near the mathematics center or work area.

1. Briefly review the previous day's worksheet.
2. Read the directions for today's assignment.
3. Ask the teacher to clarify the assignment's directions, *if necessary*.
4. Locate and retrieve the materials needed for the assignment (e.g., manipulative objects, a specific disk for the microcomputer, a metric ruler, and so on).
5. Signal the teacher when you are ready to begin work on the assignment. (The teacher provides demonstrations of or other needed instruction for the assignment; the students ask questions about the procedure and work a problem while the teacher observes; the teacher reteaches, or clarifies, when necessary.)
6. Begin work on the assignment. Check with the teacher after you do two or three problems to see if your answers are correct. If they are correct, continue to work on the assignment.
7. Complete the assignment.
8. Check your answers. If instructed to do so, check your answers against the answer key provided.
9. Place the completed assignment on the teacher's desk in the file tray.

Classroom Management

Classroom management procedures provide the structure for successful teaching. All teachers must be effective managers, and when special students are combined with their age-grade peers, effective classroom management becomes even more crucial. Two aspects of classroom management are addressed here: *instructional* and *behavioral management*. In this chapter, a distinction is made between instructional management and the instructional process (i.e., lesson planning, teaching, and assessing), even though effective instructional management is requisite to the instructional process (see pp. 172–192).

Showing a personal interest helps students stay on task.

Instructional Management

For our purposes, *instructional management* is defined as those factors that aid the delivery of classroom instruction and that require planning and supervision on a regular basis. The topics discussed here are planning and preparing, group management procedures, instructional methods, effective communication, managing student work, and managing human resources.

Planning and Preparing.   Advance planning and preparation for instruction reduces management problems. In addition to careful lesson planning, the teacher must decide which activities will be taught in large-group, small-group, or one-to-one settings, and the materials for conducting the activities must be selected. Teacher directions for activities, both oral and written, must be planned and stated precisely. The involvement of classroom helpers, whether students, parents, community volunteers, or teacher aides, requires both planning and supervision. In essence, planning for the instructional process involves answering the questions "What will be taught?" "Why should it be taught?" "Who will teach it?" "How will it be taught?" and "When and where will it be taught?" The selection and preparation of instructional and assessment materials are based on answers to the preceding questions.

Group Management Procedures.   Although some special students need frequent one-to-one instruction, this does not mean that they should be restricted from group instruction. Regular teachers often misinterpret the purpose of the IEP; the IEP is the special student's individual plan for attaining educational goals and objectives, but this does not mean that all instruction aimed at achieving the specified goals and objectives must be presented in a one-to-one manner. Special students benefit from group instruction in the same kinds of ways that regular students benefit. Alley (1977) suggests that secondary special students be grouped according to the skill areas in which they are deficient (descriptions of how to do this are contained in his article). There are a variety of grouping procedures that can be used successfully in mainstreamed classrooms. Large-group, small-group, and one-to-one procedures can be used effectively with both regular and special students.

Large-group procedures can be used for short lectures (no longer than 10–15 minutes) when the purpose is to introduce an assignment or materials, introduce a new concept, or give general directions. Class size is a factor in large-group instruction; however, a class with as many as 30 students can benefit from some large-group instruction if the content of the presentation is appropriate for all of the students. Maring and Furman (1985) describe seven teaching ideas for the improvement of reading and listening skills that can be used in "whole class" settings: once a week oral reading, pyramiding, exploring texts with students, contextual redefinition, words on the wall, guided reading procedure, and special adaptations for study guides. (Teachers interested in using these techniques are referred to Maring & Furman, 1985.)

Although large-group instruction may be appropriate for noncumulative subject matter with students who are reasonably homogeneous in learning rate and prerequisite skills, it is often misused. Prior to using large-group instruction, the skill levels, learning rates, and interests of *all* students must be considered. To determine whether a large group of students has the prerequisite knowledge and skills for a subject, a pretest can be designed and administered; only those students who attain a specified level of competency on the test are likely to benefit from upcoming large-group instruction. Some ideas for modifying large-group instruction to accommodate differences in student abilities and interests are described by Evertson, Emmer, Clements, Sanford, and Worsham (1984).

Small-group procedures include skill-specific, cooperative, and nonacademic forms of grouping. While peer-tutoring and the buddy system represent forms of small groups, they are described later in the chapter.

Skill-specific small-group procedures usually include three to seven students who receive teacher-directed instruction on a particular skill. Usually, skill-specific grouping is used with students of similar ability, and at similar levels, who need instruction in a specific skill; however, heterogeneous groups can provide lower-functioning students with models (Lewis & Doorlag, 1987). Also, learning centers can be used for small groups to practice specific skills that have been taught. (Ideas for using learning centers are described later in the chapter.) Skill-specific grouping allows direct help while providing opportunities for the teacher to gather diagnostic information related to academic and social behaviors. It also encourages participation and interaction of *all* students in the group, provides for the formation of temporary instructional groups, permits cross-age grouping for specific skill development, and allows students to get to know one another quickly, increasing productive patterns of learning and working together.

Cooperative grouping refers to the structuring of learning situations so that special and regular students work together to achieve common goals. Working cooperatively with peers not only enhances learning, but also creates positive peer relationships as students interact, encourage, and share.

According to Morsink (1984), with cooperative learning "there is a group goal and a criterion-referenced evaluation system; all members of the group are recognized on the basis of the total group's performance" (p. 101). Research findings (Bina, 1986; Johnson, Johnson, Waring, & Maruyama, 1986; Johnson, Maruyama, Johnson, Nelson, & Skor, 1981) indicate that cooperative learning assists students in retention and transfer, promotes positive student-to-student relationships, promotes students' abilities to value diversity, and facilitates the acquisition of higher-level learning tasks that involve problem solving and cognitive rehearsal. Jones and Jones (1986) offer the following guidelines for creating cooperative learning groups.

1. Cooperative group work is accomplished more smoothly and with more positive results when it occurs in classrooms in which children feel positive about their peers. Activities for creating positive peer relations can be conducted prior to group assignments.
2. Teachers must decide *when* to employ cooperative group work in the classroom. The decision of whether to employ individualized, competitive, or cooperative learning activities should be based on the learning outcomes the teacher is seeking.
3. Teachers must help students develop the specific skills necessary for working effectively in groups. This can be accomplished by providing students with group decisions or problem-solving tasks followed by discussions about which behaviors facilitated or blocked the group's completion of the task.
4. Teachers must provide groups with clear instructions and ensure that students are aware of how to solve the problems that may arise.

Nonacademic grouping can be used to facilitate management during supplementary activities and to promote social interaction among students. In subjects such as music, speech, drama, art, and physical education, opportunities arise to group students by interest, choice, proximity, counting off, or alphabetically.

Morsink (1984) points out that some students, both special and regular, may present problems when they work with others in small groups. Morsink identifies the following problems often associated with small groups and their possible solutions.

Problem	Possible Solution
Inattention to instructions	• Refuse to repeat directions. (Do this consistently.) • Make instructions brief, clear, and interactive. (Students do something in response to instruction, such as work the first problem together and check.) • Praise or reward good listeners. ("I like the way John is watching the board"; "I could tell that Sherry listened carefully because she knew what to do. I'm going to let her hold the book this time.")
Some dominate, others fail to get turns	• Go around the group in a predictable order so everyone gets a turn. Sometimes go backward or start in the middle so students do not anticipate their turn and listen only then. • Ask the question first, then state the name of the child who is to answer. You can vary question difficulty according to the student.

Problem	Possible Solution
	• Pause after stating the question to allow time for thinking and to prevent impulsive answers. (Set up a praise or point system to reward those who wait and penalize those who blurt out.)
Some finish group work too early	• Praise or reward accuracy rather than speed.
	• Have an alternative assignment for early finishers. (Print it on the board or hand them an additional task while they are in the group.)[1]
	• Set up a "checking"chain, allowing each student who gets 100% to use the answer key to check the work of the next student who finishes.
Dealing with disruptions	• Ignore if not too dangerous.
	• Restate rules: "I'll call on people when they wait quietly and raise their hands." (Then be consistent.)
	• Give choice: "You may sit in your chair or leave the group." (Be ready for a confrontation if you do this.)
	• Praise or reward those who do the right thing: "Charles, you're a superstar because Tom hit you and you didn't hit him back. That's great!" (pp. 148–149)

One-to-one procedures include teacher-to-student and tutor-to-student instruction. Exclusive use of one-to-one instruction is not recommended. It is appropriate when the teacher needs to reteach a skill that a student failed to grasp during group or independent study. One-to-one instruction should not be confused with individual interactions between teacher and student, which should occur intermittently throughout the school day as part of effective teaching. (Tutor-to-student instruction is described later in the chapter.)

Instructional Methods.   The term *instructional methods* refers to the optional ways in which content may be presented, an important component of a teacher's

---

[1] Any given intervention may have an effect that differs from the one you anticipate. Here, for example, students might begin to waste time in order to avoid the extra work! It is always important to note (better still to measure) the effectiveness of the intervention strategy. (This note and the lists of problems and possible solutions are taken from Catherine Volker Morsink, *Teaching special needs students in regular classrooms*, p.148, 149. Copyright © 1984 by Catherine Volker Morsink. Reprinted by permission of Scott, Foresman & Co.)

delivery-of-instruction system. The best teachers of all students use a variety of delivery methods to teach and assess students. The use of varied instructional methods increases student interest, thereby maintaining attention to the learning tasks, and allows students opportunities to deal with content from several perspectives. There are a number of instructional methods that are effective with special as well as regular students. Although the methods described here are designed and supervised by the teacher, they are not considered to be teacher-directed activities, in that they do not require constant teacher-student interaction. Learning centers (sometimes referred to as *learning stations*), programmed instruction, computer-assisted instruction, learning activity packets, mediated instruction, learning contracts, mastery learning, and tutorial procedures are among the methods described in the following paragraphs.

Learning centers or stations provide the opportunity for individual students and small groups to practice skills that have been acquired. They can also be constructed to provide reinforcement for teacher-taught concepts, activities for independent study, and enrichment activities. Learning centers can be developed for any subject or grade level, and they can be presented in boxes or folders, on bulletin boards or back-drop boards, or at tables.

Learning centers have specific objectives that students fulfill, representing one or more skill area in an academic area. Each center contains multilevel activities and materials, eliciting various learner response modes, designed to meet individual needs, learning styles, interests, and achievement levels. Directions for each activity are clearly and concisely written so that a student does not need constant teacher guidance. Learning centers can be used to support basic skills, supplement a unit of study, or add enrichment activities related to a content area. At the elementary school level, learning centers for mathematics, language arts, and discovery (manipulative science) are common. At the secondary level, centers can be developed to teach prevocational skills (D'Zambo, Laflex, Glenn, Webster, & Raiser, 1981) as well as English and math skills. Morsink (1984) describes how a mathematics learning center for third graders was used to supplement a math unit on metric measurement.

> It included meter sticks, metric ruler and measuring tapes, centimeter blocks, a scale and various weights including gram and a kilogram, and various sizes of containers such as liters and half liters for measuring liquids. The science table on which the center was located contained activities at different levels. Students chose activities according to their interest and ability. For example, Scott and George made up metric math problems for others to figure out. Susan, Sarah and Jane used the calculator to determine how tall everyone in the class would be if they were lying down in a long line with each person's head touching the other's feet—(3,124 cm.). Phillip used picture cards to help him structure his task. (p. 166)

Programmed instruction involves the use of commercially developed materials that present small, sequential information in either a written or mediated format, which allows students to progress at their own rate. Students who need a systematic approach to learning usually respond well to programmed materials because they emphasize factual information and provide sufficient practice. The materials are designed so that students receive immediate feedback to each of their answers. Some programmed materials include teacher-directed introductory lessons for each unit of study included in a set of materials.

Computer-assisted instruction in certain academic areas has been proven effective with special students (Hannaford & Sloane, 1981; Johnson, 1982; Joiner, 1979; Thorkildson, Bickel, & Williams, 1979; Weir & Watt, 1980–1981; Wieck, 1980). The development of microcomputers has made computer-assisted instruction an educational reality. Computers not only provide tutorial instruction, but can be used to involve students in inquiry, simulation, and problem-solving processes. Appropriate uses of the microcomputer with special students are continuing to be explored (Cosden, Gerber, Semmel, Goldman, & Semmel, 1987; Goldman, Semmel, Cosden, Gerber, & Semmel, 1987). Cosden et al. (1987) compared handicapped and nonhandicapped students' use of microcomputers and reported that while active engagement time with computers was higher for both groups (ranging from 80% to 90%) than during other instructional activities (ranging from 16% to 53%), most of the computer programs used by the students consisted of drill and practice activities; mainstreamed students were allocated longer use periods than were nonhandicapped students; and teacher contact with students during computer use periods was generally low. These findings indicate that while microcomputers hold instructional promise for both special and regular students, they can enhance the instructional process only if used creatively and selectively.

Teacher-created computer programs (lessons) can be just as useful, if not more so in some cases, as commercial programs (software). Teacher-created computer lessons can be constructed quite readily with word-processor software, which teachers can learn to use easily. Elkins (1986) recommends the use of word processors and spelling checkers by older students during composition assignments. Because microcomputers and software programs vary so widely, teachers must be careful in their selection of this equipment. Appropriate selection of computer software (programs) by teachers who are computer literate, and creative use of software are the keys to effective use of computer-assisted instruction. Review of software is ongoing and can be used by teachers in the selection of programs (Grimes, 1981; Hannaford & Sloane, 1981). Teachers can efficiently acquire computer literacy through carefully planned staff development programs (Beck, 1981).

Learning activity packets are self-instructional units prepared for a specific ability level that enable students to learn a basic concept by breaking it down into several components. The typical packet includes a set of objectives, a pretest, several instructional activities, a posttest, and suggested remediation procedures for students who do not demonstrate mastery on the posttest. Students work at their own pace through the packet. Regular teachers and resource teachers can develop learning activity packets.

Mediated instruction involves the use of media during the learning process. Commercial programs are available that combine print, tapes or records, and filmstrips to teach concepts. Teacher-created programs that combine media with textbook materials to teach skills and concepts are also effective. In addition to microcomputers and educational television, photographs, slides, filmstrips, transparencies, cassette tapes, records, videotapes, films, and electronic games can be used as supplements to printed material. By creatively combining media, teachers can enhance the quality of instruction for all students in the classroom.

Learning contracts can be used effectively with some students. A learning contract is a written agreement between the teacher and student in which the student promises to study a specific topic, using specified learning resources and procedures. The importance of the teacher and student planning the contract jointly has been emphasized by Dunn and Dunn (1974). Usually contracts include behavioral objectives and specify the amount and quality of work to be completed by a given due date. Contracts work well with students who like to choose the manner in which they learn, apply, and report information. Schulz and Turnbull (1984) indicate that emotionally disturbed students "benefit from having contingencies clearly identified in advance" (p. 116). Also, contracts can be useful with students who are poorly motivated, disorganized, or forgetful. Among the advantages of contracts are that they encourage independence, allow students to work at their own pace, individualize instruction, and help students assume responsibility for their own learning. Figure 5.3 shows a sample learning contract form.

Mastery learning methods require mastery at the end of a particular unit of instruction, whereas nonmastery methods allow students to move into a subsequent unit of instruction regardless of their performance at the end of the preceding unit. With mastery learning units, students are tested, graded, and given additional instruction and practice if they do not meet a specified criterion level. If they demonstrate mastery on the test, students are allowed to move on to the next unit after completing supplementary or enrichment activities (Morsink, 1984). The implications of mastery learning for use in mainstreamed classrooms have been described by Guskey (1981), who pointed out that mastery learning facilitates cooperative learning rather than competitive learning in classrooms. The identification and utilization of a wide variety of materials, along with specific procedures for teaching and reinforcing each concept in an academic area, are required to implement successfully a mastery learning program.

Tutorial procedures can be used to provide individualized instruction to special students. Peers, paraprofessionals, parents, and community volunteers can be trained as tutors. The use of structured tutoring and peer tutoring are recommended as tutorial procedures. The *structured tutoring model* (Von Harrison & Guymon, 1980) is characterized by a precise tutor-student relationship.

Topic/Subject Area: _____

Objective(s): _____
_____
_____
_____
_____

Procedures/Activities: _____
_____
_____
_____
_____
_____
_____
_____

Resource Alternatives   Evaluation Alternatives

_____   _____
_____   _____
_____   _____
_____   _____

_____   _____

Student _____ Date _____
                (Signature)
Teacher _____ Date _____
                (Signature)
Date Completed _____
_____

FIGURE 5.3
Sample Learning Contract Form

To ensure that the tutoring relationship is what it ought to be, it is necessary that tutors be trained in specific techniques and procedures. Tutor-training procedures must allow tutors to practice the actual behaviors rather than merely talk about them. Von Harrison and Guymon (1980) identify the following categories of training.

> (1) *General:* Including how to establish and maintain good rapport with the learner, how to use established psychological principles of learning, and how to ensure that a learner has mastered a particular step in a sequence. (2) *Material Specific:* Including prescriptions for training tutors to use materials once they are selected or prepared and for developing procedures which are responsive to the learner's interaction with the materials. (3) *Task Specific:* Including the training which must focus on techniques and procedures that are unique to the particular instructional objectives the tutors are dealing with. For example, the training a tutor would receive relative to teaching a learner to blend sounds would be markedly different from the training involved when teaching a learner to solve a specific type of math problem. (4) *Record Keeping:* Including general

aspects of record keeping as well as other aspects unique to the instructional objectives being dealt with. In either case, careful records must be kept to guide decisions, such as when to move on, to repeat, or to skip to other materials. (p. 16)

Administrators and teachers interested in establishing a structured tutoring program for special students are referred to Von Harrison and Guymon (1980). Also, because of the extensive training requirements, it is recommended that recruitment of tutors for a structured tutoring program be limited to paraprofessionals, parents, and community volunteers who have a strong commitment to the educational program.

Peer tutoring involves allowing regular students to serve as tutors to special students. Regular students benefit by becoming more accepting of the differences and likenesses among individuals, and special students benefit from the instruction and modeling provided by regular students. The effectiveness of peer-tutoring programs has been reported (Heron & Harris, 1982; Krouse, Gerber, & Kauffman, 1981; Sapon-Shevin, 1978; Strain, 1981).

All tutors must receive training before working with special students. Endsley (1980) notes that training peers to be tutors requires three or four 50-minute sessions, and that the specific areas in which training should occur include introductory techniques, general tutoring procedures, pretesting and posttesting procedures, completing student forms, tutoring from the instructional materials, completing tutor logs, determining the instructional assignments and reviews, and completing the Summative Learning Gains Record (p. 18). Each of these above topics is described in detail by Endsley (1980), whose work should be consulted by those preparing to implement a peer-tutoring program.

Teachers must develop a schedule for the peer tutors and monitor tutorial activities. Also, teachers must ensure that the learning tasks to be presented by tutors are highly structured, so that tutors can follow a specific set of procedures for presenting instruction.

Special students can serve as peer tutors as well. Not only does this improve the special student's status within a classroom, but it also provides opportunities for the special student to develop social skills and practice academic skills. The typical arrangement is for special students to serve as peer tutors for regular students in lower grade levels.

Both *same-age* (i.e., students from within the same classroom or from another classroom within the same grade level) and *cross-age* (i.e., students who are older and more advanced in school) peer-tutoring arrangements can be successful. Peer tutors have been proven successful teachers for withdrawn individuals, acting-out students, and students with deficient academic skills. Initially, a peer tutor should be prepared for rejection by a special student tutee, but this subsides as rapport develops and instruction proceeds (Gable, Strain, & Hendrickson, 1979; Lewis & Doorlag, 1987). The advantages associated with peer tutoring are that it (1) encourages social acceptance, (2) enables explanation of assignments in student terms, and (3) increases the tutor's own learning (through teaching).

The *buddy system* can be used with a special student whose handicap requires extra assistance from someone during portions of a lesson. Special students with severe hearing impairments, visual impairments, or fine motor problems can receive assistance from a classmate "buddy." Buddies can be rotated on a daily, biweekly, or weekly basis, and teachers must instruct them about how much help is needed and when help is not needed. A "hearing" buddy may be needed to make an outline or carbon copy of lecture notes, repeat directions, clarify concepts, or locate the right page in a book. A "seeing" buddy may be needed to describe a visual aid (e.g., a chart or graph), assist in retrieval of materials and resources in the classroom, or read directions and other written material. A "writing" buddy may be needed to write dictated paragraphs on worksheets or tests, mark answer sheets, and write dictated answers on math assignments.

An important point for teachers to keep in mind is that exclusive use of any one teaching method results in monotonous, boring instruction. Both special and regular students can be motivated through the use of varied instructional methods.

Effective Communication. The use of effective communication skills is the foundation of good classroom management. Both verbal and nonverbal messages can be used to facilitate instructional management.

Delivery of verbal directions in a clear, comprehensible manner is an important teaching skill. Clarity is especially crucial during content development, in that this is when nearly all new subject matter is introduced and taught. Evertson et al. (1984) describe the following as ways that teachers can enhance the clarity of lessons.

1. *Communicate lesson objectives.*
   a. State goals or objectives.
   b. Tell students what they will be held accountable for knowing or doing.
   c. Emphasize major ideas.
2. *Present information systematically.*
   a. Outline the lesson sequence.
   b. Break complex content into manageable portions, giving step-by-step directions.
   c. Summarize previous points, clearly delineating major transitions between ideas or topics.
3. *Avoid vagueness.*
   a. Provide a variety of apt examples.
   b. Use words students understand.
   c. Define new vocabulary words.
   d. Be specific, precise; refer to concrete objects if possible.

4. *Check for understanding.*
   a. Ask questions or obtain work samples to make sure students are ready to move on.
   b. Ask students to summarize main points.
   c. Reteach when necessary.
5. *Provide for practice and feedback.*
   a. Ask students to restate the lesson sequence and its major concepts.

Nonverbal signals, such as hand gestures, facial expressions, or walking over to stand beside a student who is visiting with a classmate when he or she should be working, are useful procedures for helping students attend to the learning task.

Another aspect of effective communication is the ability to listen to others. By effectively employing listening skills, teachers can create relationships that allow students to feel significant, accepted, and respected and that enable them to take responsibility for their own behavior.

The primary goal of listening is to encourage students to express their real concerns, needs, or wants (Jones & Jones, 1986). When students share personal problems, express frustration with their work assignments, or display emotions, it is often most effective (initially) just to listen. A teacher who really listens, at an empathic nonevaluative level, enables the bothered student to feel that he or she has been heard and that the feelings being expressed are acceptable. According to Jones and Jones (1986), several benefits can be derived by employing empathic listening.

> First, students learn that their feelings are acceptable, which reduces the tension and anxiety associated with having to hide one's true feelings. . . . Second, when thoughts and feelings can be expressed openly and are received non-judgmentally, students are much less likely to express feelings through un-productive behaviors. . . . Third, when adults listen nonevaluatively they provide young people with an opportunity to examine and clarify feelings that are often confusing and frightening. This exchange frequently enables youngsters to better understand a situation and to consider approaches to effectively cope with the situation. (p. 104)

Managing Student Work. Effective management of student work requires organization and consistent teacher behavior regarding student work assignments. It saves time and prevents confusion. As soon as *instructions for assignments* have been verbally communicated, the teacher should post the assignment and important instructions on the chalkboard. When writing chalkboard instructions for seatwork to several different groups, make sure the assignment for each group is clearly labeled.

Tell students the *required standards* for form and neatness and give them a due date for the assignment. Regarding standard and form, students should be told what heading to use, whether or not to write on the reverse side of the paper, whether to use pen or pencil, and whether to erase or draw lines through errors. Post a sample heading and remind students to refer to it as needed. Keep due dates reasonable, but do not extend time limits, or students may begin to dawdle rather than work. Develop a policy about work not completed on time.

Monitor progress of student work by circulating around the room and checking each student's progress report periodically. This procedure permits corrective feedback to be given when needed and helps keep students responsible for keeping pace. When notebooks, reports, or projects are not due for several days, set deadlines for completion of segments of the assignment.

Establish procedures for *monitoring the completion of assignments* and for *collecting completed assignments*. Students can place completed work on a specified corner of their desk, or they can turn it over when completed, either of which permits the teacher to determine at a glance whose assignments are completed. Assignments can be collected by having them passed in a given direction, by using designated helpers, by having them stacked in a specific spot, or by having them placed in appropriately labeled baskets.

Managing Human Resources.   Regardless of how well peers, paraprofessionals, parents, and community volunteers have been trained to tutor, perform clerical duties, and construct instructional materials, their involvement in the classroom must be managed. Administrators can establish checking-in and checking-out procedures for volunteers, locate work areas in which tutoring can take place, and locate and procure the necessary specialized instructional materials and equipment needed by volunteers as they work with special students. However, the classroom teacher needs to develop work schedules for peer tutors as well as for volunteers so that instructional periods are not disrupted by the arrival and departure of tutors and volunteers.

Also, it is necessary for the teacher to establish procedures that enable tutors and volunteers to use their time efficiently. For example, the teacher can specify the locations in the room where tutors and volunteers can obtain work assignments, pick up materials related to their assignments, and place incompleted and completed work assignments.

Behavioral Management

Teachers' classroom management skills significantly influence students' motivation, achievement, and behavior. Effective teachers manage and employ procedures designed to prevent student misbehavior, and, when necessary, they systematically use behavioristic intervention strategies to change problem behaviors.

Prevention of Misbehavior.   Jacob Kounin's book, *Discipline and Group Management in Classrooms* (1970), which is based on analyses of thousands of hours of videotapes showing classrooms with minimum disruptive behaviors and

---

What You Can Do

- Provide a positive atmosphere within the classroom and school to ensure the development of trust, which is necessary for learning to occur efficiently.

- Work toward effective communication between the regular teacher and the resource teacher.

- Use large-group procedures for lessons taking no more than 10–15 minutes.

- Provide peer tutors for special students.

- Help the special student to develop effective organization skills.

- Learn what motivates students.

- Be aware of the goals and objectives of the IEP.

- Divide skills into small steps.

---

classrooms with frequent student misconduct, reveals significant differences in the behaviors of effective and ineffective classroom teacher management *prior* to students' misbehaviors. Three areas of teacher behavior that influence students' behavior and learning are (1) a teacher's skill in organizing and managing classroom activities, (2) a teacher's skill in presenting instructional material, and (3) teacher-student relationships (Jones & Jones, 1986). Some ideas related to these areas are discussed earlier in the chapter (see pp. 137–138); the paragraphs that follow also discuss ideas and suggestions related to these areas but from a behavioral management perspective.

In general, students who are kept busy and interested in what they are learning rarely cause problems, except in the case of extremely aggressive students. Students engaged in productive and challenging learning activities usually behave appropriately. The first step to increasing appropriate classroom behavior of *all* students is for the teacher to define students' behavioral expectations or to identify for them the classroom rules that must be followed. Students need guidelines for behavior; they benefit from consistently enforced rules. Rules should be simple and clearly stated, few in number, and phrased positively. Once rules are developed, they should be posted where students can refer to them easily.

Jones and Jones (1986) have identified and discussed in detail the following instructional management skills for facilitating on-task behavior and aiding the prevention of student misconduct.

1. *Giving clear instructions:* Disruptive behavior is decreased when students know how to proceed and what to do when they need assistance to complete their work.
2. *Beginning a lesson:* Teachers should select and teach a cue for getting students' attention, remove distractions, start the lesson with a highly motivating activity, and hand out an outline, list of definitions, or study guide to help students organize their thoughts and focus their attention.
3. *Maintaining attention:* Classroom and seating arrangements; random selection in calling on students, asking the question before calling on a student, and waiting at least five seconds before answering a question or calling on another student; playing games that encourage attentive listening; asking students to respond to their classmates' answers; and providing work of appropriate difficulty—these are all tactics that help students maintain attention.
4. *Pacing:* By watching for nonverbal cues that indicate students are becoming bored, confused, or restless; breaking up activities into short segments or providing for "short breaks" during lessons that last longer than 30 minutes; and limiting the number of problems on a worksheet to indicate mastery of a skill—these are among the ways that teachers can reduce student misbehavior related to poorly paced lessons.
5. *Using seatwork effectively:* Since research shows that students spend more than half their school day working privately at seatwork, teachers should make seatwork diagnostic and prescriptive. Work through the first several seatwork problems with students, spend considerable time in presentation and discussion before assigning seatwork, relate seatwork directly to materials presented immediately prior to it, provide short segments of seatwork, and let students work together during seatwork.
6. *Summarizing:* Useful activities include asking students to state or write in a journal one thing they have learned, letting students create learning displays, providing frequent review sessions, and relating material to students' own lives and interests.
7. *Providing useful feedback and evaluation:* Feedback and evaluation can reduce anxiety among students, teachers, and parents when successes are recognized and weaknesses are constructively addressed.
8. *Making smooth transitions:* With approximately thirty major transitions during the school day, student disruptions during transitions can lead to extended periods of off-task behavior. It is important to have material ready for the upcoming lesson, to let students hand out and collect materials and do other organizational tasks, to develop and use transition activities, and to employ group competition to stimulate more orderly transitions.
9. *Handling minor disruptions:* Teachers should scan the room in order to notice and respond to potential problems or minor disruptions, respond immediately to the disruption, deal privately with the misbehaving student(s), and employ effective communication skills when resolving conflicts.

Verbal requests to behave appropriately should be directed to the student who is misbehaving. A simple, "Susie, return to your work" is better than saying, "Class get busy."

The quality of communication between the teacher and students is a factor in maintaining appropriate student behavior. Teachers who demonstrate that they accept and value students usually have fewer students with behavior problems. On occasion, the teacher may be confronted with conflict situations; when this happens, Schulz and Turnbull (1984) recommend the following guidelines for dealing with students.

1. Focus communication on the student's behavior without judging or attacking. . . .
2. Be firm and consistent in applying rules and assigning consequences. . . .
3. Angry feelings are natural, particularly when the student has engaged in behavior that is dangerous to others. Strive to express angry feelings in a rational and clear fashion without escalating the intensity of your feelings or those of the student. . . .
4. Teacher confrontations should never occur in front of an entire class. . . . (p. 344).

Sometimes students exhibit inappropriate behavior as a way of seeking attention. When teachers suspect this to be the cause of the misbehavior, they can provide extra attention to the students by assigning classroom responsibilities. Further, special students should not be overlooked when assigning classroom duties.

Involving parents in decisions about how to best motivate and discipline their child can be helpful. Parents can describe the management strategies they use with their child at home and can provide the teacher with background information useful in better understanding the student.

Sabatino, Sabatino, and Mann (1983) emphasize that the school should strive to be a place where people are courteous, where laughter is heard, and where communication is practiced. Further, the school should have democratically determined rules that everyone agrees on and that are beneficial to each individual and to the group. School administrators should actively support and practice an approach to discipline that teaches self-responsibility. Sabatino et al. (1983) provide the following general steps to good discipline.

1. Be personal, with statements to students such as, "I care about you."
2. Avoid references to the past.
3. Emphasize behavior, not feelings.
4. Stress value judgments; ask students to evaluate their own.
5. Plan, work with students to formulate successful, simple alternatives.
6. Be committed.
7. Give positive reinforcement.
8. Use behavioral contracts.
9. Decline to accept excuses.

10. Decline to punish, since punishment lifts responsibility from students.
11. Never give up but hang in there longer than the students expect. (pp. 33–34)

Development of a Behavioristic Intervention Plan.   Regardless of how effectively teachers employ procedures to prevent classroom misbehavior, some student misconduct is inevitable. A few students may need a highly structured plan to help them change specific behaviors. Most teachers find that no more than 5–10% of their students require behavior management methods. The time spent in developing an effective behavioristic intervention plan is almost always repaid many times over by reduction in student misconduct.

Behavioristic intervention is based on examining specific data and applying experimentally validated procedures to alter undesirable behavior. As a scientific approach, it is based on three assumptions: (1) behavior is influenced by the consequences following it; (2) behavior-change programs must be focused on specific, observable behavior; and (3) data collection is necessary to alter behavior thoughtfully and systematically (Jones & Jones, 1986). Therefore, several steps are involved in the development of a behavioristic intervention plan: (1) observing classroom behaviors, (2) recording the occurrence of specified behaviors before an intervention plan is implemented, (3) charting the baseline data on a graph, (4) selecting and implementing a behavioristic intervention system when results of initial observations (baseline data) indicate the need for such a system, (5) observing the occurrence of specified behaviors after the intervention plan is in place, and (6) charting all subsequent observation data on the graph containing the baseline data so that student progress can be evaluated. Although data collection is time-consuming, the advantages of possessing specific data associated with behaviors outweigh the complexity of collection procedures.

Careful observation and recording procedures are used to identify and quantify the occurrence of classroom behaviors. Direct observation of behavior and informal behavior inventories can be used to collect data and to identify the conditions surrounding appropriate and inappropriate behaviors. If an informal inventory is not used, teachers may construct their own classroom behavior instrument(s) before observation is begun. Those behaviors of interest to the teacher must be clearly specified and described so that they can be identified during the observation process. The classroom teacher, aide, trained volunteer, special educator, or student can conduct observations and record behaviors.

When possible, arrangements may be made to have two independent classroom observers involved in data collection. The use of two observers permits consensus of opinion regarding behaviors displayed, so that those behaviors identified by both observers as "occurring" are important bits of data. Observers can study the interactions between the teacher and students; it is not uncommon for observers to spot one or two mannerisms (of the student being observed, another student, or even the teacher) that may be triggering disruptive behaviors. Once the regular teacher is aware of the causes of disruptive behaviors, steps can be taken to correct the problem areas. The results of the initial observations provide baseline data and pinpoint behaviors that need modification. The term *baseline data* refers to the data collected during typical, or natural, classroom conditions *before* a management system is implemented.

Several methods for *recording observations* have been identified. Lewis and Doorlag (1987) recommend that, when possible, sequence analysis be used by observers because it is more systematic. *Sequence analysis* requires the observer to identify a behavior and to describe its antecedents (i.e., the situation or condition, or the comments or behaviors of relevant people, *just prior* to the behavior) and its consequences (i.e., the situation or condition, or the comments or behaviors of relevant people, *immediately after* the behavior). Sequence analysis provides more information than does simple observation, but it is not as easy to collect. Since behaviors do not happen in isolation, it is sometimes difficult to identify the events that precede them and the consequences that follow them. However, by doing this teachers can develop procedures that can modify both antecedents and consequences at the same time (Lewis & Doorlag, 1987). According to Walker (1979), "an example of manipulation of both antecedents and consequences would be in the case where a teacher carefully defines classroom rules and then allows children to accumulate minutes of free time for following them" (p. 46).

Other methods of recording observation data are usually some variation of either a frequency count or a time-interval measure. *Frequency count* refers to the number of times a behavior occurs, and *time-interval measure* refers to the length of time a behavior is exhibited. Frequency is recorded by making a mark beside the designated behavior each time it occurs; the marks are counted at the end of the observation period. Time-interval observations are recorded by writing beside the designated behavior the number of seconds or minutes the behavior is exhibited. Sometimes the initial observation period lasts several days, allowing observations to be recorded daily during a specified time block. The choice of recording method depends on the type of behavior(s) observed and the kind of data that will be most useful to the teacher in planning a systematic behavior management program. Sometimes teachers may choose to collect data on the behaviors of the entire class rather than on selected students. When this is done, classroom observers may choose to use a data collection form like the one developed by Jane Stallings (1983), which is shown in Figure 5.4. This form can be used to provide information on the amount and type of off-task student behavior as well as the instructional activity occurring at the time of the observed behavior. The observer makes a visual sweep of the classroom at designated intervals (perhaps every 3 or 5 minutes) and marks the appropriate symbols to describe the type of off-task behavior, the instructional activity the student should have been engaged in, and the number of the sweep. For example, suppose Bob, a student, was socializing during a listening activity on sweep 5 (see Figure 5.4). In this case, the observer would write *S/L/5* below Bob's name on the form. The data can then be used to determine the off-task percentage by using the following formula.

$$\frac{\text{Sum of no. of students off-task for each observation sweep}^3}{\text{No. of students} \times \text{no. of sweeps}}$$

Teacher's name _____ Time _____

Date _____ Number of sweeps _____

Front of classroom

Sam	Jim	Alice	Roberto
Jack	Ursula	Naomi	Bob
Sarah	Elvin	Renaldo	Katie
Ryan	Alicia	Mary	Juan
Bill	Reggie	Steve	Lionel

Student off-task codes	Time sweep	Activity codes
		(What students should be doing)
S = Socializing	1, 2, 3,	
U = Uninvolved	4, 5, 6,	S = Seatwork
N = Negative peer interaction	7, 8, 9,	O = Organizing
D = Other disruptive behavior	10	L = Listening
		R = Oral reading
		Q = Question answering
		W = Waiting quietly

FIGURE 5.4

Data Collection Form (Source: J. Stallings [1988], *Staff development and administrative support* [Houston, TX: Houston Center for Effective Teaching, 1988]. With permission.)

It is often useful to know how all students are behaving during selected instructional activities.

After the initial observations are completed, teachers *chart the baseline data.* Charting data on either line or bar graphs facilitates interpretation of baseline data. It is not uncommon for teachers to discover that one or more of the behaviors observed did not occur as often as they originally believed; in this case, teachers would not include these behaviors in the group to be modified.

When the baseline data warrant use of a behavioristic intervention plan, teachers must choose *specific behavioristic intervention strategies* and use them consistently. Each reinforcement system, or strategy, if used consistently, contains the structure needed to bring about a change in behavior. The age and behavioral levels of the students, the resources available, and the preference of the teacher should be considered when selecting behavioristic intervention strategies (Schulz & Turnbull, 1984). The paragraphs that follow describe the roles of positive and negative reinforcement as well as some specific intervention strategies.

Positive and Negative Reinforcement. Since *behavior is learned*, it is strengthened, weakened, or shaped by the behavior's consequences. According to Carter (1979), teachers may either (1) *reward behavior to increase* its frequency of occurrence or (2) *not reward behavior to decrease* its frequency of occurrence. Teachers may also *punish behavior to decrease* its frequency, but this may result in undesirable side effects in the student's behavior. In general, teachers should reward desirable behavior and not reward undesirable behavior. Positive reinforcement increases the likelihood that a behavior will be repeated. According to Schulz and Turnbull (1984), for positive reinforcement to work, it must come *immediately after* the desired behavior, and the reinforcer (consequence) must be favorable (positive) so that it increases the frequency of the desired behavior. Also, positive reinforcement must be continuous and given in sufficient quantity. Selection of appropriate positive reinforcers may take some time; the teacher can observe the student carefully to determine likes and dislikes, talk with the student about the different things that could be used to help him or her acquire a desired behavior, or eventually arrange events so that a specific reinforcer (consequence) can occur and observe its effect on the student. Rewards may be extrinsic or intrinsic. *Extrinsic rewards* are given to the student by someone else, whereas *intrinsic rewards* come from within the student in the form of interest in engaging in a certain behavior (i.e., the behavior supplies its own rewards). Extrinsic rewards are often initially needed to strengthen a desired behavior.

Just as positive reinforcement brings about desirable behavior, negative reinforcement reduces or eliminates undesirable behavior. Effective negative reinforcement methods include providing alternative behaviors (e.g., "You may not color, but you may work a crossword puzzle with Sue"), reinforcing incompatible behaviors (e.g., "John, I'm pleased to see you are working on your math rather than walking around the room"), and ignoring undesirable behaviors (e.g., ignoring students who call out answers rather than first raising their hands). *Punishment* should be used only when effective behavior change cannot be accomplished with positive or negative reinforcement, or when the safety or welfare of the student or others in the setting is at risk. Alternatives to physical punishment include verbal reprimands, response cost (i.e., a positive reinforcement is withdrawn), and timeout (i.e., isolating the student for a specific period of time). The effects of punishment are not always predictable and can produce undesirable side effects, such as avoidance of the punisher (teacher), aggression, fear, withdrawal, or anxiety. Because of the potential problems associated with punishment, teacher(s) should use punishment only as a last resort.

Behavioristic Intervention Strategies. Many behavioristic intervention strategies are described in the literature (Wood, 1984; Sulzer-Azaroff & Mayer, 1977). Several strategies are briefly described in the following paragraphs.

Shaping is the process of reinforcing a student's behavior so that it more closely approximates the desired behavior. Shaping can be used to teach new behaviors or to increase the occurrence of desirable behaviors. For example, shaping could be used with a student who completes only small portions of worksheets, when the desired behavior is to complete the whole worksheet; as the student increases the portion size completed, he or she is reinforced.

Chaining techniques are used to teach behaviors that occur in a sequence; that is, the complete behavior is broken down into small steps to be learned one at a time and then chained together to obtain the desired behavior. Reinforcement is withheld until after the last step is attained. Chaining can be used to teach a set of classroom procedures for beginning instruction. For example, to teach students to wait for the teacher's instruction before going to their desks, the teacher would guide students through the following steps: (1) on entering the classroom, first go to your mailbox to get the daily assignment; (2) go to your seat to read the directions; (3) locate and retrieve the materials you will need for the assignment; and (4) motion to me when you are ready to begin the assignment.

Fading involves the use of a stimulus to bring about a desired behavior, and after the behavior is acquired, the stimulus is gradually removed. As an example, fading techniques could be used to teach a student to keep vertical numbers properly aligned when doing addition. Small squares on paper could be used initially for each numeral of a two-digit number; later, the vertical lines could be removed; and finally, the horizontal lines could be removed. However, it is important to note that if fading is done too quickly, the response may be lost; waiting too long to fade may result in student dependence.

Modeling is particularly useful in teaching social, self-help, and motor skills. Modeling involves a model (the teacher, peer, or volunteer) who demonstrates a desired behavior while the student observes. The intent is that the student will learn to imitate the model and the desired behavior will be reinforced. However, for modeling to be effective, students must receive immediate reinforcement when they emulate the desirable behavior of the model. Teachers can use social reinforcement or tokens as reinforcers.

Cueing consists of increasing the salience of an antecedent event. For example, if a student is to identify a triangle by pointing to it, a cue can be provided by the teacher or tutor who points to the triangle while giving the verbal command. Physical prompts (e.g., holding or directing the student's hand while he or she performs a given task), instructions (e.g., "Follow me" or "Pick up the card I touch"), and increasing the stimulus dimension of an antecedent (e.g., making the triangle just mentioned larger than the other shapes, so that its difference is made more obvious) are other types of cues.

Tangible rewards (reinforcers), such as cookies, crackers, stickers (e.g., smiley faces, stars), raisins, or potato chips, are effective with students who exhibit extreme behaviors that need immediate change and who have not responded to social and activity reinforcers. When paired with praise and approval, tangible rewards can establish a framework for nontangible reinforcers learned later on. The tangible reinforcer can be faded gradually so that it is eventually replaced by a nontangible (social) reward. Students who do not receive tangible reinforcers need to understand that rewards differ but that all appropriate behavior will be rewarded in some way.

Social reinforcement, such as special recognition by the teacher and peers, smiles and pats, verbal expressions of approval, written notes on completed assignments, or notes of praise to parents, is easy to deliver and is a powerful reinforcer. When using social reinforcement, it is important to tell students what they did to deserve the praise or special attention given.

The *token system* can be used when social reinforcement has not been effective. The token system can be used with one student, a small group of students, or the whole class. Students are presented with tokens after a specified behavior has occurred. When a student accumulates a previously agreed upon number of tokens, or if at the end of a specified amount of time a token is earned, the student trades the token(s) for other reinforcers known as *backup reinforcers* (e.g., candy, extra free time, gum, a free lunch, and the like). As with tangible rewards, tokens should be paired with social reinforcers and gradually withdrawn.

A *contingency management system* can be effective with individuals and the entire class. The teacher changes a student's behavior by arranging enjoyable contingencies for desirable behavior. For example, if a student completes a math worksheet, he or she can watch 15 minutes of television; or, when a whole class works quietly all morning as they complete their assignments, they are granted an extra 10-minute recess in the afternoon. A contingency system involves students in the decision-making process—the students make the decision to do what is necessary to get the reward, a decision that leads toward self-management.

Verbal reprimands consist of giving students verbal feedback about their behaviors. A statement such as, "I don't like it when you draw pictures rather than complete work assignments," or a sharp command like, "Stop rocking," lets the students know specifically what they are doing that is not desirable. Verbal reprimands should last only a few seconds.

Timeout periods (i.e., removal to an isolated spot) can be used to reduce the occurrence of inappropriate behaviors. A timeout period should never exceed 5 minutes, with 3 minutes usually being sufficient. Students should always be told why they are being sent to timeout. It is easy to overuse timeout, which decreases its effectiveness. Barton, Brulle, and Repp (1987) have demonstrated that differential scheduling of timeout is effective in reducing target maladaptive behaviors and that it allows students to develop self-control within a structured setting.

Response cost results in the loss of some portion of a desired activity or tangible item. The student pays the cost of emitting an undesirable act by giving up something he or she desires. It is important that the student know the exact reason for the response cost and that he or she be given the opportunity to regain the lost activity or item by emitting desirable behavior. Response cost procedures can be used effectively in conjunction with token systems.

Behavior contracts are specific, written agreements designating the exact behaviors a student agrees to perform. The contract usually contains a time frame and the specific reinforcement or punishment associated with performing or failing to perform the behaviors agreed to in the contract. The student should be involved in determining the terms of the contract. After the contract has been negotiated, the student should be asked to paraphrase or outline the conditions of the contract to make certain that he or she understands what has been agreed to.

Observation and recording of behavior should continue after intervention strategies are implemented, so that the effectiveness of the program can be evaluated. Sufficient time must be allowed for behavior change to take place. It may be necessary for the observer(s) to record behavior for several days during a given intervention period. Further, the *behaviors observed during intervention should be charted on the graph* containing the baseline data, so that comparisons of baseline and subsequent data can be made. Graphic display of the data enables the teacher and student to see the progress being made as a result of intervention. Also, the graph indicates to parents, administrators, and professional team members that the student's misbehavior is being dealt with in a conscientious manner.

Development of Self Management. Teachers must keep in mind that the ultimate goal of a behavior management system is to assist students in the development of *self-management skills.* Readiness for responding to self-management strategies is indicated when the value of tokens, tangible rewards, and reinforcing events (activities) has decreased and the satisfaction of succeeding in school has become more important. The teacher's role in helping students acquire self-management skills is most important. After teaching students how to behave appropriately in the classroom, the teacher must provide encouraging feedback to students involved in self-management. The teacher should also allow students to make decisions about behavioral choices.

Silverman (1980) suggests that students be taught to use a systematic approach to behavioral choices that includes (1) consideration of all their choice alternatives, (2) identification of the consequences associated with each alternative, (3) consideration of how each alternative would make them feel, (4) selecting the most appropriate alternative in light of everything considered, and (5) evaluation, and reflection, about the choices they made after having acted on their decisions. When students realize that they *can* control their own behavior and that the consequences of that control are pleasant, they no longer require external control. It is at this point that the teacher functions to facilitate student growth in self-management. (Readers interested in more information should consult Jones and Jones, 1986, who describe procedures designed to facilitate student growth in self-management skills.)

The Instructional Process

As soon as a multidisciplinary evaluation team has determined that the results of the comprehensive evaluation indicate that a student does possess a handicap and that the most appropriate educational setting for the student is the regular classroom, planning for instruction takes place at two levels. First, there is planning by the evaluation team as they write the student's IEP based on strengths and weaknesses identified during the evaluation process. Although in practice regular teachers do not usually participate in the formation of a student's IEP (Goldstein, Strickland, Turnbull, & Curry, 1980), *they should be included* in the procedures because their input can be of great value to the team. Schulz and Turnbull (1984) emphasize the importance of involving a regular teacher in the development of an IEP.

> The time is ripe for classroom teachers to assume a much greater role in the IEP meeting. Since they are responsible for teaching handicapped students, it is critically important for them to have a strong voice in planning a program that can be effectively implemented in their classroom. . . . In the area of goals and objectives teachers have valuable information to share concerning the scope and sequence of the regular curriculum. (pp. 90–91)

In addition to basic demographic information related to the special student, an IEP contains specific educational requirements relevant to the special student (see Chapters 1 and 2).

The second level of planning for instruction takes place as the regular teacher plans instruction appropriate for the special student. The student's IEP, along with specific information derived from several other sources, provide the data base for planning, teaching, and assessing student performance. The paragraphs that follow describe how the instructional process can be adapted to meet the needs of mainstreamed students.

An Interactional Scheme

The instructional process can be divided into three major components: planning, teaching, and assessing. The interaction among these components, each of which is influenced by teacher-student interaction, reflects the circular nature of the

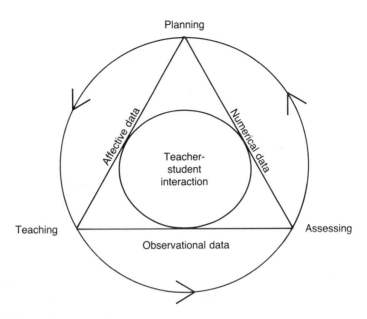

FIGURE 5.5
The Instructional Process: An Interactional Scheme

process, which can be schematically represented as shown in Figure 5.5. The core of the instructional process is teacher-student interaction through which important affective and observational data may be discerned. Affective and observational data obtained through teacher-student interaction during each component of the instructional process, along with numerical data, are used by successful teachers as assessment data on which to base their planning and teaching behaviors. The use of data-based instruction provides both special and regular students with appropriate learning experiences. Aspects of planning, teaching, and assessing, integral to the instructional process, are addressed here in terms of their applicability to special students.

Planning for Instruction. In addition to study of the special student's IEP, the regular teacher may want to consult with the student's resource teacher as plans are formulated for daily, weekly, or monthly lesson plans. People who offer other special services to the student may be consulted as well, as can special education teachers and consultants. The student's parents can assist the regular teacher by sharing information about their child's current academic and social/emotional functioning. Other sources of data available to regular teachers include the student's cumulative records, teachers who have taught the student previously, and samples of *recent* classroom assignments completed by the student. Roffman (1983) describes several ideas that may be useful during examination of a student's cumulative folder and emphasizes the importance of reviewing the student's cumulative folder, in that it may "contain diagnostic tests that have been administered by specialists but that have not been fully interpreted on paper" (p. 27). Information in the cumulative folder should identify the special student's current level of achievement within each academic area of the school's curricula.

If available assessment and evaluative data for a special student do not indicate the student's preferred mode of learning (i.e., learning style), the regular teacher should arrange to collect this information. Perhaps the regular teacher and resource teacher can work together to collect the information. According to Wood (1984), "knowledge of the different ways a student may approach a learning situation and awareness of the influences on these approaches pave the way for successful teaching" (p. 88). (For those interested in reading more about learning styles, Wood, 1984, describes learning and learning styles in detail and lists several excellent references.)

Student Placement Within the Curricula. The content to be taught to special students comes from two major sources: (1) the school's curricula and (2) the instructional needs of the student, which are contained in the student's IEP. In most cases, schools have established for each subject area an appropriate sequence of skills that reflects the subject area curriculum in the special student's current grade placement. The evaluation team that wrote the student's IEP should have assessed the special student's performance on each of the appropriate skills in the subject areas. Those grade-level skills that had not been mastered by the student were written as IEP instructional goals or objectives to be taught. By examining the sequence of skills for a given subject area, the teacher can locate the skill described as an IEP objective and identify the prerequisite skills or tasks that lead to attainment of the objective (skill). Therefore, a special student's placement within a given subject area is determined by identifying the prerequisite skill (within the hierarchy of skills underlying the IEP objective) that has been *mastered* by the student and by using the subsequent skill as the point of entry into the instructional sequence.

If a skill sequence is not available for a given subject area, or if each sequenced skill in a given subject area represents large learning tasks, it will be necessary to conduct a task analysis of the content that comprises the subject area. *Task analysis* involves breaking down a complex task into its component parts and identifying the prerequisite skills associated with each component; the result is a hierarchical arrangement of learning tasks that lead to an instructional goal (Gagne, 1974; Gagne & Briggs, 1979). A concise summary of the task analysis method is provided by Thiagarajan and Stolovitch (1974) along with a flowchart. The flowchart, shown in Figure 5.6, shows how the method is used to establish the learner's level of performance. Task analysis can be used to determine a student's entry level within an instructional sequence as well as the student's level of competence after instruction. However, the usefulness of a skill sequence, or a task analysis, is related to its degree of precision; that is, sometimes a skill sequence represents rather large tasks that must be broken down into smaller, more discrete steps. [Readers interested in a thorough de-

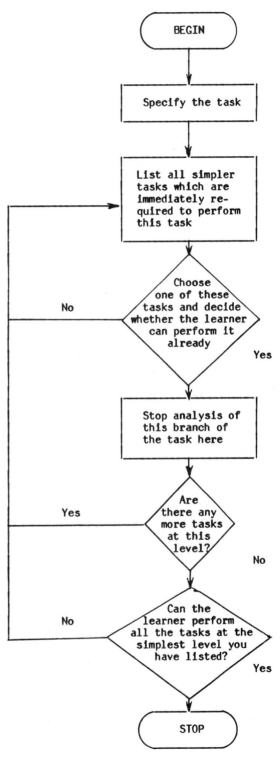

FIGURE 5.6
*Task Analysis Flowchart
(Source:* S. Thiagarajan & H.
Stolovitch [1974], *Before and
beyond behavioral objectives
[a report on an intensive
institute on writing
performance objectives.*
Sponsored by the Michigan
Department of Education
(Waldenwoods Conference
Center).] Reproduced by
permission.)

scription of task analysis may refer to Gagne & Briggs (1979), who discuss three different aspects of task analysis—information processing analysis, task classification, and learning task analysis.]

Adapting Lesson Plans. Lesson plans developed for use with regular students can be adapted to meet the instructional needs of special students. Adaptations should be made in light of the instructional goals and objectives specified on the special student's IEP. Since the remaining chapters of this textbook address lesson plan adaptations in specific academic areas, the points mentioned here are of a general nature, providing background information for later chapters. Lesson objectives can be adapted to specify both the behaviors and the criteria for successful attainment, which must be demonstrated by the special student to indicate that specified skills have been acquired. The behavior and criterion level specified in each objective are usually based on teacher judgment, which includes knowledge of the content difficulty and the student's capabilities.

The teaching procedures and learning activities outlined in lesson plans can be adapted to meet the needs of special students. Introductory, developmental, and concluding teaching procedures and activities should be included. Introductory teaching procedures and activities are used to develop interest in the lesson. Developmental teaching procedures and activities provide step-by-step guidance during acquisition of the lesson content; the procedural and learning steps should be sequenced, in terms of content presentation and task assignments, from lower to higher difficulty levels. Developmental teaching procedures and activities should facilitate acquisition, retention, and transfer of content and should require active involvement on the part of the student. Concluding procedures are designed to help students summarize their learning in some fashion.

Materials needed to teach the adapted lesson should be identified and listed in the lesson plan. If modifications are to be made in the materials (e.g., if a worksheet needs to be reformatted or a portion of a text rewritten at a lower reading level), a notation regarding the change should be made in the adapted lesson plan, as a reminder to make the change. All media, equipment, and other resources to be used in the lesson should be identified.

Adaptations in the assessment component of a lesson plan are easily developed when lesson objectives are written behaviorally, in that they specify the response or behavior a student must demonstrate to show mastery of a skill or concept. Ideas relevant to the development of instructional objectives, learning activities, and assessment procedures appropriate for special students are discussed in the following paragraphs.

Writing Instructional Objectives. Assuming that the school has established a skill sequence for each academic area, the regular teacher can use the skill sequences to devise an appropriate instructional program for the special student based on the student's IEP goals and objectives. The IEP objectives can be treated as target objectives or instructional goals to be attained during the school year. From the target objectives, the teacher can develop lesson objectives, or enabling objectives, when writing daily or weekly lesson plans for use with a special student. Gagne and Briggs (1979) define *target objectives* as "those to be attained at the end of a course of study" and *enabling objectives* as "those which must be attained during a course of study because they are prerequisites" to target objectives (p. 97). (The terms *target objectives* and *enabling objectives* are used in this chapter.) Teachers should keep in mind that it may take several sequentially arranged enabling objectives with corresponding learning activities for a special student to acquire the skill specified in one IEP target objective. The determination of how many lessons are necessary for a student to accomplish an IEP target objective "is based on the complexity of the objective and the learner's current abilities" (Schulz & Turnbull, 1984, p. 100).

When writing enabling objectives, the teacher must consider the prerequisite skills for learning the task and the sequential steps involved in learning the task (skill). If an available skill sequence, or task classification, for the subject area is extremely detailed, the teacher can construct enabling objectives from the prerequisite tasks (steps) associated with larger tasks. The importance of knowing that a special student possesses the prerequisite skills for learning a subsequent skill and of appropriately sequencing enabling objectives cannot be overemphasized. It is also important to construct enabling objectives that contain the essential characteristics identified by Mager (1975): a well-constructed instructional objective stipulates the *specific behavior* expected, delineates the *conditions* under which the student is to display the specified behavior, and provides a *criterion* against which the specified behaviors associated with attainment of the skill can be evaluated. Not only do precisely written instructional objectives, whether they are target or enabling objectives, specify the purposes of instruction, but they define what is to be assessed as well, emphasizing the interaction between the planning and assessment components of instruction. Consider the following examples of enabling objectives that might be constructed by a regular teacher, after reviewing the annual goal and related target objectives contained in a special student's IEP.

IEP annual goal—Development of ability and desire to read independently for information and pleasure.
Related IEP target objectives—(1) The student will be able to answer, orally or in writing, at least 85% of the literal and inferential comprehension questions formulated from content material he or she has read; and (2) the student will self-select and read for pleasure at least three short stories during a 3-month period.

Example 1: Teacher-constructed enabling objectives for the first IEP target objective (assuming the academic area is science).

After reading and studying about plants in the science textbook, the student will be able to:

1. Match on a worksheet five science terms with their definitions by drawing lines from terms to definitions, with 100% accuracy.
2. Answer orally ten factual recognition/recall questions asked by the tutor, with 90% accuracy.
3. Illustrate the *effects* that four specified *conditions* (causes) might have on plants by drawing pictures, one per condition, to show the possible effects of too much water, too little water, too much fertilizer, and poor soil, with 75% accuracy.

Example 2: Teacher-constructed enabling objectives for the second IEP target objective.

After self-selecting and reading for pleasure at least three short stories, the student will be able to:

1. Tell a classmate at least three things about a specified short story that made it an interesting one, during a 5–10-minute, student-paired conversation.
2. Describe on a tape recorder the setting of a specified short story, giving at least six specific details.
3. Retell to the teacher a specified short story in correct sequence, including at least ten events or details, with 100% accuracy.

As indicated by the set of teacher-constructed enabling objectives in example 1, sequential arrangement is most important. That is, for a student to answer literal and inferential (i.e., information implied but not explicitly stated) comprehension questions about content read (in this example, science), terms and definitions must be acquired first, followed by practice in answering factual questions, and eventually, opportunities to predict or discover cause and effect relationships (only one of several types of inference) must be provided. In a similar manner, the teacher-constructed enabling objectives in example 2 are arranged in order of difficulty. It is easier to tell a classmate why a story is interesting than it is to recall a small portion of a story (in this example, the setting—assuming, of course, that the student knows the meaning of story setting). Also, it is easier to recall the story setting than it is to recall the whole story in proper sequence and with sufficient detail.

Although the preceding examples do not identify the prerequisite skills associated with each of the enabling objectives, a teacher can determine those skills through task analysis when it seems appropriate to do so. By working backward from an enabling objective, a teacher can determine the skill sequence that leads to successful attainment of a given task. According to Gagne and Briggs (1979), "the learning of a new skill will be accomplished most readily when the learner is able to recall the subordinate skills which compose it" (p. 150). Therefore, an occasional teacher-student discussion to recall the prerequisite skills for accomplishing a learning task is recommended.

Each of the teacher-constructed enabling objectives in the preceding examples contains the three essential characteristics of a well-constructed objective. By dissecting the first enabling objective, shown in example 1, the following characteristics are identified.

Condition:	After reading and studying about plants in the science textbook,
Specific behavior:	the student will be able to match on a worksheet five science terms with their definitions by drawing lines from terms to definitions
Criterion:	with 100% accuracy.

It may take some special students several instructional periods (days) to accomplish one enabling objective, whereas other special students may be able to complete two or three enabling objectives during one instructional period. However, it is better to have students work toward attainment of only one enabling objective per instructional period until the regular teacher feels certain the student can accomplish more enabling objectives during a given period.

Designing Learning Activities.　For each enabling objective, teachers must design learning activities that will lead to attainment of the objective. The activities should be of sufficient variety to meet the learning needs of students. Also, learning activities associated with a specific topic should result in different kinds of learning outcomes (i.e., different types of learned capabilities). Gagne and Briggs (1979) identify five types of learning outcomes—motor skills, verbal information, intellectual skills, attitudes, and cognitive strategies—and recommend that lesson activities for a given topic should be planned in terms of the different kinds of learning outcomes that will result.

The special student's preferred mode of receiving and expressing information should also be considered when designing learning activities. Smith and Bentley (1975) emphasize that *all* students have preferred modes of receiving information (input) and expressing information (output). They describe a model that shows how different instructional strategies can be used to teach the same skill or concept; the input methods are shown in Table 5.3. The five input methods could be used in planning learning activities and the five output methods could be used in planning evaluation procedures. Some teachers may prefer to suggest several activities, representing a variety of approaches to learning, and allow students to select the activities they want to use in learning each lesson. Other teachers may prefer to specify which activities are required for each lesson and which are optional.

Learning activities should be designed so to teach effectively the skill (task) specified in the lesson's enabling objectives and to facilitate transfer of learning and generalization. Since assessment procedures often evaluate the learner's ability to apply acquired knowledge to a variety of situations, the interaction

TABLE 5.3
Alternative Input and Output Methods

Input/Data Synthesis

View/Observe	Read	Listen
visuals	books	radio
bulletin boards	comic books	records
banners	pamphlets	T.V.
posters	posters	speeches
transparencies	newspapers	lectures
slides	bulletin boards	debates
films/filmstrips	flash cards	discussions
flashcards	reports	dramatics
T.V.	wall graffiti	interpretive readings
graphs	letters	concerts
community events		interviews
field trips	**Smell/Taste/Touch**	
dramatic presentations	objects	**Try/Do/Use**
nature/animals	textures	games
	foods	experiments
	temperatures	exercises
	chemicals	manipulative materials

Output/Data Synthesis

Make/Construct	Verbalize	Write
diorama	oral report	theme
collage	panel	research paper
scroll	debate	report
sand painting	discussion	workbook answers
diary	games	blackboard problems
pictograph	brainstorm	poems
media presentations	oral questions and answers	essays
maps	**Solve**	**Perform**
models		
timelines	puzzles	simulation
leaf prints	mazes	role play
paintings	problems	sociodrama
food	equations	concern
clothing	games	pantomime
bulletin board	riddles	interpretive reading
banner		
graph		
work wall drawings		

Source: P. B. Smith & G. Bentley (1975), *Facilitator manual, teacher training program.*
Mainstreaming mildly handicapped students in the regular classroom (Austin, TX: Education
Service Center, Region XII). Reprinted by permission.

between the teaching and assessing components of the instructional process must be carefully considered.

When designing learning activities to teach enabling objectives, the following principles of presentation, identified by Schulz and Turnbull (1984), should be kept in mind.

1. The tasks should be uncomplicated.
2. The tasks should be brief.
3. The tasks should be presented sequentially.
4. Each learning task should allow for success.
5. Overlearning must be built into the lesson.
6. Learning tasks should be applied to objects, problems, and situations. (p. 292)

By following these principles of presentation in designing learning activities, teachers can arrange activities that represent the stages of learning acquisition: initial acquisition, proficiency, maintenance, and generalization (Hart, 1981). The following example, based on the first enabling objective for the first IEP target objective in the preceding example 1, illustrates how lesson activities might be devised to represent each of the stages of learning acquisition.

After reading and studying about plants in the science textbook, the student will be able to:
1. Match on a worksheet five science terms with their definitions by drawing lines from terms to definitions, with 100% accuracy.

Activities for Initial Acquisition
   The student may:
1. Locate the boldface terms on the three pages to be read in the science book, and copy the terms and their definitions on notebook paper.
2. During a teacher-directed activity, locate and read aloud the definition of each term read aloud by the teacher.
3. Get the packet of materials labeled "Plants" from the science area and
   a. Remove the word cards, pictures, and cards with definitions from the packet.
   b. Match the word cards to the pictures they represent (by using the textbook as a reference or by interaction with the teacher or a peer tutor).
   c. Add the definition word cards to the paired word cards and pictures (check for corrections by using the textbook, teacher feedback, or tutor feedback).

Activities for Proficiency
4. Remove pictures from word cards and definition cards, rescramble cards, and match word cards to definition cards without the aid of pictures (check for corrections by using teacher feedback).
5. Give definition orally after a tutor or classmate selects a term and says it.

6. Give terms, orally, after a tutor or classmate reads aloud the definition.

Activities for Maintenance
7. Write a definition for each term, using his or her own words.
8. Get the word-processor disk titled "Plants" and type in the term that will correctly answer each question in the program (give a print-out copy to the teacher for feedback).
9. On a worksheet, fill in the missing term in each of the statements about plants.

Activities for Generalization
10. During a small-group activity, participate in the group's effort to group terms together meaningfully after having viewed the filmstrip titled "Healthy and Unhealthy Plants" (e.g., terms for plant parts, terms associated with healthy plants, terms associated with unhealthy plants, and so on).
11. Take part in small-group discussion about terms; each group will discuss and answer the following (one member of the group will act as the recorder for the group's answers):
    a. Identify synonyms that could be used for the following terms: moisture, stem, nutrients, pollination
    b. Describe how the following sets of terms are related:
       (i)   pollination, germination, fertilization
       (ii) annuals, perennials, biennials
       (iii) sunlight, water, soil
    c. Describe which plant terms could be analogous (related to) the following human body parts: feet, legs, face, heart, arms (defend your answers).

It might be necessary for some students to do all of the above activities, plus others, in order to demonstrate 100% mastery on a test of the terms and their definitions, whereas other students could demonstrate 100% mastery after doing only one activity in each of the stages of learning acquisition. The preceding activities indicate the variety of learning activities that can be used at each stage of learning acquisition. Hart (1981) cautions teachers that the frustration level of the special student during the initial stage of acquisition is usually low; however, "if a good job is done at this stage, as far as teaching is concerned, the other stages usually follow uneventfully" (p. 128).

In summary, for each enabling objective, there are many activities that can be designed to teach the skill or concept. Teachers need to combine their knowledge and creativity with input from the resource teacher, as well as from the special student for whom the activities are being specified, as they plan instructional activities.

Teaching.   When constructing enabling objectives and related learning activities, teachers must consider the teaching techniques that will be used to ensure successful learning experiences. The importance of using a systematic teaching approach with special students has been emphasized by many authorities (Lewis & Doorlag, 1987; Schulz & Turnbull, 1984; Stephens, Blackhurst, & Magliocca, 1982; Wood, 1984).

Systematic instructional approaches have two elements—sequential arrangement and presentation consistency—that make the approaches appropriate for teaching special students. The following instructional sequence, composed of five phases, is representative of most systematic approaches (although specific approaches may label the phases differently): lecture/demonstration, imitation, production, practice, and application. During the *lecture/demonstration phase*, the teacher explains, describes, models, or demonstrates information and students are encouraged to ask questions for better clarification and understanding of the material presented. The *imitation phase* allows students the opportunity to imitate the responses or tasks that were presented or to repeat what was said or done. During the *production phase*, students perform the response or task under the supervision of the teacher; feedback from the teacher is immediate. The *practice phase* allows the student opportunities to practice the response or task independently; in this case, teacher feedback is delayed until completion of the practice exercises. *Application*, the final phase, occurs when the student's practice exercises are adequate; then, the student performs the response or task similar to the original learning task. If the student is unsuccessful during any phase of the teaching sequence, the teacher has the student return to the phase immediately preceding it and instruction at that phase is repeated.

The imitation, production, and practice phases of this teaching approach allow the student to model procedures or responses presented by the teacher. Teaching techniques that involve modeling are most effective with special students. Omizo, Cubberly, and Cubberly (1985) examined the effects of observer modeling and participant modeling on perceptions of self-efficacy and arithmetic achievement of learning disabled students. They found that students in both types of modeling groups achieved higher self-efficacy and arithmetic scores than students who worked individually on identical instructional packets, with the participant modeling group receiving the highest score.

All systematic teaching approaches provide for some type of direct instruction from the teacher. *Direct instruction* involves direct teaching of skills supplemented by teaching activities that require behaviors or responses similar to those specified in the enabling objectives. The effects of *preteaching*, a direct instruction technique, have been examined by Kameenui and Carnine (1986). They hypothesized that "preteaching a critical component skill *prior* to teaching the entire operation would result in more rapid acquisition of the entire operation than concurrent teaching of all its component skills" (p. 104). Kameenui and Carnine found that skill-deficient second graders who received preteaching of a selected component skill of a subtraction algorithm before they worked the entire algorithm outperformed the comparison group of students who, from the beginning, received systematic instruction in working the entire algorithm.

Further, the authors suggested that requiring students to master specific component skills is a tightly designed direct instruction sequence that may save instructional time. Among the benefits of direct instruction are that students (1) are given more opportunities to respond to what is being taught, (2) receive immediate feedback to their responses or behaviors, and (3) spend more time on task (i.e., actively involved in the learning process). The positive effects of direct instruction also have been reported by Morsink, Soar, Soar, and Thomas (1986).

Another component of systematic teaching approaches is *positive reinforcement*. Although all students respond well to pleasant consequences, special students have more difficulty completing classroom assignments successfully. Thus, positive reinforcement of special students' desirable responses and behaviors is crucial. Many kinds of positive reinforcement can be used to encourage special students to repeat accurate responses and desirable behaviors, including student knowledge of results (feedback), praise, teacher attention, special privileges, awards, and special activities. When possible, positive reinforcement should be given as soon as students' correct responses or behaviors occur and it should be used consistently.

There are several *general strategies* that may be applied to various teaching situations. For example, teachers may find it useful to make format changes in order to accommodate students who display short attention spans, distractibility, hyperactivity, or memory problems. Schulz and Turnbull (1984) recommend that assignments be divided into smaller units or reduced in length for students with short attention spans or who are hyperactive. Other examples of format changes are shortening work periods, providing more frequent activity changes, and scheduling preferred and less-preferred activities alternately.

Students with memory problems often forget directions or are confused about the sequence of steps they should follow to complete an assignment. Teachers can deal with students' memory problems by simplifying directions, using cues that prompt correct responses, having students repeat directions or steps, and letting them demonstrate their understanding by working one or two problems while the teacher observes. Memory problems displayed by hyperactive students may be alleviated through biofeedback and relaxation training. Omizo, Cubberly, Semands, and Omizo (1986) examined the effects of biofeedback and relaxation training on memory tasks among 48 hyperactive boys randomly assigned to experimental and treatment conditions. The results of their study revealed that the boys exposed to biofeedback and relaxation training achieved higher scores on memory tasks than those who did not receive the training.

Morsink (1984) offers the following general instructional strategies for teaching students who have mild learning and behavior disorders.

1. Measure the effectiveness of your instruction so that procedures that are not working can be identified and changed.

2. Base instruction on a carefully designed plan that focuses on an objective to be learned.
3. Be exact when telling a student what you want him or her to learn or do.
4. Simplify instructions or demonstrate what you want students to do, especially for students who have language problems.
5. Use concrete materials whenever possible.
6. Concentrate on essential attributes of concepts by eliminating irrelevant details.
7. Show how words are associated with objects or ideas (label and sort objects, describe functions, state rules).
8. Divide material to be learned into smaller tasks, and sequence learning tasks from easy to difficult.
9. Provide overlearning through appropriately spaced practice using a variety of methods to help students remember what they learn.
10. Establish an atmosphere for success and provide incentives for learning.
11. Give students constructive feedback immediately after their performance.
12. Encourage students to use mnemonic devices for recall of information.
13. Use peer tutors to assist students in those subjects in which they have weaknesses (e.g., if there is a reading disability, allow a peer tutor to read assignments aloud).
14. Use procedures appropriate for the specific learning problem (e.g., if students exhibit extreme weaknesses in learning through listening, use techniques applicable to students with hearing impairments).

Most of the teaching techniques described so far are effective with both elementary and secondary special students. Powers (1979) provides the following suggestions for mainstreaming secondary level educable mentally-retarded (EMR) students.

1. Design and use learning centers in the classroom. Activities and materials should be developed from course-specific objectives. A student or group of students may be scheduled into centers as an alternative to traditional instruction, or as a supplement, reinforcement or extension of such instruction.
2. Design and use learning modules. As self-contained instructional units, these learning packets should include all necessary directions and materials to provide students with specific sets of skills in a designated area of instruction.
3. Use interstudent tutoring. Peer tutoring may involve students in the same classroom or students from other classes or organizations at the school.
4. Use volunteers. Parents, retired teachers, preservice university students and others can provide valuable assistance in tasks such as record keeping, materials construction, and direct student assistance.
5. Analyze the current approach to teaching. If a verbal learning, lecture-oriented approach is predominant, consider devising strategies for in-

tegrating more activity-based experiences into the teaching style. Direct involvement in meaningful activity enhances learning at all levels.

6. Consider the use of multiple project assignments in a single classroom. Assign different groups of students different activities. Such a procedure recognizes that the same goals may be accomplished in various ways and that students differ in learning style and activity preference.

7. Use variable evaluation methodologies. Consider demonstration, construction, dramatization, oral examination and other procedures rather than only pencil and paper testing.

8. Design and develop learning contracts with individual students or groups of students. Joint contracts, involving several regular classroom teachers and special educational personnel are especially valuable.

9. Develop activities which integrate several areas. For example, a student mainstreamed into an English class and a bricklaying class might write an essay on the topic of masonry. Evaluation could then involve joint efforts on the part of the vocational teacher for content and the English teacher for structure.

10. Encourage the participation of EMR pupils in extracurricular organizations and activities. (pp. 102–108)

Although special students need consistency in routine and instructional approach, it is also necessary to *implement new techniques* for various reasons and under certain conditions. The most common reason for implementing a new technique is to help students learn how to deal with change. After special students feel comfortable with a specific routine or approach, teachers can gradually make small changes in the routine. Before the changes are actually introduced, teachers should first inform special students of each change, of how it will affect them, and of how long the change in routine or approach will last. The teacher should plan with students ways to help them remember and respond to the change. Further reason or reasons for the changes should be given with comments such as "We need to change our routine because of an assembly program," "The routine will be changed to help reduce noise during small-group work," or "I want to change the routine so that we can try something new."

New techniques also are implemented because certain conditions may require them. For example, when an approach or technique is not as efficient as it could be or when it is not producing desired learner responses or behaviors, teachers should implement new techniques that will meet these goals. As teachers monitor student progress, they can determine whether new techniques are needed. The results of teacher observation, progress checklists, daily or weekly exams, and analyses of errors can be used to make changes in instructional approaches and techniques. As with changes in routine, the teacher should inform students of the changes that will be made in instructional techniques and tell them why the changes are needed.

Assessing Student Performance. Assessment procedures typically used in regular classrooms compare students with each other. It is obvious that the classroom performance of special students should not be compared to regular students' performance. Increasingly, educators are advocating informal rather than formal assessment procedures to evaluate special student performance (Evans & Evans, 1986; Salvia & Ysseldyke, 1985). *Formal assessment* procedures include standardized or norm-referenced tests that compare an individual's performance to that of a nationwide normative sample. *Informal assessment* procedures are not norm-referenced, may or may not provide a score, may be published tests or teacher-made tests, and are designed to assess student performance in an academic area, in behavior, or in ecological aspects of the learning environment. Although formal assessment does serve some useful purposes in evaluation of special and regular students, it is not discussed here because our focus is on the regular, ongoing assessment of special student performance.

Informal assessment of special students' performance should be based on the curriculum they have been taught and on their test-taking capabilities (Schulz & Turnbull, 1984). The test-taking skills and capabilities of special students must be ascertained prior to assessment. It may be that specific training in test-taking skills may be particularly beneficial to students who have learning or behavior problems. Scruggs and Mastropieri (1986) found that students trained in test-taking skills scored significantly higher than untrained students on the word study subtest of the Stanford Achievement Test. Thus, the interaction between assessment of student performance and the curriculum taught provides the data to determine (1) the level of performance achieved, (2) the effectiveness of the teaching procedures and curriculum offered, and (3) if and where changes are needed.

Curriculum-based assessment uses the curriculum to be learned in the local school setting as the basis for assessment. Gickling and Thompson (1985) define *curriculum-based assessment* as "a methodology used to determine the instructional needs of students based upon their performances with existing course content" (p. 217). Direct observation and analysis of the learning environment, analysis of the processes used by students in approaching tasks, examination of pupil products, and control and arrangement of tasks for students are among the benefits provided by curriculum-based assessment (Salvia & Ysseldyke, 1985). The approach focuses on assessment of a student's ongoing performance within the existing curriculum, and it includes the use of many informal procedures to examine performance.

Frequency of assessment should be determined by the needs of the special student. Curriculum-based assessment permits both continuous and periodic data collections. Some special students may need daily assessment because of the severity of their learning or behavior problems, or because they need to be reassured of their progress, in which case the assessment data become a form of positive reinforcement. Other special students may require or prefer less frequent assessment. Research by Fuchs and Fuchs (1986) indicates that, although frequency of assessment (e.g., daily, twice per week, or three times per week) is related to academic achievement, it is not as significant as are some other variables. Fuchs and Fuchs found that teachers who incorporate behavior modification as part of a formative evaluation process, who graph student performance data rather than simply recording it, and who use systematic data evaluation rules rather than personal judgment to make changes in students' programs produce higher academic achievement among students than teachers who do not employ these methods.

Both *master and proficiency levels* obtained during assessment should be used to make decisions about student advancement in a given skills sequence. Evans and Evans (1986) make a distinction between mastery and proficiency and emphasize that both should be considered when making decisions about advancement. Their definition of *mastery* includes three characteristics: "(a) performance or knowledge of a skill; (b) a specific skill level expected (percent or rate correct); and (c) the quality of the performance expected"; and they state that *proficiency* "implies a level of fluency beyond mastery, in which performance is automatic, consistent, and comfortable" (p. 11). Therefore, assessment of student performance not only indicates whether the student has acquired a skill, but also how proficient the student is at performing the skill. Further, by using a *variety of informal assessment procedures*, data relevant to mastery and proficiency can be collected. Some informal assessment procedures are criterion-referenced measurement, teacher observation, checklists and rating scales, error-analysis measurement, and self-reports.

Criterion-referenced tests can be constructed for each enabling objective in a lesson plan as well as for a related group of skills in a specific academic area. However, specialists should be involved in the development of criterion-referenced tests. Teachers should construct criterion-referenced tests to measure student performance related to enabling objectives contained in lesson plans for special students. Since enabling objectives state the level of mastery that the student is expected to demonstrate on each objective, the teacher and student have a clear understanding about what constitutes acceptable performance prior to assessment. There is an added benefit derived from the stated level of mastery—it lets the special student know that the teacher *expects him or her to achieve mastery*. Schulz and Turnbull (1984) point out that criterion-referenced tests are appropriate for special students because they assess the progress of students "in relation to their starting point rather than to an arbitrary normative standard" (p. 127). (Readers interested in a more thorough description of criterion-referenced measurement should consult Swezey, 1981.)

When appropriate, *teacher-made tests* prepared for regular students can be adapted to meet the assessment needs of special students. These tests can assess the skills specified in the enabling objectives. Two versions of the same test can be constructed, one for regular students and the other for special students who have difficulties with reading or writing. When only one test is constructed, teachers can make every second or third item of the test appropriate for special students and instruct them to answer only those items. Teachers may also choose to modify only certain sections of a test for use with special students, or to make other modifications such as those suggested by Warger, Aldinger, and Okun (1983) as follows:

- Tape the instruction and questions for a test on an audio cassette.
- Use teacher aides, tutors, or other students to administer test orally.
- Record unit summaries on tape cassettes for students to review.
- Correct for content only and not for spelling and writing problems.
- Underline the key words in test questions.
- Permit the use of a typewriter in class for tests.
- Allow some flexibility in the amount of time given to complete tests and make adjustments if more time is needed.
- Use several items to test the major objectives in a unit.
- Cut down the number of objectives measured in a given test.
- Use objective rather than essay tests.
- Provide study guides to help the student focus on the main facts and concepts to be covered in the test.
- Provide the student with practice tests.
- Allow the student to recycle work in order to improve achievement.
- Allow students to take pretests that help them focus on the required material. (p. 28)

Still other adaptations in teacher-made tests are suggested by Roffman (1983) as follows:

1. The physical presentation of the test is very important.
   - Try not to cram too much writing on one page, as this creates visual figure-ground difficulties and is psychologically intimidating to even the stronger students.
   - Type or legibly print the test. Many students miss items simply because they cannot read the teacher's handwriting.
   - Use caution when mimeographing test papers on both sides. The ink often bleeds, making it extremely difficult for the student to decipher the content.
2. Be sure to leave enough work space for the students. . . .
3. Avoid shortcuts when making up tests. Unnecessary abbreviations and ditto marks may confuse the student.
4. Provide clear, concise directions. It is often helpful to read them aloud to the class. . . .
5. Test for understanding of concepts rather than for mastery of writing mechanics. . . . (pp. 109–110)

Teacher observation is one of the most convenient methods of measuring student performance. Through direct observation techniques teachers can identify aspects of the classroom environment that affect the special student adversely or positively during the instructional process. Mercer and Mercer (1981) suggest that teachers observe the special student's learning along the following four dimensions.

Expectancy—Does the student expect to fail? Are the demands and expectations either unrealistically high or so low that little effort is required?

Stimulus events—Does the student work best in a quiet area or in a particular location? Is large- or small-group seatwork, one-to-one seatwork, or peer tutoring effective? Does the student respond better to verbal or visual instruction, to using equipment or concrete materials, to charting scores, or to using games?

Response types—Does the student prefer one-word responses or longer discussions? Does the student prefer responses that require touching, writing, or manipulating objects?

Subsequent events—Does the student respond to verbal praise or humor? Does the student like smiles, hugs, or handshakes? Does the student prefer immediate or delayed feedback, and from teachers or from peers?

Further, teachers can invite the resource teacher and other members of the professional team to visit the regular classroom to observe the special student's instructional performance and to share observation results in a follow-up discussion. Likewise, the resource teacher can invite the regular teacher to the resource classroom to observe the special student. Observations may be recorded in narrative or checklist format, or shared orally with the appropriate person. In addition to on-the-spot observations, written assignments, tests, and video- and audiotapes of student responses can be examined by the teacher and other members of the professional team to obtain an overview of a student's day-to-day classroom performance (Bulgren & Knackendoffel, 1986).

Checklists and rating scales may be used to collect assessment data. Although checklist and rating-scale data are often based on observation, the data can be derived from written work samples as well. Checklists may be used to monitor special students' progress in general or in a particular content area. For example, the following items might be included on a yes/no checklist to monitor progress in word recognition performance.

	Yes	No
1. Student can read previously taught sight words	___	___
2. Student can read the following types of basic sight words:		
Verbs	___	___
Nouns	___	___
Prepositions	___	___
Adjectives	___	___
3. Student can sound out words accurately	___	___
4. Student can read words containing consonant blends	___	___
5. Student can identify base words in affixed words	___	___
6. Student can use context to determine unknown words	___	___

Both commercially produced and teacher-constructed checklists and rating scales can be of value to teachers. Checklists for specific content areas can be constructed from skill lists. Most checklists elicit a yes/no response that is tallied, whereas rating scales usually elicit a likert-scale response (e.g., poor, average, good, excellent) from the person completing the scale. Observation checklists and rating scales are especially useful when measuring social adjustment, peer interaction, and work habits.

Error analysis is used by teachers who want to identify the type and causes of errors made by students. Howell and Kaplan (1980) state that, because "errors are not just the opposite of corrects" (p. 245), systematic error analyses can suggest reasons for students' errors. That is, identification of response patterns and the student's rationale for the response can provide the basis for effective instructional planning. Error-analysis procedures can be used effectively in the instructional areas of mathematics, reading, writing, and spelling. Detailed descriptions of how to apply error analysis to the work samples of special students are provided by Hart (1981) and Schulz and Turnbull (1984).

Self-reports by special students and by regular teachers can be used periodically to evaluate the instructional program. The reports may be either written or presented through oral discussion about self-perceived strengths and weaknesses. Self-reports may be given in response to open-ended statements, a series of questions, or a single global question. Examples of global questions are "What are your strengths and weaknesses?" "What do you need to do to improve?" and "Do you generally feel you are successful?" The questions used to obtain self-reports are determined by the purpose of the assessment.

Regardless of the assessment procedures used for the frequency of assessment, teachers must assign and report grades to special students and their parents. The best procedure for *grading and reporting grades* for mainstreamed students remains a controversial issue among educators. Michael and Trippi (1987) compared the opinions of administrators, special education teachers, and regular teachers about the appropriateness of fourteen grading procedures that have been used with mainstreamed students. They found that the Individually Written Report (IWR) and the Individual Education Plan (IEP) were favored by all respondents, with the Multiple Grade System (MGS) and Goal Attainment Scaling (GS) ranking third and fourth, respectively. The MGS permits three grades for every subject area, representing ability, effort, and achievement. GS includes all involved persons in the establishment of a set of goals, assignment of weights to the goals, and development of a set of expected outcomes and corresponding scores for each goal (a summary of the outcome scores across the goal permits calculation of a grade). In general, report cards should include information on achievement and effort. Schulz and Turnbull (1984) suggest the following alternative ways of reporting grades.

1. Use criterion stated in IEP objective so that if a student masters an objective to 80 percent accuracy, a grade of B would be assigned. The subject grade would then be computed as an average of the objective grades.
2. A more global, IEP-based system could be used according to a scale such as:
   A—the student surpasses the expectations of the IEP

B—the student meets IEP expectations

C—the student performs somewhat below IEP standards and expectations

D-F—the student performs significantly below IEP standards and expectations

3. Letter grades can be used to indicate the extent of the student's progress in various subject areas:

S—progress is satisfactory

I—improving but not completely satisfactory

N—needs to improve

U—progress is unsatisfactory

X—not being evaluated at this time (pp. 130–132)

Reporting grades on the student's efforts can also provide helpful information. This can be done by using the preceding satisfactory/unsatisfactory scale or by using numbers, as follows:

1—best effort

2—good effort but could work harder

3—poor effort; needs much improvement

Other areas that can be included in the grading system are social adjustment, work habits, and peer relationships (Schulz & Turnbull, 1984).

Vasa (1981) suggests some alternatives to grading special students at the secondary level, such as the use of (1) contracts (in which teacher and student outline the objectives, activities, and performance criteria); (2) pass/fail grades (given in reference to some predetermined standard); and (3) checklists (indicating specific areas of competence and needed improvements). Morsink (1984) also recommends that grades for secondary students be based on completion of an instructional packet or special project.

Research and Instruction

Mainstreaming as a research area in education continues to receive much attention. Preservice and in-service teachers and administrators are encouraged to study research findings. In general, reported research studies related to mainstreaming are well-designed studies, controlling factors that could have threatened internal and external validity. Among the contemporary topics being examined are metacognitive strategies (especially self-regulated learning); instructional communication and feedback; acquisition, use, and transfer strategies; content area instruction; and assessment of the learning process. The research findings related to these topics provide direction for the creation and development of successful experiences for teachers and students involved in mainstreamed programs.

Summary

Designing an appropriate mainstreamed environment is a complex issue. However, it is necessary for educators to plan carefully for the physical, instructional, and behavioral environments of the mainstream program in order to lay a good foundation for meeting the instructional needs of special students.

Discussion Questions

1. Discuss some things a teacher can do to prevent behavior problems among students.
2. Discuss aspects of effective instructional management.
3. Discuss the circular nature of the instructional process and its application to mainstreamed classrooms.
4. Discuss why the use of a systematic approach is essential when designing a mainstreamed environment.
5. Discuss the phases of instructional sequence that are common to most of the systematic approaches designed to teach special students.
6. Discuss the instructional importance of the IEP for mainstreamed students.

Individualizing for Language Arts

JERRY ALDRIDGE
University of Alabama at Birmingham

Chapter Objectives

After reading Chapter 6 the student will be able to

- Describe instructional approaches for the mainstream student in the areas of listening, speaking, reading, writing, and spelling
- Discuss characteristics of the mildly handicapped reader or language learner
- Explain how to coordinate language arts instruction with the resource or reading teacher
- Devise and produce specific activities for language arts instruction to be used with the mainstream student
- Facilitate computer learning in language arts more efficiently

Development of the language arts is necessary for the mainstreamed student to succeed in everyday communication. Language arts instruction is a broad topic that includes listening, speaking, reading, writing, handwriting, and spelling. This chapter provides information about instructional strategies and adapted activities for each of these language arts areas. Computer application to language arts is provided and several different types of resources for the mainstream language arts teacher are listed within the categories of commercially published tests, supplementary materials, microcomputer software, and professional organizations.

Listening

Listening is the foundation for the language arts. Although listening is required more than speaking, reading, or writing in most classrooms, it is given less attention than the other language arts. Researchers have learned much about how listening affects school achievement. For example, Chenfeld (1978) reports that:

1. Children listen best early in the morning after a good night's rest and breakfast.
2. Children listen more effectively if the teacher gives wait time after questions and makes those questions open-ended.
3. Children listen better when they are active participants in the experiences being discussed.
4. Children listen better to meaningful and relevant information.
5. Children listen better when the material is presented in a variety of ways.
6. Children listen better in an atmosphere free of humiliation.
7. Children listen better when they are encouraged to express themselves.
8. Children listen better when they help form the listening rules for the class.

Further, Anderson and Lapp (1979) report that, according to a study of high school students in Detroit, 30% of a student's time is spent speaking, 16% reading, 9% writing, and 45% listening. Thus, listening is used more than any other language art. They also note a wide range of differences in listening, including that girls appear to be better listeners than boys in the United States.

Instructional Approaches

Listening is a skill that must be taught. To be able to teach listening to mainstreamed students, it is helpful to understand the developmental nature of listening. Listening can be divided into three hierarchical levels (Taylor, 1969). The lowest level of listening is *hearing*. Hearing involves receiving sounds but does not necessarily require comprehension. Although some students may hear the teacher's voice, they may not be listening or comprehending what is being said. The term *listening* comprises the second level of the listening process. *Listening* can be defined as the process of constructing meaning from what is heard. Finally, the highest level of listening, known as *auding*, refers to critical listening and problem solving based on what has been comprehended. The auding student is able to use the information that has been comprehended through listening.

Another important point to remember when developing a listening program is that slower students prefer to obtain information from listening rather than from reading (Rubin, 1985). Reading can be a difficult task for some students. Many of these students are first taught to be proficient at listening and comprehending information when the teacher reads to them. Listening comprehension is always at a higher level than reading comprehension; for example, a teacher can read information at the fourth-grade level and many mainstreamed students, who may not read above the first-grade level, will comprehend the information through listening. Listening is very important to mainstreamed students' learning and it is a necessary foundation for the other language arts.

Teachers must learn to develop a listening environment for mainstream students. The creation of an appropriate listening program must include a proper emotional background and specific instructional techniques. The *emotional background* refers to the level of acceptance and intensity that the teacher makes clear through interaction with students. Although teachers should expect and teach high standards of listening, this must be tempered with a balanced level of acceptance. For example, when students are asked to talk, they should feel free from ridicule or humiliation because the teacher has created an emotional background that encourages their comments and in which others are expected to listen with respect.

Specific instructional techniques should be developed to maximize students' auding abilities. The teacher should model listening for students and communicate how important listening is to learning. Instructional processes should include both teacher-pupil interaction and pupil-pupil interaction. To facilitate teacher-pupil interaction, teachers can have students listen to tape-recorded reading lessons and allow them to dramatize stories. To promote pupil-pupil interaction and listening, the teacher can have students work in pairs or small groups to accomplish tasks dependent on listening. Students can be encouraged to discuss content area material and prepare oral reports to be shared with the class. Remedial learners can benefit from specific activities. Although all of the following activities can be used to teach active listening, activities 1–5 are designed for use with younger children and activities 6–10 for use with older students.

1. *What's that noise?* Encourage students to bring in objects that make different noises (such as rubber bands, toy cars, and so on). Place the objects in a bag and arrange the class in a circle on the floor. Have one child come

to the front of the class and be the noisemaker. The other students are instructed to close their eyes and guess what noise is being made. The first child to guess the noise gets to be the new noisemaker.

2. *Taped sounds.* Tape the following sounds on a tape recorder: shoes shuffling, phone ringing, bell, door slamming, a whistle. Students should be able to identify these sounds quickly.

3. *Who is it?* Describe a child in the classroom but do not mention the child's name. Let the students guess who it is. Then let each child take a turn describing a classmate.

4. *How many bounces?* Have one child bounce a ball. The other children close their eyes and count as they listen to the ball being bounced. The children are encouraged to listen carefully and to tell how many times the ball was bounced.

5. *The story we heard.* Read a book or story to students. Place a long sheet of butcher paper on the bulletin board or long table so that the children can make a mural. Students can illustrate the story immediately after it is read.

6. *The listening team.* Divide the students into groups of two. Make sure that mainstreamed students are paired with compatible classmates. One child in each group is chosen to be the listener and the other is instructed to talk for 1 minute. The listener must then repeat what the speaker said. The activity is repeated by asking the students in each group to reverse roles.

7. *What's the title?* Read a short story or poem to the students but do not reveal its title. Ask the students to supply the missing title and to give reasons for their choice.

8. *Which does not fit?* Read to students a paragraph in which one sentence does not fit. Have them determine which sentence is the misfit and explain why.

9. *Drawing conclusions.* Choose a content area subject and read a series of paragraphs from the text. Then ask students to decide on a concluding statement for each paragraph read.

10. *Politics or commercials.* As the class listens to a commercial or a political speech, they are asked to listen for words used to sway the listeners and to name those words.

Although the preceding activities help develop listening in both regular and handicapped learners, some students, such as the hard-of-hearing, need special listening considerations. To develop listening skills in these students, Heward & Orlansky (1988) recommend the following considerations.

1. Provide preferential seating for the hard-of-hearing student. Let the student sit where he or she can hear best—usually to the front of the classroom.

2. Keep noise distractions to a minimum in the room, hall, and outside the classroom whenever possible. (Background noise can interfere with hearing.)

3. Speak naturally and do not exaggerate mouth movements.

4. Try to talk to the child at a distance in which he or she can see mouth movements during the giving of information and instructions. A distance of 6 feet is recommended for the student to see clearly the instructor's natural mouth movements.
5. Do not talk or lecture while writing on the blackboard.
6. Encourage the student to ask questions when he or she is confused, and ask the student to signal you when he or she cannot hear what is being said.

Speaking

Speaking is important for everyday communication. A mainstream student with speech or language difficulties needs special considerations in the regular classroom. Any student's receptive language ability (i.e., what he or she can take in and understand) is always ahead of the student's expressive language ability (i.e., what he or she is able to express). The difference between receptive and expressive language ability may be much greater for the learning disabled child than for the normal child.

Teachers can teach oral language skills to mainstream students through two important techniques. Just as listening is taught through modeling and activities, speaking and oral communication also can be taught through observational learning and activities designed for speaking. Teachers can model appropriate oral language not only by providing a good example but also by expanding students' statements. For example, if a child says, "Cat scratch," the teacher can expand on the child's comment by saying, "Yes, the cat scratched you on the arm. I see." Modeling can also be accomplished by self-talk, in which the teacher talks through the manual task, or by parallel-talk, in which the teacher talks about what the child is manually doing. Specific activities designed to improve oral language are often necessary with the mainstream student. Show-and-tell, storytelling, and naming objects are ways that teachers can encourage speech development.

Instructional Approaches

To improve the mainstreamed child's speaking, certain adapted activities and remedial strategies are recommended for use in the regular classroom. Many of these activities can be used with the entire class even though they especially benefit the mainstreamed student. The following twenty activities have been designed by regular classroom teachers for use in helping the spoken language of mainstreamed students.

1. Students can learn to follow oral directions by following instructions given a song format. For example, "Mulberry Bush" is a song that is excellent for direction following.

2. When teaching students to speak in a clear and understandable manner, use songs. Break each song into small segments. The teacher sings each segment and students repeat the segment.

3. Students can practice speaking in complete sentences by modeling the teacher. The teacher can hold up an object and say, "This is a _____ ." Students can repeat after the teacher.

4. When dictating stories, use the language experience approach. Plan a visit to a special place or event. After the visit, have the students tell the teacher what they did. The teacher can record the story on the chalkboard.

5. In assisting students in retelling stories in proper sequence, place the story parts on picture cards. As the teacher reads the story, place the corresponding story picture on the chalkboard. When the story is completed, let the students repeat the story in sequence, using the visual story picture clues.

6. When teaching students to follow oral directions, state the directions one at a time. Also, place the directions on the chalkboard for visual cues. Have students repeat the directions to you.

7. In assisting students in listening to questions and in giving appropriate answers, use the tape recorder. Record questions and have the students respond at the pause.

8. When asking students questions, be sure that the question is on the level of the student's functioning. If the teacher is working on oral language, it is important for the student to be comfortable with the answer and to concentrate on the spoken response.

9. When teaching students how to introduce a friend, use the modeling technique. The teacher demonstrates the first step in an introduction and the student repeats the step.

10. In assisting students in staying on the topic in conversations and discussions, show a movie on a topic of interest in order to provide a topic for discussion. Organize a list of questions that sequentially follow the movie.

11. Following a series of directions, begin with one direction and progress to two or more. Use visual models for each direction.

12. Students can practice producing basic speech sounds by playing "I Spy." The student locates an object in the room and gives clues to its size, color, shape, and location. The remaining students try to guess the object.

13. Use puppets for assisting students in using formal conversation and reports. Provide a script for the students to follow or let students create their own script.

14. Let students prepare their own stories for storytelling. Provide a folder with "story starters." Students select a starter and begin to complete their story. For special needs students, use the tape recorder.

15. Use sentences displayed on the board for assisting students in distinguishing between the pitch and tone of voice intonation. Have the students read sentences punctuated with periods, question marks, commas, and exclamation marks. Discuss the correct intonation. Use modeling for students who

may need assistance in reading; the teacher reads the question and the student repeats.

16. Read a play to the class. Discuss the different character roles. Let the students role play to express themselves.
17. Students can give accurate directions by presenting an oral report to the class on how to make something. The student is asked to present each step sequentially. The teacher records the steps in order to see that all steps were included in the proper sequence.
18. When teaching students how to give a speech, have them practice outlining and talking from their outline.
19. Students can present a speech to the class by using character cards. The cards serve as prompts to organizing what will comprise the content of the speech (See Figure 6.1).

Character Card—Dentist

I. Model to be used _____	I. Dentist
II. What does the dentist do?	II. The dentist takes care of teeth.
_____	
III. What would the dentist say to you? ____	III. Describe how to clean teeth.

FIGURE 6.1
Sample Character Card Used by Students to Present a Speech to the Class

20. Assist students in participating in class discussions by providing questions for the students to ask in class. This promotes students' ideas for beginning the discussions.

Reading

Reading can be defined as obtaining meaning from printed words. Handicapped learners often face many obstacles in their attempts to derive meaning from print. Many already have failed by traditional methods of teaching reading and need a corrective or remedial program designed to meet their individual learning style and needs. A reading program for the mainstreamed student should include an assessment of where the student is functioning, a list of goals and objectives for the student, a variety of well-planned instructional approaches, and adapted activities that help the individual meet the goals and objectives.

Reading Assessment

Assessment of reading should occur with a specific purpose in mind. Assessment of mainstreamed students in reading should identify their strengths and weaknesses, measure their ongoing progress, and be used to individualize instruction. Informal assessment is a useful tool for instructional decision making. *Informal assessment* can be defined as "any assessment that involves collection of data by anything other than a norm-referenced (standardized) test" (Salvia & Ysseldyke, 1985, p. 22). There are several procedures that can be used to determine reading ability, including the cloze procedure and the Informal Reading Inventory.

The Cloze Procedure. The cloze procedure can be used to help determine a student's appropriate level of reading material. The procedure is appropriate for use with the mainstreamed student in that it uses the actual text content or reading material in which the student could be placed. The cloze procedure answers the question "Can this student read this book?" Steps for conducting a cloze procedure are listed in Table 6.1.

The cloze procedure is scored by counting the number of words the student reads correctly. In scoring the cloze procedure, only the exact words found

TABLE 6.1
Steps for Conducting a Cloze Procedure

---

1. Select a passage of approximately 250 consecutive words from the textbook. This should be a passage that the pupils have not read, or tried to read, before.

2. Type the passage, leaving the first sentence intact and deleting every fifth word thereafter. In place of the deleted words, substitute blanks of uniform length.

3. Give the pupils the passage and tell them to fill in the blanks, allowing them all the time they need.

4. Score the test by counting as correct only the exact words that were in the original text. Determine each pupil's percentage of correct answers. *If a pupil had less than 44 percent correct, the material is probably at that individual's frustration level and is too difficult.* Thus, you should offer alternative ways of learning the material. If he or she had from 44 percent to 57 percent correct, the material is probably at the instructional level for that student, and he or she will be able to learn from the text if you provide careful guidance in the reading by developing readiness, helping with new concepts and unfamiliar vocabulary, and providing reading purposes to aid comprehension. If the child had more than 57 percent correct, the material is probably at his or her independent level, and he or she should be able to benefit from the material when reading it independently (Bormuth, 1968).

Source: Burns, Paul C., Betty D. Roe, and Elinor Ross. *Teaching Reading in Today's Elementary Schools.* Fourth Edition. Copyright © 1988 by Houghton Mifflin Company. Used with permission. (Italics added.)

in the text are counted as correct. If the student reads less than 40% of the words correctly, then the text is probably too difficult and another should be chosen. Often the selection of another text is not possible, in which case the existing text will need to be adapted. Suggestions for adapting texts are made later in the chapter (see pp. 212–221).

Informal Reading Inventory.   Another widely used instrument for determining reading levels is the Informal Reading Inventory (IRI). The IRI procedure can be teacher constructed or selected from several commercially produced inventories. The IRI is an instrument used to determine the independent, instructional, frustration, and capacity levels of a student. The *independent level* is the level at which the student can read alone without assistance; the *instructional level* is the level at which the student should be taught; the *frustration level* is the level at which a student has great difficulty; and the *capacity level* is the highest level at which a student can listen to and comprehend a passage read by someone else. Burns, Roe, and Ross (1984) have described four steps to constructing an Informal Reading Inventory; these steps are described in Table 6.2.

TABLE 6.2
Steps in Conducting an Informal Reading Inventory

Four steps are involved in devising an inventory to establish a child's reading level.
1. Selection of a standard basal series
    a. Use any series that goes from preprimer to the sixth level or above.
    b. Choose materials that the child has not previously used.

2. Selection of passages from the basal reading series
    a. Choose selections that make a complete story.
    b. Find selections of about these lengths:
        Preprimer—book 1 (grade 1): approximately 75 words
        Book 2: 100 words
        Book 3: 125 words
        Book 4: 150 words
        Book 5: 175 words
        Book 6 and above: 200 words
    c. Choose two selections at each level; plan to use one for oral reading and one for silent reading. Take the selections from the middle of the book.

3. Questioning
    a. Develop five to ten questions for each selection at each level.
    b. Include at least one of each type of question: main idea, detail, vocabulary, sequence, and inference.

4. Construction
    a. Cut out the selections and mount them on a hard backing.
    b. Put the questions on separate cards.
    c. Have a duplicate copy of the oral reading passage for marking purposes.

Source: Burns, Paul C., Betty D. Roe, and Elinor Ross. *Teaching Reading in Today's Elementary Schools*, Third Edition. Copyright © 1984 by Houghton Mifflin Company. Used with permission.

There are pros and cons of using the IRI with the handicapped learner. The IRI does help indicate the frustration level of the handicapped student. Often mainstreamed students are asked to read on their frustration levels and the IRI is quick to determine their frustration levels based on school basal texts at various grade levels. However, the limitations of the IRI procedure are that (1) comprehension is treated by questions that emphasize literal facts and (2) the levels are usually determined quantitatively, meaning they are based on the number of mistakes or miscues made by the student. Another criticism of the IRI is that it often stresses oral reading before silent reading has developed (Caldwell, 1985).

Informal assessment of reading includes other types of information gathering besides the cloze procedure and the Informal Reading Inventory. Structured and organized teacher observation can be used as an indicator of reading progress. Assessment can be a daily ongoing activity through the use of a continued record of the student's progress. A simple assessment procedure that involves teacher observation on a continuous basis is the completion of a form each time the student reads orally. This assessment procedure is completed while the student is reading. The form is sent home to parents, who are encouraged to serve as partners in helping their child progress. A sheet of paper serves as the form; it is divided into two sections—"What I Did Well" and "What I Need to Work On." The handicapped student can help provide input into this process through self-evaluation while the teacher is also providing feedback.

Interest inventories, which usually involve asking students what they are interested in reading, can be helpful as well. Most basal reader companies also provide tests for measuring progress through graded programs. There are graded word lists such as The San Diego Quick Assessment and the Slosson Oral Reading Test, which give a grade level placement based on the student's recognition of words. Standardized tests (norm-referenced or criterion-referenced) can be chosen on the basis of information needed about the student's reading functioning. There are numerous commercially produced tests that can be used to pinpoint specific reading information (e.g., reading readiness tests, comprehensive reading tests, reading achievement tests, decoding and word attack tests, intelligence tests, and reading potential tests) (Burns, Roe, and Ross, 1984). In using these formal instruments, the teacher can ask three important questions about them: (1) "'What do I want to know about the student?" (2) "Does this test measure what I need to know?" and (3) "Will the information gathered from this test be helpful in instructing the student?" (Since there are so many different types of standardized reading tests, it is impossible to describe them all here; however, many of the tests are listed in the Resources section at the end of the chapter.)

There are many purposes of assessment but three of the most common are (1) to determine the reading level, (2) to determine the strengths and weaknesses with regard to skills, and (3) to see what specific reading disabilities the mainstreamed student might have. Since *reading* has been defined as acquiring meaning from print, the assessment procedure should include finding out how the student attempts to get meaning from print.

Reading Goals and Objectives

Once the reading level, the strengths and weaknesses, and the specific reading problems of the student have been identified, goals and objectives can be developed according to the instructional level of the student. In planning goals and objectives in reading for the mildly handicapped student, certain considerations influence planning: (1) the characteristics of the mildly handicapped reader, (2) the coordination of reading with the resource teacher or reading teacher, and (3) the most effective way to group the students for instruction. The overall goal of any reading program should be the development of the student's ability to comprehend the printed word. In the primary and elementary grades, specific reading objectives are oriented toward learning how to read. In the secondary grades, the specific objectives shift in emphasis to helping the student compensate for his or her reading difficulty and to guiding the student in determining the meaning from print even when text materials are too difficult. Activities for meeting these goals and objectives are presented later in the chapter.

Characteristics of the Mildly Handicapped Reader. In planning goals and objectives for any child, it is good to note that mildly handicapped readers are a diverse and heterogeneous group. One student's strengths could be another student's weaknesses. There are, however, certain patterns or characteristics that appear in many handicapped readers. Buttery & Creekmore (1985) have identified the following generalizations that can be made about these students.

1. Mildly handicapped students can achieve in reading commensurate with their mental ages but they usually do not achieve even at this level.
2. Mildly handicapped students usually do better in reading achievement when they are taught in the regular classroom than when they are taught in special classrooms.
3. Mildly handicapped girls usually do better in reading than boys with the same type of handicap.
4. Mildly handicapped children may be good at word recognition or word calling, but their major limitation in reading achievement is related to comprehension.
5. Mildly handicapped readers tend to be less able to use context clues and require more words to be pronounced for them when reading orally.
6. No one method of teaching the mildly handicapped is superior to any other based on research.
7. The teacher is the most important factor in the development of successful reading in the mildly mentally handicapped.

8. The same assessment measures used for normal children can be used with the mildly mentally handicapped.

Looking further at the characteristics of the mildly handicapped reader reveals that there are distinct differences between good and poor readers (Raykovicz, Bromley, & Mahlois, 1985). In general, good readers look at reading as enjoyable, are able to get involved in the visual images of what is being read, and find reading to be an interesting leisure time activity. In contrast, poor readers think of reading as the study of the pronunciation and meaning of words, rarely refer to reading as requiring thinking, are less active in questioning than better readers, and are less likely to use mental pictures as often as good readers. Raykovicz, Bromley, and Mahlois (1985) conclude that "perhaps less classroom time could be spent in reading orally and more time spent in teaching poor readers how to improve their own comprehension monitoring abilities, including memory and use of visual images" (p. 90).

The differences between good and poor readers are often more related to how goals and objectives are implemented than to learner characteristics. There is often a discrepancy between the way teachers teach good and poor readers; that is, good readers are taught using goals and objectives that involve more meaningful tasks whereas poor readers are more often taught using objectives that involve phonics and decoding skills. Further, good readers spend over one-half of their reading instruction time (57%) on reading selections whereas poor readers only spend about one-third (33%) on reading selections (Gambrell, Wilson, & Gantt, 1981). Also, poor readers are much more likely to be passive in their approach to reading than are good readers. One possible cause for this is that many poor readers are placed at their frustrational level. Even good readers focus less on making sense out of reading when they are placed at a reading level higher than their instructional level. When planning reading materials for poor readers, it is better to place them in material that is too easy than in material that is too difficult. Poor readers need to have a sense of control over their reading, and placing them in easier materials can help them comprehend the material. Students should always be placed at or below their instructional level so that they can focus their attention on comprehension (Bristow, 1985).

Coordination of Reading Objectives with the Resource or Reading Teacher. Goals and objectives for the reading program can be coordinated with the resource or reading teacher. Handicapped students benefit more from instruction if they are not taught by conflicting approaches in the regular class and resource room. Students with special needs are often served through what are sometimes referred to as *pull-out programs* (i.e., students are "pulled out" and sent to these classes). A problem can exist with pull-out methods if the exceptional readers are being taught by one approach in the resource room and a different approach, such as the basal reader, in the regular class. This is particularly a problem if the student is expected to return to the regular class and progress through the basal readers. Further, if instruction is not coordinated with the resource teacher, the student in the pull-out program may be learning isolated skills that are not transferred to instruction in the regular class. Cooperation and coordination of goals and objectives between the regular and resource teacher can solve this problem. Costabile and Costabile (1985) recommend the following simple guidelines for working cooperatively with reading specialists and resource teachers.

1. Does the reading specialist know what text you are using with the child? The specialist also needs to have a copy of the text and its manual.
2. Does the specialist know what the child's daily assignments are?
3. Is the specialist planning activities that directly support the classroom content?
4. Is there frequent feedback between yourself and the specialist? (p. 374)

One suggestion for coordinating the reading program for the mildly handicapped student is for the resource teacher and the regular classroom teacher to work with the mildly handicapped student within the setting of the regular classroom. Bean and Eichelberger (1985) have researched the changing role of the reading specialist by looking at pull-out and in-class programs. They conclude that, "because the in-class program has potential for developing a more consistent, focused program for students and for increasing the efficiency and effectiveness of instruction, we support this notion" (p. 652). This can be accomplished in several ways. The resource teacher may be invited to observe the handicapped student interact in the regular classroom and then make suggestions for instruction. The resource teacher can act as a consultant for recommending teaching strategies. Although it is often not possible for the resource or reading teacher to spend considerable time in any one regular classroom, it is still recommended that the resource teacher assist in actual instruction of the handicapped student within the regular class. A resource teacher who can teach the student in the regular class once a week can help implement the suggestions made.

Effective Grouping for Reading Instruction. Meeting the mainstreamed student's individual needs through grouping and individualizing is a major goal of reading instruction. The most commonly used grouping method in schools for reading instruction is *ability grouping.* Research studies show that this form of grouping is not always appropriate for those with reading difficulties. Jongsma (1985) has reported that in lower groups, teachers spend more time with discipline problems, less time with preparation, and move at a slower pace with less challenging and less interesting materials. Further, students in the slower groups are often held in lower esteem by the other students, and placing students in ability groups can be detrimental both educationally and socially to those in the lower groups (Manning & Manning, 1981).

Other methods of grouping that can be used include (1) skills grouping, (2) interest grouping, (3) tutorial grouping, (4) project grouping, (5) buddy grouping, and (6) cooperative learning grouping (Ekwall & Shanker, 1985; Burns, Roe, & Ross, 1984).

Skills Grouping.   Skill grouping is accomplished by placing all students having difficulty with a particular reading skill in one group. For example, if the teacher has determined that four students are having problems with context clues, these four students are grouped together temporarily to teach this skill. Average and above-average students sometimes have difficulty with the same skill as a slower student and can be placed with this slower student for instruction with skills grouping (Matthes, 1977).

Interest Grouping.   Interest grouping can be used on occasion to group students based on topics they are interested in reading about. Students in these groups can read books on their individual levels and share information based on what they have learned with each other. The slower student will share some of the same interests with other students in the class (Miller, 1977).

Tutorial Grouping.   Tutorial grouping is useful with some students. Peer tutoring, mentioned in several other chapters, also can be used effectively in reading instruction. Grouping students for peer tutoring is often done by grouping a more able student with a less able student or an older student with a younger student. Although ability grouping can sometimes be harmful to the slower students (Esposito, 1973), placing slower students together in a tutoring group can bring results. Handicapped students and students who are having trouble with the same reading skill can also serve as tutors for each other in learning selected reading skills. This is accomplished by grouping three students with the same difficulty in the same group. Each day a different student in the group serves as a tutor and the other two are tutees. The leader or tutor must practice the skill in order to help the other two students. The benefits of this tutoring model are social and self-esteem as well as academic. As the tutor's self-esteem increases, the reading achievement should also improve (Harris & Aldridge, 1983).

Project Grouping.   Project grouping is a procedure in which students are grouped to complete a selected project. Since reading is important to other content areas such as science and social studies, project grouping may be helpful for students in content area learning classes. For example, each group may be given a science experiment to present to the class. This project involves reading about how to perform the experiment. A handicapped learner placed in one of these groups can benefit from seeing how other students approach the assignment.

Buddy or Friendship Grouping.   Buddy grouping, sometimes useful in reading, is defined as placing students in a group with friends for the purpose of sharing ideas about what they have read. Students are encouraged to read several books and discuss them with their friends. The handicapped learner who has difficulty reporting orally in front of the class still has the opportunity to share information in a less threatening method by using buddy grouping for instruction.

Small-Group Cooperative Learning. Cooperative learning is another method of grouping students heterogeneously. A cooperative learning group is given a specific task to accomplish in a certain amount of time. In cooperative grouping, it is necessary to have a specified goal and procedure and there should be an accountability system built into the program. With this approach, guidelines for group participation include that:

1. Each member make a serious effort to do the work.
2. Each member follow the directions for the assignment.
3. A member who disagrees with an answer to a question should defend his or her point of view by giving specific reasons based on the reading or text.
4. No member dominates or withdraws from the activity; each member must add something to the discussion about the reading.
5. Each member display a positive and encouraging attitude toward every other group member (Maring, Furman, & Blum-Anderson, 1985).

Heterogeneous cooperative learning groups can work together to learn a particular task and then teach it to another group. If all groups are given different tasks to learn, students from each group will have an opportunity to teach something to someone in another group, regardless of their achievement level. This same type of grouping can be used to have students rewrite a chapter or produce an abstract of a chapter in their own words. The abstract or rewritten chapter may be used by a mainstream student as the reading source in the place of the more difficult text. Johnson & Johnson (1980) have researched cooperative learning extensively and their results indicate that cooperative learning results in higher achievement for all students, greater friendships, and social acceptance.

Whatever grouping technique is chosen by the regular classroom teacher for reading instruction, it is important to remember that heterogeneous grouping is more conducive to the handicapped student's self-esteem and produces a more positive interaction among all students in the classroom. Teachers tend to give equal amounts of time to heterogeneous groups, but when ability grouping has to be used, teachers must work harder to maintain quality instruction for all groups—especially those needing extra help.

Individualization of reading is often necessary beyond grouping. Since no two students have the exact same needs, individualization of reading is necessary for meeting goals and objectives of reading instruction. Individualization in reading has been found to improve rate of reading, fluency and vocabulary, increase a student's overall knowledge base, and create a more positive attitude

What You Can Do

- Teach students how to listen.

- Work with the speech therapist in developing classroom activities for students with speech impairments.

- Include in your reading program a well-developed assessment plan, objectives, and adapted activities for each student.

- Coordinate the regular class reading program's objectives with the reading objectives in the resource room.

- Remember that heterogeneous grouping is more conducive to the handicapped student's positive self-esteem.

- Focus remedial strategies on students' strengths.

- Sequence reading activities from less difficult to more complex.

toward reading—all worthy goals of reading instruction. Individualization frees the teacher to work with poorer and special needs readers who need more help (Bagford, 1985). (Individualization is discussed more specifically later in the chapter.)

Instructional Approaches

Instructional approaches are selected for the handicapped students with the previously determined goals and objectives in mind. Remembering that the ultimate goal of reading is getting meaning from print will make the selection of instructional approaches for the handicapped more appropriate. Starr and Bruce (1983) have suggested that "one cause of students' difficulties has been the emphasis on teaching reading as a series of discrete skills isolated from each other and from the process of reading. In many classrooms, children spend their reading time learning phonics and the meanings of individual words. They receive very little instruction that will help them understand and think about what they read. . . ." (p. 2).

Although reading skills such as word attack and phonics are important for handicapped learners, comprehension activities are crucial and cannot be postponed until word attack and phonic skills have been learned. Traditional reading programs for the handicapped have emphasized the remediation of weaknesses that are often considered to be deficiencies in word attack. Remedial strategies that focus on students' strengths are more beneficial than those that focus on students' weaknesses. Comprehension-oriented strategies more often deal with children's reading strengths (Gentile, Lamb, & Rivers, 1985). Instructional approaches for reading include survival skills, adapted activities for nonreaders and beginning readers, and adapted activities for more advanced readers.

Survival Skills.   Handicapped students often have more trouble with incidental learning. Just as the regular teacher may need to guide the handicapped student through a reading assignment, the teacher may also need to teach important survival skills that many regular students acquire without assistance. *Survival skills* are defined as those skills that are absolutely essential in reading, writing, spelling, and computing to function in everyday life. Table 6.3 lists the basic survival information developed by the staff of *Academic Therapy*. A checklist can be made from the information in Table 6.3 and the mainstream student can be checked at regular intervals to determine which survival skills the student has and which still need to be learned.

TABLE 6.3
Basic Survival Skills for the Handicapped Student

What the Student *Must* Know

When teaching learning disabled youngsters to read, compute, write legibly, or spell, it is easy to bypass the teaching of other important information. It is too easy to believe that they already know it. And yet, if reports from teachers are accurate, large numbers of learning disabled children and adolescents are really quite unclear on critical information relating to their own lives.

What kinds of basic, survival information should they have at their "fingertips" and should you check on to make sure they know?
—How to write their full names
—Their parents' names
—Names of their brothers and sisters
—Their telephone numbers
—Their addresses
—Where their parents work and how to reach them
—The city in which they live
—Names of adjoining or nearby cities
—The county or parish they live in
—Their birthdate, including the year in which they were born
—Their Social Security number (if they have been issued one)
—The school they attend
Prepare a simple form that you can use to check this information regularly. Give it to your students at frequent intervals and make sure they are able to complete all of the items on the form. It will pay big dividends—to you and to them.

Source: IDEAS: What your students must know. *Academic Therapy,* 21 (3), 322. Reprinted by permission.

Adapted Activities for Nonreaders and Beginning Readers.   Adapted activities in reading should be used when a student is not able to comprehend and use the regular class reading materials. The following are adapted activity suggestions that can be used in the regular classroom. The activities are sequenced from less difficult to more complex and are adapted for nonreaders to more advanced students in the secondary grades.

The handicapped nonreader or beginning reader probably has failed to learn to read by the traditional reading methods. The regular class teacher can select appropriate reading activities for this student who cannot read or is in the beginning stages of the reading process. Activities that are recommended for the nonreader and beginning reader include LOGO learning, individual picture reading, newsflash, rebus reading, predictable books, and phonics in context.

Logo Learning.   Logo learning is an appropriate activity for nonreaders and beginning readers. Several research studies have been conducted using logos as reading material for young and high-risk children (Cloer, Aldridge, & Dean, 1981–1982; Goodman & Altwerger, 1980; Wepner, 1985). For young mainstreamed students who are at the reading readiness level, the development of a logo learning or environmental print program can be effective. Logo learning or environmental print learning is simply using familiar neighborhood, television, newspaper and magazine print to aid in beginning reading. Food products and advertisements serve as the prime source for such activities. Common neighborhood products are selected such as soft drink cans, french-fry packages, and other items containing logos.

The *first* step in logo learning is to have students bring in local logos such as candy-bar wrappers from home. Logo items are placed at a reading center or table, and children are asked to identify the different logos during reading period. After the mainstreamed student can automatically recognize the collected logos, the *second* step of logo learning is used. The collected products are copied on a copy machine. Students can then identify the copy of the logo. Research has shown that transfer to this stage is usually automatic. The *third* step of logo learning involves a copy of the product but without the supporting detail of stage 2. All background pictures and information are removed and only the printed words of the logo are shown to the student. Transfer at this stage is also automatic. The *fourth* stage of an environmental print program, at which direct instruction occurs, is the most difficult for handicapped nonreaders. The product is written on the board or paper in standard manuscript handwriting. Studies have indicated that transfer to this stage is the most difficult for handicapped nonreaders. At this stage the students practice reading and writing the name of common products in standard manuscript. Finally, at the *fifth* stage students develop sentences about the logos while the teacher writes them down. Language experience activities using logos can be used at this level. Figure 6.2 shows the developmental steps of print awareness.

Step 1	The actual object with its logo (a Band-Aid box, for example) is shown.
Step 2	A copy of the object, made on a copy machine, is shown.

Step 3	A copy of the product is shown but without the supporting detail of Step 2.

Step 4	The product name is written on the board or paper in standard handwriting.

Band-Aid

Step 5	The product name is used in a sentence.

I put a <u>Band-Aid</u>
on my cut finger.

FIGURE 6.2
Developmental Steps of Print Awareness

Individual Picture Reading. Picture reading is an instructional procedure for nonreaders. In preparation for this method, the teacher sections an 8-1/2 × 11-inch sheet of paper for each student so that it has a 1-inch left margin and a 3-inch bottom margin. Each nonreader is asked to draw a picture in the top section of the paper. As each student finishes, he or she brings the picture to the teacher. The teacher takes each child individually and asks the child to describe the picture. While the student describes the picture, the teacher writes down exactly what the student says with a highlighter or a yellow felt-tipped pen. The student then reads back what he or she has said and is directed by the teacher to trace over with a pencil what the teacher has written for the student with the highlighter. In some cases, the child may not want to draw a picture but may choose instead a magazine picture to describe. Pictures from several students can be bound into a book of collections. These books can be used for beginning reading with handicapped nonreaders. The making and binding of the children's books in the classroom is shown in Figure 6.3.

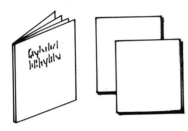

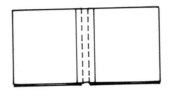

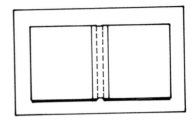

1. Cut two pieces of heavy cardboard slightly larger than the pages of the book.

2. With wide masking tape, tape the two pieces of cardboard together with a ½-inch space between.

3. Cut the outside cover 1½ inches larger than the cardboard and stick it to the cardboard (using thinned white glue if the cover material is not self-adhesive).

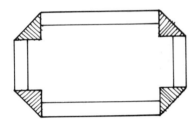

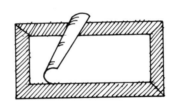

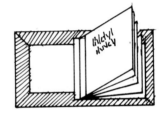

4. Fold the corners first, then the sides.

5. Measure and cut the inside cover material and apply as shown.

6. Place the stapled pages of the book in the center of the cover. Secure with two strips of the inside cover material, one at the front of the book and the other at the back.

FIGURE 6.3
Steps in Making and Binding a Book of Pictures Drawn by an Individual Student or the Class (Source: R. Canady, Reading for meaning (1980), Highlights for Children, 3 (4) [Newsletter: Parenting], 5.)

As students progress with individual picture reading activities, they will develop proficiency with writing their descriptions without the teacher's help. There is a sequence the teacher can use in moving the child toward this independence. After the child has traced several times what the teacher has written with a highlighter, he or she should be ready to copy what the teacher writes. This is done by the teacher writing down exactly what the student says under the picture, but leaving space for the student to copy under the teacher's writing. As time progresses, the teacher can write what the child says on another sheet of paper and the child can copy what he or she has said from that paper to the space provided under the picture the child has drawn. The last step in the sequence requires the student to write a sentence by him- or herself (Gentry, 1985).

Newsflash.   This activity may be used with the mainstreamed student who is moving from nonreading to beginning reading. Newsflash consists of the day, the date, the weather report, and something interesting about the day. The student dictates the sequence and the teacher writes it on the board. A typical day's newsflash might read like this:

Newsflash

Today is Monday, January 9, 1989. It is sunny and cold outside. We will play in the snow today.

The same sequence of writing skills described in the previous section on individual picture reading may also be used with newsflash. Students who cannot copy newsflash from the board may need to have it written by the teacher with a highlighter pen. Later the teacher can write it with a pencil on the child's paper for him or her to copy. Still later the student can copy it from the board.

Rebus Reading.   Rebus reading is appropriate for some handicapped learners in the beginning stages of reading. Rebus reading involves a picture that is drawn in a sentence in the place of the word it represents. Olson (1985) has described a technique for teaching high-frequency words through the use of a rebus story. A rebus story is made so that there is ample space for a rebus picture to be drawn. The teacher types or writes the story so that there is ample space for a rebus picture to be drawn. Students are instructed to make their own stories by drawing what they want in the blanks. Students can read their story to a classmate and a collection of these stories can be made into a book. Figure 6.4 shows an example of high-frequency words used in a rebus story.

Rebus stories are an effective way of teaching high-frequency words. Handicapped students in the beginning stages of reading need extra practice with high-frequency words. Since they may have trouble with transfer of learning from isolated skills to use in practical context, these high-frequency words should not always be presented in isolation. The rebus story is a good way to present the words in context.

Handicapped learners become more proficient at reading if they are given opportunities to read real books. Predictable books are recommended for reading practice with remedial readers so that they will develop a sense about what is to come next. These books help develop active comprehension and predicting strategies. A good example of a predictable book is *Brown Bear, Brown Bear* (1970) by Bill Martin. McClure (1985) has listed over seventy predictable books that can be used with the handicapped learner.

As students learn from predictable books they acquire important comprehension strategies. Determining what happened before, during, and after a picture can also be an effective way of teaching predicting skills to beginning readers. Policastro (1985) has suggested an activity directed around a single picture. The first step is to collect pictures that show children or adults in action. The sec-

FIGURE 6.4
Examples of a Rebus Story Using High-Frequency Words (Source: M. O.
Olson (1985), Practicing high frequency words with rebus stories, *The
Reading Teacher, 39* (3), 820. Reprinted with permission of Mary Olson and
the International Reading Association.)

ond step is to mount the pictures in the middle of a large piece of construction
paper. Students are directed to describe what they think happened before the
picture, what is happening during the picture, and what will happen after the
picture. This instructional strategy is effective with one student or a small group.
An example of the strategy is shown in Figure 6.5.

Some students in the beginning stages of reading will need extra help in
phonics. Teaching phonics in context can help the student better use phonics
skills to comprehend reading. Phonics is an abstract skill that can be taught
in context in several ways. Using concrete, tangible objects is one way to teach
phonics. Students are asked to bring in objects or simply identify items already
in the room. Items can be discussed with regard to beginning, ending, or medial
sounds. Students can be encouraged to develop their own alphabet books of
pictures that begin with certain letters.

Adapted Activities for More Advanced Readers.   More advanced readers need
practice with reading. Durkin (1978–1979) has found that teachers spend little time on background information, new vocabulary, or prereading questions
when they teach the basal readers. Handicapped readers need to be taught active prereading strategies before they can attempt to read a passage. These
strategies include (1) students asking themselves questions before reading (this
can be taught by changing subheadings into questions); (2) providing purpose
setters for reading or asking handicapped students to invent their own purpose setters; and (3) introducing new vocabulary with transfer of learning in
mind. Students should be encouraged to find the vocabulary words in the story
and read each word in context of the sentence in which it appears (Hahn, 1985).

FIGURE 6.5

Example of a "Before, During, and After" Strategy (Source: M. M. Policastro (1985), What's happening: Predicting before, during, and after the picture, *The Reading Teacher, 39* (3), 929. Reprinted with permission of Margaret M. Policastro and the International Reading Association.)

More advanced students can be taught to determine the main idea of reading passages. The following general activities promote proficiency in finding the main idea of a passage (Greene, 1985).

1. Select the best title of a selection from a provided list.
2. Write a title for a given paragraph or story.
3. Mark the words that best describe the characters or events discussed in a passage.
4. Reread a selection to determine which scenes can be dramatized.
5. Match the pictures with the paragraphs they illustrate.
6. Draw a mural indicating the main event of a passage.

RATE. RATE is an activity appropriate for more advanced readers. Self-selection of reading materials must be taught to students. "*RATE* (Read and then Evaluate) is a program that provides opportunities for learning disabled students to self-select appropriate reading materials, form and communicate opinions about what they have read and gain confidence in themselves as readers" (Jamison & Shevitz, 1985, p. 47).

The following is an adaptation of the RATE approach. A disabled reader is given the opportunity to read and rate books. The teacher first meets with the reader to define what the evaluation process will be for recommending or not recommending a particular book. Reasons are given by the student and these are listed in two separate columns on the board. Next, the instructor reads a book and lets the student rate it using the criteria just chosen. The student then works at his or her own rate, evaluating books based on the criteria. The student begins by selecting a simple picture book or other similar book which he or she can read. Student pairs can be assigned to compare books and recommendations and a sharing and discussion time is held periodically to see how a student rated the books read.

Peer Tutoring.   Peer tutoring is mentioned as a technique for reading improvement with the mainstreamed student. More advanced learners can become peer tutors in reading. Klumb (1985) recommends peer tutoring in reading as a reward for disabled learners who have satisfactory classroom behavior. A mildly handicapped fourth grader who is reading at the second-grade level could be used to help a first grader by listening to the first grader read, by reading alternative pages with the first grader, or by reading to the first grader.

General Organizational Strategies.   These strategies need to be taught to more advanced readers. Many handicapped readers fail to organize their reading strategies before, during, or after reading. Many have not been taught how to organize what they read. Clewell & Haidemenos (1982) have presented three graphic organizers that can improve active comprehension abilities—webbing, pyramiding, and think sheets.

Webbing is a visual representation of what one reads. The middle of the web is the main idea and the spokes contain the supporting information. Webbing is used to show the relationship of the ideas in a passage. In webbing, a circle is drawn in the middle of the page. Next, the main idea of the paragraph, page, or passage is written in the center. Related ideas are then placed on the spokes. Finally, subideas are placed on new spokes, and the process continues until all important information is webbed.

The teacher can use webbing to show students comparisons, problems and solutions, descriptions, collections, and cause and effect relationships. Students can design webs before or after reading, and they can be used to organize information for outlining, take notes from a written report, present oral reports, or just to study information about the chapter. Webbing facilitates memory by providing a visual image of the author's message. It requires active thinking on the part of the learner before, during, and after reading—especially if the students are directed to produce two webs, one before and another after reading. Figure 6.6 presents an example of a web.

Pyramiding (modified) is also a visual representation of a selected chapter or passage. It is used to organize information at the main-idea level, the middle-idea level, and the supporting-details level. The pyramid is organized from a bottom-to-top passage or a detail-to-main-idea sequence. Students are asked to read a short passage such as a section of a chapter or a chapter summary. This can be done in student pairs or the teacher can work directly with individual students. One student reads aloud sentences or facts from the summary while

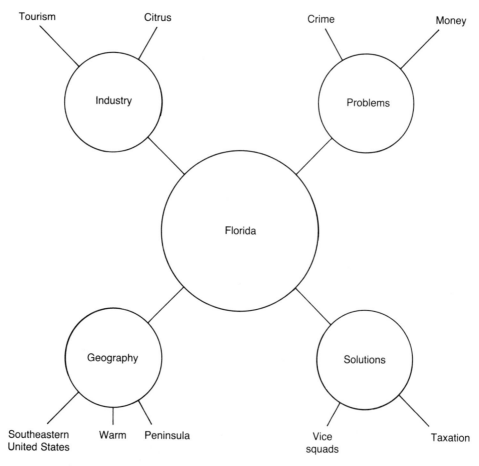

FIGURE 6.6
Example of the Webbing Technique (Source: Adapted from S. Clewell & J. Haidemenos (1983, May), Organizational strategies to increase comprehension, *Reading World, 22* (4), 13–30. Used with permission.)

the other student or the teacher writes these facts on large index cards, placing only one fact on a card. These facts are then placed in a horizontal row. Next, the statements are divided into categories and the categories labeled, one category per card, to become the next row of index cards. For the next level, only one large index card is needed. The students must decide what the whole passage is about and write a summary statement on this card. One more card is used at the top to serve as a title for the passage. A completed pyramid is shown in Figure 6.7.

The teacher can use the pyramid method to help the mainstreamed student organize a review for tests. It also can be used as the actual test format to measure a student's learning. Students can use the pyramid to study for tests

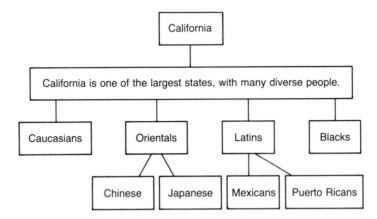

FIGURE 6.7
Example of the Pyramiding Technique (Source: Adapted from S. Clewell & J. Haidemenos (1983, May), Organizational strategies to increase comprehension, *Reading World, 22* (4), 13–30. Used with permission.)

and to organize information for essays and oral reports. The method is helpful in distinguishing lower-level information from mid-level and topic information. Students are encouraged to see relationships and become better able to remember the concepts presented in print.

Think sheets (modified) help students learn to set a purpose for reading. They serve as a framework for predicting what information might be included in the chapter. Think sheets are centered around a chapter or section of a text. The students are instructed to list all headings and subheadings in the chapter, leaving space between each so that predictions can be made. Think sheets can also be used with a student partner or with the teacher. Each student in the pupil pair is to predict what that subheading might be about and write about it in the space provided. The student then reads the chapter to see how accurate the predictions were. Correct answers are then recorded under the student's predictions. The procedure is especially helpful in getting readers involved in active comprehension through predicting what the material will be about. It also gives pupil pairs a chance to interact with each other's background experiences. Figure 6.8 is an example of a think sheet.

Other organizational strategies to be used with handicapped readers include the following (Dinsmore & Isaacson, 1986).

1. To clarify the topic and improve comprehension, provide background information about the topic before having students read about it.
2. Occasionally, give handicapped students the test questions before they read a selection. This will serve as an organizer for the material that is to be studied.
3. Sometimes, let handicapped students prepare their own test questions.

How Can Weather Be Observed and Described?

WEATHER CAN BE OBSERVED WITH BINOCULARS AND DESCRIBED ON T.V.

By Using Sattellites and Comeras.

Temperature

TEMPERATURES FROM DIFFERENT LOCATIONS

The weather bureau and thermometers

Condensation

WATER IN THE AIR COLLECTS ON GLASS WHEN WARM.

They block the passage of energy from sun to earth

Precipitation

THE AMOUNT OF RAIN OR SNOW IS MEASURED.

A rain gauge is a cylinder funnel that measures rainfall

Measuring Precipitation

AMOUNT OF RAINFALL ANNUALLY

Rain, Snow, hail, sleet and fog etc.

Changing Air Pressure

HOT AIR RISE AND COLD AIR STAYS LOW

Changing air pressure causes storms

Observing Wind Direction

WIND DIRECTION IS DETERMINED BY WEATHER VANES

Using wind funnels like at the airport

FIGURE 6.8

Sample Think Sheet (Sources: Text material from Laidlaw (1970), *The new Laidlaw science program, modern science, level 6* (pp. 114–118); think sheet technique adapted from S. Clewell & J. Haidemenos (1983, May), Organizational strategies to increase comprehension, *Reading World, 22* (4), 13–30. Used with permission.)

4. Use drills of vocabulary words only after the students have read them in context and understand them.

Vocabulary and Sight Word Considerations

Teaching vocabulary and sight word selections to mainstream students can require special considerations. There are at least six ways to better improve the teaching of sight words and vocabulary to slower students. These include (1) beginning with concrete, tangible words; (2) teaching the language associated with words (such as letter, word, sentence, and paragraph); (3) helping students acquire and use phonics skills; (4) having students use vocabulary in context immediately after presenting the words; (5) teaching function words through a better presentation of the words; and (6) teaching students how to use syntactic and semantic clues. Vocabulary for mainstream students can begin with concrete, tangible words. Introducing vocabulary based on the senses is a good place to begin. Show objects that can be seen, heard, touched, smelled, and tasted and introduce vocabulary words associated with these senses. Words such as *loud* and *soft* or *sour* and *sweet* can be experienced directly by the students as they learn to associate the written word with a concrete experience.

Sight words and vocabulary are difficult for mainstream students because many of them do not understand the language or printed communication. These students need specific instruction and examples using the terms *letters, words, sentences,* and *paragraphs.* Students need to be provided practice in finding the last word in the sentence or the first letter on the page. While many students pick up the concepts of letters, words, and sentences, it cannot be assumed that mainstream students have these concepts. It is helpful to provide practice in having them identify these terms in familiar contexts.

Some approaches to vocabulary and sight words are look-and-say approaches or whole-word approaches whereas others encourage the use of phonics to sound out words. Phonics, although only one tool that can be used to determine words, should be taught. Whether phonetics is taught incidentally or sequentially is dependent on the program used in many cases. A more important consideration for the mainstream student should be how he or she learns. A common phonics sequence is to teach consonant sounds first, then short vowel sounds, consonant blends, consonant digraphs, vowel digraphs, and diphthongs. Teaching phonics may be more important to spelling and writing than to reading in that many handicapped students have been taught to sound out almost every word, which later leads to slow word-by-word reading and faulty comprehension. When phonics is taught sequentially to handicapped learners, it is most helpful when it is presented and used in a meaningful context.

Many vocabulary and sight words are taught at the beginning of a basal reading lesson. Students are shown words that will appear in the story. Mainstream students may need extra help with these words. Strategies to help them recognize these words include (1) using the words in a sentence for them, (2) having them use each word in a sentence, and (3) most important, having them find the words in the story or passage that is to be read. Transfer of learning is often difficult for these students. When any word is shown on the board, a flashcard, or any form of isolation, the word should immediately be used in a meaningful situation.

Function words are sometimes hard for students. These are words that have no concrete meaning but are meaningful only in context. Many word lists include function words. Some students can recognize the words when presented to them on a flashcard but have trouble reading them in context. A simple way to present these words to mainstream students is to present only a few at a time that are dissimilar in size, letters, and configuration. The words should be printed in isolation and in context. Students identify the words, read them in context, and are then given multiple-choice selections in context to choose the correct word (Burns, Roe, & Ross, 1984).

Teaching children to think about what the word might be in context is often helpful. Semantic clues can be used in which the child tries to discover the word by the meaning of the words around it. Syntactic clues can be used by helping students look at where the word is found in the sentence. Certain words appear in special places in a sentence. For example, in English, it is rare that the subject of the sentence is the last word. Students can be taught to look at word order to help them in determining words.

Comprehension Considerations

Comprehension is the main reason people read in the first place—to understand the printed word. Comprehension is an active process that often gives mainstream students particular difficulty. There are two important reasons that comprehension seems elusive to many students. One reason is that many of them have been given passages that are not meaningful. Some approaches to reading advocate learning skills such as phonics first and later transferring emphasis to comprehension. Some mainstream students have spent so much time in the decoding phase that they never make it to the comprehension phase. For this reason, it is important to have meaningful reading material from the beginning. Another reason students fail at comprehension is because of learned helplessness. Comprehension is an active process which requires the reader to actively seek information needed for understanding. Some readers view reading as something done unto them rather than something that they do. For these and other reasons, comprehension is often a problem for the mainstream student.

Comprehension can be taught to students by requiring active interaction with the material. The activities mentioned earlier—webbing, pyramiding, and think sheets—are designed to challenge students to organize the information for better understanding. There also are other techniques that can be used with mainstream learners for active comprehension. Most of these strategies require questioning by the students. Three of these strategies are the Directed Reading Thinking Activity (DRTA), the Directed Inquiry Activity (DIA), and the Question Only strategy.

The *Directed Reading Activity* is a process that requires students to make predictions from the title and the picture clues. Students then read the material to determine if their predictions were correct. This procedure is helpful in content area material. Students are actively involved because the purpose is to compare their predictions with the author's message.

The *Directed Inquiry Activity* was developed by Keith Thomas and published in Manzo, 1980. With this procedure, students look at a reading passage after they have predicted what the passage is going to be about. The terms *who, what , when, where, how,* and *why* are placed on the board and students guess what the passage will be about using each one of these questions. These predictions provide an active reason for reading the passage (Manzo, 1980; Burns, Roe, & Ross, 1984).

The *Question-Only* strategy can be used to help students learn to ask better questions in content area passages (Manzo, 1980). The teacher tells the students that they must learn as much as possible about the topic by asking questions. Students are told they will be given a test based on what the book said about the topic. The teacher then answers all questions. Students are given the test to see if they asked good questions. Then they read the passage to see what types of questions they might have asked. Of course, the test is not recorded. Since test anxiety can be a problem for the mainstream students, this activity can be adapted to a guessing game format. The purpose of the activity is to give a purpose for understanding the material and actively participating in asking questions. Modifying the technique to a game instead of a test might help some students.

Adapted Reading Activities that Involve Specific Situations.   Situation-specific reading activities are sometimes necessary in the reading class. Teaching the mildly handicapped student to read math problems may be necessary. Sullivan (1985) recommends a procedure for helping learning disabled students understand and read math problems. The method requires four steps. First, the child is asked to underline the most important words found in the problem. In the next step, the student places the key words on index cards. Cards are then divided into either a quantitative or a descriptive category. The last step requires the student to simplify the cards and attempt to answer the problem. If this technique seems too confusing or time consuming, the procedure can be shortened to just requiring the student to underline the most important words in the problem.

Another specific situation is teaching the hard-of-hearing or the deaf child in the regular classroom. Deaf children have a distinct way of communicating, especially those who are taught American Sign Language (ASL). ASL utilizes a distinct language pattern. For example, in ASL, the question "What kind of soda do you want?" might be signed "Soda you want which?" Adaptations need to be made for these students to help them learn to read. Some adapted strategies for the deaf child include the following (Carlsen, 1985).

1. Use the whole-language approach rather than the phonetic method (the student cannot hear the speech sounds).
2. Use a modification of the language experience approach. The student does better if he or she experiences the topic firsthand. Then, the vocabulary and sentence structure are easier to learn.

3. Analyze your reading material and list the most important concepts that you will teach. Remember that deaf children may be literal in their interpretation and will have difficulty with statements like "The refrigerator is running."
4. Teach vocabulary by using as much visual media as possible to illustrate the concepts and words, and limit the number of new words in the reading assignment.
5. Use bookmaking with the deaf child but reverse the procedure. Instead of asking the child to draw a picture and describe it, the teacher writes a sentence or story and has the student illustrate it. This serves as a revealing comprehension check.
6. Make as many visual aides as possible and constantly ask questions to check comprehension.

Although reading instruction in the regular class requires adaptations, progress can be made. Instruction begins with an assessment of reading abilities and then goals and objectives are developed based on individual needs. Individual instructional needs also exist in the area of written language. As we see in the following section, a student's needs in reading are almost always related to the student's needs in writing.

Case Study

INDIVIDUALIZING FOR LANGUAGE ARTS

In addition to self-contained spelling and reading classes, Lynn Mitchell teaches language arts to all sixth graders at Rutledge School in Midfield, Alabama. She is a dedicated and energetic teacher who draws on countless resources to enrich her instructional program and stimulate the learning environment of her students. Lynn encourages creative writing and has been rewarded with the obvious improvement her students have made in the various areas of language and communication. They have written stories, poems, journals, and original plays that have been performed in the school. There is an excitement about learning that fills Lynn's classroom and is obvious to all who enter.

Much of Lynn's success as a teacher comes from her own positive, accepting, and encouraging attitude toward others. Her students absorb this attitude and soon begin to reflect it. Also important is Lynn's patience. Without it she would have been overwhelmed when the sixteen learning disabled and seven educable mentally retarded students were mainstreamed into her classes this year, making her already difficult task even more challenging.

To better meet the needs of these special students, Lynn worked close-ly with the special education teachers. Her colleagues note that Lynn is receptive to suggestions that prove effective with these students. Lynn used a variety of instructional methods including repetition, increased in-dividual attention, and peer tutoring in small groups. She incorporated many critical thinking activities into her curriculum, which proved effective with all her students, but particularly those with special needs. She has worked closely with parents as well, often meeting with them before and after school. While Lynn is willing to recognize the special needs of her students and make the necessary adaptations within her own techniques and expectations, she refuses to accept less than each person's best effort. The results of these positive yet realistic and encouraging expectations, coupled with effective and appropriate methodology, have increased academic achievement as well as greatly improved self-confidence and ac-ceptance within the peer group.

Two students who illustrate Lynn's success are Johnny and Karen. Johnny has problems with his speech and was for the most part nonverbal. He rarely made eye contact when he did speak. The change in Johnny this year has been remarkable. Through encouragement and acceptance from his teacher and classmates, Johnny has come to be the star of several of the original plays mentioned earlier. His self-confidence has swelled and with it his desire to communicate with others. Lynn first discovered his abilities through individual writing assignments at the beginning of the year. She worked closely with Johnny, encouraging him continuously, so that now he performs before his own class and in front of other students, too.

Karen is an EMR student who lacked many social skills that further hindered her learning abilities. Karen used to be ridiculed by her classmates but now she is one of the more popular girls in the class. This dramatic change is due partly to Lynn's efforts and attitudes. She has fostered an easy acceptance of Karen's abilities and inabilities. Karen did have very poor personal hygiene skills but now she bathes daily at the school with the assistance of some of her classmates. Karen's reply to direct questioning used to be a shrug of the shoulders at best. She now talks freely to everyone without being prompted. Her sullen and angry look has been replaced with a ready smile. She used to stare blankly at a piece of paper when given a writing assignment and now she easily fills several pages.

Karen and Johnny certainly indicate that all such students can be suc-cessfully mainstreamed if the teacher is willing to be realistic, accepting, encouraging, and adaptive. Lynn Mitchell is all of these and more.

Writing

Written expression is necessary for functional living. People who have difficulty writing also have difficulty in other academic subjects because written expression is required in all content areas. Writing is important because it not only communicates but serves as an emotional outlet as well. Writing is an avenue in which the student can learn to communicate, release feelings, reflect, analyze, review, and better understand him- or herself. Here we discuss ideas for writing instruction with the mainstreamed student. The development of a creative writing program through individualized instruction is presented as are assessment, goals, and instructional approaches for both handwriting and spelling.

Creative Writing

Since the 1970s, much research has been conducted concerning the writing process (Graves, 1983). Previous to this time many teachers of writing believed a child had to master the mechanics of writing before he or she could be a creative writer. Research now indicates that there are developmental stages of art and writing. Teachers aware of this development can allow even the slowest child to develop creative writing skills.

Brittain (1979) has described stages in young children's art. The young child begins drawing by random scribbling and later moves into the stage of controlled scribbling. The child then progresses into what Brittain calls "scribbling." In this stage, the lines drawn represent something. The next stage is the early representational stage, in which the child produces a symbol for an object even though the teacher may not be able to recognize what the child has drawn. Finally, the child progresses to the preschematic drawing stage, in which objects and people are portrayed and the sizes and shapes are more proportional. At this stage, the adult may recognize what the child has drawn.

Similarly, there are beginning stages to children's writing and spelling. Gentry (1981) has described at least four stages that children go through as they learn to write and spell. He calls the first stage the *deviant stage*, in which the child simply writes letters in a random order to represent a word. (e.g., the child might write *gFnTb* for *cookie*). The next stage, termed the *prephonetic stage*, appears when the child uses one-, two- or three-letter spellings for a word in which there is some letter-sound correspondence. For example, *CKE* might represent *cookie* in the prephonetic stage. At the *phonetic stage*, there is almost a perfect match between the letters and sounds. The child might write *kookE* for *cookie* in the phonetic stage. The final stage before correct writing and spelling is the *transitional stage*, in which the child spells phonetically but there is now a vowel in each syllable.

Help students build writing experiences from life events.

Other researchers have studied the beginnings of art, writing, and spelling and have described beginning literacy in different ways (Ferreiro & Teberosky, 1982; Temple, Nathan, & Burris, 1982). The important point to remember is that all children go through developmental stages of becoming creative writers. A teacher aware of this can develop the attitude that all children can write. A child who is still at the scribble stage or prephonetic stage can still be given the opportunity to be a creative writer. The product will simply be at a different stage than other children. The following recommendations can be made for teaching children in the beginnng stages of writing: (1) develop the attitude that all children can write creatively; (2) accept the child's developmental writing level; and (3) provide opportunities for all children to write creatively. The *individual picture reading* and *newsflash* activities described earlier can also be used for written expression practice with beginning writers.

For more advanced writers the teacher might use the writing process described by Graves (1983). In the writing process, students are taught to write through the sequence of drafting, revising, editing, and publishing. Conferencing takes place throughout the writing process. Drafting is simply writing thoughts and ideas down on paper. A student begins to write creatively by first getting his or her thoughts down on paper. After the first draft, the student is then taught to revise and place the thoughts in a coherent sequence. After revising comes editing. The teacher can serve as the final editor before the product is finally ready for classroom publishing.

Managing creative writing can be difficult if the teacher does not have an organized plan for implementing an individualized writing program. Gurosky (1986) has described the following classroom management plan for creative writing used with a second-grade class to develop creative writing abilities.

1. Everyone writes at a set time for 30 minutes a day using the drafting, revising, editing, and publishing process.
2. The teacher holds daily conferences. With twenty-five children in the class, five are assigned as Monday children, five as Tuesday children, and so forth.
3. Monday children have the opportunity to share with the class what they are writing about on Monday; Tuesday children have the opportunity to share their writing with the class on Tuesday; and so on. This sharing time is optional and occurs after the 30-minute writing period.
4. Drafting, revising, and editing occur 3 weeks out of the month. The last week of every month is set aside for publishing. *Publishing* here is defined as binding a story into a book or booklet.
5. A child is free to choose the writing he or she wishes to publish. The teacher helps with the editing but the choice of topics is left to the students.
6. No story starters are provided. Children are encouraged to think of their own topics to write about.
7. Good children's literature is often presented as a springboard for writing. Poetry, predictable books, picture books, and books from selected authors are read to children in hope that the books will spark ideas for creative writing.

Slower students benefit from the writing process as much as gifted students because they work at their own pace. They also develop an understanding of what written communication is all about because they are directly involved in the process (Gurosky, 1986). Creative writing is possible with slower students if the teacher understands that everyone is a writer. This attitude often carries over to the student who develops the attitude "I am a writer."

Mechanics of Writing

How do mainstream students learn about the mechanics of writing? There are two general approaches to teaching the mechanics. The first is the *whole-language approach*, which can be used with the creative writing process described in Graves' (1983) model. Through their own creative writing, students are taught about sentence sense, word usage, subject-verb agreement, pronoun usage, capitalization, and punctuation. These skills are specifically taught through individualized instruction during the editing part of the process. When students are involved in the first two steps (drafting and revising), the focus is on content and getting ideas down on paper. When it comes to edit, emphasis shifts to structure and organization of these ideas.

The second approach to teaching mechanics of writing is the *skills approach*, in which skills are taught through direct lessons in capitalization, punctuation, and sentence structure. The skills are first applied to sentences. The skill emphasis at the sentence level is on structural development. Once students are proficient at this stage, they are taught organizational strategies that go beyond sentence development. Organizational strategies are taught for writing paragraphs and larger compositions. The skills approach is a part-to-whole approach in which students are given direct, systematic instruction and practice in capitalization, subject-verb agreement, punctuation marks, pronoun usage, and vocabulary development and usage. After acquisition occurs, application of these skills to other common writing activities such as letter writing, note taking, preparing outlines, and writing summaries or reviews are stressed.

Table 6.4 compares the skills approach and the whole-language approach to teaching the mechanics of writing. The advantages of using the whole-language method to teach basic grammar, syntax, and other writing skills are many. First, children have a purpose for learning these skills, in that they are using them in their own writing to communicate ideas to others. Secondly, since they are using them in context, transfer is more likely to occur than learning the skills in isolation. The disadvantage of using whole-language approaches to teach writing skills is that the skills are developed incidentally and not sequentially. Some mainstream students may need extra practice on some skills. For this reason, some teachers prefer to use the skills approach to teach grammar and syntax sequentially, following a prescribed course of study.

The advantages of using the skills approach to teach basic writing skills involve sequence and practice. Students are taught step by step the writing skills needed for appropriate written communication. Students practice these skills by learning how to construct sentences. Later they develop paragraphs and stories based on the knowledge they have acquired through skills training. In the past, this approach has been used most often with handicapped students. However, this method also has its disadvantages. When the skills approach is used, many of the slower students never have the opportunity to write stories. They are so consumed with learning the mechanics of writing that they never become proficient enough to get beyond the sentence construction level. This approach is often based on children's deficits and may give them the feeling that they are not writers until they learn all of the prerequisite skills. Students who have great difficulty with grammar and syntax may not have trouble coming up with interesting content.

Assessing Handwriting

In the beginning stages of handwriting, assessment involves prewriting and readiness. There are certain prerequisite skills that are necessary before formal handwriting instruction can begin. The following abilities are considered important before formal instruction of handwriting occurs. This list can serve as an informal assessment for handwriting instruction (Hildebrand, 1986).

- Recognizes and discriminates between and among the letters of the alphabet
- Establishes a dominant hand
- Follows directions
- Makes circles, squares, straight lines
- Knows left and right
- Draws with a brush
- Uses crayons
- Manipulates puzzles and blocks
- Uses scissors
- Copies simple shapes
- Shows visual memory for letters

Although this list is not sequential, it can serve as an indicator of readiness for formal handwriting instruction. Perhaps the most important prerequisite for handwriting instruction is the student's interest and desire to learn how to form letters correctly.

Goals of Handwriting Instruction

Handwriting instruction has been criticized during the past few decades because of the emphasis on mechanics rather than communication (Rubin, 1985). The goal of any handwriting instruction program should be the communication of ideas. Handwriting instruction should be taught with this purpose in mind. The overall goal of handwriting instruction is the legibility of writing so that communication is most effective. The handicapped student may need help in understanding why legible writing is so important. This might be accomplished by asking questions similar to the following.

TABLE 6.4

The Skills Versus the Whole-Language Approach to the Mechanics of Writing

Mechanics	Whole-Language Approach	Skills Approach
Punctuation	The use of a period, question mark, comma, hyphen, colon, apostrophe, exclamation mark, and semicolon are taught using a student's writing as they occur incidentally.	The use of a period, question mark, comma, hyphen, colon, apostrophe, exclamation mark, and semicolon are taught sequentially, using some predetermined list of sequential skills. Students then construct individual sentences to practice using these skills.
Capitalization	Students are taught to capitalize through their own writing selections. Each sentence is looked at for capitalization.	Students are taught specific lessons on capitalization and are asked to develop sentences applying principles of capitalization learned in the specific lessons.
Subject-verb agreement	Subject-verb agreement is also taught through a student's own composition. Students are asked to look at their writing and see if they detect errors in agreement. The teacher also points out errors that have been made; students are shown how to correct them and are encouraged to apply this learning to their future writing.	Students are taught direct lessons and rules about subject-verb agreement. Practice activities are provided in which students select the appropriate verb for the sentence provided.
Word usage	Students are taught vocabulary through the use of their own writing. If they use a word too frequently, they must find a synonym for it.	Words are taught in isolation, and then sentences are constructed using those words.

TABLE 6.4
(continued)

Mechanics	Whole-Language Approach	Skills Approach
Sentence sense	Students are taught to edit their own sentences so that fluency occurs and content makes sense. Students are taught to watch for run-on sentences, short choppy sentences, and sentence fragments during the editing process.	Students are taught to construct sentences and then paragraphs. As they move from sentence writing to paragraph construction, they are taught about run-on sentences, choppy sentences, and sentence fragments.

1. If someone has given you directions to their house and you have trouble recognizing the letters they wrote, what could happen?
2. If you are taking a spelling test and don't write neatly, what could happen?
3. If you write a letter to a friend and the friend cannot read your writing, what might happen?

Instructional Approaches to Handwriting

Handwriting instruction usually begins with manuscript writing. There are several reasons why formal handwriting begins with manuscript rather than cursive writing. First, the pencil is lifted from the paper after each part of a letter is made. Young children and handicapped learners who do not have the fine motor coordination to make continuous strokes learn better through manuscript writing first. Second, the letters are not connected, which means that connecting the letters does not have to be taught first. Probably the major reason manuscript writing is taught first is because of the fine motor coordination needed for cursive writing. When teaching manuscript writing, there are some basic principles that teachers should understand.

1. Right-handed people pull their pencil across the page. Left-handed people push the pencil. This means that right-handed children can see what they have just written as they pull their pencil and are less likely to smudge the paper. Left-handed children immediately cover what they have written with their hand and are more likely to smear the page.
2. Letters in manuscript are usually written with vertical, horizontal, slanted, and circular strokes.
3. Perceptual motor skills have to be developed. This can be accomplished through (a) multisensory stimulation, (b) stressing self-correction, (c) work-

ing on comparison and improvement rather than quantity, and (d) emphasizing consistency of letter formation (such as the difference between a *b* and a *d*).

There are several commercially produced handwriting programs such as the Zaner-Bloser, the D'Nealian manuscript alphabet, and the Palmer method. The Zaner-Bloser method utilizes a standard manuscript format whereas the D'Nealian alphabet more closely resembles the letters made in cursive writing. Those students in the mainstream still having trouble writing legibly may need remedial strategies to help them since most were taught by traditional methods and are still having difficulty.

Cursive handwriting instruction is usually taught at the end of the second or the beginning of the third grade. Students are thought to have developed enough fine motor coordination to begin cursive writing. Cursive writing is different from manuscript writing in several ways. First, in cursive writing the pencil is not picked up until a word is completed. This means that the letters *i* and *j* are not dotted and the *t* not crossed until the word is completely written. One of the biggest differences between manuscript and cursive writing is the fact that cursive writing requires connecting one letter to another, which means that teaching how to connect the letters is important. Another difference between cursive and manuscript is the slant of the paper. Manuscript writing does not usually require the slant of the paper but in cursive writing left-handed children are taught to slant their paper at a 30-degree angle to the right, and right-handed children to slant their paper at a 30-degree angle to the left.

Cursive writing can pose a problem for the exceptional student. A major problem with cursive writing is often spacing (Groff, 1984). "The single most negative influence on handwriting legibility, however is speed" (p. 12). Other problems include irregular slant and the inability to align letters with the lines of the paper. Letter size can also be a problem for the handicapped writer using cursive writing. There are techniques that can be used to help correct these problems. "Almost all disabled writers, it is found, can slow down when directed to do so, can put greater distance between letters they write, can increase the regularity of the slant and alignment of the letters they write, and can write letters in two distinctive sizes" (p. 13).

There are other special situations that the mainstream teacher may have to consider. Children with orthopedic handicaps (particularly cerebral palsy) may have great difficulty with handwriting, which causes frustration and fatigue in the student. A child with cerebral palsy may know what he or she wants to write but the child's body will not cooperate. Such a student usually expends more energy per task than the average child—especially in handwriting. Special pencil grips may be used with this student to provide a better grasp of the pencil. Occupational therapists are specially trained to provide help with self-help and fine-motor abilities. An occupational therapist may need to be consulted for writing aids for the orthopedically impaired child. The partially sighted child could also have writing difficulties. This student has difficulty with contrasts—

especially when the lines of the paper are too light. The student will sometimes need special equipment such as bold-lined writing paper, a writing kit, script-letter aids, or other devices that can be purchased to help with writing. Such devices may be purchased from the American Printing House for the Blind (see the "Resources" section at the end of the chapter).

Graham and Miller (1980) have provided guidelines for teachers working with slower students on handwriting (see Figure 6.9). Whatever program of hand-writing is chosen, the guidelines listed in Figure 6.9 can be used as principles for better handwriting instruction.

Handwriting Activities

Extra practice in handwriting for students with special needs should include visual, auditory, kinesthetic, and tactile activities to help the handicapped stu-

---

1. Handwriting instruction should be direct and not incidental.
2. Because handicapped students exhibit a diverse range of handwriting achievement, instruction should be individualized.
3. The handwriting program should be planned, monitored, and modified on the basis of assessment information.
4. Successful teaching and remediation depend on the flexible use of a wide variety of techniques and methods.
5. Handwriting should be taught in short daily learning periods, during which desirable habits are established.
6. Skills in handwriting are overlearned in isolation and then applied in meaningful context assignments.
7. Teachers must stress the importance of handwriting and must not accept, condone, or encourage slovenly work.
8. Effective handwriting instruction is dependent on the attitudes of both student and teacher.
9. The instructional atmosphere should be pleasant, and motivation should be promoted through incentives, reinforcement, success, and enthusiasm.
10. Teachers should practice lessons prior to presentation and should be able to write a "model" hand.
11. Students should be encouraged to evaluate their own handwriting and, when appropriate, to participate actively in initiating, conducting, and evaluating the remedial program.

FIGURE 6.9

Guidelines for Teaching Handwriting to the Handicapped (*Source:* S. Graham & L. Miller (1980), Handwriting research and practice: A unified approach, *Focus on Exceptional Children, 13*(2), 5–6. Used with permission.)

dent remember and improve handwriting skills. The following is a list of hand-writing suggestions for students who need extra practice.

1. Use "finger frolics" for teaching basic shapes. The teacher draws shapes in the air and the student models them.
2. Teach basic shapes by using cardboard models for students to trace.
3. Use sandpaper letters for students to trace when reproducing letters of the alphabet.
4. Place cardboard models of letters under white paper and have students make crayon rubbings of the letters. Combine to make an alphabet book.
5. When teaching left-right progression, use a green dot for go and a red dot for stop.
6. Prepare a 9 × 12-inch piece of paper with the student's name written in solid letters on the top half of the paper. On the bottom half of the page, write the student's name with a highlighter pen. The student traces over the highlighter.
7. Provide kinesthetic learning as students form letters by touching/tracing letters in sand, salt, or made from sponges as they view a given model.
8. Use hand puppets made from paper bags to assist students in construct-ing a story on a given topic. The teacher records the story on the chalkboard as it unfolds.
9. In teaching sentence writing, provide a simple check sheet of the steps necessary for constructing the sentence. Students check off each step as it is completed.
10. When writing friendly letters, provide a form letter with lines drawn for the letter parts. The student completes the blanks.
11. Design learning centers with various activities for handwriting.
12. When selecting main ideas for paragraph writing, let students select an idea from the "main idea box" and develop a paragraph centered around the main idea selected from "the box."
13. When reading or listening to a story and retelling it in written form, tape record the story and provide a structured format of the story for students to complete. This provides a written prompt for rewriting the story.
14. Teach descriptive paragraph writing by providing an oral demonstration. The teacher describes a person, object, or place and writes it on the board.
15. When assisting students in writing a paragraph containing a main idea and several supporting details, provide a visual aid in the form of an art object, picture, or other concrete item. As the students decide which details are supportive, include them on a chart. After the list is made, have the group develop the paragraph.
16. When requiring students to write poems, (limerick, haiku, blank verse) displaying varied rhyme schemes, provide copies of the poems with miss-ing last lines. The limerick is a good place to start.
17. In writing letters (friendly, business, and so on), provide a visual model with lines representing the letter parts. Students fill in the model's format. The

second time around, have the students write a letter while using only the model as a prompt.

18. When gathering and organizing information for reports, provide the student with a structured form in which to gather and organize the information.

Spelling

Just as there are developmental stages of art and writing, there are developmental stages of spelling. Forester (1980) has described the stages as (1) scribbling, or pretend writing; (2) one-letter spelling; (3) two- and three-letter spelling; (4) self-programming of simple spelling rules; and (5) overgeneralization of rules and patterns (such as phonetic spelling or transfer of spelling patterns from known to unknown words. Several other attempts have been made to describe the developmental sequence of spelling (Ferreiro & Teberosky, 1982; Gibson & Levin, 1975; Henderson, 1985; Read, 1971). When looking at the spelling errors of a student, it is often helpful to look also at the developmental level of the student.

Graham (1985) points out that "most learning disabled, mentally retarded, and emotionally disturbed children who are mainstreamed have spelling problems" (p. 299). Many of these children are taught from spelling texts that rarely take into account individual differences. These poor spellers "often have a limited vocabulary and may not have access to a wide variety of spelling skills" (p. 300). Graham recommends that remedial spellers should have at least some instruction directed toward increasing spelling vocabulary, interest in spelling words correctly, perfecting the ability to find and correct spelling errors, and improving phonics and dictionary skills. Some handicapped spellers can benefit from visual imagery training and auditory training.

Instructional Approaches and Remedial Strategies

Spelling programs should be highly structured, direct, and not incidental. Although a whole-language approach is recommended for the language arts, spelling programs should not be based solely on the other language arts, in that research shows that poor spellers do not acquire many words developed outside of the spelling lesson period (Graham, 1985). Both whole-word and phonemic approaches can be integrated in such a way as to include direct phonic instruction and words used most often in the child's writing. Basic spelling vocabulary recommended by most spelling programs can also be used.

Remedial spelling programs should be based on research findings such as the following.

1. The test-study-test method produces better results than the study-test method. In this procedure, the students take a pretest to determine which words they do not know. The students are then taught the words they misspelled and then are given the test again (Graham, 1985).
2. Learning spelling by a whole-word method is more effective than learning words by syllables. Research indicates that directing student attention to the whole visual image of the word is more appropriate than syllabication. In fact, syllabication may produce negative effects on spelling achievement (Graham, 1985).
3. Students should correct their own spelling tests under teacher supervision immediately after taking the test. This has proven to be the single most helpful instructional technique in spelling improvement (Graham, 1985).
4. Each student should be taught systematic ways of studying unknown spelling words. Handicapped students usually do not generalize without direct instruction on word-study techniques (Graham, 1985).
5. Direct modeling is effective in teaching the handicapped speller. Specifically, "showing a child how *not* to spell a word followed by showing him the correct spelling (may) be more effective than merely showing him the correct spelling. . . . The effect of such sequences of negative-positive instances . . . [appear] to be more effective for the more difficult concepts such as phonetically irregular words" (Kauffman et al., 1978, p. 37).
6. Handicapped spellers may be more different than alike. There appear to be significant differences between good readers/poor spellers and poor readers/poor spellers (Graham, 1985).
7. Teachers should emphasize the positive through praise, structure spelling assignments for success, provide for meaningful practice, and use interesting games and activities (Henderson, 1985).

Spelling can be included as part of an integrated language arts program. Whole-language approaches to language arts encourage the incorporation of spelling into the reading and writing process. For this reason, vocabulary and word lists used in reading also can be used for spelling. The following approaches are ways spelling can be taught in conjunction with the other language arts.

1. When teaching *survival words* in reading, use some of them in spelling. Words such as *poison, danger,* and *stop* can be used to teach survival spelling as well as survival reading. A resource for choosing the most essential survival words can be found in Polloway and Polloway (1981).
2. *Environmental word-list approaches* can be used with the logo learning activities described earlier in the chapter. Students who are learning to recognize logos such as "K-Mart" and "McDonalds" can be taught to spell them and incorporate them into their language experience writings.

3. The *key-words approach* to reading can be modified to include the spelling of words. With this approach, each child meets individually with the teacher to tell the teacher a word. The teacher writes the word for the child on a sentence strip. The child says each letter as the teacher writes the word; then the child traces the word with the index and middle fingers several times (spelling the word as he or she traces). The child then writes the word. The word can be incorporated in spelling. Children often want to learn how to spell words they have used or thought of themselves. The words can be stored on shower curtain rings or kept in file boxes (Veatch et al., 1979).

4. A *concrete-objects approach* can be used with spelling and language. The teacher chooses one concrete object a day for the reading/writing/spelling list. The word can be any object that the teacher can point to or hold. The word for the day might be *chair, pencil, glass, masking tape,* or some other. After students are shown the object by the teacher, the name of the object is written on the board and the teacher names each letter of the object's name as it is being written. Students then make up sentences about the object, which the teacher also writes on the board. Students are instructed to write the word and construct their own sentence using the concrete object.

5. The *labeling approach* to spelling can be incorporated into language arts by placing labels on various objects in the classroom (chair, desk, clock, door, and so on). This approach is similar to the concrete-objects approach, except the items are always visible in the room. One or two labeled items a week can be used in the language arts period for reading, writing, and spelling.

Games also can be used effectively with remedial spellers. Brown (1985) notes that, although there are certain pitfalls with using games, there are ways to avoid them. He suggests that spelling games should be used for specific instructional objectives. Other recommendations include selecting players who are compatible, encouraging self-competition, allowing students to correct their own mistakes as they happen, and analyzing student responses for further instruction. Some selected spelling games are described in Figure 6.10.

Computer Applications for Language Arts

Computers are helpful to the mainstreamed student in reading and writing. Handicapped students can use the computer as a tool for writing their own stories. To use the computer for this purpose, the student needs to be taught about the computer and the vocabulary needed for using it appropriately. Writing stories on the computer and building computer vocabulary can be accomplished in the following manner.

Spelling Game Pattern

1. *Tachistoscope.* For rhyming word patterns tachistoscopes are useful. They can be teacher-made or student-designed and made. The movable portion of the tachistoscope can be the letter in the initial, medial, or final position of the words being practiced. The example shows a baseball tachistoscope with beginning and ending consonant sounds.

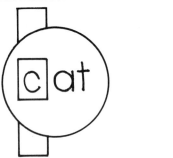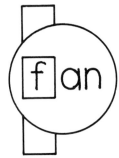

2. *Star speller.* The star pattern can be used for numerous spelling activities. The points of the star are matched with the center. Several cut-up stars are placed together in one envelope so students can match star points to their centers.

3. *Mini-puzzle match.* Blends, digraphs, and spelling beginnings or endings can be matched up in the mini-puzzle format. Only one correct answer should be possible, however, or students will become confused in trying to match items.

FIGURE 6.10
Spelling Activities and Games for Handicapped Students

4. *Poke-and-peek the right spelling.* A spelling picture can be pasted on an index card with a selection of several spellings at the bottom and a hole punched beneath each choice. The correct spelling is marked on the back with a highlighter. Students put their pencils through the hole beneath their selection. The answer can be checked on the back.

5. *Car wheels.* Car wheels can be used for matching any type of graphophonic information. (The student places all matching words on top of the wheels.) Homonyms, synonyms, antonyms, and many others are possibilities.

FIGURE 6.10 *continued*

Computer Stories

The *Bank Street Writer* program for computers is useful for helping students with reading difficulties (Hedley & Hedley, 1984). The following program sequence can be used to help teach mildly handicapped students to write creatively.

1. Type a story dictated by a remedial student. The student should be able to see the screen as you type and allowed to recommend adjustments to the story as he or she wishes.

2. When typing the story, leave enough room for the student to insert illustrations.

3. Later, the student can participate in group stories on the computer with the idea that one student begins a story and the next one adds to it.

Hedley & Hedley (1984) stress that there are many benefits of using the *Bank Street Writer* with the mildly handicapped, including that (1) children learn left-to-right sequencing, spelling, letter recognition, sentence formation, editing, and how to complete their work; (2) students move at their own rate; (3) writing is seen as an active process; (4) small-group instruction, peer tutoring, and individualization can be incorporated into this method; (5) parents become involved by reading the books produced on the computer by their child and classmates; and (6) the wholeness of reading and writing is stressed (pp. 18–19).

Computer Vocabulary Building

The computer brings with it its own vocabulary. Dreyer, Futtersak, and Boehm (1985) have previewed thirty-five software programs and listed the most common words used by them. When students are taught how to use the computer, these words, which often appear in the computer programs the students will be using, can be taught in reading as essential vocabulary words. The words can be taught in context on the computer itself. The most commonly found words found in at least ten of the thirty-five software packages are:

arrow	key	press
choose	loading	program
continue	menu	return
enter	name	sound
escape	number	spacebar
game	please	type

--------------------------- *Summary* ---------------------------

Language arts instruction is one of the most important educational areas for the mainstream student. Adaptations often have to be made in reading, writing, spelling, speaking, and listening if the exceptional learner is to succeed in the regular classroom. Adaptations are usually based on assessment, indicating the student's strengths and weaknesses. Once this has been determined, goals and objectives for an individual language arts plan can be written. The student will need varied instructional approaches and adapted activities, which are often coordinated with a resource teacher. Language arts instruction for the mainstream learner can be time consuming but the rewards and benefits of individualizing instruction are worth the effort.

Discussion Questions

1. Select one adapted instructional strategy from each of the following areas: listening, speaking, reading, creative writing, spelling, and computer applications in language arts. Describe each activity in detail and explain why it is appropriate for a mainstream student.
2. Describe the major differences between good and poor readers. Why are these differences often more related to instructional strategies than to learner characteristics?
3. What is the importance of coordinating reading goals and objectives with the resource or reading teacher? What possible problems result in reading instruction when the efforts of the regular and resource teachers are not coordinated?
4. Compare and contrast the following grouping methods for the mainstreamed student in language arts instruction: skills grouping, interest grouping, tutorial grouping, project grouping, and buddy grouping.
5. Devise a method of teaching slower students the most commonly used computer terms. Be sure that the terms are to be taught in context.

Resources

Commercially Published Language Arts Tests

Auditory Discrimination Test, Language Research Associates, Chicago, IL. This is a norm-referenced test appropriate for children 5 to 8 years old. Forty word pairs are given and the child must indicate if each word pair is the same or different.

Carrow Elicited Language Inventory, Learning Concepts, Austin, TX. This is a measure of expressive grammatical competence. Use of pronouns, prepositions, conjunctions, articles, adverbs, adjectives, and other expressive competencies are measured. The test is not recommended for students with severe articulation problems or echolalia.

Criterion Reading, Random House, New York, NY. This is both a diagnostic tool and a teaching system for individualized instruction. Reading skills (450) are criterion-referenced in the following areas: comprehension, syntax, verbal information, structural analysis, phonology, auditory input-motor response, visual input, and motor response and skills.

Diagnostic Reading Scales, CTB/McGraw-Hill, Monterey, CA. This test measures oral reading, silent reading, and auditory comprehension skills. There are twenty-two reading passages and supplementary phonics and word-analysis tests.

Goldman-Fristoe Test of Articulation, American Guidance Service, Circle Pines, MN. This test measures a child's ability to produce speech sounds. It is divided into the areas of sounds-in-words, sounds-in-sentences, and stimulability. In the last section, the examiner goes back to the sounds misarticulated by the child and sees if the child can produce them correctly.

Illinois Test of Psycholinguistic Abilities, University of Illinois Press, Champaign, IL. This is an individually administered norm-referenced test with norms for children between 2 and 10 years of age. It is divided into the following sections: auditory reception, visual reception, visual association, verbal expression, manual expression, grammatical closure, auditory closure, sound blending, visual closure, auditory sequential memory, and visual sequential memory.

Northwest Syntax Screening Test, Northwestern University Press, Evanston, IL. This is an individually administered test of a child's language structure. The child is instructed to point to the picture that best illustrates a sentence. In part 2 of the test, expressive language is supposedly measured. The child has to repeat a correct sentence from a sentence pair.

Phonological Process Analysis, University Park Press, Baltimore, MD. This is an individually administered criterion-referenced device that measures sixteen phonological rules related to speech production.

Prescriptive Reading Inventory, CTB/McGraw-Hill, Monterey, CA. This is a criterion-referenced test that measures reading ability at the elementary level. The test also includes prereading measures such as auditory discrimination, visual discrimination, knowledge about the alphabet, language experience, attention skills, comprehension, and beginning reading.

Slingerland Screening Tests for Identifying Children with Specific Language Disability, Western Psychological Services, Los Angeles, CA. There are nine regularly administered subtests designed to measure several aspects of written language disability. These include copying from a wall chart; copying words in isolation; recalling words, numbers and letters; matching words to samples; drawing from memory; writing letters, numbers, and words from memory; writing the initial and ending letters in words; recalling words, letters, and numbers; and writing answers to questions.

Test of Auditory Comprehension of Language, Learning Concepts, Austin, TX. This test is reported to measure the developmental level of a child's auditory comprehension as well as language comprehension difficulties in the content areas. It is individually administered and recommended for children 3 to 6 years of age.

Test of Adolescent Language, Pro-Ed, Austin, TX. This is a norm-referenced test used to measure language functioning in the following areas: listening/vocabulary, listening/grammar, speaking/vocabulary, speaking/grammar, reading/vocabulary, reading/grammar, writing/vocabulary, and writing/grammar.

Test of Written Language, Pro-Ed, Austin, TX. This test measures written abilities of the school-aged child. It looks at spelling, word usage, punctuation and capitalization, handwriting, vocabulary, and sentence production.

Selected Instructional Materials

Cartloads of Creative Story Starters, The Learning Works, P.O. Box 6187, Santa Barbara, CA 93111. This is a word bank of story starters that includes such topics as sports, occupations, seasons, holidays, good things to read, and animals.

Composition Skills, Basic Learning Corporation, Williamsville, NY 14221. *Composition Skills* comes in grade-level packages; each set contains story starters that address specific skills.

Creative Writing Roundup, The Learning Works, P.O. Box 6187, Santa Barbara, CA 93111. This book contains help for the primary or intermediate student in written expression. It includes poetry, story starters, brainstorming activities, and other motivators.

Desk Top Story Starters, Creative Teaching Press, Inc., Huntington Beach, CA 92649. Cut-out props are used to help students in starting their stories. It is appropriate for grades 1–3.

Far Out Story Starters, Enrich, Inc., 760 Kifer Road, Sunnyvale, CA 94086. Reading comprehension and writing skills are stressed through story characters and comic strips. These serve as story starters. This is appropriate for grades 1–4.

Fingerprint Funnies, Frank Schaeffer Publications, Inc., 26616 Indian Peak Road, Palos Verdes Peninsula, CA 90274. This is a book for primary-level students that contains twenty story starters.

Flannelboard Kits, Instructo/McGraw-Hill, Paoli, PA 19301. Individual flannel board kits can be ordered on the following stories: "The Three Pigs," "Goldilocks and the Three Bears," "Gingerbread Boy," "Little Red Riding Hood," "Three Billy Goats Gruff," "Hansel and Gretel," and "Rumpelstiltskin."

Language Arts Box, Educational Insights, Inc., 20435 South Tillman Avenue, Carson, CA 90746. This box contains activities for many of the language arts areas such as vocabulary development, spelling, dramatics, informational writing, and public speaking.

Reaction Cards, Developmental Learning Materials, 7440 Natchez Avenue, Niles, IL 60648. Students react to six different situations found on reaction cards. There is one main card and several cards that show alternatives. Students are to discuss the alternatives and they may choose one as a story starter.

Reading for Comprehension Series, Educational Insights, Inc., 20435 South Tillman Avenue, Carson, CA 90746. This is a set of reading paragraphs presented in increasing difficulty. Multiple-choice answers are provided throughout the series, which measure reading phrases, make inferences, predict outcomes, note the main idea, note details, draw conclusions, use context clues, and find sequence.

Story Starters, Curriculum Associates, Inc., Esquire Road, North Billerica, MD 01862. This is a set of thirty-two open-ended situation cards with questions to be used as story starters.

Storytelling, Pitman Learning, Inc., 6 Davis Drive, Belmont, CA 94002. This book is divided into nursery rhymes, tell-a-story, fairy tales, and finger puppets.

Storytelling Pictures, Developmental Learning Materials, 7440 Natchez Avenue, Niles, IL 60648. This is a set of twelve color pictures that promote making up stories, which can be told aloud or written.

Super Reader, Frank Schaeffer Publications, Inc., 26616 Indian Peak Road, Palos Verdes Peninsula, CA 90274. This is a group of reading and writing activities that helps with comprehension, vocabulary development, phonics, and alphabetizing. It is appropriate for students who are at the fourth- to eighth-grade levels.

Working with Stories, Curriculum Associates, Inc., Esquire Road, North Billerica, MD 01862. This is a collection of beginning paragraphs for stories to be used by students in developing their own stories.

Selected Microcomputer Software

Alphabet Critters, Aquarius Software, P.O. Box 128, Indian Rocks Beach, FL 33535. This program presents individual letters, words, and book titles for teaching the use of alphabetical order.

Auditory Memory, Aquarius Software, P.O. Box 128, Indian Rocks Beach, FL 33535. This program provides practice in remembering numbers, letters, and words. Audiocassettes are included with the program.

Cloze-Plus, Milliken Publishing Co., 1100 Research Blvd., P.O. Box 21579, St. Louis, MO 63132-0579. This program includes six packages of four diskettes per package, each representing a particular skill. Exercises are built around comprehension, vocabulary skills, comparison, and other reading skills.

Learning Ways to Read Words, Intellectual Software, 798 North Avenue, Bridgeport, CT 06606. This program is for all ages and includes everything from the study on alphabetizing to the use of the dictionary to the use of long and short vowels. Prefixes, suffixes, and root words are also used in the program.

Letter Recognition and Alphabetization, Milliken Publishing Co., 1100 Research Blvd., P.O. Box 21579, St. Louis, MO 63132–0579. This program teaches lowercase letters, uppercase letters, and sequencing and is good for teaching alphabetizing skills at all levels.

Memory Match, Hartley Courseware, Inc., 123 Bridge Street, Box 419, Dimondale, MI 48821. This is a matching series that includes matching rhyming words, homonyms, and number words and can be programmed for use with words that the teacher chooses.

Reading Pacer, Intellectual Software, 798 North Avenue, Bridgeport, CT 06606. This program is used to help students increase their reading pace. The material is brought on the screen at one of five speeds.

Organizations

Association for Childhood Education International (ACEI), 71141 Georgia Ave., Suite 200, Wheaton, MD 20902. Publishes *Childhood Education*, a journal concerned with the total development of the child through adolescence, including language arts instruction.

International Reading Association (IRA) 800 Barksdale Rd., P.O. Box 8139, Newark, DE 19711. Publishes *The Reading Teacher* for elementary teachers and *The Journal of Reading* for secondary and postsecondary reading education.

Chapter 7

Individualizing for Arithmetic

DEBORAH A. BOTT
University of Kentucky

Chapter Objectives

After reading Chapter 7 the student will
be able to

- Describe a comprehensive process for
  assessing arithmetic skills in the
  mainstream classroom
- Discuss important considerations when
  selecting arithmetic objectives for exceptional students
- Describe how features of effective instruction may be used when teaching
  mathematics to students with special
  needs
- Provide examples of how to present a
  mathematical concept at each level of
  representation: concrete, semiconcrete,
  and abstract
- Cite a variety of practice activities
  designed to promote mastery and
  maintenance of arithmetic concepts
  and skills by students with learning
  problems
- Devise a survival skills mathematics
  curriculum for secondary students experiencing learning problems

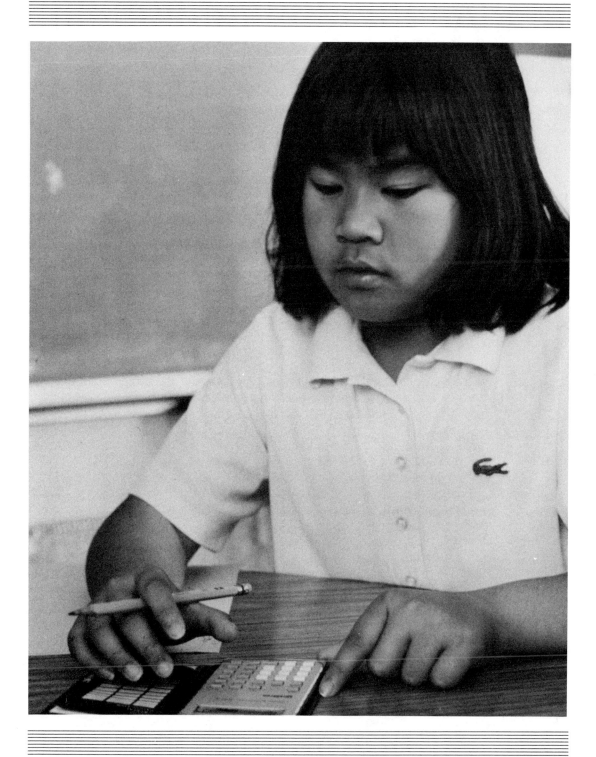

Arithmetic skills are vital for success in school and independent living. Learners with handicaps need success-oriented arithmetic instruction designed to remediate and accommodate their unique disabilities if they are to leave school with these indispensable skills. This chapter begins with a description of assessment tactics and instruments in arithmetic, as individualized instruction cannot begin without the proper assessment information. A discussion of arithmetic goals and objectives is followed by descriptions of approaches appropriate for arithmetic instruction in the mainstream classroom. For teachers of middle and high school students, a section dealing with survival skills in arithmetic is provided. A discussion of the use of microcomputers is also included. Specific adapted activities are presented for the major skill areas of counting, basic facts, language of mathematics, and algorithms. Finally, several different types of resources for the mainstream teacher are listed within the categories of commercially published tests, supplementary materials, microcomputer software, and professional organizations.

Assessing Arithmetic Skills

Individualized arithmetic instruction in the mainstream classroom begins with assessment of each student's arithmetic skills. Assessments done during the first few days of school provide the mainstream teacher with the information needed to plan and start individualized instruction in arithmetic. The mainstream teacher does not need to instruct each student individually, but students do need to be placed in groups with other students working at about the same level.

Individualized arithmetic programs that begin in September are still individualized in February only if the mainstream teacher continues to assess each student's progress throughout the curriculum. Just as learners begin at different levels, they progress at different rates, and they experience unique problems along the way. Frequent and continuous assessments allow the teacher to determine if students are working on appropriate skills and if they are succeeding. Decisions to move to a higher skill, change materials, alter a practice strategy, or reteach a skill are more likely to be successful if they are based on assessment data. The following sections contain an overall assessment strategy for the mainstream arithmetic class and information on test and assessment tactic selection.

Assessment Strategy for the Mainstream

The mainstream teacher needs an efficient assessment strategy that yields useful and timely information about students' arithmetic skills. The assessment

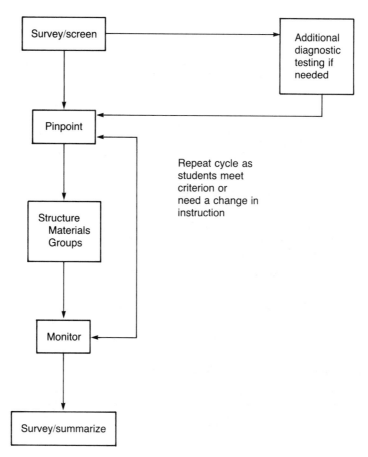

FIGURE 7.1

Assessment Strategy for Mainstream Arithmetic Instruction from Beginning to End of School Term or Year

strategy illustrated in Figure 7.1 begins on the first day of class or the first day with a new student. It provides the teacher and student with feedback throughout the school year, and results in data for progress reports at the end of a term or the school year.

The different assessments provide information that allows the teacher to:

1. Survey the class and screen for students experiencing difficulty.
2. Document referrals to diagnosticians for additional testing.
3. Place learners at a starting point on a skills hierarchy or within curricular materials.
4. Place learners in homogeneous groups for instruction.
5. Monitor progress.

6. Diagnose specific difficulties.
7. Summarize and report progress.

The assessment strategy for the mainstream includes several different types of tests and interviews, each with a different purpose.

Survey/Screen

The first step in the arithmetic assessment strategy, the *survey/screen assessment*, gives the mainstream teacher an overall picture of the levels at which students are presently performing. The previous year's achievement test results or curriculum-based records can help the teacher select the range of skills to be tested, but they do not indicate starting points for instruction. Amazing things can happen to arithmetic skills during the summer months, especially for handicapped learners. The survey test is usually a pencil and paper test based on a hierarchy, or sequential list, of arithmetic skills (Underhill, Uprichard, & Heddens, 1980). It may be either commercially prepared or teacher-made, and is usually administered to the entire class at the same time.

The survey/screen assessment also can help identify students at risk for difficulties in readiness, computation, or problem-solving skills. Some of the students in the class already may be identified as handicapped. However, if the mainstream teacher finds that one or more unidentified students scores well below his peers or well below his own ability level, then the teacher may want to refer the student(s) to a diagnostician for additional testing.

Pinpoint

Based on the results of the survey/screen assessment, the mainstream teacher then identifies specific instructional objectives for each student. These objectives are the lowest-level arithmetic skills not yet mastered (Resnick & Ford, 1981). This step, called the *pinpoint* step, may involve an analysis of the survey test or additional, more fine-tuned testing such as a unit pretest or a test restricted to a single arithmetic objective.

Whenever possible, the teacher also identifies factors that will promote more efficient learning. For example, a student may score 100% on a basic facts test but may be the last one in the class to finish because the student finger-counts to find the facts. This student would need instruction and practice designed to make calculating basic facts more automatic and thus more functional.

The pinpoint step recurs during the school year as students pass mastery tests and move on to new skills, or as students do not reach criteria and need a different approach or lower-level skill. Informal diagnostic interviews or tests can help the mainstream teacher pinpoint students' difficulties. Each instructional decision is based on data collected on the student's test performance.

Structure

The purposes of the *structure* step are to place students at appropriate points within curricular materials and to group students for instruction. Warning: there are no perfect matches between students and groups and time available. Given the single period typically devoted to arithmetic instruction, some compromises need to be made.

First, the teacher needs to decide how many different groups could be taught each day (Silbert, Carnine, & Stein, 1981), and then divide the students according to the results of survey/screen and pinpoint assessments. Teachers in the upper grades might choose not to meet with each group every day. The best compromise is usually to have two or three groups for teacher-directed instruction and to supplement this arrangement with individual practice, peer tutoring, and time for the teacher to circulate to assist individual students.

The structure step also recurs during the school year. Groups are not permanent, and a variety of instructional materials may be needed. The makeup of the groups and students' placements in curricular materials will change, depending on the students' performance.

Monitor

The mainstream teacher continuously *monitors* student progress throughout a unit of study (a single objective or a single unit or chapter in materials). Quick minitests, some only lasting one minute, can give the student and teacher frequent, even daily, feedback on learning. Posttests indicate whether the student is ready for the next skill or whether reteaching is required. The monitoring step is key to keeping instruction individualized and appropriate.

Handicapped learners are typically behind their peers in mathematics achievement. Frequent monitoring allows the teacher to detect problems before they become serious, or to move the student ahead the instant he or she is ready for a new skill. Performance charts or graphs give a quick, visual picture of progress on arithmetic skills on both an individual and group basis (see Figure 7.2). Monitoring can make instruction more efficient and can reinforce both the teacher and the student with a sense of progress and success.

The monitoring step is part of a cycle that is repeated many times during the school year. When monitoring indicates that the student has reached criteria, or has not reached criteria and needs different instruction or a lower level of skill, the cycle is repeated beginning at the pinpoint stage so to identify a new skill or unit of study.

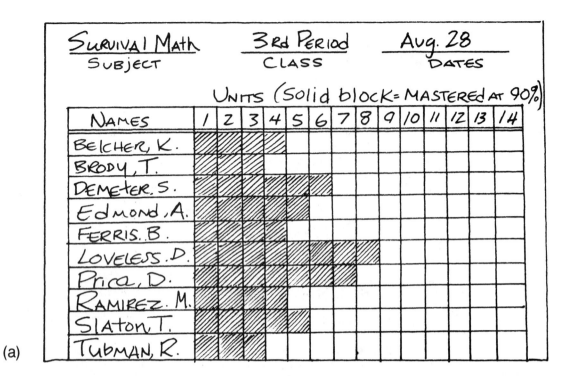

(a)

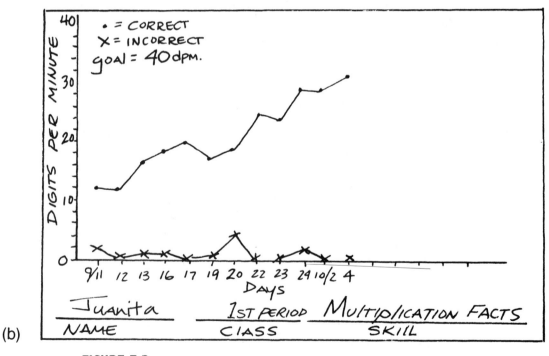

(b)

FIGURE 7.2
Sample Student Performance (a) Chart and (b) Graph Illustrating Progress in Mathematics Skills

Survey/Summarize

At the *survey/summarize* step, mainstream teachers need to assign grades and usually need to test for arithmetic achievement at the end of a school term or year. Much of the data collected during the monitoring stage can help with assigning grades, but the teacher may want to give a summary test that is an overview of all the skills taught to each group.

Many school districts and states assess students' arithmetic achievement or mastery of essential skills, typically at the end of the year. If the same test was used at the beginning of the term or year during the survey/screen stage, the teacher can estimate how much progress students made during the school term or year.

Test and Tactic Selection: The Right Assessment at the Right Time

Mathematics tests and assessment tactics give the teacher different types of information about students' skills. It is important to know what types of data are needed. For example, if the purpose of a test is to find out which students are achieving below grade level, then the test selected must give grade-level scores. However, if the purpose is to determine if students have mastered converting fractions to decimals, then a grade-level score is not appropriate. Norm-referenced, criterion-referenced, observational, and oral interview data are described below in the following sections. (Selected commercial mathematics tests are identified in the "Resources" section at the end of the chapter.) All four types of assessment data have their place within the strategy for individualizing for arithmetic. Assessment results indicate starting points and instructional objectives, as well as when a goal has been achieved.

Norm-Referenced Data

Norm-referenced data compare a student's test score to the scores of a group of peers either on the basis of age or grade-level placement. Standardized achievement tests usually give norm-referenced data in the forms of grade-level scores, percentile ranks, and so forth. The students taking the test are compared to a norm group, usually a large sample of students from different geographic areas. Norm-referenced tests would typically be used during the survey/screen and survey/summarize stages of assessment. They may also be one piece of information used by diagnosticians testing for eligibility for special education placement.

However, there are limitations to what may be learned from a norm-referenced test. Typically, achievement tests sample each arithmetic skill with few items, and scores reflect only one day's performance. There is also the question of how well the items on the achievement test match the mathematics curriculum studied during the year. Ashlock, Johnson, Wilson, and Jones (1983) point out that arithmetic skills are usually assessed only at the abstract, pencil-and-paper level of understanding, and that scores on subtests can be misleading unless the teacher knows what types of items were missed. Norm-referenced test results do not indicate exactly which skills are mastered unless the teacher looks at the individual test items.

Gregory's (1979) results indicate yet another problem involved in using standardized test data as the sole basis for instructional decisions. Gregory found that students' clerical errors on standardized test forms result in misleading scores. In this study, students who recorded answers to an arithmetic test on an answer sheet made a total of 1,255 errors, but the same students taking the same test and recording answers in the test booklet made only 66 errors—a dramatic difference. In view of this, students should be allowed to record answers on the test itself whenever possible.

Despite the shortcomings of standardized tests, the mainstream teacher can use norm-referenced data in several ways. The grade equivalents can give teachers and administrators a rough estimate of overall student progress from the beginning to the end of the school year. For students with below-average intellectual abilities, Reisman (1982) suggests calculating an "expected grade equivalent" (p. 46) that indicates what levels may reasonably be expected of students with lower IQ scores. For example, a sixth-grade student with an IQ of 85 is achieving as expected if the student's arithmetic grade level score is at 4.9 or above. This concept is helpful in reminding teachers that not all students performing below grade level are performing below potential. A norm-referenced test score is only one piece of the puzzle; by itself it is not a satisfactory indicator of ability, skill, or improvement.

Criterion-Referenced Data

Test information indicating performance on specific skills is *criterion-referenced data*. Students are not compared to other students; their performance is compared to a criterion, or goal, such as 80% accuracy, 40 correctly written digits per minute, or nine out of twelve items correct. However, if the grades on a test are curved, the data are no longer criterion-referenced in that the student is being compared to other students rather than a standard of performance.

Criterion in computation skills is commonly stated in terms of accuracy (85% correct), but fluency or speed is also an important aspect of performance. Smith (1981) emphasizes that speed is especially important in mastery of the basic facts in addition, subtraction, multiplication, and division. Fluency is measured by counting correct and incorrect movements per minute (White & Haring, 1980).

A number said aloud or a written digit is counted as a single movement. For example, the written numeral *39* is counted as two movements, the 3 and the 9. The criterion for mastery in written facts is in the range of forty to ninety digits per minute with two or fewer errors (Mercer, Mercer, & Evans, 1982). Fluency may be assessed with 1-minute timings. A sample procedure for administering timings to groups is outlined in Figure 7.3.

Preparation

The following procedures for administering a group timing may be used with a small group or an entire class. It is not necessary for all students to have the same worksheet or probe. Students may have individualized probes that contain written problems at their present skill level. Probes should have several more problems than the student will be able to complete in 1 minute.

Materials

Written probe for each student
Pencil for each student
Timing device (stopwatch or digital watch are best)
Answer key(s)
Colored correcting pens or pencils
Progress chart for each student

Procedures

1. Distribute written probes and be sure each student has a pencil.
2. Direct students to keep the probes turned face down until they are given the direction to begin.
3. Instruct students to work as quickly and accurately as possible for 1 minute. Students may skip an item if they do not know the answer (a skip is better than a wild guess).
4. Simultaneously begin the timing device and say, "Please begin."
5. Allow students to work undisturbed for 1 minute; then say, "Please stop."
6. Distribute correcting pens or pencils and direct students to put the pencils under their desks.
7. Make answer keys available. Either distribute a copy to each student, project it on a screen using an overhead projector, or display it on a blackboard that is covered by a screen or map during timing.
8. Allow students to self-correct probes, calculate the number of correct and incorrect digits, and enter their results on progress charts.
9. Recognize and praise students who improve over previous timing or reach a performance goal.

FIGURE 7.3
Suggested Procedures for Administering Group Timings to Assess Students' Fluency on Math Skills

One of the most popular commercially published criterion-referenced mathematics tests is the Key Math Diagnostic Arithmetic Test (which also gives grade-level scores). The test is administered individually, and most items are read to the student. Individual test items correspond to instructional objectives provided in the test manual. If the student misses a single item, the corresponding objective is assumed to be appropriate for instruction. The small sampling of each skill is a limitation of this test. In some sections of the test, missing one item can drop the student's score one grade level. Due to the limited sampling of items, the Key Math test is best used as a starting point for more in-depth diagnosis. Price (1984) compared the Key Math with the California Achievement Test (CAT) (Forms C and D), which also is a standardized test with behavioral objectives associated with each item. Price concludes that the CAT saves administration time because it may be given to groups, gives more complete diagnostic data, provides more test items per instructional objective, and is available in a wider range of skill levels.

Curriculum-based assessments such as the pre- and posttests available with many commercial mathematics materials are usually criterion-referenced tests. Teachers may also make criterion-referenced tests to assess specific skill areas and different levels of understanding such as concrete, semiconcrete, and abstract (Underhill et al., 1980). For example, the teacher may assess the concept of 6 at different levels by asking the student to put six pennies on the desk (concrete), draw six boxes (semiconcrete), and write the digit that represents a set of six blocks (abstract).

Criterion-referenced data may be used at every stage of the assessment strategy. If grade-level scores are not relevant, criterion tests may be given as part of the screen/survey to get an overall picture of the skills students have mastered. (A sample survey test that may be duplicated for noncommercial purposes is available in Silbert et al., 1981.) Smaller tests covering fewer items may be used to pinpoint, structure, and monitor. A mastery test covering all skills presented during the school year may be used for the survey/summarize stage.

Observational Data

Arithmetic is a process, sometimes a very complicated process. Simply judging that an answer to an exercise is right or wrong does not indicate why or how the learner arrived at the final answer. A great deal may be learned by observing how students approach computation or problem-solving. *Observational data* are obtained by analyzing work samples, watching students as they work exercises, and asking students to verbalize what they are doing during computation (Ashlock, 1986; Baroody, 1984; Pieper, 1983; Schoen, 1979; Skirtic, Kvam, & Beals, 1983). Random or careless mistakes do occur, but often students apply an incorrect procedure in a systematic and consistent way (Resnick & Ford,

1981). Reys (1975) emphasizes identifying systematic errors because such errors can be remediated.

Categories of errors are important to identify, as they indicate the type of corrective feedback the student needs. Roberts (1968) identified types of errors found in children's arithmetic work as (1) wrong operation, (2) obvious computational error, (3) defective algorithm, and (4) random response. For example, if a student's errors are primarily of the wrong operation type, the teacher may instruct the student first to circle the operation sign to cue the student before calculation is begun. Ashlock's book, *Error Patterns in Computation* (1982), is an excellent reference for examples of common error patterns and suggested remediation approaches. Figure 7.4 illustrates several examples of error analysis.

Oral Interview Data

The *oral interview* is a valuable diagnostic tool for the mainstream teacher. It may be a very quick assessment as the teacher is assisting a student. The teacher may simply say, "Tell me how you did that problem." The oral interview may also be done more systematically, with the teacher preparing two copies of a worksheet with six to eight problems (Pieper, 1983). The student works on one copy while the teacher records responses and observations on the other copy. The student is instructed to say aloud every step of the process. The teacher may ask for more information but is not to instruct or assist the student. The teacher looks for efficient and inefficient algorithms for computation. For example, the teacher may discover that the student understands the concept of multiplication but needs fluency training on the multiplication facts until they become automatic and more functional.

Oral interviews may also take place during a group lesson. Valuable diagnostic information may be gained by asking the right questions. McAloon (1979) offers the following guidelines.

1. Questions should require the student to give an explanation or a mathematical answer. Avoid questions that may be answered with a "yes" or "no."
2. Questions should help identify students' strengths and weaknesses. An example is, "Why do I need to use two steps to solve this word problem?"
3. Encourage students to ask questions of the teacher and of classmates.
4. Base further questioning on answers given by students.
5. Remember that listening is an important teaching behavior, and giving students information is only half of the process.

Observational data and oral interview data may be used at any point during the assessment strategy, but it is particularly important during the monitoring stage. Teachers need to look for incorrect algorithms or strategies and correct them as soon as possible.

Addition error pattern

$$
\begin{array}{r}
74 \\
+56 \\
\hline
1210
\end{array}
\qquad
\begin{array}{r}
67 \\
+18 \\
\hline
715
\end{array}
\qquad
\begin{array}{r}
56 \\
+97 \\
\hline
1413
\end{array}
\qquad
\begin{array}{r}
88 \\
+39 \\
\hline
1117
\end{array}
$$

This common error pattern indicates that the student does not understand the concept of place value. The sum of the ones and the sum of the tens are recorded separately. Concrete experiences with place value charts and sample 2-digit plus 2-digit addition problems are recommended.

Subtraction error pattern

$$
\begin{array}{r}
147 \\
-20 \\
\hline
120
\end{array}
\qquad
\begin{array}{r}
624 \\
-323 \\
\hline
301
\end{array}
\qquad
\begin{array}{r}
527 \\
-304 \\
\hline
203
\end{array}
\qquad
\begin{array}{r}
805 \\
-200 \\
\hline
600
\end{array}
$$

This student consistently writes zero as the difference for any subtraction fact involving a zero, even if the minuend is a number greater than zero. The basic subtraction facts involving zero need to be retaught. Concrete and semiconcrete experiences could illustrate the concept that any number minus zero is that number.

Multiplication error pattern

$$
\begin{array}{r}
\overset{2}{2}7 \\
\times 4 \\
\hline
88
\end{array}
\qquad
\begin{array}{r}
\overset{2}{1}8 \\
\times 3 \\
\hline
34
\end{array}
\qquad
\begin{array}{r}
\overset{1}{2}4 \\
\times 4 \\
\hline
86
\end{array}
\qquad
\begin{array}{r}
\overset{1}{3}5 \\
\times 3 \\
\hline
95
\end{array}
$$

In this error pattern the student records the number of tens to be added but does not actually add them after multiplying in the tens column. Recording the tens to be added below the bar in a small numeral and then writing the final answer for the tens column over that in a larger numeral may help the student remember to deal with the tens to be added.

Division error pattern

$$
\begin{array}{r}
37 \\
5\overline{)465} \\
45 \\
\hline
15 \\
15
\end{array}
\qquad
\begin{array}{r}
14 \\
4\overline{)164} \\
16 \\
\hline
4 \\
4
\end{array}
\qquad
\begin{array}{r}
67 \\
3\overline{)228} \\
21 \\
\hline
18 \\
18
\end{array}
$$

This student recorded answers in a way that would have been correct for the other three operations—from right to left. It must be made clear to the students that division is an exception: answers are recorded from left to right. An arrow pointing left to right written in colored pen above a sample division problem at the top of a worksheet can provide a visual reminder. Teaching students to estimate a quotient before dividing can help them check the reasonableness of their answers.

FIGURE 7.4

Examples of Arithmetic Error Patterns and Analysis. (Source: R. B. Ashlock [1986], *Error patterns in computation,* 4th ed. [Columbus, OH: Merrill]. Copyright © 1986 by Bell & Howell Co. Adapted by permission.)

Selection of Arithmetic
Goals and Objectives

Having a goal and knowing what objectives must be met to reach that goal can make management easier for the teacher and learning more meaningful for the student. Individualized instruction in arithmetic means careful selection of objectives. The goals and objectives selected for each student should represent the lowest relevant arithmetic skill not yet mastered. This section includes options for selection of arithmetic objectives and a discussion of the importance of mastery of objectives.

The ultimate goals of mathematics instruction for all students are application and problem solving, but problem solving can take place at many different levels. Some mainstreamed handicapped students achieve at or above grade level on mathematics skills, and those students should have little difficulty in moving through the regular curriculum with their nonhandicapped peers (Smith, 1981). However, many handicapped students do experience significant difficulties in arithmetic (McLeod & Armstrong, 1982), and for these students the goal of arithmetic instruction should be to develop those skills needed in typical employment, family, and community situations. Chandler (1978) estimates that only a fourth-grade skill level in arithmetic is required of adults in the typical employment situation; these skills typically include numeration, computation, measurement, and simple problem solving. (Later in the chapter we describe basic math survival skills in more detail.)

The mainstream teacher has several options for selecting arithmetic objectives. Regardless of the source, the goals and objectives selected for the mainstreamed student must match his or her skill level and be relevant to the student. Instructional time is precious. Careful selection of goals and objectives can mean that time spent in arithmetic class is providing mainstreamed students with the arithmetic skills they need for success in school and life after school.

Scope and Sequence Lists

A sequence of learning objectives is an important guide for the arithmetic teacher because simple concepts and operations are the tools for more complex computation and problem solving. Scope and sequence lists include the range of objectives within the mathematics curriculum (scope) ordered from simple to complex (sequence). For example, Resnick, Wang, and Kaplan (1973) note that learning numerals is easier once rote counting is fluent, and therefore rote counting should precede numeral recognition on a scope and sequence list.

Teachers using scope and sequence lists should consider them to be flexible. Not all scope and sequence lists are based on research involving how children best learn arithmetic; sometimes the lists are based on tradition (Thornton, Tucker, Dossey, & Bazik, 1983) or best guesses by authorities. Handicapped learners may need a single skill in a sequence broken down into several component skills (see Figure 7.5). Some skills may not be relevant for all students. For example, a mentally handicapped student should probably not spend time on a unit introducing the binary number system, as this will probably not be a functional skill for that student. Grade-level indications on scope and sequence lists are estimates, and it is more important to consider the skills that students can or cannot perform.

Scope and sequence lists can help the teacher identify prerequisites for a particular skill (those items listed before the target objective) and where to pro-

---

Terminal Objective

Given a calendar that only shows the number 1 in the first day of each month, the student writes in the correct days of the week, names of the months, and number of days with 90% accuracy.

Component Objectives

1. Given a calendar, the student points to the correct label when asked to identify the name of the month, the names of the days of the week, specific dates, and the year with 100% accuracy.
2. Given the direction, "Say the days of the week in order," the student states the correct sequence with 100% accuracy.
3. Given the direction, "Write the days of the week in order using the complete spelling," the student writes the days in correct sequence with accurate spelling with 100% accuracy.
4. Given a month's calendar containing all labels except the days of the week, the student writes the names of the days in the appropriate boxes with 100% accuracy.
5. Given the direction, "Say the months of the year in order," the student states the correct sequence with 100% accuracy.
6. Given the 12 months on calendar sheets in random order, the student arranges the sheets in correct sequence with 100% accuracy.
7. Given the direction, "Write the months of the year in order using correct spelling," the student writes the months in correct sequence with accurate spelling with 100% accuracy.
8. Given a year's calendar containing all labels except the months of the year, the student writes the names of the months in an appropriate place with 100% accuracy.
9. Given the name of each month, the student states how many days are in that month with 100% accuracy.
10. Given a year's calendar containing all labels except the numbers for each day of the month, the student writes in the appropriate numbers with 100% accuracy.

FIGURE 7.5
Sample Arithmetic Skill Sequence Including Component Skills

ceed after a skill is mastered (the next higher skill on the list). Lists of arithmetic objectives are often available from state or local education agencies, and may also be found within the teacher's guides that accompany instructional materials. Many textbooks for educators also provide arithmetic scope and sequence lists (Ashlock et al., 1983; Mercer & Mercer, 1985; Silbert et al., 1981; Thornton et al., 1983; Underhill et al., 1980).

Essential Skills Tests

Many states and school districts are requiring students, including mainstreamed handicapped students, to pass essential skills tests in order to progress to the next grade level or graduate from high school. The mainstream teacher should be aware of the content areas covered by the tests and the types of responses required. This does not mean that the instructor should "teach the test." It does mean that there should be a match between objectives selected for arithmetic instruction and arithmetic skills assessed by the essential skills test.

In addition to content objectives, essential skills tests may indicate the need for an objective related to test-taking skills. If possible, the mainstream teacher also should prepare students to produce the type of response required by the test. For example, answering an arithmetic problem in a multiple-choice format may be new to some students. Practice on teacher-made tests that require the same response format as the essential skills test may help handicapped students who often perform poorly in novel situations.

Mastery of Arithmetic Objectives

Teaching skills in mathematics is much like laying bricks for a wall. If the lower pieces—the objectives—are missing or weak, the whole structure may not be functional. Ashlock et al. (1983) describe learned disabilities in arithmetic that are the result of students not understanding concepts completely before being moved to drill activities or the next skill level. Management by objectives—breaking down topics into sequential behavioral objectives and requiring mastery at each level—has proven to be an effective instructional approach with mentally handicapped learners (Boehmer & Hofmeister, 1978). To reach the goal of application and problem solving, learners must first master the components of the larger skill—understanding, accuracy, and speed. Only then can students apply the process to more difficult tasks and procedures.

Time allowed to reach objectives is an important instructional variable for many mainstreamed students. Handicapped learners are likely to need additional time to master objectives (Callahan & Robinson, 1973; Garnett & Fleischner, 1983). This reinforces the importance of the monitoring stage in the assessment strategy; that is, only by continuous and frequent monitoring of students' performances can the teacher determine when learners have mastered a skill.

Criteria for mastery should be high enough to make the arithmetic skill functional for the learner. For example, requiring 80% mastery on basic subtraction facts could mean that the student has not learned twenty different subtraction facts. This could result in serious difficulties when the student is expected to use basic facts in more complex calculations. It is not unreasonable to expect 100% accuracy in basic facts. And accuracy is only one part of mastery. Students should be able to explain what they are doing in any operation or calculation (understanding) and perform the work quickly (fluency). The time spent in reaching mastery can result in precise and confident performances on higher level computation and problem-solving skills.

Instructional Approaches

A few basic teaching practices can make mainstream instruction productive and enjoyable for both teachers and students. Students with learning problems do best if their teachers (1) provide direct instruction, (2) are in control of the arithmetic lessons, (3) are aware of each student's skill level, and (4) require students to master arithmetic skills before moving ahead in the curriculum (Fleischner & Hathaway, 1984). Certainly all students need to know they can learn—success experiences are key to keeping students interested and involved in mathematics. Teachers who set reasonable goals, break down complex skills into achievable subskills, and provide intense instruction can convince each learner that they can "do math."

Selection of materials is an important factor in successful arithmetic instruction. The basal series can be a starting point, but many times handicapped learners need additional practice activities and adapted materials. McLeod and Armstrong (1982) surveyed teachers working with students with learning problems and found the consensus among them to be that basal arithmetic texts typically do not provide enough practice exercises to establish mastery. (See the "Resources" section for a list of selected arithmetic materials.) Chandler (1970) offers the following guidelines in teaching arithmetic to learners with special needs.

1. Provide for physical activity (in addition to pencil-and-paper tasks).
2. Keep each learner involved in the learning process.
3. Promote success with small instructional steps and simple tasks.
4. Make the task meaningful by drawing from situations familiar to the student.
5. Present novel activities and avoid uninteresting presentations and monotonous drill.

The remainder of this section provides more detail on instructional approaches, including instruction according to levels of representation, cognitive strategies, and techniques for teaching word problems. Since practice is so important for mainstreamed students, several different practice strategies are described.

Levels of Representation

When students see the digit *8* written on a piece of paper, the symbol itself gives no clues as to its meaning. It is only through experiences in counting objects, seeing pictures of sets of 8, and using the digit *8* in calculations that students learn the meaning of the symbol. Drill and rote memorization cannot teach students the meaning of numbers and their relationships; systematic presentations of number concepts at the concrete, semiconcrete, and abstract levels can promote mathematical understanding rather than rote performance (Underhill, 1981). When students understand the meaning of numbers, operations, and algorithms, then they have the skills needed to solve application problems in school and in everyday life.

The Concrete Level.   Prior to pencil-and-paper activities, teachers should model math concepts and students should use concrete materials, or manipulatives, to illustrate concepts (Dunlap & Brennan, 1979; Skirtic et al., 1983; Underhill et al., 1980). This step is especially important for students with learning problems, as abstract thinking is frequently a weakness for such students. Skirtic et al. (1983) found that 92% of the learning disabled adolescents tested were still functioning at the concrete stage of mathematical operations. Concrete materials also are an efficient way to demonstrate arithmetic concepts for visually impaired and hearing impaired students.

In a summary of the literature on manipulatives, Dunlap and Brennan (1979) offer guidelines for using concrete materials with students experiencing learning problems. First, the manipulatives must accurately represent the mathematical concept or process. One excellent example of this is the Add Card Math Strategy (Creekmore & Creekmore, 1983) illustrated in Figure 7.6. As much as possible, the arrangement of the concrete objects should closely resemble the way written digits represent the operation or calculation. The teacher should demonstrate the arrangement of the manipulatives, but each student should have direct experience moving the objects or device. The purpose of manipulatives is not fulfilled if students are passive observers in the lesson.

Dunlap and Brennan (1979) also recommend that more than one manipulative aid be used to promote generalization and flexibility. For example, learners should not learn that addition only applies to a particular set of red blocks. Kevra, Brey, and Schimmel (1972) recommend making a kit of manipulatives for each learner that contains a variety of common objects such as buttons, stones, beans, paper clips, and the like. Similarly, fractions may be taught using various parts of regions (i.e., circles, squares, and so on) and parts of sets of objects (e.g., two-thirds of a set of six bottle caps is four bottle caps).

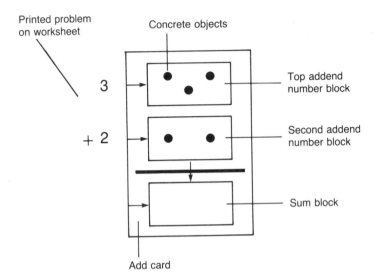

Steps for the Add Card Math Strategy

1. Place the add card so that the arrows line up with the printed problem.
2. The student says the top number (addend), selects the proper number of counting objects, and places the objects in the top block.
3. Repeat the above step for the second addend.
4. Move the objects from both number blocks down to the sum block below the line.
5. Count the objects in the sum block and write the digit on the worksheet.
6. Check the answer by counting again.

FIGURE 7.6
The Add Card Math Strategy, Instruction at the Concrete Level of Representation. (Source: W. N. Creekmore & N. N. Creekmore [1983], Math strategy for MH children, *Academic Therapy, 19*(1), p. 69. Reprinted by permission.)

In addition to the guidelines already mentioned, teachers should consider students' age level and fine motor skills when selecting manipulatives. Young students or physically handicapped students may have difficulty picking up and moving very small or flat objects. Older students may be offended if the objects appear babyish. Instead of using 1-inch cubes, older students may be more willing to work with coins, paperclips, or peanuts (especially if they get to eat them when the lesson is completed).

The Semiconcrete Level.   Learning at the semiconcrete level is defined as a visual experience (Underhill, 1981). This includes looking at illustrations that appear on a worksheet, in a textbook, or on a computer monitor. Illustrations may be pictures of objects (e.g., a line drawing of three ducks) or graphic representations (e.g., a four-by-five array of hash marks that illustrates the multiplication fact 4 × 5). Watching a demonstration with manipulatives and viewing a film also are semiconcrete experiences because the learner is not directly handling the objects. Kevra et al. (1972), suggest arranging manipulatives on the stage of an overhead projector to provide a large group with a semiconcrete demonstration. Figure 7.7 illustrates using a felt board to demonstrate subtraction basic facts at the semiconcrete level.

The Abstract Level.   At the abstract level of mathematics, learners use written digits and symbols or spoken and written words. One goal of instruction at the abstract level is to relate the concrete and semiconcrete experiences to the abstract symbols or words. When instruction at the abstract level is preceded by concrete and semiconcrete experiences, learners are more likely to understand the mathematical concept behind the numbers (Underhill et al., 1980). This background is key to the ability to apply basic facts and operations in ap-

A flannel board may be used to demonstrate basic subtraction facts at a semiconcrete level of representation. Sadowski (1982) recommends using felt pieces with a contrasting color on each side. To illustrate the subtraction fact, first place pieces (all one color) in a line to represent the minuend, or top number in the fact.

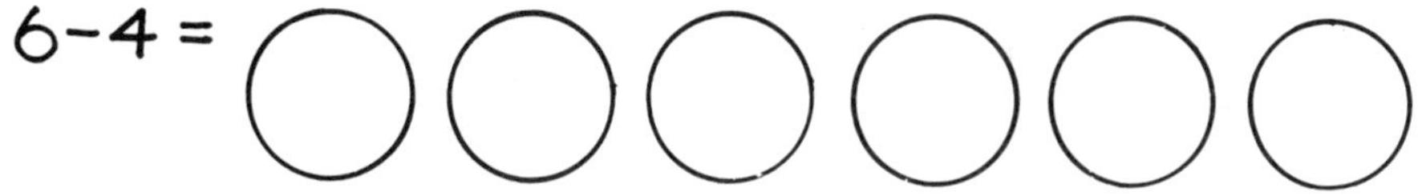

Next, turn over the number of pieces that represent the subtrahend, or second number in the subtraction fact.

The last step is to count the pieces remaining in the original color.

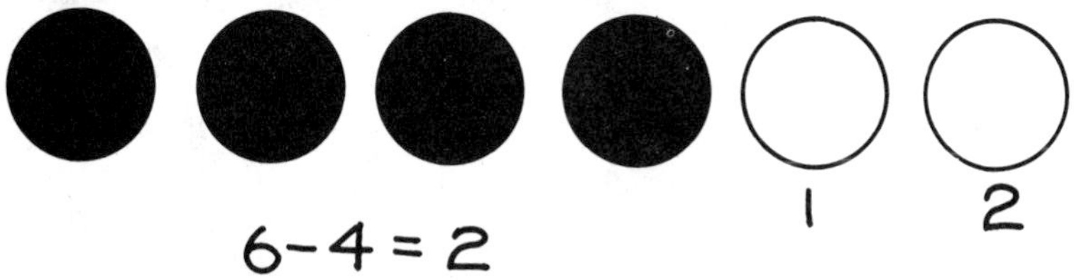

FIGURE 7.7
Using a Felt Board to Illustrate Basic Subtraction Facts at the Semiconcrete Level of Representation

plications and problem solving. When learners are capable of learning at the abstract level, they are ready for drill activities that focus on accuracy and fluency. If drill activities are introduced before mathematical understanding is established, learners may be frustrated and unable to apply the skill in a meaningful way (Ashlock et al., 1983; Cawley, 1970; Dunlap & Brennan, 1979).

Transitions Among the Levels of Representation

For arithmetic lessons at the three levels of representation, mastery is again a key concept in successful instruction. Learners should demonstrate understanding at the concrete level before lessons involving the same skill proceed to the semiconcrete; in turn, semiconcrete representations must be understood before work is begun at the abstract level (Underhill et al., 1980). Dunlap and Brennan (1979) suggest that one way to check for mastery at the concrete and semiconcrete levels is to present the student with a written number sentence (abstract) and to ask the learner to describe the process using objects (concrete) or illustrations (semiconcrete). Next, manipulatives or illustrations are presented that describe a process and ask the learner to write the correct number sentence. When the learner can work in both directions, he or she is ready for work at the next level. This sequence—concrete, semiconcrete, abstract—is repeated for each new arithmetic skill. Pretesting can determine if students need direct and intense instruction at any of the three levels. A suggested remediation technique is to use the previous level for explaining concepts or procedures to learners who are experiencing difficulty.

Cognitive Strategies

A growing number of theorists and researchers are advocating the use of cognitive strategies in mathematics instruction (Cawley, 1985; Dunlap & McKnight, 1980; Resnick & Ford, 1981). According to Resnick and Ford (1981), "strategies organize the thinking process and call upon various components of knowledge to put together a plan of action capable of solving the task at hand" (p. 214). Left without direct instruction in successful and efficient strategies, students will frequently develop their own strategies for problem solving, which may or may not result in correct answers. Students with learning problems can benefit from instruction and practice dealing with problem-solving strategies.

Strategies may be simple. For example, using the phrase "Does McDonald's sell burgers?" to remember the mnemonic "D.M.S.B." can help students execute the correct series of steps in long division—divide, multiply, subtract, bring-down the next number. Mosconi (1984) successfully used self-instruction strategy training to teach a learning handicapped student subtraction with regrouping—a skill that had previously frustrated the student. Baroody (1984) recommends teaching the missing addend strategy for subtraction basic facts, in which the student starts with the subtrahend and counts up to the minuend. Another subtraction strategy developed by a special education teacher (see Figure 7.8) uses visual cues initially and later encourages students to use the strategy without drawing the picture (Weill, 1978).

Formal research in cognitive strategies in mathematics is relatively new, although people have probably used strategies (efficiently and inefficiently) since the beginning of the history of numbers. There is evidence that one difference between successful learners and learning disabled students is the ability to devise strategies. Mainstream teachers should be aware of this emerging instructional technique, and should be alert to materials and techniques that emphasize strategy instruction.

Teaching Word Problems

Word problems are intended to stimulate real-life applications of arithmetic skills. They are an extremely important part of the mathematics curriculum, but they offer a variety of difficulties for special needs learners. Moses (1982) identifies three levels of barriers to solving word problems. The first level involves interest and motivation; students, especially many handicapped students, are more likely to work to solve a problem if it appears relevant and realistic to them. The second level of potential barriers are basic skills, which includes not only computation but also reading, language, and the ability to use formulas. Cognitive skills are the third level of barriers for problem solving. Solving word problems requires devising appropriate plans, visualizing the solution process, flexibility in thinking, ignoring irrelevant information, and many other cognitive skills—all of which are potential difficulties for many handicapped learners.

Mainstreamed students can learn to solve word problems, but lessons must be carefully planned and problem-solving must be recognized as the desired end result of all other arithmetic instruction. Following are several suggestions for word problem instruction that can lead to a successful experience for both teachers and students.

Selection of Word Problems.   Not all word problems are created equal, and simply because a word problem appears at the end of a unit is no assurance that it is appropriate for students who have completed that same unit. Teachers need to be aware of the characteristics of word problems and to work toward achieving the best possible match between types of problems and students' skills. Reading level is a key factor. Problems need to be written at students' independent reading level, or some type of adaptation must be made. Story problems may be tape-recorded, or handicapped learners may be paired with a peer who is able to accurately read the written problem. Formats for word prob-

"Mrs. Weill's Hill" is designed to help students by providing a visual cue for calculating the answers to subtraction problems with minuends from 11 to 18.

First, students are taught to put the numbers from a subtraction problem on a hill with the minuend at the top and the subtrahend at the bottom.

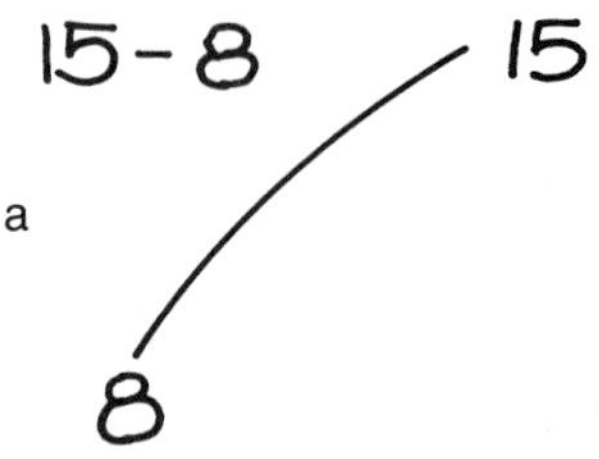

$$15-8$$

Next students write a "10" in the middle of the hill under the line.

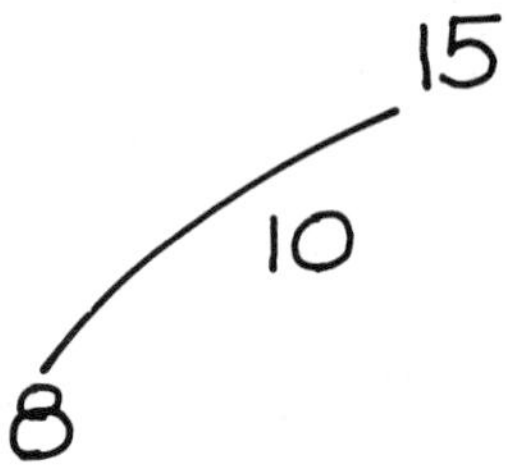

Above the hill on the lower portion, students write how many steps from the subtrahend to 10.

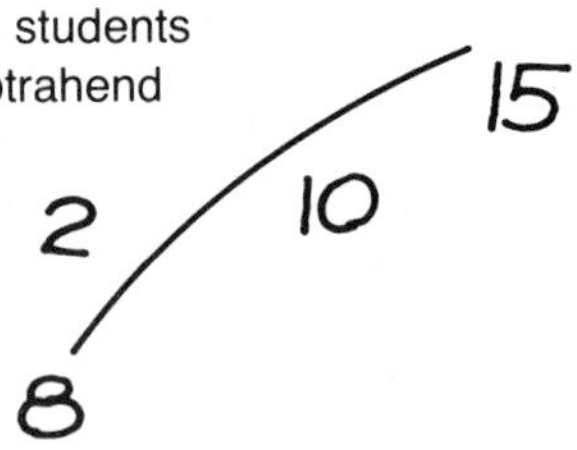

Above the hill on the upper portion, students write how many steps from 10 to the minuend.

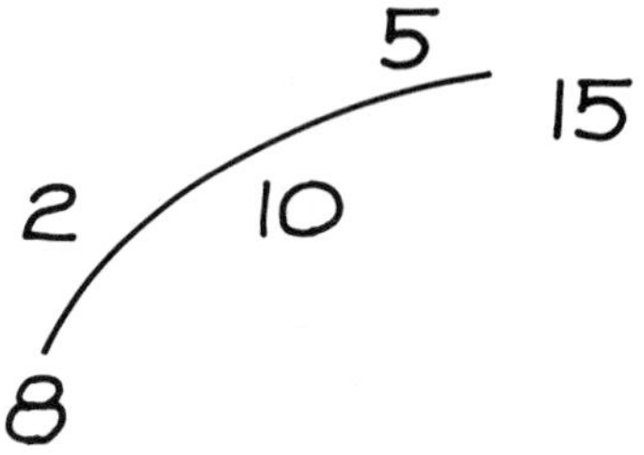

Students add the steps noted above the line (a simple addition fact) to get the answer.

$$2+5=7, \quad 15-8=7$$

The last step is to encourage students to visualize, or make a mental picture of, the hill without actually drawing it.

FIGURE 7.8

Strategy for Computing Subtraction Facts with Minuends 11–18 (Source: B. F. Weill [1978]. Mrs. Weill's hill: A successful subtraction method for use with the learning disabled child *Arithmetic Teacher, 26(2),* pp. 34–35. Adapted by permission.)

lems vary; they may require more than one operation or contain irrelevant information as distractors. Table 7.1 lists types of word problems for addition according to degree of difficulty. Blankenship and Lovitt (1976) recommend systematic instruction for the different types of story problems: (1) identify the specific type of problem to teach, (2) select appropriate examples, and (3) teach to mastery before beginning instruction on a different type of word problem.

Word problems are an ideal opportunity to illustrate to students that mathematics is functional for them in their lives outside of school. Story problems that describe situations to which students can relate are likely to be more motivating. For younger students such situations might include television programs, pets, spending money, and sports (Moses, 1982). For older students scenarios could include cooking, caring for a car, shopping, banking, calculating sports statistics, and realistic job situations. Some students may enjoy describing their own situations. For example, teachers could give students incomplete problems such as, "Trent wanted to buy his _____ a _____ that originally cost $_____ and is on sale for 25% off. How much will he pay including 5% tax?" In this format the teacher controls the level of difficulty, but the student controls the subject matter.

Promote Careful Reading.   Many students make mistakes in solving word problems not because of a computational error but because of a reading error. Just telling students to read carefully does not give them any idea as to *how* to do so. Blankenship and Lovitt (1976) used a series of techniques to promote more careful reading of word problems and improve students' accuracy in solving problems. If students did not meet criterion in pretesting, students were required to read each problem orally before writing an answer. If that answer was not correct, students were to make a written copy of each incorrect problem. Both techniques required students to attend more carefully to the word problem.

Frequently, word problems presented in a practice exercise all require the same operation. This arrangement does not promote careful reading because pupils quickly learn that once the first problem is solved, all others use the same operation. Presenting a series of problems that require two or more operations can require the students to analyze carefully each problem (Carpenter, Corbitt, Kepner, Lindquist, & Reys, 1980).

Blankenship and Lovitt (1976) found that, in problems containing extraneous information, students frequently use the first two numbers found in the problems even if one of the numbers is irrelevant information. If teachers notice this error pattern, it may be helpful to instruct students to locate the irrelevant information, cross it out, and underline the data required to solve the problem (Hoy, 1984; Moses, 1982).

Concrete and Semiconcrete Representations.   Just as arranging objects and drawing pictures can help students learn basic mathematical concepts, concrete and semiconcrete representations can be valuable aids in solving word problems.

TABLE 7.1
Sample Addition Problems for Each Class of Story Problems

Class Number	Description	Example
1	Constant noun *apple*	John had 2 *apples*. Tom gave him 4 *apples*. How many *apples* did John have then?
2	Twenty-five different nouns	John had 2 *zebras*. Tom gave him 4 *zebras*. How many *zebras* did John have then?
3	Introductory sentence	*John worked at the zoo.* John had 2 zebras. Tom gave him 4 zebras. How many zebras did John have then?
4	Extraneous information in only the fourth sentence	John worked at the zoo. John had 2 zebras. Tom gave him 4 zebras. *John had 3 pencils.* How many zebras did John have then?
5	Extraneous information in either the second, third, or fourth sentence	John worked at the zoo. John had 2 zebras. *John had 3 pencils.* Tom gave him 4 zebras. How many zebras did John have then?
6	Pronoun *he* for John	John worked at the zoo. *He* had 2 zebras. *He* had 3 pencils. Tom gave him 4 zebras. How many zebras did *he* have then?
7	Several names	*Sam* worked at the zoo. Sam had 2 zebras. *David* gave him 4 zebras. How many zebras did *Sam* have then?
8	Constant question sentences	Sam worked at the zoo. Sam had 2 zebras. David gave him 4 zebras. How many zebras did Sam *have*?
9	Passive verb tense	Sam worked at the zoo. Sam had 2 zebras. *He was given* 4 zebras. How many zebras did Sam have?
10	Blank in question sentence	Sam worked at the zoo. Sam had 2 zebras. He was given 4 zebras. Sam then had _____ zebras.
11	Mode of numeral	Sam worked at the zoo. Sam had *two* zebras. He was given 4 zebras. Sam then had _____ zebras.
12	Five different verbs	Sam worked at the zoo. Sam had two zebras. *Then he purchased* 4 zebras. Sam then had _____ zebras.

Source: C. S. Blankenship & T. C. Lovitt (1976), Story problems: Merely confusing or downright befuddling? *Journal for Research in Mathematics Education*, 7(5), p. 293. Used by permission.

Several reseachers have found that use of pictorial aids improves handicapped students' accuracy in solving word problems (Blankenship & Black, 1985; Goodstein, Bessant, Thibodeau, Vitello, & Viahakos, 1972).

Strategies for Solving Word Problems.   To avoid a haphazard or inaccurate approach to solving word problems, mainstreamed students may benefit from direct instruction in a strategy to solve word problems. Teachers should first model the strategy, clearly identifying each step as it is performed. Next, students should imitate the teacher's model on the same problem and then practice applying it to a similar problem using different numbers. The teacher should be ready to give immediate reinforcement or corrective feedback. Finally, students should have the opportunity to practice the strategies independently. A sample strategy includes the following steps.

1. Read the problem silently and then read it aloud.
2. Cross out any information you do not need.
3. Circle the numbers you will need to solve the problem.
4. Draw a picture that shows what the problem is about.
5. Decide how many steps are needed to find the answer.
6. Decide if you need to add, subtract, multiply, and/or divide.
7. Write the number sentence(s).
8. Solve the number sentence(s).
9. Decide if the answer is reasonable.
10. Label your answer.

This strategy or any other strategy could be displayed on a large poster within clear view during the arithmetic period. Students may also make their own copies of the strategy outline to keep at their desks or to use when completing homework assignments. After students use the strategy following a written list of steps, they should practice saying the steps of the strategy from memory. When grading word problems, giving partial credit for each step of the strategy that is demonstrated can encourage students to apply the strategy during independent practice or on tests.

Practice Procedures

Exceptional students often require exceptional amounts of practice before skills are learned and retained across time. Research has established the value of both mastery of concept and adequate practice in promoting student achievement (Silbert et al., 1981). Students are assigned practice activities for several different purposes: to become accurate in applying arithmetic skills, to become fluent in using these skills, and to review previously learned arithmetic skills periodically.

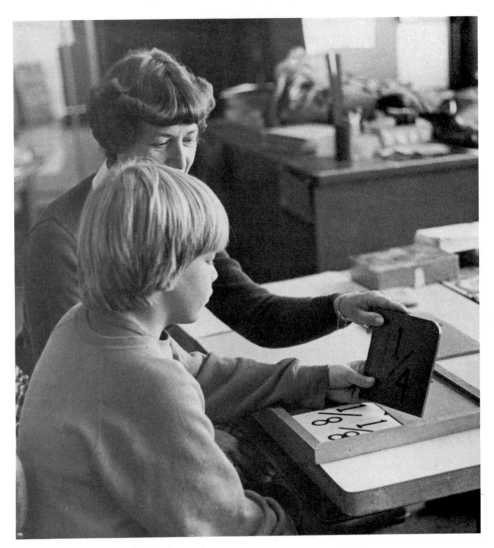

Practice must be carefully planned.

Practice must be carefully planned—both the timing and the format of practice activities are important. According to Ashlock et al. (1983), "mathematical ideas must be understood before we attempt to fix and maintain those concepts through controlled practice" (p. 18). Practice activities should be assigned after the student is fairly accurate in applying an arithmetic concept or skill. It is not appropriate to require learners to practice skills independently that are at the acquisition stage of learning (i.e., when performances are relatively slow and not yet accurate). Learners who are still at acquisition need teacher-controlled lessons and closely supervised practice trials; independent practice at this point could lead to frustration or repetitions of incorrect procedures. The following practice procedures and guidelines can help the mainstream teacher design productive, individualized practice activities.

The Importance of Variety

Students with learning problems sometimes groan at the mere sight of a deck of arithmetic flashcards. No wonder, for many students have been overexposed to the traditional flashcard drill, and the result is probably not improved retention but decreased motivation. As Chandler (1970) aptly states, "A change is as good as rest" (p. 197). Variety is an important factor in any individualized arithmetic program. Fuson and Brinko (1985) compared use of flash cards and microcomputers to present similar drill on basic arithmetic facts. They found that for both types of practice, students tended to improve significantly immediately after conditions were switched, making a strong case for the power of novel practice activities.

Since students with learning problems require large amounts of practice, a variety of practice formats may be needed for a single arithmetic skill. One way to accomplish this is to make several different practice activities for the same skill available to students and allow them to choose among options. Older students especially appreciate the element of choice, and students are likely to self-select the activity that they are most motivated to complete.

The principle of variety should be kept in mind when reading the following sections dealing with practice. All of the procedures have been found to be successful, but none of them will work all of the time for all students.

Peer Tutoring

A valuable instructional resource found in every mainstream classroom is the students themselves. A series of investigations has found that handicapped and nonhandicapped peers ranging from third graders through high school students have successfully tutored students with learning difficulties (Bullard & McGee, 1983; Lancioni, 1982; Roach, Paolucci-Whitcomb, Meyers, & Duncan, 1983). Tutors need to be trained in presentation techniques, positive reinforcement, and simple correction procedures. Bullard and McGee (1983) called their tutors the "Super Tutor Crew" and gave them printed sheets outlining the necessary materials and the steps of the practice activity. The privilege to serve as an arithmetic tutor may be used as a reward for mastering a specific arithmetic skill. The peer-tutoring format can provide valuable review for the tutor as well as an enjoyable practice activity for the tutee.

Instructional Arithmetic Games

There is virtually an endless variety of teacher-made and commercial arithmetic games available at all skill levels. The same format may be used for different concepts and different game formats may be used for the same concept. Instructional games can look like fun and still provide serious drill and practice. Ashlock et al. (1983) offer some guidelines for arithmetic games: (1) items should appear in random order, (2) students should receive immediate feedback after making a response, (3) a time limit should be set for making a response, and (4) errors should be penalized only by lack of progress, not by losing points or position.

Instructional arithmetic games have been found to be an effective alternative to more traditional worksheets and drill activities. Beattie and Algozzine (1982) have reported that educable mentally retarded students who practiced arithmetic skills using instructional games performed significantly better on a teacher-made test, received higher grades, and were on-task appproximately 20% more than peers who received comparable drill presented via worksheets. One student who practiced arithmetic skills using games was heard to say, "It sure beats doing math" (p. 258).

Self-Correcting Materials

During independent practice it is not possible for the mainstream teacher to monitor each student closely. Students working independently can still receive immediate feedback as to the correctness of a response by using self-correcting materials (Mercer, Mercer, & Bott, 1984). These materials make mistakes private events, a feature that is important to many students with learning problems. They also can prevent every arithmetic teacher's nightmare: the student who practices over and over again 7 + 8 = 14. Self-correcting materials are available commercially or may be teacher-made. Perhaps the most common self-correcting arithmetic material is the flashcard with the basic fact on the front and the answer on the back. Mercer et al. suggest twelve different formats for self-correction: answer on the back, matching, puzzles, holes, packets, strips in a folder, colored acetate, stylus, cassette recordings, light, flap, and windows. An example of a self-correcting material is illustrated in Figure 7.9.

As with any other practice procedure, teachers must carefully plan when and how to use self-correcting materials. It is not appropriate to expect a self-correcting material to teach a skill; these materials are best used for practice and review. Also, students must understand that the only thing that "counts" is how they perform on a mastery test, not how well they do on a self-corrected practice activity. This one provision has been successful in preventing students from cheating, as they quickly come to understand that looking at an answer before making a response does not help when it comes time for the mastery test.

Windows: Money

Pinpoint

See pictures of coins and amounts in numbers—match equivalents

Aim

To complete the puzzle successfully by matching coins and amounts

Feedback Device

When the puzzle is completed correctly and viewed through the window, a message appears.

Materials

6" x 8" piece of poster board cut into puzzle pieces showing coins and amounts in numbers

Piece of cardboard or a box with a 7" x 10" opening cut in it

8½" x 11" piece of acetate covering the 7" x 10" opening in the box

Envelope to hold the puzzle pieces

Directions to the Learner

[Write on the envelope]
1 Sort all the pieces so the numbers face up.
2 Match the coins to the same amount in numbers.
3 Make the puzzle on top of the window in the box.
4 When you have finished, lift the box and look in the window. If the secret message appears, you completed the puzzle correctly.

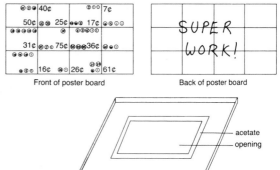

FIGURE 7.9

Self-Correcting Math Material (Source: C. D. Mercer, A. R. Mercer, and D. A. Bott [1984], *Self-correcting learning materials for the classroom* [Columbus, OH: Merrill], p. 59. Copyright © 1984 by Bell & Howell Co. Reprinted by permission.)

Fluency Practice

After students have learned the meaning of the operation and can perform the computation fairly accurately, it is appropriate to introduce practice in making responses quickly, called *fluency practice*. The difference between a student who can write the answers to subtraction basic facts at forty digits per minute and the student who finger counts and can write only twelve digits per minute is often the difference between a skill level that is functional and a skill level that hinders the student's future progress in arithmetic.

Certainly, some physical disabilities such as cerebral palsy prevent quick physical movement, but most handicapped students can learn to perform arithmetic operation fluently. There is evidence that learning disabled students are less able than their nonhandicapped peers to recall basic facts automatically (Garnett & Fleischner, 1983), but given intense and appropriate instruction, students with learning problems can perform arithmetic facts as accurately and quickly as their age-mates (Bullard & McGee, 1983).

One format for fluency practice appropriate for the mainstream classroom is Coble's (1982) "beat your record" technique. Students rotate to an arithmetic station where they take timed tests of 1 or 2 minutes each. Time is kept using an egg timer or a cassette tape on which tones are recorded at 1-minute intervals. Students correct their own work from answer keys and calculate the number of correct digits per minute. (It is important to count digits rather than answers, as the answer "36" takes longer to write than the answer "8.") Students record their rate on a chart and receive a reinforcer if they were able to beat their own score. The reinforcement may be in the form of a certificate, a sticker, or the student's name posted on a list of winners. Students are allowed to take a second test if they did not beat their previous score and would like to try again.

Hasselbring, Goin, and Bransford (1987) offer some guidelines based on their research dealing with fluency practice. First, it may be helpful to begin with facts that are already fairly automatic for the student and then gradually introduce more difficult facts. Facts should be presented in small sets—two or three facts and their reciprocals—and the facts should be practiced until the student responds without hesitation or finger counting. Hasselbring et al. also suggest the use of a challenge time, a limit on the latency period between when the student sees the fact and when he or she answers. The suggestion is to begin with a challenge time of approximately 3 seconds and work down to a challenge time of 1 second or less. This type of fluency practice may be effectively delivered by computer-assisted drill and practice programs.

Learning Modalities

During a typical arithmetic lesson, students may be presented arithmetic problems both verbally (e.g., "What is the answer to 39 minus 17?") and visually (e.g., the teacher writes 39 − 17 on the blackboard). Students are also expected to respond in a variety of ways, by saying the answer, writing the answer, moving blocks to represent the answer, drawing a picture to illustrate the answer, or entering the answer on a computer keyboard. There is some evidence that students experiencing difficulty in arithmetic respond to certain input-output modality pairings differently than their arithmetic-proficient peers (Webster, 1980). There is not yet any reliable diagnostic test that can tell teachers the modality strengths and weaknesses of their arithmetic students, but teachers can make practice activities more effective if the factor of modality is taken into consideration. Two concepts should be kept in mind: (1) multisensory experiences can improve arithmetic performances and (2) practice activities should at minimum incorporate the same input-output pairs used to test mastery.

Multisensory experiences are activities or tactics that incorporate more than one modality. For example, Lovitt and Curtiss (1968) have found that requiring students with behavior disorders to look at a printed problem, say the problem aloud, and then write the answer can improve their performance. Saying the problem aloud possibly causes the student to be more deliberate. Verbalizing the problem results in better accuracy than when the student simply looks at the problem and writes an answer.

There is also evidence to support the concept that students should receive practice involving modality pairs that match those used to test mastery. Bott (1983) has examined the arithmetic performances of students with learning problems across six different input-output modality pairs—see-say, see-write, see-touch a key on a keyboard, hear-say, hear-write, and hear-touch a key on a keyboard. Given intense and direct instruction, the students learned to perform in the different modality pairs. But the learning frequently did not generalize to performing the same arithmetic facts in a different modality pair. This has implications for the typical flashcard drill (see-say) used to prepare students for the typical achievement test (see-write). It is possible that some handicapped students are less flexible in performing arithmetic calculations across different input-output pairs than are their nonhandicapped peers. All arithmetic practice need not be restricted to see-write because of achievement tests, but practice does need to incorporate directly those formats required for students to demonstrate achievement.

What You Can Do

- Provide direct instruction to students.
- Set reasonable goals, break complex skills down into achievable subskills, and provide intense instruction.
- Promote success.
- Provide word problems that simulate real-life applications of arithmetic skills.
- Promote arithmetic survival skills specifically at the secondary level.

Arithmetic Survival Skills

For many handicapped students, middle school and high school mathematics classes represent their last formal instruction in arithmetic. These students will go on to take jobs and become homeowners, consumers, and taxpayers. All of these roles require the application of arithmetic skills. These are not always high-level skills, but they are certainly important arithmetic skills if the handicapped individuals are going to function as independent adults. For many handicapped students in secondary mainstream classes, arithmetic survival skills are an appropriate and vital curriculum (Cawley, Fitzmaurice, Shaw, Kahn, & Bates, 1979; Chandler, 1978; McLeod & Armstrong, 1982; Schwartz & Budd, 1983).

Arithmetic survival skills may be defined as those math skills required to carry out everyday functions at home, at work, and in the marketplace. The Charles County Board of Education (1981) in Maryland published a list of curricular objectives thought to be arithmetic competencies required for independent living. Skill areas include money, making change, paychecks, budgeting, banking services, savings accounts, loans, credit, comparative shopping, taxes, time, linear measurement, liquid and dry measurement, measuring temperature, measurement devices for operation of a vehicle (gas pumps, pressure gauges, odometers, and so on), graphs and charts, and determining clothing sizes. Handling money is probably the most important survival skill in arithmetic. Halpern (1981) estimates that 83% of the arithmetic used by adults is concerned with buying and selling, and another 11% deals with other aspects of finances. Halpern maintains that arithmetic instruction should emphasize those skills students will need as adults. Pike (1985) describes a year-long classroom simulation of checking accounts in which she uses checkbooks, check registers, and deposit slips without account numbers donated by a local bank. Students earn $3 for each assignment successfully completed, and that amount is credited each week to their fictional bank accounts. Students must pay a $30 weekly rent for work space, and can write checks to receive play money to be used to buy computer time, pencils, paper, and so forth. Each month the students are given statements they must balance, and at the end of the school year students practice filling out state and federal income tax forms.

Use of calculators may also be part of the arithmetic survival skills curriculum. Block (1980) recommends that calculators not be used before the fifth grade because mastery of basic facts and operations without calculators represents greater freedom; that is, teachers should not promote reliance on a calculator when students are capable of learning arithmetic skills. Students must understand what the operations mean before calculators can be viable tools, in that students still need to make choices concerning which numbers to enter and which operations to use. If the decision is made to use calculators, teachers need to recognize that students need direct instruction in their use. Two important skills in calculator use are estimation and rounding. Students need to judge if answers are reasonable, and since most calculators show answers to division problems in decimals, students must learn to round answers to whole numbers when appropriate.

Microcomputer Applications

The mainstream teacher can make good use of microcomputers for delivering individualized arithmetic instruction, but just as with any other instructional tool, effective use of computers requires careful planning and appropriate applications. This section describes the features of computer-assisted instruction (CAI) in math, suggests when microcomputer use is appropriate, and discusses the results of research dealing with microcomputers and mathematics. Selected computer software pieces are given in the "Resources" section at the end of the chapter.

Features of Computer-Assisted Instruction for Arithmetic

The microcomputer has many features that make it an ideal tool for arithmetic instruction. Arithmetic assessments may be presented and evaluated by a computer, and based on the results of the assessment, the learner may automatically receive appropriate tutorial and practice activities also presented by the computer (Trifiletti, Frith, & Armstrong, 1984). Computer software can be designed to provide immediate feedback in terms of both the speed and accuracy of the learner's responses. CAI arithmetic programs can be written to provide automatic additional practice on errors, or even better, to deliver a short tutorial lesson on the concept or procedure. It is possible to program software that can record students' performance and to provide the teacher with individual or group reports, either on the computer monitor or on a written copy from a printer. The microcomputer never tires of repetition of a drill activity, and a wide variety of software programs can provide several different activities on the same arithmetic skill. Finally, the microcomputer may be a motivator for those students who are reluctant to complete another ditto worksheet.

When to Use Microcomputers

Computers will never replace teachers because teachers have to decide when it is appropriate to use a computer and what kind of software the computer should run. These instructional decisions are at present beyond the capabilities of the classroom microcomputer. The different types of computer software are tutorial, drill and practice, simulations, problem-solving software, and instructional games. Each has a different purpose and is appropriate for learners at different times during instructional sequences.

When learners are beginning to learn a skill, they need demonstrations, examples, nonexamples, and feedback. These are characteristics of *tutorial* programs designed to introduce and teach skills and concepts. After learners are somewhat accurate and fluent, practice is appropriate, and this is when *drill and practice* software may be used. Some instructional computer games are also designed to provide drill and practice in more exciting and appealing formats. When learners are ready to apply skills, *problem-solving* and *simulation* software are suitable. Simulation programs present realistic situations such as running a business (see the description of the *Whatsit Corporation* program in the "Resources" section), and students must make decisions and then proceed based on the consequences presented by the computer. Finally, when students need periodic review of previously learned concepts, teachers may use either drill and practice or *instructional games* software pieces.

Before students are assigned to work at a computer, however, they must be taught some prerequisite skills. Students must know how to turn on the computer and monitor and how to insert a disk or tape. Other prerequisite skills include selecting options from a menu, or list of choices, and escaping from the program if the student does not or cannot finish the activity. Teachers should clearly describe when students should call for the teacher's help; these situations may include when the computer "locks" (the cursor disappears and pressing appropriate keys has no effect) or when error messages appear on the screen. For most arithmetic programs, students will primarily use the number keys, but they should receive some instruction in how to locate and use the keys on the keyboard. If a joystick or some other type of device is used with the computer, the teacher should first demonstrate its use before students are expected to work independently.

Research Results

Although several researchers have investigated the use of microcomputers, there are still many unanswered questions, especially in regard to the use of CAI with handicapped students. The two studies reported here (Trifiletti et al., 1984 and Fuson & Brinko, 1985) both have interesting results. They have been selected because of their relevance to mainstream instruction and the relative soundness of their research designs.

Trifiletti et al. (1984) compared the effectiveness of the SPARK-80 arithmetic program—a combined CAI and management system—and arithmetic instruction in a resource room that primarily used workbooks. The students involved had learning disabilities and were working below grade level in arithmetic. After one academic year of instruction, the CAI group mastered an average of 21.16 arithmetic skills, whereas the resource room students mastered an average of 2.28 arithmetic skills. Both groups were tested before and after instruction using the Key Math Diagnostic Arithmetic Test, and the CAI students gained an average of 8 months, whereas the resource students showed an average of 3 months' progress. The research study does not report many details about the resource room instruction, but the CAI approach includes reports of daily assessment of speed and accuracy, assignment of activities based on level of learning and previous performance, mastery of skills, and computer games as a reinforcement for completed homework.

The principle of variety is supported by the findings of Fuson and Brinko (1985). These researchers compared basic facts drill presented by a microcomputer and by flash cards. Both activities were designed to be similar and to provide individualized sets of facts, immediate feedback, recycling of incorrect facts, and a measure of both accuracy and speed. The second, third and fourth graders involved in the study were exposed to both the computer drill and the flash card drill. After 4 weeks in one condition, the groups switched for 2 weeks in the opposite condition. The two practice activities resulted in equivalent levels of learning in equivalent amounts of time, although 63% of the students said they preferred using the computer. In discussing their results, Fuson and Brinko point out that flash cards are a less expensive instructional material than the microcomputer. They also note that for both conditions, students' scores improved significantly right after the conditions were switched; apparently, when both conditions are similar, novel practice situations can result in improved performance.

These two studies illustrate that well-designed CAI programs can result in equal or superior achievement when compared to more traditional instructional approaches. If teachers make careful selections when purchasing software and consider individual learners' needs when assigning microcomputer activities, the microcomputer can deliver effective and efficient instruction.

Adapted Activities for Arithmetic

The activities presented here are examples of instructional and remedial strategies that the mainstream teacher may implement to address specific difficulties in arithmetic. Several different subskills are included for the major skill areas of counting, basic facts, language of mathematics, and algorithms. For each subskill, one potential difficulty is described and one adapted activity is recommended.

Counting

Counting skills are the basis for many problem-solving strategies and higher-level calculations. Counting means more than reciting the numbers 1 through 10 or counting a set of three pennies. In addition to rote and rational counting, students should be able to count backward and forward from numbers other than 1 (Silbert, Carnine, & Stein, 1981).

Backward Counting

Difficulty. When asked to count backward from the number 8, Jeffrey took a long time to respond, and then said, "Eight, nine, ten." His teacher decides that Jeffrey does not know the meaning of the word *backward*.

Adapted Activity. Provide students with concrete examples of what it means to count backward. Give each student a number line, a card on which an arrow is printed, and five buttons. Model placing one button on the numbers 1 through 5, and place the arrow card above the number line pointing toward zero. Say, "When we count backward, we move closer to zero. Listen and watch me: Five, four, three, two, one, zero." As each number is said aloud, take away one button. Model again, but this time ask the students to imitate what is said and done. When each student can follow the teacher's lead, ask individual students to demonstrate they can count backward using the buttons and number line. Repeat the procedure using larger numbers as starting points.

Counting from Irregular Beginnings

Difficulty. Angela can accurately count forward from numbers other than 1, but she is extremely slow and hesitant in her responses. Her teacher concludes that Angela needs more drill and practice on the skill.

Adapted Activity. A board game for two to four students is designed to provide drill and practice in counting from irregular beginnings. The game board is a generic design with 50 spaces, some of which have chance messages such as "Take an extra turn" or "Go back one space." To take a turn, the student draws from a deck of cards on which the numbers 2 to 50 are written and then rolls a die. The student begins counting at the number printed on the card and counts forward one number for each dot on the die. If the student counts correctly, he or she may move a marker on the board one space for each dot on the die. The first student to reach the end wins. A printed list of numbers from 2 through 50 is available to make the game self-correcting.

Basic Math Facts

Many handicapped students need prolonged intense instruction to master the basic math facts in the four operations, but it is possible for most students to learn to perform basic facts accurately and quickly. The *basic facts* are defined by Garnett and Fleischner (1983) as including all single-digit addition and multiplication problems (e.g., $9 + 5 = 14$ and $6 \times 3 = 18$) as well as the subtraction and division problems that are the reverse of the addition and multiplication facts (e.g., $14 - 9 = 5$ and $18 \div 6 = 3$).

Math facts can be mastered in a variety of ways.

Addition

Difficulty.   Timmy has impaired vision and suffers from eye strain when he is required to do excessive reading and writing. He is falling behind his nonhandicapped peers in learning the addition facts because he is not able to complete as many written practice exercises as his classmates. Timmy's teacher knows he needs some alternative practice activities.

Adapted Activity.   Use of an abacus can provide visually impaired students with alternative practice in additon. Kang and Masoodi (1978–1979) suggest the following instructional sequence.

First, familiarize the student with the abacus and explain how it is used. Begin by saying a number and demonstrating how to count a number. Next, arrange beads to represent numbers and ask the student to read the number. Finally, demonstrate how to calculate the addition facts by counting beads on the abacus and touching beads to find the answer.

Subtraction

Difficulty.   The basal arithmetic series used in Michael's class presents subtraction facts in two large groups: minuends 1 through 9 and minuends 9 through 18. Michael's teacher used concrete and semi-concrete materials to illustrate the subtraction process, but Michael continued to make a large number of errors when he completed practice worksheets. His teacher decided that Michael probably needed to work with a smaller number of subtraction facts at one time.

Adapted Activity. One way to task-analyze subtraction facts is to arrange facts according to the subtrahend (i.e., $n - 1, n - 2, n - 3$, and so on). Baroody (1984) recommends a practice activity using these groups of facts and dominoes. Students play according to regular domino rules, only the matches are made not with equal numbers but with numbers one less if the student is practicing the $n - 1$ group of facts, two less for $n - 2$ facts, and so on. This may also be adapted to serve as an independent practice activity.

Multiplication

Difficulty. Elizabeth's teacher did an error analysis on her mastery test involving all the multiplication facts. Her teacher noticed that Elizabeth consistently made errors on seven different facts, but that she always wrote the correct answers for the inverse facts. For example, the student knew that $5 \times 3 = 15$, but she missed 3×5. Elizabeth did not understand the commutative property of multiplication.

Adapted Activity. After demonstrating the commutative property with manipulatives and requiring the student to demonstrate understanding at the concrete level, practice using semiconcrete materials may be helpful. One practice strategy recommended by Nelson (1979) is a game called "Table Tangle"; the game's objective is to help students recognize that products may be represented several ways.

The materials for "Table Tangle" include a large playing board that displays the multiplication facts in a table format, a set of eighty-one pictorial array cards, and a deck of thirty-six product cards (one card for each of the products of the basic facts and six wild cards). The procedures for the game are as follows.

1. Both decks of cards are kept in separate piles, shuffled, and put face down.
2. The dealer gives each player seven array cards, and the players arrange these cards face up.
3. The first player turns up a product card and places it on the game board over a fact with a matching product.
4. That player or any other player(s) may place any array illustrating that product on the board. For example, if the "12" product card was drawn and placed over 3×4, players may use arrays illustrating $4 \times 3, 2 \times 6$, and 6×2.
5. If the player drawing the product card cannot play an array, that player draws another array from the deck. The player may use the drawn card if possible.

If not, the card is placed face down in front of the player, and the next player takes a turn.
6. If a wild card is drawn, the player may say what product it should be.
7. The winner is the first player to place all of his or her array cards on the game board.

Division

Difficulty.   Sam can demonstrate division facts accurately at the concrete and semiconcrete level, but when given a printed worksheet containing the division facts, he has been unable to score above 45% correct. Sam's teacher thinks he is just guessing at the answers, as all of his errors appear to be random mistakes. Sam needs a strategy to help him work at the abstract level.

Adapted Activity.   Provide the student with a number line from 0 to 81 that is sized for a desktop and laminated, and a grease pencil or washable acetate marker. Demonstrate how to use the number line to find quotients (Silbert et al., 1981). First, read the problem aloud, "Eight divided by four means start at eight and make jumps of four." Draw a series of arcs over the number line, 8 to 4 and 4 to 0. Then say, "Then I count how many jumps I made—one, two. The answer to eight divided by four is two." After modeling the procedure, guide the student in following the steps. Ask the student to demonstrate the strategy without any hints or cues. Require 100% mastery in using the strategy before assigning the student to independent practice.

―――――――――― *Case Study* ――――――――――

INDIVIDUALIZING
FOR ARITHMETIC

James Patrick teaches all second-grade math groups at the Second Street School in Frankfort, Kentucky. Mainstreaming has been a big part of his job this school year. Not only has James been part of a team working to implement adaptive instruction at his school, but he also is Nick's math teacher. Nick has cerebral palsy and is mainstreamed for all of his academic instruction, including math.

Writing is very difficult for Nick, so he sits at a specially designed desk that puts his books and papers at an angle to make it easier for him to write and to see his work (there is a small rail at the bottom edge to prevent things from sliding off the desktop). When Nick has an assignment requiring a large amount of writing or if James notices Nick is fatigued, James assigns an aide or a peer tutor to record Nick's answers for him.

James feels it is important to give Nick assignments that are comparable to those given his peers; his handicap should not mean that he gets less practice in math skills. Nick's parents are supportive of James's philosophy and frequently help Nick with practice papers at home.

Early in the school year James tried to help Nick use manipulatives to introduce and illustrate math operations. Nick was extremely slow in moving the objects and had great difficulty in picking them up and placing them accurately. James felt that the effort required of Nick to work with manipulatives took away from learning the concepts rather than enhancing the lessons.

To substitute for the concrete objects, James has done two things. First, he has taught Nick to use a number line. There is a number line attached to Nick's desk, and number lines are placed in other places he works such as the computer center. Second, since Nick's finger manipulation is not accurate even for simple counting, James showed him how to count using larger body parts—two arms, two legs, one head. James began by touching Nick's body and counting aloud. Now Nick is able to visualize his own body or other peoples' and count without the touch cue.

Like many other physically handicapped children, Nick has had a series of surgeries that have caused absences from school. During Nick's most recent hospital stay and recuperation, James kept in touch with Nick and his parents. James sent work home when Nick was ready, and as a result, when Nick returned to school he was able to stay in his same math group.

Learning centers are an important part of the adaptive instruction program used in Nick's class. In addition to Nick's daily math assignments, he may choose from a variety of math centers. Movement around the classroom is difficult for Nick, but James tries not to let this factor restrict Nick's experience with the learning centers. When Nick is ready to choose a center, either the center is brought to him, or an adult helps him move to the learning center.

James's classroom is a good example of school and home working together to provide the least restrictive learning environment for a handicapped child. As much as possible, Nick's math instruction is the same as that of his classmates, but when he has a special need, his teachers and family work to see that it is met.

The Language of Mathematics

Many students with learning problems have difficulty learning language skills. A language disability is just as problematic during arithmetic instruction as it is during reading, writing, or speech lessons. Teachers in the mainstream need to teach the language of mathematics, as understanding of mathematics vocabulary can be a key to understanding mathematical concepts.

Listening Skills

Difficulty. Nathan is a middle school student who is known to have a receptive language disability. He must concentrate very hard in order to gain understanding from spoken directions and explanations. Nathan's teacher notices that he frequently loses interest in lectures, even if they are concise and lively. The teacher would like to find some way of motivating Nathan to attend more closely to class discussions and lectures.

Adapted Activity. To promote more careful listening, tell students that they will hear the teacher use an incorrect vocabulary word periodically and that their job is to catch the teacher in the intentional mistake. At first, mistakes are obvious and absurd (e.g., "In order to find the answer, we first *cook* the top number in the fraction"), but later on the mistakes can be more subtle. Keep a running tally on the blackboard with students earning one point for every mistake they catch, and the teacher earning one point for every mistake the students do not correct. It is important never to allow an intentional verbal error to go uncorrected. If students do not catch an error within a set time period (e.g., 10–20 seconds), the teacher points out the error, makes an accurate statement, and records the point.

Mathematics Vocabulary

Difficulty. When Sheila's teacher asks her to read aloud directions from her arithmetic text, she can pronounce every word but she cannot restate the directions in her own words or accurately follow the directions. Sheila's teacher did some informal vocabulary testing and found that she does not know the meaning of many mathematical terms used in the directions. More formal testing by Sheila's speech and language therapist supported this conclusion.

Adapted Activity. The mainstream teacher and the speech and language therapist should work closely in developing mathematical vocabulary skills for students with language disorders. Mainstream teachers can anticipate those new vocabulary words that will be used in future units and provide the language therapist with a list to be used in therapy. Students may also benefit from practice using self-correcting materials. Vocabulary terms may be written on one set of cards and the definitions on another set. The backs of the matching cards can be color-coded with matching colored shapes. Students may practice matching terms with definitions and then turn pairs of cards over to check their answers. The mainstream teacher should be conscious of consistent use of those terms that have been the object of direct instruction.

Algorithms

After students have mastered basic facts, they then must learn to apply the facts within more complex calculations. Arithmetic problems requiring more than one step are called *algorithms*.

Place Value and Subtraction with Regrouping

Difficulty.   Monica always finished her subtraction worksheets before her classmates. She did not understand what was so difficult about the subtraction exercises. Monica's teacher told her that the problems required something called *regrouping*, but Monica found it easier to take the smaller number from the larger number instead. Monica's teacher discovered this error pattern after analyzing her written work and determined that Monica did not understand place value.

Adapted Activity.   Many students need concrete experiences that illustrate the concept of place value. Skirtic et al. (1983) recommend a backward trading game that provides practice in the regrouping procedures required for subtraction. Students playing the game each have a place value chart with columns marked ones, tens, hundreds, and so on, as well as markers placed in the columns to represent the same value. (The amount selected for the beginning number depends on students' skill level.) The first player rolls a die or spins a spinner and removes that value from the number represented by the markers on the chart. The next players take turns in the same way. Eventually, trading, or regrouping, will have to occur. Play continues until all players have removed all markers from their boards.

Sequencing Steps in an Algorithm

Difficulty.   Pedro's written work in arithmetic is extremely difficult to read. When copying problems, he usually misaligns the columns of numbers. Pedro also has trouble sequencing the steps within an algorithm. It is not unusual for him to raise his hand and tell his teacher, "I'm lost." Pedro's teacher knows he needs some strategies to help him become better organized in his approach to written work in arithmetic.

Adapted Activity.   Using large-square graph paper for work in arithmetic can help many students align columns of numbers properly and achieve more legible written work. In addition to this adaptation, Young (1984) recommends a procedure designed to help students remember the steps in an algorithm and identify the digits to use at each step. First, students write the problem on large-square graph paper using one square per digit. Then they cover each digit with a piece of colored paper cut to the size of the squares on the paper. The rule for this procedure is that students may uncover only those digits needed at each step. The teacher should demonstrate the procedure, ask students to imitate the model, and then question students about which digits should be uncovered at each step of a sample problem. For large-group instruction, presentations may be made using an overhead projector.

Summary

Although many handicapped students experience difficulty in learning mathematics, these difficulties can be overcome. The mainstream teacher who conducts careful and frequent assessments, delivers well-planned individualized instruction, and requires students to master skills before moving on to more difficult ones can be confident that students are gaining a solid foundation in the arithmetic skills and concepts needed for success in school and in real-life experiences outside of school. The most important characteristic of a successful teacher may be the conviction that all students can learn mathematics if the classroom environment is adapted to meet their individual needs.

Discussion Questions

1. What is the purpose of the monitor stage of the assessment strategy for arithmetic? How does this stage differ from the other stages of assessment? Why is it especially important when working with learners with handicaps?
2. Compare and contrast direct observation of students' math work and oral interviews in terms of (a) purpose, (b) procedures, and (c) information collected. Discuss the strengths and limitations of both procedures.
3. Define each level of representation for math operations (i.e., concrete, semiconcrete, and abstract) and give an example of how the process of division could be described at each level. Discuss the role of manipulatives within arithmetic instruction.
4. State a rationale that would support the importance of providing learners with handicaps a variety of practice activities in mathematics. Briefly describe at least four different types of practice activities for mathematics.
5. Define *survival skills* in mathematics. Why should survival skills be part of the mathematics curriculum? For whom are they most appropriate? What key skills should be part of the survival skills curriculum in mathematics?

Resources

Selected Commercially Published Math Tests

Adston Mathematics Skills Series, Adston Educational Enterprises, Inc., 945 East River Oaks Drive, Baton Rouge, LA 70815. Four separate tests are available in this series: Readiness for Operations, Working with Whole Numbers, Common Fractions, and Decimal Numbers. The tests involve a combination of group and individual administrations and are criterion-referenced.

Brigance Diagnostic Comprehensive Inventory of Basic Skills, Brigance Diagnostic Inventory of Essential Skills, Curriculum Associates, 5 Esquire Road, North Billerica, MA 01862. The *Inventory of Basic Skills* includes math skills at grade levels k–9, and the *Inventory of Essential Skills* includes math skills found in survival skills and vocational skills curricula in grades 4–12. The inventories must be administered individually and are criterion-referenced.

California Achievement Tests (CAT), California Test Bureau, McGraw-Hill Division, Del Monte Research Park, Monterey, CA 93940. This test may be administered to groups and covers academic skills from grades k–12. There are two mathematics subtests—computation and application—that take approximately 70 minutes to administer. The CAT is both a norm-referenced and criterion-referenced test.

Diagnostic Mathematics Inventory, California Test Bureau, McGraw-Hill Division, Del Monte Research Park, Monterey, CA 93940. This inventory is a series of multiple-choice tests that covers math objectives at grade levels 1.5–8.5 and may be administered to a group of students. The inventory is criterion-referenced and each objective is accompanied by specific suggestions for teaching the skill. The inventory has several purposes including diagnosis, placement of students in instructional groups, and evaluation of progress.

Diagnostic Test of Arithmetic Strategies, Pro-Ed, 5341 Industrial Oaks Blvd., Austin, TX 78735. This instrument measures the procedures used in basic calculations of addition, subtraction, multiplication, and division. It is appropriate for students working at an elementary level in math and gives information about both correct and incorrect strategies. Suggestions for remediation of incorrect strategies are also included.

Key Math Diagnostic Arithmetic Test, American Guidance Service, Inc., Publishers' Building, Circle Pines, MN 55014. This test is administered individually and covers math skills from grades k–8. There are fourteen subtests within the areas of content, operations, and application and the test takes approximately 30–40 minutes to administer. The Key Math is both a norm-referenced and criterion-referenced test.

Kramer Preschool Mathematics Inventory, Teaching Resources Corporation, P.O. Box 4000, One DLM Park, Allen, TX 75002. The inventory is designed for children ages 3–6.5 years and assesses precalculation skills and concepts. It is intended to identify those children in need of remedial instruction. A 21-item screening test may be administered to a group of children, but the inventory requires individual administration.

Sequential Assessment of Mathematics Inventory—Classroom Test: Sequential Assessment of Mathematics Inventory; Individual Assessment Battery, 555 Academic Court, San Antonio, TX 78204. The SAMI covers math skills from grades k–8. The *Classroom Test* may be administered to groups and requires approximately 40 minutes. The *Individual Assessment Battery* requires individual administration and involves use of some concrete materials. The tests are criterion-referenced and include objectives for the language of mathematics, ordinality, number and notation, measurement, geometry, computation, word problems, and mathematical applications.

Stanford Diagnostic Mathematics Test (SDMT), Harcourt Brace Jovanovich, Inc., Test Department, Orlando, FL 32887. This test may be administered to groups and is available in four different levels covering skills at grade levels 1.5–12. At each level there are three subtests—Number System and Numeration, Computation, and Applications. The SDMT is both a norm-referenced and criterion-referenced test.

Test of Mathematical Abilities (TOMA), Pro-Ed, 5341 Industrial Oaks Blvd., Austin, TX 78735. The TOMA may be administered to groups and is designed to identify math difficulties of students in grades 3–12. The test is norm-referenced and covers the areas of computation, story problems, attitude, vocabulary, and general cultural application.

Selected Instructional Materials

Computational Arithmetic Program (CAP), Pro-Ed, 5341 Industrial Oaks Blvd., Austin, TX 78735. Designed for students needing instruction in basic calculations in the four operations, this program helps students learn to perform calculations quickly and accurately. Support materials include assessments, error-analysis forms, monitoring system, intervention suggestions, and certificates of mastery.

Corrective Mathematics, SRA, 155 North Wacker Drive, Chicago, IL 60606. This remedial series is designed for individuals in grade 3 through adult and applies direct instruction teaching techniques. Modules are available for each of the four operations. Each module provides instruction and practice in basic facts, computation, and story problems. Lessons are designed for either small groups or an entire class.

Fraction Bars Step by Step, Opportunities for Learning, Inc., 20417 Nordhoff St., Dept. FE, Chatsworth, CA 91311. This kit includes materials designed to teach fractions using concrete, semiconcrete, and abstract materials. The fraction bar model represents denominators as number of parts on a bar and numerators as shaded parts on the same bar.

KeyMath Teach and Practice, American Guidance Services, Inc., Publishers' Building, Circle Pines, MN 55014. Concepts and skills in this remedial program are correlated with objectives from the KeyMath Diagnostic Arithmetic Test. The material can help teachers identify specific difficulties and provide appropriate instruction using concrete materials and pictorial representations. Drills, games, and extensions are included.

Math in Action: Word Problems, Janus Book Publishers, 2501 Industrial Pkwy. West, Dept. MIA, Hayward, CA 94545. These high interest/low vocabulary materials are appropriate for students in intermediate and secondary grades who have difficulty solving word problems. Workbooks present concepts in small, structured units providing a variety of practice activities and applications in everyday situations. Individual books are available on the topics of math vocabulary, understanding word problems, use of calculators, estimation, and solving word problems.

Paying with Cash and *Paying with Promises*, Quercus Corporation, 2405 Castro Valley Blvd., P.O. Box 20158, Castro Valley, CA 94546. These high interest/low vocabulary workbooks (Spache reading level of 2.5) are designed to teach consumer skills. *Paying with Cash* gives students practice in recognizing and counting money, making change, reading receipts, and so on. *Paying with Promises* teaches students the advantages and disadvantages of money orders, layaway plans, credit cards, and the like, and how to take out a loan.

Pre-Math: The Success Training Program of Increasingly Complex Number Skills, Communication Skill Builders, Inc., 3130 N. Dodge Blvd., P.O Box 42050, Tucson, AZ 85733. Aimed at children up to 7 years of age who are experiencing learning problems, this material includes seven separate programs: matching numbers, showing numbers, naming numbers, rote counting, counting objects, selecting from a greater amount, and sequencing numbers. Directions to the teacher are precise and thorough.

Real Life Math, EBSCO Curriculum Materials, Division of EBSCO Industries, Inc., Box 486, Birmingham, AL 35202. Designed for students with learning problems, this kit provides practice in math skills required to make transactions with banks and other companies. Students simulate a variety of occupational roles as they solve realistic math problems associated with the workplace.

Speak and Math, Texas Instruments, P.O. Box 10508, Mail Station 5849, Lubbock, TX 79408. This hand-held electronic device (battery-powered) presents math problems and feedback in both visual and auditory modes. Students may independently practice basic math facts at three different levels.

Step-by-Step Series, DLM Teaching Resources, P.O. Box 4000, One DLM Park, Allen, TX 75002. Designed for students experiencing difficulty learning the basic operations (addition, subtraction, multiplication, and division) this series of black-line masters covers both basic facts and computation. Appropriate for students in grades 2–8, the series emphasizes frequent review and small instructional steps.

Supermath, Special Child Publications, 4535 Union Bay Place NE, Seattle, WA 98105. This book is aimed at junior high school students who are working below grade level in math. The material is age-appropriate and includes descriptions of activities using manipulatives in geometry, addition, subtraction, multiplication, and division.

Teams Assisted Individualization, The Johns Hopkins Team Learning Projects, TAI, Johns Hopkins University, 3505 N. Charles St., Baltimore, MD 21218. This math curriculum and management system is appropriate for mainstream classrooms, third grade and above. Small homogeneous groups cooperate to earn rewards and incentives for mastery of math skills. Units are task-analyzed and the program incorporates periodic review.

Selected Microcomputer Software

Academic Skill Builders in Math, DLM Teaching Resources, P.O. Box 4000, One DLM Park, Allen, TX 75002. These arcade-like math games promote both accuracy and fluency. The student or teacher may control the level of difficulty, speed of presentation, and run time. Programs are available in each of the four operations.

Basic Number Facts Practice, Control Data Publishing Company, Inc., P.O. Box 261127, San Diego, CA 92126. This well-designed drill program covers basic facts in all four operations using a car racing theme. Objectives include increased speed and accuracy on basic facts and discrimination among the operations. Visual cues are available and learners receive feedback in a variety of forms.

Basic Skills in Math, Love Publishing Co., 1777 South Bellaire St., Denver, CO 80222. Four separate programs are available, one for each operation. Students take assessment tests on the computer and are automatically presented with an appropriate practice level. Tutorial help is available after errors are made or when the student requests it. The system includes mastery tests, a computer game for reinforcement, and a student record-keeping feature.

Challenge Math, Sunburst Communications, 39 Washington Ave., Box 40, Pleasantville, NY 10570. This set of three game programs provides practice in basic calculations and estimation of whole numbers and decimals. Teachers may control run time, operations included, speed of presentation, sound, and whether or not decimals are included.

Computer Math Games, Volumes 1–7, Addison-Wesley Publishing Co., 2725 Sand Hill Rd., Menlo Park, CA 94025. This series of games features immediate feedback to the learner, clear directions, and attractive graphics. Each volume emphasizes a different set of math skills.

Fractions, Edu-Ware Services, 28035 Dorothy Drive, Agoura, CA 91301. Students using this program begin with an assessment test and the program then presents practice activities at the appropriate level. Behavioral objectives are included.

Learning About Numbers, C & C Software, 5713 Kentford Circle, Wichita, KS 67220. This program, aimed at learners k–5, provides drill and practice in counting, telling time, and basic math facts. Learners receive corrective feedback, and the program includes a management and record-keeping system for the teacher.

Stickybear Numbers, Weekly Reader Family Software, 245 Long Hill Rd., Middletown, CT 06457. Intended to support teacher-controlled instruction, this attractive program provides practice in counting sets of objects and number recognition for 0–9. Appropriate for primary-aged students.

The Whatsit Corporation: Survival Math Skills, Sunburst Communications, 39 Washington Ave., Box 40, Pleasantville, NY 10570. This simulation program requires students (either as individuals or teams) to apply math skills in running a small corporation.

Organizations

National Council of Teachers of Mathematics (NCTM), the largest national association for teachers interested in mathematics, publishes *The Arithmetic Teacher*.

National Council of Supervisors of Mathematics (NCSM).

School Science and Mathematics Association publishes *School Science and Mathematics*.

Research Council for Diagnostic and Prescriptive Mathematics; membership focuses primarily on those students who have difficulty in the area of mathematics.

Chapter 8

Individualizing for Science and Social Studies

JAMES R. PATTON
University of Hawaii at Manoa

KATHERINE E. ANDRE
Department of Defense Schools

Chapter Objectives

After reading Chapter 8 the student will be able to

- Provide a rationale for teaching science and social studies in regular education settings to students with special needs
- Present and analyze the most commonly used approaches to assessing and teaching these subject areas
- Suggest techniques that increase the accommodative capacity of regular classroom settings
- Highlight selected resource materials that can help regular classroom teachers meet the needs of special learners

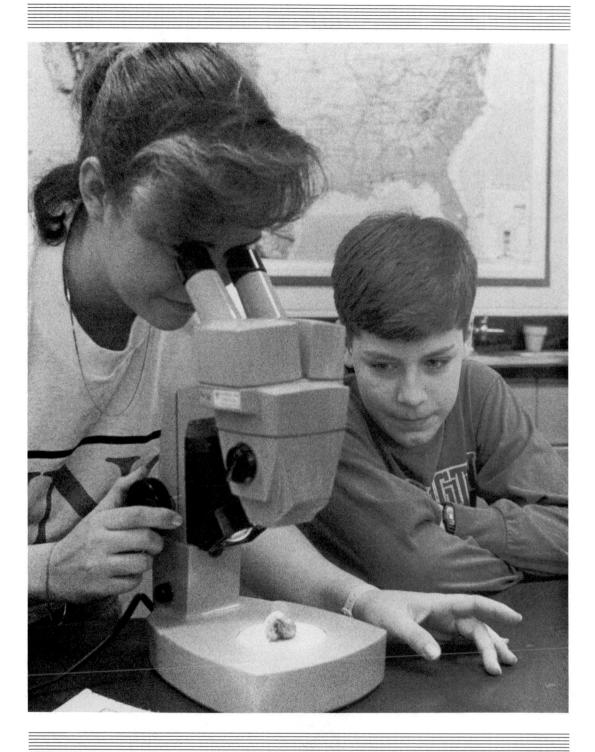

S tudents are typically very interested in their surroundings and the events that occur in these various environments. Astute teachers can take advantage of students' natural curiosity by engaging them in science and social studies topics related to their world. However, this is often difficult to accomplish, as teachers are constantly faced with the challenge of presenting appropriate instruction to students with diverse educational needs.

Many students in regular science and social studies classrooms display characteristics that can interfere with their academic performance. Students requiring special attention might include those with learning, behavioral, physical, sensory or communicative problems. It is important to realize that some of these students will never have been officially labeled "handicapped." Other students who display high potential or giftedness can also present challenges to the regular classroom teacher. The value of science and social studies instruction for many handicapped students is reflected in the following possible outcomes.

1. Experimental backgrounds can be expanded; many of these students are experience poor (Mathias & Johnson, 1981).
2. Information and skills required for successful adult adjustment can be addressed.
3. Basic skills can be integrated into relevant and meaningful subject matter.
4. Much of what is taught can be done so in active, hands-on ways.
5. Students can further develop important skills related to thinking and problem solving.

Unfortunately, for many students with learning-related problems in special educational settings, science and social studies are often treated as priority subject areas (Polloway, Payne, Patton, & Payne, 1985). Data collected on the status of science and social studies instruction in special education settings (Patton, Polloway, & Cronin, in press) indicate that these subject areas are often not taught, and, when they are taught, less time as compared to regular education is devoted to them. Interestingly, science and social studies are the subject areas into which handicapped students are often first "mainstreamed."

Regular educators have identified a number of areas that contribute to the difficulty of adequately teaching students with diverse needs. First, many feel that they have not been trained to deal with these student populations. Second, they feel that existing curricula may not be sensitive to the specific needs of certain students. Third, appropriate instructional materials and equipment are viewed as lacking for this group. Fourth, sufficient support and assistance from resource personnel is usually not available. These are formidable barriers.

Individualizing instruction for such diverse student populations requires awareness, knowledge, skills, and competence. The intent of this chapter is to provide information that will assist teachers in accommodating the special needs of certain students in the areas of science and social studies.

Assessment

For the purposes of this chapter, *assessment* is considered the process whereby information is gathered about students and their learning environments. All too often assessment is equated with testing; however, many different techniques can be used to collect information (e.g., observation, interviews, self-reports, cumulative folders, and formal/informal testing). Collecting information on students and their learning environments can assist in making decisions about them (Salvia & Ysseldyke, 1985).

Assessing Students

There are three major assessment issues for teachers who teach science and social studies to special learners. First, we are concerned about a particular student's *strengths* and *weaknesses.* This information will help in planning instruction and choosing specific activities. For instance, knowing that a student has limited upper-body strength due to muscular dystrophy would suggest that this student may not be able to perform some laboratory activities. This type of data should be available if a comprehensive diagnostic workup was done on a student; often it can be obtained from former teachers.

Teachers should also take time to assess the individual interests of their students. Finding out what the students like and dislike can be used for planning purposes. Rossman (1983) states that science curriculum can be anything that catches a student's attention. Determining what students find interesting can lead to capturing their attention.

The most common reason for assessing students is to evaluate their levels of knowledge and skill attainment (i.e., progress). This can be done on an ongoing basis (formative) or at the end of a longer specified period of time (summative). It is imperative that teachers monitor the progress of their students to make prudent decisions about instruction and goal attainment. For this reason, we emphasize here the need for more formative measurement.

A number of different techniques are available for assessing student progress in science and social studies. Which one to use depends on certain variables such as "the objectives to be evaluated, the conditions under which children are working, and the type of behavior involved" (Michaelis, 1985, p. 388).

Formal Standardized Tests. Formal standardized tests are norm-referenced devices that provide information on a student's performance relative to some comparison group. They are usually composed of many different subtests, covering a range of subject and skill areas and typically include science and social studies. However, data obtained from these measures may be of limited value for determining the progress of students in a given science or social studies curriculum if the instrument tests areas that were not covered in the curriculum. Table 8.1 presents some of the more commonly used *group-administered* in-

TABLE 8.1
Selected Standardized Group Achievement Tests

Test	Publisher	Age/Grade Appropriateness for Science/Social Studies	Subtests		Type of Derived Scores	Remarks
			Science	Social Studies		
Iowa Test of Basic Skills (ITBS)	Riverside Publishing (1982)	3–9	(X)	(X)	Percentiles Age and grade equivalents Stanines Standard scores Normal curve equivalents	Science and social studies are supplementary tests Special percentiles—National and Special
Metropolitan Achievement Test (MAT) (5th ed.)	Harcourt, Brace, Jovanovich (1978)	1.5–9.9	X	X	Percentiles Grade equivalents Stanines Scaled scores Normal curve equivalents	Science and social studies are included in the "survey" battery

Test	Publisher (year)	Grade range			Scores	Comments
Sequential Tests of Educational Progress (STEP) Series III	Educational Testing Service (1979)	3.5–12.9	X	X	Converted score Percentile ranks Percentile bands	No grade equivalents are reported There is no general science subtest at the upper levels of this test—it has been replaced with separate tests in the areas of biology, chemistry, and physics
SRA Achievement Series	Science Research Associates (1978)	4–12	X	X	Percentiles National percentile band Grade equivalents Stanines Normal curve equivalents Growth scale value	Test provides an ability measure (Educational Ability Series) All items on the social studies test are based on the analysis of graphic information
Stanford Achievement Test	Harcourt, Brace, Jovanovich (1982)	3.5–9.9	X	X	Percentiles Age and grade equivalents Stanines Standard scores	Science and social studies subtests combined at the early levels (1.5–3.9); subtest called "environment"

struments, with particular attention to the assessment of science and social studies.

Curriculum-based Assessment. Curriculum-based assessment techniques may be the most helpful if such measures are designed to show how well a student does in a defined area within a specific curriculum. The format of this informal methodology will vary according to the nature of the skill or topic being evaluated; that is, the data collected can be from written, oral, or performance activities. Often in science and social studies, formats might incorporate situational items and questions based on pictorial and graphic material.

Observation. Another valuable technique for evaluating students is to observe them in action. Many opportunities exist in science and social studies classes for students to be engaged in some activity. For example, in science, students can perform science activities or conduct experiments; in social studies, role playing is often used as a way of covering subject matter. These types of activities can be observed and evaluated by teachers.

Assessing the Learning Environment

Not all problems displayed by students are the result of a condition they possess. Sometimes, learning-related problems can be caused by weaknesses in the learning environment. For instance, a student who has trouble following directions may have a difficult time in a science classroom where the procedures for performing a given activity are not presented clearly. In general, we are concerned about the following features of what happens in the classroom: classroom management/organization, lesson planning and execution, efficient use of instructional/learning time, adequate opportunity for practice, appropriate feedback to students, and thoughtful decision-making.

Assessing Instructional Materials

Another consideration in meeting the needs of students is the selection of appropriate instructional materials. A substantial number of students may encounter difficulty dealing effectively with science and social studies because they cannot successfully use the curricular materials chosen for a particular course. With this in mind, teachers are advised to examine the following features when selecting instructional materials: readability, organization, linguistic demands, and conceptual complexity. Readability levels can be determined in a number of ways, including information provided by the publisher, formulae (e.g., Fry and Spache), or the use of microcomputer utilities programs. The way a material is organized and some of the features that characterize its organization (e.g., headings and margin notes) may be useful to certain special learners. Related to the problems of readability levels is the issue of language usage, which may also be beyond the levels of learners. Sometimes this reality cannot be avoided; if so, teachers may have to address the problem alternatively. Finally, the conceptual level of some topics and the way they are presented in written materials can also be problematic. Background information, preliminary discussions, and regular checks of student understanding may be needed.

Science

Goals and Objectives

The goals and objectives for most students with special needs in regular science classrooms are not any different than for other students. Cain and Evans (1984) have highlighted three major goals of science education: content goals, process goals, and attitudinal goals.

Content goals relate to the presentation of certain facts, concepts, and principles that students need to acquire. Although some controversy exists as to how much emphasis should be given to the acquisition of content, the fact remains that a certain amount of basic information is essential and useful to students. The primary science disciplines covered in the K–12 curriculum are as follows:

1. Life science: zoology, botany, ecology.
2. Physical science: chemistry, physics.
3. Earth/environmental science: astronomy, meteorology, geology.

Process goals refer to the development of investigation and problem-solving skills. For the most part, this involves providing students many opportunities to use a variety of primary and higher-level inquiry/process skills.

1. Primary skills:
    a. Observing
    b. Classifying
    c. Measuring
    d. Using spatial relationships
    e. Communicating
    f. Predicting
    g. Inferring
2. Higher-level skills:
    a. Defining operationally
    b. Formulating hypotheses
    c. Interpreting data
    d. Controlling variables
    e. Experimenting

Attitudinal goals underscore the need to develop an appreciation for and an interest in the world. Moreover, students should be encouraged to be objective and base their thinking on the facts they gather.

Major Approaches to Teaching Science

The nature of science instruction has changed over the years. Prior to the late 1950s, science education usually consisted of using a textbook with very few hands-on activities. As Polloway et al. (1985) highlight, science appealed to a select few: "Those who found science enjoyable probably liked to read and liked to write definitions to selected scientific terms" (p. 339). After the initiation of major reforms in the 1960s, science education took on a more inquiry-oriented character, resulting in the development of a number of federally funded programs. Recently, there seems to be a trend that has been characterized as a return to the more traditional approaches (i.e., heavy reliance on textbooks) to teaching science (Prince, News, & Stitt, 1982).

The four major approaches to teaching science are the textbook, process/inquiry, specialized program, and customized approaches. Each of them is examined in terms of its benefits and drawbacks for use with special learners, and all of the information presented here is summarized in Table 8.2.

Textbook Approach. Teachers can use commercially produced textbooks in a variety of ways, from using them as the primary vehicle for providing science education to using them only as resource or reference materials. In practice, textbooks are used extensively as a major instructional tool. Penick and Yager (1986), in highlighting the findings of Project Synthesis (an effort to synthesize the problems of current science programs), point out that "over 90% of all science teachers use a textbook 95% of the time" (p. 428). In a national study sponsored by the National Science Teachers Association, Teters, Gabel, and Geary (1984) found that while many teachers claim to use hands-on activities to teach elementary science, there remains a heavy emphasis on textbooks as well, particularly in grades 4–6.

As indicated in Table 8.3, using textbooks as the primary way of teaching science to special learners can be problematic. As the most likely students to be mainstreamed are those with various learning disabilities, their ability to handle the reading demands of textbooks is usually limited. Suggestions on how to address this problem include using textbooks that are activity-oriented and minimize the need to read.

Process/Inquiry Approach. The process/inquiry approach to science instruction stresses the importance of students actively "doing" and "discovering" science. Students are required to use the inquiry skills identified earlier in the chapter. Teachers act as facilitators of learning rather than distributors of information. Three of the most popular programs are described in Table 8.3.

Although there is limited data on the effectiveness of these types of programs with special students, there is some indication that they can be successful (Atwood & Oldham, 1985; Davies & Ball, 1978; Esler, Midgett, & Bird, 1977).

A number of features make process/inquiry programs attractive for use with special learners. First, they require students to be actively engaged in learning. Second, these programs can be used to augment other less activity-oriented approaches, thus making them more hands-on. For instance, most of the units of the *Elementary Science Study* series could augment similar topics covered in a textbook. Third, as Atwood and Oldham (1985) note, regular education teachers feel that handicapped students can be effectively integrated into these types of programs.

Specialized Program Approach. A few programs have been developed specifically for various handicapped populations. The major programs of this type are presented in Table 8.4. The *Me Now, Me and My Environment,* and *Me in the Future* programs were originally developed by the Biological Sciences Curriculum Study (BSCS) for students with limited intellectual capacity. The *Science Activities for the Visually Impaired* (SAVI) program was designed for students who are blind or visually impaired, perhaps the most challenging and difficult group to the science teacher. These materials are also believed to be appropriate for use with other handicapped students as well, and as a result the Science Enrichment for Learners with Physical Handicaps (SELPH) program has evolved.

Customized Approach. In some settings, teachers choose to develop their own curricula. The content of customized programs is often determined by student and teacher interests. Rossman (1983) provides a refreshing way to conceptualize this orientation: "I teach that each place we cast our attention is worthy of attention. . . . I teach that it's a natural act to *really pay attention* to what we encounter and behold. . . . It's an easy curriculum even without microscopes, since everything's grist for the mill" (p. 78). Scope and sequence charts might be helpful for some teachers who desire more structure when designing a customized curriculum.

Instructional Methodologies

A wide variety of specific techniques is available for teaching science. The major instructional options include teacher-led lecture/discussion/demonstration, workbooks, media (films, filmstrips, television, videotapes), microcomputers, simulation games, hands-on activities, field trips, and guest speakers (Coble, Matthis, & Vizzini, 1982; Patton et al., in press). All of these techniques can be used effectively; however, an overreliance on any one can create problems. For this reason, it is a good idea to vary instruction as much as possible. Sometimes the choice of methodology is determined by the nature of the topic, the types of special learners in the class, or the availability of resources. For example, soft-

TABLE 8.2
Analysis of Various Approaches to Teaching Science

Approach	Issues Related to Special Learners		Remarks	Examples
	Positive Features	Negative Features		
Textbook	Organized science program	Readability problems	Certain series have deemphasized the need to have good reading skills (Addison-Wesley Science and Houghton-Mifflin Science)	(Almost all major publishers of educational textbooks)
	Useful for beginning teachers	Geared for average students		
	Excellent resources	Can be too content-oriented	Checklists exist to help teachers evaluate textbooks (see Cain & Evans, 1984; Price, Ness, & Stitt, 1982)	
	Certain series contain many hands-on activities	May become only source of information		*Quercus*
	Teacher's guide may contain suggestions for working with special learners	Content may be covered too quickly	Newly published texts of high interest, low readability are now available	*Project Earth*
	Most textbook series come with material kits	Content often presented apart from activities		
Process/ Laboratory	Stress inquiry/problem solving	May be too discovery-oriented for some students	With some modifications these programs can work with special groups	*Elementary Science Study* (ESS)
	Minimize the need to be a good reader	Less teacher-directed instruction, which some special students may require	Can be effectively used in combination with other programs	
	Activity-oriented		Some of these programs have developed additional materials for working with special populations (e.g., *ESS/ Special Education Teacher's Guide*)(Ball, 1978)	*Science Curriculum Improvement Study* (SCIS/SCIIS)
	Curricularly flexible	Require special instructional skills, which not all teachers demonstrate or are comfortable with		*Science . . . A Process Approach* (5-APA)
	Can be used with older students			

308

			May not address concept development appropriately for some students	
Specialized Programs	Developed with special populations in mind Minimize reading skills Programs designed for older students are functionally-oriented	May not cover some important science topics May differ from a school system's other science programs Probably will be used in noncredit generating courses	There are relatively few programs of this nature currently available Little empirical research exists validating their value Activities from these programs can be integrated into regular science programs	*Me Now* *Me and My Environment* *Me in the Future* *Science Activities for the Visually Impaired/Science Enrichment for Learners with Physical Handicaps (SAVI/SELPH)*
Customized Programs	Can be based on interests, current issues, local needs Relevant Typically very "Hands-on"	Requires much teacher time May not cover some important science topics May not match the scope and sequence of the school system May not address concept development appropriately	Success depends on the following qualities of the teacher: Resourcefulness Organizational skills Instructional skills Curriculum development abilities For older students this approach may better prepare them for adulthood	

TABLE 8.3
Description of Selected Process Programs

Program	Publisher	Grade Range	Features	Topics/Content	Components
Elementary Science Study (ESS)	McGraw-Hill	K–9	56 individual units that can be used as a complete program or as supplementary materials Flexibility–units can be used at different grade levels Units are interesting and can be tailored to the needs of special students Reading is minimized Students are actively involved Provisions for special students, *ESS/Special Education Teacher's Guide* (Ball, 1978) is available	Biological science units Physical science units Earth science units	Typically, each unit has a teacher's guide and requisite materials Some units have supplementary materials

Program	Publisher	Grade	Description	Scope	Materials
Science Curriculum Improvement Study (SCIS)	Rand McNally	K–6	Complete science program Program is sequential 13 units (one unit for K and 2 units for each of grades 1–6) Emphasis on the concept of interaction Employs a teaching strategy referred to as *exploration-invention-discovery* Reading is minimized	For kindergarten (one unit) For each grade (1–6) One unit on life/earth science One unit on physical/earth science	Materials in kit form Teacher's guide Supplementary materials
Science . . . A Process Approach	Ginn and Company	K–6	Sequential modular program (must be used in this fashion)	Program addresses 13 skill areas K–3: 8 skills 4–6: 5 skills	Each module has a kit Instruction booklet Supplementary materials

TABLE 8.4
Description of Specialized Programs

Program	Publisher	Grade Range	Features	Topics/Content	Components
Science Activities for the Visually Impaired (SAVI)/ *Science Enrichment for Learners with Physical Handicaps* (SELPH)	Center for Multisensory Learning (Lawrence Hall of Science University of California, Berkeley)	1–10	Life and physical science program designed for students with visual (SAVI) or physical and *learning* problems (SELPH) SAVI and SELPH contain the same content Activity-oriented Multisensory Can be used in a range of settings	Measurement Structures of life Scientific reasoning Communications Magnetism and electricity Mixtures and solutions Environments Kitchen interactions Environmental energy	Activity folios for each module Training manual Materials kit (special equipment designed for visually impaired students is available)
Me Now	Hubbard	Upper elementary	Life science program designed for mildly retarded students Two-year sequence Primary focus on systems of the human body Activity-oriented	Digestion and circulation Respiration and body waste Movement, support, and sensory processes Growth and development	Teacher's guides Multimedia supplementary materials Supplies kit Student worksheets Evaluation material

Program	Publisher	Level	Characteristics	Topics	Materials
Me and My Environment	Hubbard	Junior high school	Environmental science program designed for mildly retarded students; Three-year sequence; Activity-oriented; Inquiry-oriented; Reading minimized; Functional language used; Reading minimized; Activities present in small, discrete units	Exploring my environment; Me as an environment; Energy relationships in my environment; Transfer and cycling of materials in my environment	Teacher's guides; Multimedia supplementary materials (e.g., slides, games); Supplies kit; Student worksheets
Me in the Future	Hubbard	High school	Career education focus; Culmination of other Hubbard programs; Activity-oriented; Adult interest level; Low readability level	Vocations; Leisure; Daily living skills	Teacher's guides; Multimedia supplementary materials; Supplies kit

ware may not have been developed for certain science topics; some field-based activities may be inaccessible to students in wheelchairs; or due to limited supplies, individual hands-on activities must be replaced by teacher-directed demonstrations.

Adaptations and Modifications

On inspection of the literature on adapting instruction for handicapped populations, suggestions on what can be done are available but little empirical data supporting their effectiveness can be located (Lovitt, Rudsit, Jenkins, Pious, & Benedetti, 1985). Nevertheless, most teachers can share personal accounts of changes they have made that have worked well with special needs students.

There are a number of techniques for accommodating special learners vis-a-vis science instruction. Suggested modifications can be divided into three categories: classroom environment, materials, and instructional modifications. Table 8.5 provides specific suggestions for making modifications in these three areas for different handicapping conditions.

Classroom Environment Modifications.   Most handicapped students benefit from classroom settings that are well-organized and structured. The most important organizational dimension in the classroom is seating. Attention to this factor can help students be more successful and reduce the amount of noninstructional time that teachers may be required to give certain students.

As safety is a major concern in science, it should be considered regularly. Special recognition should be given to students who experience seizures and loss of consciousness by seating them so that they will not harm themselves. For visually impaired students, it is beneficial to establish a "geographic work area" with which they can become familiar and which does not change. The use of trays and containers that hold science materials is also helpful.

Materials Modification.   Although Table 8.5 presents many ideas for modifying instructional materials, there are some additional suggestions worth noting. The one area that demands the most attention is modification of written materials.

Logical suggestions such as taping or rewriting textual materials have two serious drawbacks—time and effort. For those students who can handle the readability of texts but need assistance in mastering content, the use of framed outlines may prove helpful (Lovitt, Rudsit, Jenkins, Pious, & Benedetti, 1986). These materials outline the text passages with key words deleted for the student to fill in. Lovitt et al. also found the use of vocabulary practice sheets to be effective in helping students deal with the linguistic demands of a seventh-grade physical science text. These vocabulary exercises required students to fill in blank spaces associated with particular definitions with words contained in a vocabulary list.

TABLE 8.5
Modifications in Science

Disability	Classroom Environment Modification	Materials Modification	Instructional Modification
Learning disabilities	Students seated away from distracting noises	Concrete, relevant materials	Immediate feedback Short activities Cueing of relevant details Social praise Pairing of an object and its symbol Eye contact and priority seating for discussion Multisensory activities
Behavior disorders	Students seated away from distracting noises	Training with equipment prior to use	Motivation Immediate reinforcement Cueing of relevant details Short activities Eye contact and priority seating for discussions Social praise
Mental retardation (and slow learners)	Students seated away from distracting noises	Low-reading-level materials Training with equipment prior to use Concrete, relevant, tangible materials	Social priase Eye contact and priority seating for discussions Short activities Repetition Active involvement Practice in a variety of settings Contact with real objects Immediate feedback *(continued)*

TABLE 8.5
(continued)

Disability	Classroom Environment Modification	Materials Modification	Instructional Modification
			Pairing of an object with its symbol
			Adaptations of reading material
			Cueing of relevant details
Visual impairment	Materials kept in predictable place	Large-print or Braille reading materials	Hands-on activities—use of other senses to observe
	Students seated near activity	Taped lessons	More verbal description and use of touch
	Sighted guide to aid in giving directions	Sighted tutor to read directions or guide movements	Contact with real objects
	Well-lighted work area	Training with equipment prior to use	
		Braille writer, slate and stylus, Braille typewriter or large-print typewriter	
Hearing impairment	Students seated near activity so they can hear better and lip read if necessary	Captioned films, filmstrips	Hands-on experience to develop concept
		Visual text to accompany tapes	Visual aids to accompany lectures
	Students seated away from distracting noises	Model or repetition of directions	List of new vocabulary before verbal presentation
			Eye contact before speaking
			Clear enunciation
			Contact with real objects
			Repetition of instructions and verbal presentation as necessary

TABLE 8.5
(continued)

Disability	Classroom Environment Modification	Materials Modification	Instructional Modification
Health impairment	Removal of things that could aggravate health condition (e.g., no sugar for diabetic; no plant pollen for allergic child)	None	None
Physical impairment	Adequate space for movement; desk and table height adjusted for wheelchairs Seats near exits whenever possible for safety Barrier-free access	Training with equipment prior to use Peer to help with manipulation of materials Mechanical aids for manipulation of materials as necessary	Contact with real objects

Source : Adapted by permission from S. E. Cain & J. M. Evans (1984), *Sciencing: An involvement approach to elementary science methods* (2nd ed.) (Columbus, OH: Merrill), pp. 237–240.

For students whose reading skills do not allow them to handle grade-level materials, the following suggestions are offered.

1. Deemphasize the use of textbooks and focus science instruction on "doing."
2. Use alternative means for students to get the printed information (e.g., taped texts and readers).
3. For secondary level students, obtain science texts that are considered easy reading (i.e., topical but written at low reading levels). Table 8.6 contains selected examples of this type of material.

Other strategies that can assist in comprehending written materials include a variety of activities that can take place before, during, and after the student reads. Preview and self-questioning techniques have been shown to be effective with learning disabled students (Wong, 1985). Another technique is cognitive mapping (Novak & Gowin, 1984), in which students graphically relate concepts that they read, thus enabling them to see and understand relationships. See Table 8.6 for additional ideas to help students comprehend textual material.

TABLE 8.6
Easy-Reading Science Materials

Topic	Janus Books	Quercus Corporation[a]
Life science	Life Science[b]	Human Biology
	Green Plants	Biology of Plants and Animals
	Animals	Help: First Aid and Biology
	The Five Senses	Take Care of Yourself
	Human Systems	
Physical science	Physical Science[b]	Chemistry
	Sound	Physical Science
	Machines	
	Electricity	
	Energy	
Earth/environmental science	Earth Science[b]	Earth Science
	The Solar System	Environmental Science
	Earth Resources	
	Weather	
	Changing Earth	

[a] All texts are supplemented by lab books, except *Help* and *Take Care of Yourself.*
[b] Hardcover texts.

Some materials given to students can be confusing and difficult to follow. It may be necessary to modify commercially prepared worksheets and other handouts. For example, a data collection sheet used in an activity may need to be simplified for some students. Moreover, do not expect all students to be able to develop their own materials in an organized and useful manner.

Instructional Modification. For many students, it is essential that they are prepared for the instruction that will be presented. Science teachers may find it helpful to explain what is to happen and what they expect from students at the beginning of the lesson. Further, assisting special learners to organize themselves and providing clear directions are advisable as well (Sheinker & Coble, 1981). Lastly, actual classroom instruction needs to be lucid and conceptually understandable.

It is strongly suggested that students become as actively engaged in learning as possible. One characteristic of many handicapped students is that they are inactive learners. The subject area of science provides an excellent forum for students to participate actively in their learning. Stallings (1982) has noted that science instruction that primarily involves the use of workbooks and little or no interaction with materials or teacher demonstrations is ineffective, particularly for low achieving students.

Many students with learning problems will prosper from *teacher-directed instruction* where the teacher plays an active role during instruction. Obviously, the amount of teacher-directed activity will vary with the nature of the lesson. Blosser (1986) captures the importance of this component: "instructional techniques which help students focus on learning (preinstructional strategies, increased structure in the verbal content of materials, use of concrete objects or realism) are effective in promoting student achievement in science" (p. 169). Good (1983) has persuasively argued that teachers engaged in active instruction do make a difference in student learning.

What You Can Do

- Deemphasize the use of textbooks and focus science instruction on "doing."

- For secondary level students, obtain science and social studies texts that are considered easy reading.

- Use preview and self-questioning techniques.

- Modify commercially prepared worksheets and other handouts.

- Provide clear directions.

- Explain what is to happen and what is expected from students at the beginning of the lesson.

- Provide study guides as a review before tests.

Another important instructional practice that should be included in science instruction is the *demonstration-prompt-practice* sequence. This sequence is utilized when introducing a new routine or skill and is characterized by instruction that proceeds through the stages of teacher demonstration of the behavior, student performance of the behavior with teacher assistance, and then student performance without assistance. Many situations exist in the science classroom where this technique would be appropriate, such as establishing safety rules and procedures, introducing the proper operation of a new piece of equipment, or teaching students how to graph data. Some specialized strategies worth considering in modifying instructional programs are listed here.

1. Use of all of the senses—multisensory learning (Sheinker & Coble, 1981).
2. Teach students to use mnemonic illustrations to facilitate the recall of science facts (Scruggs, Mastropieri, Levin, & Gaffrey, 1985).
3. Consider the use of mastery learning—it has been found to be a successful strategy (Willett, Yamashita, & Anderson, 1983).

4. Utilize the strategy of concept analysis—identify the critical and noncritical dimensions of the concept to be taught. (Cole, Kitano, & Brown, 1981).
5. Use wait time—the amount of time allocated before a student responds or a teacher replies to a student (Cain & Evans, 1984; Tobin, 1980).
6. Provide informational (i.e., to help the learner modify responses in specific ways) and motivational feedback.
7. Program for generalization—relate instruction and activities to real-life situations (Keller, 1981).

Learning environments that provide students with much instructional and interactive teacher contact have been found to promote significant learning gains (Brophy, 1979). When this scenario is accented by a positive, supportive, and nurturing classroom climate, the probability of student success is maximized.

Social Studies

Social studies, like science, is an exciting curricular area. However, this subject area seems to be "locked in a rigid instructional pattern of lecture-type class activities in which teachers present information and students receive it" (Memory & McGowan, 1985, p. 177).

Social studies is a complex and difficult discipline. A number of factors contribute to this situation. Many social studies concepts are abstract (e.g., community, country), requiring adequate cognitive and conceptual skills. In most social studies classes, reading and writing are essential. Shepherd and Ragan (1982) have warned that elementary social studies textbooks are likely to have the highest reading levels of all curricular areas. Further, students with rich experiential backgrounds are likely to find social studies more interesting and relevant. Much of what is covered in social studies is based on previous exposure to or interaction with various topics. Hallenbeck (1974) summarized the plight of many students with diverse needs: "realizing the difficulty of the subject for the average grade school student, one can expect the special student to have an even rougher time" (p. 18).

Goals and Objectives

There are many different definitions of social studies and, not surprisingly, various interpretations of its goals and objectives. Variations notwithstanding, much of what is done in social studies (regular education) focuses on citizenship education (Shaver, 1981). The intent is to develop an informed, active participant in community life and consumer of community resources.

One way to conceptualize the goals of social studies education is to examine the four major categories identified by the National Council for the Social Studies (NCSS) (cited in Osborn et al., 1979):

Social studies brings the world into the classroom.

1. Knowledge: an understanding of the world and its peoples gained through study of the social sciences and social issues.
2. Abilities: refers to thinking, data-processing, and human relation skills, which are obtained from the study of social studies and required of competent adults.

3. Values: relates to decision making and personal value systems.
4. Social participation: provision of actual experiences or opportunities to apply knowledge, skills, and value-related decision making in self-directed ways.

These goals can be found throughout the social studies curriculum.

For most special learners who are in regular education social studies classes, these goals are just as important as they are for nonhandicapped students. For some mainstreamed students, we must look at these goals in different ways, as Ochoa and Shuster (1980) suggest.

> Obviously with certain kinds of handicapped learners, instructional goals for social studies must be tempered by reality. . . . The fact that some learners will not attain these goals fully is not a reason to alter the goals; rather, the challenge to teachers is one of finding ways to increase the likelihood that learners will achieve these goals. (p. 19)

On inspection of the curricular pattern of social studies found in most schools in the United States, there seems to be little diversity (Superka, Hawkes, Morrissett, 1980). This conflicts with statements that social studies is a discipline lacking in uniformity. However, even though certain topics are typically found in the curricula of most schools, there is less information regarding the specific content of the courses that cover these topics. From other evidence, which will be addressed in the next section, it is safe to say that there is much similarity in content as well. This typical curricular pattern is comprised of two major stages: a *7-year expanding environments* sequence (K–6) and a *recurrent contracting environments* sequence (7–9, 10–12) (Superka et al., 1980). The curricular pattern reflecting these sequences is presented in Table 8.7.

TABLE 8.7
Typical Social Studies Themes by Grade Level

Grade Level	Social Studies Topics
K	Self, school, community, home
1	Families
2	Neighborhoods
3	Communities
4	State history, geographic regions
5	U.S. history
6	World cultures, Western Hemisphere
7	World geography or history
8	American history
9	Civics or world cultures
10	World history
11	American history
12	American government

Major Approaches to Teaching Social Studies

Professional thinking about the social studies curriculum has changed over the years and with it so has the emphasis on how it should be taught. At the elementary level, social studies instruction seems to have shifted toward a back-to-basics orientation (Birchell & Taylor, 1986). Instruction at the secondary level has been influenced by this movement as well, especially in terms of competency testing.

There are a number of discernable approaches to teaching social studies, although they may be labeled differently by various people. The major approaches discussed here are summarized in Table 8.8. The table highlights some of the most obvious advantages and disadvantages of each in regards to the needs of special learners; however, it is not an exhaustive listing. In addition to the textbook, inquiry, and topical approaches, there is the informal (Maxim, 1987) or incidental (Shepherd & Ragan, 1982) approach, which is characterized by the use of bulletin boards and learning centers. This particular orientation is not addressed here.

Textbook/Lecture/Discussion Approach.   At the heart of this approach is the textbook, which serves as the primary vehicle for disseminating information or reinforcing information provided in class. Its importance within the social studies curriculum has been documented extensively (Memory & McGowan, 1985; Superka et al., 1980; Woodward, Elliott, & Nagel, 1986). Woodward et al. note that "the development of textbook programs by commercial publishers and the selection and implementation of textbooks by teachers appears to have all but replaced other forms of curriculum development in the elementary school" (p. 50).

The heavy reliance on textbooks has brought mixed reactions from the professional community. Most of the positive comments are associated with various improvements made over earlier editions (Garcia & Logan, 1983; Superka et al., 1980). Yet others note little improvement over earlier editions (Elliott, Nagel, & Woodward, 1985). Elliott et al. point out that current texts do not cover topics in enough depth, are not well integrated, have too narrow a focus (too little on international topics), and overemphasize map and globe skills (underemphasize thinking skills). Additional concerns include less utilization of outside reading materials (Memory & McGowan, 1985) and diminished use of supplemental materials and activities (Woodward et al., 1986).

When considering the needs of special learners, the dominance of the textbook approach and the findings associated with their use induce mixed feelings as well. That publishers have reduced the readability levels of recently published texts (primarily at the secondary level) is good news for many special learners, as this is often troublesome for them. However, the fact that teachers faced with time limitations do not use many supplementary materials and activities, probably resulting in fewer hands-on activities, is unfortunate for many of these same students. The resultant scenario of social studies instruction (large

TABLE 8.8
Analysis of Various Approaches to Teaching Social Studies

| Approach | Issues Related to Special Learners | | Remarks |
	Positive Features	Negative Features	

Textbook	Most recently published series have been simplified (Birchell & Taylor, 1986)
	
	Good aesthetic features (e.g., illustrations)
	
	Good resource/reference materials
	
	Introduce content-related terms (Armstrong, 1984)
	
	Lessen workload (i.e., preparation time) on teacher
		Readability problems
		
		Language complexity
		
		Concept development—too many, too quickly
		
		Lack of organizational aids (e.g., headings & subheadings) (Adams, Carnine, & Gersten, 1982)
		
		Superficial and disconnected coverage of topics makes under-standing difficult (Woodward, Elliott, & Nagel, 1986)
		
		Teacher's guides not too helpful for accommodating special learners
		
		Typically used in combination with discussion only
			Components:
			  Teacher's guide
			  Student text
			  Student workbook
			  Supplemental materials (e.g., filmstrips)
			
			Texts can be used in various ways (see Turner, 1976, for an interesting continuum of use)

Inquiry	Accentuates organizational and problem-solving skills	Requires organizational and problem-solving skills	Components:
			  Tradebooks
			  Reference materials
			  Library work

amounts of reading, teacher lecturing, and class discussion) is one in which special students can have problems.

On close examination of commercially available social studies textbooks, one finds that the suggestions for meeting individual needs are not too helpful. Ochoa

TABLE 8.8
(continued)

| Approach | Issues Related to Special Learners | | Remarks |
	Positive Features	Negative Features	
	Student-centered Capitalize on student curiosity and interests	Demands self-directed behavior (i.e., independent learning) Requires the use of outside materials, which may not be readable or available (e.g., in Braille or on tape) Requires special skills of the teacher	Field work Media Resource persons Student reports (orally written) Microcomputers Few inquiry-oriented materials developed in the 1960s and 1970s are being used (Superka, Hawke, & Morrissett, 1980)
Topical (customized)	Student- and teacher-focused Relevant to students' interests and experiences Local context Can be student-generated Should be activity-oriented Can include a combination of instructional practices Can integrate curricular areas	Typically requires considerable teacher effort May be conceptually confusing Could result in too narrow a focus	Components: no set list but may include: Texts Trade books Media Role playing Simulations Group work Microcomputers Excellent source of ideas: *My Backyard History Book* (Weitzman, 1975) Another example: minisociety (Kourilsky & Ballard-Campbell, 1984)

Source: Polloway, E. A., Payne, J. S., Patton, J. R., & Payne, R. A. (1989), *Strategies for teaching learners with special needs,* 4th ed. (Columbus, OH: Merrill).

and Shuster (1980) have analyzed seven major textbooks in relation to how well they assisted teachers in modifying instruction for special groups. Although the series they reviewed has since been revised, what they found in this earlier examination still holds for the more recent editions. There are too few specific suggestions for adapting the text or modifying activities to help handicapped students. On the positive side, some of the publisher-supplied supplemental materials that accompany textbooks can be helpful. For instance, the *Heath Social Studies* series provides reading worksheets (i.e., study guides) for each chapter. This material can assist in better comprehending what is read, as suggested in the next section. However, if students are having trouble with the readability of the text, they will probably have difficulty with the readability of the material as well.

Inquiry Approach. Not unlike the process/inquiry approach used in science instruction, the inquiry approach for social studies focuses on problem-centered learning. It has been called "interest-driven learning" and "self-impelled learning" (Maxim, 1987) and is usually characterized by students engaged in independent pursuit of finding answers to some problem. The inquiry approach demands that students and teachers possess certain abilities and prerequisite skills.

Evolving out of the thinking associated with the New Social Studies movement of the late 1960s and early 1970s, inquiry-based instruction emphasizes concepts, generalizations, and methodologies. Currently, it is not being used much in social studies classes across the country. Jarolimek (1981) suggests that teachers find this method unattractive because they (1) do not feel comfortable with the procedures, (2) find it too time-consuming, and (3) feel that it does not transmit the substantive knowledge of social studies as well as they would like.

The information contained in Table 8.8 presents many of the concerns of using the inquiry approach with special populations. Although this instructional option may have its limitations, it can and has been used successfully with special learners (Curtis, 1974). Nevertheless, some general guidelines for using the approach with students displaying diverse learning needs are warranted (Polloway et al., 1985).

> The use of a total inquiry-oriented approach for teaching social studies to special learners is questionable. As in science, the use of process approaches with special students is not prohibited but a certain amount of structured instruction will probably be necessary. In other words, it will be very important to (a) assess whether students can effectively use inquiry skills and (b) present some substantive information via a systematic teaching paradigm. (p. 358)

Topical Approach. The topical approach covers subject matter that is determined in a number of ways. It may follow the scope and sequence set by the school district or the adopted textbook series. The topical sequence also might be customized by the teacher, students, or both. Moreover, what is covered might develop spontaneously, following Rossman's (1983) idea that anything of interest is worthy of study.

The topical approach to social studies instruction can be exciting and relevant to students. However, it has drawbacks as well. For the most part, the factor that weighs most heavily in being able to set up and provide a custommade program is the amount of time and effort required. For educators who must teach an array of subjects, with the accompanying daily preparation, this approach may not be desirable.

Some examples of ideas that could be used as a basis for structuring a topical curriculum include the following.

1. Teaching units on various subjects of interest and concern (e.g., homeless people or Middle East politics).
2. Addressing social issues through popular music (e.g., Madonna's "Papa Don't Preach").
3. Using another source as a guide (e.g., at the elementary level, the stories contained in the basal reading series)(Patton & Oyama, 1987).

These are only selected samples from a large assortment of possibilities.

Some Additional Considerations.   Much of what can be done to accommodate the needs of special learners in the regular social studies classroom is similar to what can be done in the science classroom. Many of the modifications presented in Table 8.5 and discussed in the section on modifying science instruction are appropriate to social studies as well and are not repeated here (see pp. 314–320). However, other specific suggestions, particularly in the area of instructional practices that may differ, are addressed here.

Table 8.9 graphically presents information helpful to social studies teachers in meeting the needs of special students. The table is organized according to

TABLE 8.9
Adaptations and Modifications in Social Studies

Instructional Practice	Specific Presenting Problem	Recommendation	Reference
Textual material	Readability	Taped texts and readers Teacher Other students Volunteers Recordings for the blind	Hallenbeck (1974) Barnard (1981) Tyo (1980)
		Multilevel texts, lower-level materials	Memory & McGowan (1985)
		Transcribe into Braille or print in larger type-face	

(continued)

TABLE 8.9
(continued)

Instructional Practice	Specific Presenting Problem	Recommendation	Reference
		Read basal reading series of appropriate level that relate to topic (collateral reading)	Garcia & Logan (1983)
		Cooperative learning arrangement	
		Rewrite materials	Gregory (1980)
	Vocabulary level	Teacher-prepared glossaries	Armstrong (1984)
		Go over terms prior to reading	
	Comprehension	Prereading: Preview reading selection; go over photographs, illustrations; inspectional reading	Downey (1980) Schneider & McGee-Brown (1980)
		Formulate hypotheses and questions	Yeager & Edwards (1980) Wong (1979)
		Use advanced organizers (i.e., participatory graphic organizers, structured overviews)	Bender (1985) Hawk & McLeod (1984)
		Actual reading: Study and reading guides (e.g., comprehension level, pattern, concept, assistive guides)	Schneider & McGee-Brown (1980)
		Teach students to monitor and evaluate their reading	
		Post reading: Have students retell what they read, but structure this activity	Adams et al. (1982)

TABLE 8.9
(continued)

Instructional Practice	Specific Presenting Problem	Recommendation	Reference
		Projects (e.g., editorials, debates)	
		Role playing/ simulation activities	
		Timelines	
		Practice worksheets	Schlick, Gall, & Riegel (1981)
		Games (e.g., word hunts, cryptograms)	Schneider et al. (1980)
		Relate graphics (e.g., pictures) from other sources to reading; make scrapbook	Turner (1976)
		Use language experience approach to recreate sections of reading	Turner (1976)
		Have students redo graphs, charts, etc, in their own way	Danzer (1980)
	Study skills	Teach study skills *directly*	Adams et al. (1982)
	Visual impairments	Encourage the acquisition of information through other means (e.g., telephone)	Singleton (1979)
		Use technological devices (e.g., Kurzweil Reading Machine)	
Map, globe, picture, and graph skills	Visual impairments	Use tactile materials	
		Certain textures, patterns, and symbols are more legible	Orlansky (1981)
		Avoid graphics that are too cluttered	
		Enlarge and use high contrasting colors	

(continued)

TABLE 8.9
(continued)

Instructional Practice	Specific Presenting Problem	Recommendation	Reference
		Check out specialized equipment	American Printing House for the Blind (n.d.)
	Conceptual development	Begin with maps of immediate environment	
		Draw maps on floor	Dunne & Knudsen (1981)
Media	Comprehension	Use previewing, viewing, postviewing activities	
		Avoid introducing a historical topic with a film/filmstrip—they are too factual—students need more background	Casteel (1981)
	Language level	Introduce vocabulary, concepts, names ahead of time	
	Visual impairments	Good to use	
		Pair with other student	
	Hearing impairments	Discuss afterward	
Field trips	Physical impairments	Inform—call ahead	
		Portable ramps	
	Wheelchairs	Appropriate seating	
	Motor involvement	Few stairways	
		Preview trip	
	Visual impairments	Utilize hands-on exhibits	
		Pair with sighted guide	
		Inform—call ahead	
		Preview trip	
	Hearing impairments	Interpreter	
		Pair with another student	
		Inform—call ahead	

TABLE 8.9
(continued)

Instructional Practice	Specific Presenting Problem	Recommendation	Reference
	Outside readings	Teacher assistance will be needed in selection	
		Encourage acquisition of information from variety of sources	
Projects	Understanding directions	Clarity and teacher follow-up	
	Organizational skills and self-direction	Cooperative learning	
		Time management (i.e., scheduling and deadlines)	
	Conceptual development	Encourage concrete activities—total immersion	Hallenback (1974) Karlin & Berger (1964)
		Make relevant (e.g., teach social issues through music; use newspaper)	Karlin & Berger (1964) Gregory (1979)
	Physical/sensory limitations	Team with other students	
		Alternative projects/reports	
	Writing skills	Deemphasize this area for the project	
		Allow alternative products—oral reports, art work, photographic essay	
Lecture	Attention	Use self-monitoring strategies	Hallahan, Lloyd, & Stoller (1982)
		Seat students appropriately	
		Use students' names regularly—keep active	Simms (1984)
		Small groups	

(continued)

TABLE 8.9
(continued)

Instructional Practice	Specific Presenting Problem	Recommendation	Reference
		For visually and hearing impaired students—take breaks	
	Comprehension	Prelistening: Advanced organizers Checklist of readiness behaviors Go over new terms and vocabulary	
		Actual Listening: Study guide Tape-record Teach students to ask questions Highlight major points Give written information to sensory impaired students	
		Postlistening: Have students evaluate their listening-checklist (see suggestions in text)	Kopp (1967)
	Notetaking	Teach notetaking	
		Prepared outlines	Simms (1984)
		Framed outlines	
		Write out unfamiliar terms, names, and so on	
		Have students share notes—make copies	
	Visual aids Pictures	Explain to visually impaired students	Singleton (1979) provides excellent guidelines for using and adapting visual materials
		Enlarge	
	Illustrations	Adapt, using tactile materials	
		Enlarge	

TABLE 8.9
(continued)

Instructional Practice	Specific Presenting Problem	Recommendation	Reference
	Guest speakers	Contact ahead of time; notify regarding types of students in class	
		Obtain handouts ahead of time; adapt as necessary	
Discussions, role playing, simulations, debates	Understanding directions	Use clear wording and check for understanding	Bender (1985)
	Participation	Encourage students to use reference materials (e.g., study guides)	
		Have students prepare questions ahead of time	
		Use small groups	
		Create a supportive atmosphere	
		Do not force students with communication disorders to speak	
	Comprehension	Review and summarize frequently	
		Relate discussion to experiences	
		Supplement with concrete activities	
Inquiry-oriented programming	Independent learning skills	Cooperative learning	
		Teach these skills	
	Conceptual development	This approach may need to be more structured	Polloway et al. (1985)
		Some teacher-directed instruction may be needed	

Source: Polloway, E. A., Payne, J. S., Patton, J. R., & Payne, R. A. (1989). *Strategies for teaching learners with special needs*, 4th ed. (Columbus, OH: Merrill).

TABLE 8.10
Easy-Reading Social Studies Materials for Secondary Students[a]

American History	Civics and Government
Highlights of American History, Janus (2^2)	*Government in Action,* Janus (2^2)
Famous Americans, Janus (2^2)	*The Government and You,* Follett (3^2)
America's Story, Steck-Vaughn (2^2–3)	*The Law and You,* Follett (3^2)
Foundations in History, Opportunities for Learning (4)	*Citizens Today,* Steck-Vaughn (3–4)
America's Early Years, Steck-Vaughn (4–5)	*Government and Law, Level I,* McGraw-Hill Paperbacks (3–4)
Twentieth-Century America, Steck-Vaughn (4–5)	*United States Government,* Bowmar/Noble (4–6)
American Nation, Follett (4–7) (JHS)	*Democracy in Action,* Steck-Vaughn (5–6)
New Exploring American History, Globe (5–6) (JHS)	*Exploring American Citizenship,* Globe (5–6)
The United States in the Making, Globe (5–6)(JHS)	*Civics: Citizens and Society,* Webster/McGraw-Hill (5–6)
Building the American Nation, Harcourt Brace Jovanovich (5–6) (JHS)	*Civics,* Follett (6–7)
Foundations in American History, Globe (5–6)	**World History**
Life and Liberty, Scott, Foresman (5–6) (HS)	*World History and You,* Steck-Vaughn (4)
American History, Follett (5–7)	*Building the Modern World,* Harcourt Brace Jovanovich (5–6)
Exploring Our Nation's History, Globe (6–7) (HS)	*World History for a Global Age,* Globe (5–6)
Building the United States, Harcourt Brace Jovanovich (7–8) (HS)	*Exploring World History,* Globe (5–6) (HS)
	World History, Follett (6–8)
Geography and World Cultures	*Scholastic World History Program,* Scholastic
Culture Studies Program, Addison-Wesley (5)	
Exploring a Changing World, Globe (5–6)	
World Geography, Follett (6)	
Scholastic World Cultures, Scholastic (6–8)	

[a]The numbers and letters in parentheses are readability levels.
Source: D. M. Memory & T. M. McGowan (1985). Using multilevel textbooks in social studies classes, *The Social Studies, 76,* 178. Reprinted with permission of the Helen Dwight Reid Educational Foundation. Published by Heldref Publications, 4000 Albemarle St., NW, Washington, DC 20016. Copyright © 1985.

the type of instructional practice being used, provides relevant problems associated with the practice, and recommends ways to address the problem area. Citations are listed so that teachers can pursue certain suggestions in greater depth. Further, a list of social studies materials of lower readability levels is

TABLE 8.11
Additional Easy-Reading Social Studies and Science Materials

Topic	Quercus Corporation	C.C. Publications
American history	To the New Land	The First Americans
	In the Colonies	Explorers and Discoverers
	Statehood, the West and Civil War	Colonial Times
	Industrial Giant	Revolution and Independence
	The Americans Since 1914	Westward Expansion
	American History Activities	Civil War and Reconstruction
		Industrial Revolution
		Immigration
		World War I
		Roaring Twenties and the Depression
		World War II
		The Nuclear Age
Geography and world cultures	Geography One: The Earth and Its Resources	Geography
	Geography Two: The Earth and Its People	
Civics and government	Government Is News	
	State and Local Government	
World history	World History: I, II, III	

provided in Table 8.10. These texts will be particularly attractive to teachers at the secondary level. Some additional materials not included here are presented in Table 8.11.

In general, social studies teachers should keep the following points in mind.

1. Keep students as actively engaged in their learning as possible (i.e., supplement textbooks, lectures, and discussions with hands-on activities).
2. "It matters little *how* a student learns the content; the issue is how *well* the student learns what needs to be learned" (Memory & McGowan, 1985, p. 177).

Computer Applications in Science and Social Studies

The use of microcomputers in science and social studies is another instructional practice that can have positive outcomes and benefits for special learners. First, this technology possesses features that enhance traditional classroom instruction in ways that are advantageous to special populations. Second, hardware and software exist that provide specific functions that certain disabled individuals cannot perform (e.g., speech).

Although most software development to date has focused on content areas other than science and social studies, there are a number of exciting and instructionally sound programs now available in these areas. On a general level, there are three principal educational uses of microcomputers: (1) computer-assisted instruction (CAI)—student usage; (2) computer-managed instruction (CMI)—teacher usage; and (3) computer-assisted management (CAM)—administration usage. Although all of these uses are important, this section covers various ways microcomputers can be used instructionally with special groups in the areas of science and social studies. In addition, selected educational software appropriate for use with special learners is described.

Science Applications

Although science software is available in all the different areas of computer-assisted instruction, only certain selected examples are included in the following list.

1. Use drill and practice software to review different types of animals and their characteristics.
2. Tutorials can cover information that is difficult for students to understand through lecture.
3. Specific chemical experiments can be simulated, thus avoiding any potential danger or allowing physically disabled students to actually carry out the activity.
4. Student logs and notes on activities can be stored in data bases or on word-processing programs.
5. Students who have problems in math can make use of calculation software.
6. Commercially prepared data bases (e.g., *Animal Life Databases* available from Sunburst Communications) can help students retrieve relevant information.
7. Graphics programs can assist students who have trouble drawing visually pleasing charts and graphs.
8. Communication software allows students to go on "electronic field trips" (Adams & Bott, 1984), which can expand the experimental backgrounds of students who are limited in this area.

9. Various probeware that measures a number of variables can be helpful to students whose skills or physical abilities do not allow them to do so in traditional ways.

The availability of science software is growing everyday. It is important for teachers to evaluate carefully the quality of these programs before purchase. This is particularly noteworthy as much of the software has the potential to assist teachers in accommodating special needs learners. Some of the programs that science teachers may find useful are listed in the "Resources" at the end of the chapter.

Social Studies Applications

Social studies is an ideal subject area for using microcomputers. It lends itself well to using simulations, tutorials, interactive video, and the many utility applications. Some exciting software programs have been developed commercially in recent times. Further, many social studies teachers have developed their own applications for using data bases and word-processing programs. The following list represents some of these teacher-developed uses for regular and special students.

1. Word processing:
   a. Report writing
   b. Developing editorials
2. Data bases:
   a. Organizing information about community resources
   b. Filing information of world leaders and newsmakers (Mendrinos, 1986)
   c. Classifying inventions/technology or information about presidential elections (Hunter, 1985)
3. Graphics:
   a. Graphing demographic information about a population
4. Spreadsheets:
   a. Economics
5. Communication:
   a. Obtain information from on-line data bases
   b. Establish local school-to-school networks

From an ever-increasing number of good social studies software, we have selected a few examples that are not only exciting but useful for a wide range of students; these may be found in the "Resources" section. See Schug and Kepner, 1984, for suggestions for evaluating microcomputer simulations in social studies.

Research Implications

Although much of science and social studies education is suited to research study, only limited data-based information exists that increases our knowledge of special learners in these subject areas. Further, this is even more surprising when we consider that these subject areas are some of the first into which these students are mainstreamed.

A number of issues that could be systematically studied are described here, including instruction, curriculum, learning, school environment, and diffusion of new ideas. This structure is based on a model contributed by Ehman and Hahn (1981), which they present as a way to conceptualize the categories of research in social studies education. Although their original model contains six categories, only five are discussed here. Further, the research questions highlighted here are particularly relevant to diverse student populations.

Instruction

Are the many suggested adaptations and modifications really effective? Which ones? How are they effective?

Can the textbook adaptation techniques found to be successful by Lovitt et al. (1986) work in other areas? With younger student populations? Is it reasonable to think that teachers can make such adaptations regularly?

Have the commercially produced instructional materials ever been verified as leading to student success?

Can special learners succeed in inductive approaches?

Can alternative approaches to teaching special groups be developed?

How actively engaged are special students when they are in mainstreamed science and social studies settings?

Which microcomputer uses can be validated as effective with handicapped students?

Are cooperative learning arrangements advantageous when special students are using microcomputers?

Curriculum

Are customized and topical approaches to teaching science and social studies efficacious?

Can integrative curriculum programming be used successfully with special learners?

What constitutes a "functional" science or social studies curriculum at the secondary level?

Learning

Do students actually learn from textbooks?

Do textbooks assist in developing the critical thinking skills of special students?

Do special learners prosper from science and social studies instruction where they are taught information via direct instruction?

Are handicapped students developing more positive attitudes toward science and social studies?

Can mastery learning work successfully in these subjects?

What are some ways to help students generalize various concepts to real-world situations?

School Environment

What are the prevailing attitudes of science and social studies teachers about handicapped students? About teaching handicapped students?

How are students with diverse needs treated in the classroom?

Are special students being accepted in these classes?

Diffusion of New Information

How are in-service teachers provided new information about teaching handicapped students?

Are in-services designed for science and social studies teachers effective?

Do preservice methodology courses cover the topic of accommodating students with special needs? How is this done? What is covered? What effect does it have?

Do mainstreaming courses address the issue of integrating special pupils into science and social studies?

The preceding questions represent only some of the many areas that could be examined; however, they do suggest that much remains to be learned.

_____ *Case Study* _____

INDIVIDUALIZING FOR SCIENCE

Peter is an 8-year-old student with a unique combination of features—a learning disability and cerebral palsy. Peter uses a walker to get from place to place. Further, he was required to be in a prone stander for two 20-minute periods everyday.

He was in a science class that met four times per week for 40 minutes. This class was held during one of the times when he was in the prone stander. He participated in all science activities enthusiastically. Actual lessons did not have to be altered for him; however, changes were necessary in scheduling.

Many activities were scheduled around his "nonambulatory" time. For example, any outdoor work (such as, collecting samples) had to be set up either before or after this 20-minute block.

When Peter was in his stander, he had a portable desk. Although the desk was larger than a standard desk, it was not as stable. Therefore, again proper scheduling became essential. To minimize frustration and accidents, the use of glassware, other specialized equipment, and chemicals were not planned during this 20-minute period of nonambulation. These activities were performed at other times when he was at his standard desk. Another alternative that was used was to clear one of the teacher's desks and let him use this while he was in his stander. This provided him with a sturdier work area.

When Peter used his own work table, he had to take all of his school supplies with him. Often his materials (e.g., pencils) would fall off his desk. He was not able to bend down and pick them up and, if the teacher was elsewhere, he might not be able to continue with the activity and time would be wasted. As a result, a thin rubber sheet that he would usually sit on so he wouldn't slide was placed directly on the table to hold his supplies securely in place. All of his supplies were deposited into a small box at the end of this sheet to make it easier for him to transport his supplies independently.

When the class activities involved the use of liquids or required the utilization of potentially dangerous equipment, Peter was assigned a partner. As the whole class worked with partners, this technique for helping him did not make him stand out or feel different.

Peter was required to participate in all activities and as it turned out few major adaptations were required. He got so excited about this subject area and the activities that were a regular part of it that he would "walk" to where other action was occurring while in his stander by holding onto desks and pulling himself. All students assisted the teacher on a scheduled basis by distributing and collecting materials and equipment to the rest of the class. Peter was no exception, as he executed this duty eagerly and competently.

Peter is a good example of a student who has special needs but who can be accommodated easily into the regular routine of a class. He wanted to participate to the greatest extent possible and was encouraged to do so. Science instruction, particularly if it is activity-oriented as Peter's was, could be a difficult area in which to have such a student. However, with minor adaptations his needs were met successfully.

Roles and Responsibilities

The roles and responsibilities of regular education teachers, special education teachers, and ancillary personnel seem clear. Nevertheless, some confusion can occur. Who is responsible for whom?

Most mildly handicapped students can be handled effectively in regular education. As the severity of the disability increases, the probability that the student will need special education services also increases. Yet, this is not a strict linear model as many moderately handicapped students (e.g., visually impaired, hearing impaired, and learning disabled) can be accommodated in regular science and social studies classes. It is even reasonable to consider the integration of some severely handicapped individuals (e.g., severe forms of cerebral palsy) into such classes, assuming these students possess the requisite cognitive skills.

Some confusion as to roles and responsibilities can arise in regard to older students who still lack some of the basic skills. Wiseman, Van Reusen, and Hartwell (1981) describe one such situation.

> Basic skill proficiency should be a priority goal for secondary schools, but the false notion persists that students improve in basic skills while involved in content-centered instruction. Regular and high-achieving students do improve, but low-achieving students do not. Low-achieving students need direct instruction by trained personnel with appropriate materials and controlled practice in order to show growth in the basic skills. The teachers of social studies courses should not be expected to be responsible for the basic instruction of reading, writing, or spelling. Their responsibility is teaching content in any manner that it can be learned. (p. 58)

It is important for regular classroom teachers to appreciate how other personnel can help them in meeting the needs of a diverse student population. The special education teacher can assist by diagnosing student problems, providing instructional support, helping develop curriculum, and modifying materials and activities. Other members of the professional staff including specialists (vision, hearing, speech), school nurse, school psychologist, counselor, social worker, and media/computer specialist can provide valuable advice and information about special students and their needs.

Summary

This chapter presents information related to meeting the needs of students with diverse needs who are in regular education science and social studies classes. It begins by establishing the importance of these subject areas as well as some of the realities of teaching handicapped students. For each subject area, we discuss its goals and objectives, approaches to teaching, and suggested adaptations and modifications. The many ways in which computers can be used with special students in these subject areas is also presented. Finally, we focus on future areas of research and the roles and responsibilities of various personnel in working with handicapped students in regular education.

Science and social studies instruction should be engaging and exciting. Nevertheless, teaching is challenging, and working with diverse student populations is demanding. Whether or not students with varying needs succeed is largely dependent on classroom teachers. Effective teachers understand the individual differences of their students and are willing to make the effort to help them.

Discussion Questions

1. Explain what is meant by the assessment of the three following areas: students, learning environment, and instructional materials.
2. Analyze the major approaches to teaching science in terms of the potential problems as well as the positive features for special populations.
3. List specific instructional modifications and considerations for teaching science to learners with special needs.
4. Given that many students with special needs have difficulty in the area of reading and that the textbook approach to teaching social studies dominates most classroom routines, suggest some alternative ways to help these students acquire skills and knowledge in this subject area.
5. Discuss how microcomputer technology can enhance social studies education for students who encounter difficulties with traditional methods of instruction.

Resources

For both science and social studies, the resource materials are listed according to the following types: (1) materials that assist in teaching science to diverse student populations, (2) materials that can be used with special learners, and (3) computer software materials.

Science

Resources on Teaching Science to Special Groups

Ball, D. W. (1978). *ESS/special education teacher's guide.* St. Louis: Webster/McGraw-Hill. This guide is designed to help teachers in developing science programs for handicapped students through the use of ESS. It augments the teacher's guides that accompany each ESS unit and contains information regarding 31 ESS units.

Cain, S. E., & Evans, J. M. (1984). *Sciencing: An involvement approach to elementary science methods* (2nd ed.). Columbus, OH: Merrill. This textbook provides an excellent introduction to various approaches for teaching science, major curricular modes, and teaching techniques. Chapter 8 is devoted to teaching science to students with special needs.

Corrick, M. E. (Ed.). (1981). *Teaching handicapped students science.* Washington, DC: National Education Association. This edited work contains nineteen relatively short articles on teaching science to a wide range of handicapped groups. Articles are organized according to the following sections: goals, prerequisites, approaches, materials, barriers, and evaluation.

Hadary, D. E., & Cohen, S. H. (1978). *Laboratory science and art for blind, deaf, and emotionally disturbed children: A mainstreaming approach.* Austin, TX: PRO-ED. This book provides examples of science and art activities and how they can be interrelated. Suggestions are also appropriate for handicapped groups other than those mentioned in the title.

Jacobson, W. J., & Bergman, A. B. (1987). *Science for children: A book for teachers.* Englewood Cliffs, NJ: Prentice-Hall. This textbook provides information for teaching science and serves as a reference for obtaining explanations of scientific concepts. Chapter 9 is devoted to the topic of science for handicapped students and contains many suggestions.

Taylor, F. D., Artuso, A. A., & Hewett, F. M. (1973). *Exploring our environment: Science tasks for exceptional children in special and regular classrooms.* Denver: Love Publishing. This book or set of cards provides 108 simple science activities. The most attractive feature is that each activity includes a real-world example related to the science concept being addressed.

Instructional Materials Relevant for Special Groups

Brown Paper School Books, Little, Brown & Co., 200 West Street, Waltham, MA 02254. This series of books is designed to provide an exciting collection of ideas on various topics. The guiding principle on which this series has been developed is "that learning happens only when it is wanted, that it can happen anywhere, and that it doesn't require fancy tools." The titles related to science are *The Reasons for Seasons (The Great Cosmic Megagalactic Trip Without Moving from Your Chair); Blood and Guts (A Working Guide to Your Own Insides); The Night Sky Book (An Everyday Guide to Every Night); Good for Me (All About Food in 32 Bites); Beastly Neighbors (All About Wild Things in the City or Why Earwigs Make Good Mothers); Gee Wiz! (How to Mix Art and Science or the Art of Thinking Scientifically).*

Foundations Approach to Science Teaching (FAST), Curriculum Research and Development Group, College of Education, University of Hawaii at Manoa, 1776 University Avenue, Honolulu, HI 96822. FAST is an intermediate level interdisciplinary, environmental science program. It is designed to provide investigative experiences and inquiry activities in the physical, biological, and earth sciences.

Hawaii Nature Study Program, Curriculum Research and Development Group, College of Education, University of Hawaii at Manoa, 1776 University Avenue, Honolulu, HI 96882. This program is an environmental education program for elementary students comprised of out-of-door, action-oriented, problem-solving observations and investigations about the natural environment. Even though it is designed with Hawaii in mind, most of the activities and ideas can be replicated in other parts of the world.

Laboratory Science Series, C. C. Publications, P.O. Box 23699, Tigard, OR 97223. This is a science program designed for students with low reading abilities and for teachers with little or no science background. It contains ten different topics presented in workbook format. The value of this series would be as supplemental material.

Quercus Publications: *Project Earth* and *Project Explore*, Project Earth, Box 31, Sauk Centre, MN 56378. This program is designed for handicapped and remedial high school students. It contains twelve magazine-style text-workbooks and covers earth, life, and physical sciences.

Earth Science, Physical Science, Environmental Science, Human Biology, and Biology of Plants and Animals, Quercus Corporation, 2768 Pineridge Road, Castro Valley, CA 94546. This program is designed for high school students whose reading levels are as low as second grade. The intent is to relate simple science concepts to students' own lives.

Your World of Facts, C. C. Publications, P.O. Box 23699, Tigard, OR 97223. This program is designed as a supplement to any science or social studies curriculum. The most noticeable feature of this program is the teacher-directed instruction of key facts and relationships. This two-part program can be used with students in grades 3–6 or with older remedial students.

Computer Software

Chem Lab, Simon & Schuster, Gulf & Western Bldg., One Gulf & Western Plaza, New York, NY 10023. (Grades 6–12.) Chem Lab is a simulation of fifty different experiments. Each activity uses realistic supplies and equipment.

Odell Lake, Minnesota Educational Computing Consortium, 3490 Lexington Ave., North St. Paul, MN 55112. This is not a new program, but it is worth discussing because of its features. Odell Lake is an ecological simulation in which students are placed in the situation of being a specific type of freshwater fish and react to certain situations. This program illustrates the need for students to have some understanding of the content being simulated and the directions they are to follow. If not, frustrated students could turn this simulation into a *Pac-Man*.

Science Toolkit, Broderbund Software, 17 Paul Drive, San Rafael, CA 94903. (Grades 4–12.) This software is an example of probeware. It includes measurement instruments and interfacing software which allow students to measure temperature, light intensity, and time. Supplemental equipment that records additional measures is also available.

Sky Lab, Minnesota Educational Computer Consortium, 3490 Lexington Ave., North St. Paul, MN 55112. (Grades 5–8.) Sky Lab is an astronomy simulation that addresses the following topics: rotation of the earth, paths of planets, Halley's Comet. It includes different vantage points for examining these topics.

The Voyage of the Mimi, Holt, Rinehart & Winston, 383 Madison Avenue, New York, NY 10017. (Grades 4–8.) This program is actually a multimedia package including videocassettes, teacher's guides, student books, and software. There are thirteen dramatic episodes accompanied by thirteen documentary-type expeditions. Four software modules that use a variety of types of CAI techniques cover: Introduction to Computing, Maps and Navigation, Whales and Their Environment, and Ecosystems.

Social Studies

Resources on Teaching Science to Special Groups

Adams, A. H., Coble, C. R., & Hounshell, P. B. (1977). *Mainstreaming language arts and social studies: Special ideas and activities for the whole class.* Santa Monica, CA: Goodyear Publishing. Organized on a 36-week basis, this guide provides many different activities that can be used with a range of elementary-aged students. The use of these activities with the entire class is emphasized.

Herlihy, J. G., & Herlihy, M. T. (Eds.). (1980). *Mainstreaming in the social studies* (NCSS Bulletin 62). Washington, DC: National Council for the Social Studies. This book presents many different topics related to mainstreaming. It is a good introduction to what mainstreaming is all about. A useful overview of the individual educational program (IEP) is provided.

Ochoa, A. S., & Shuster, S. K. (1980). *Social studies in the mainstreamed classroom, K–6.* Boulder, CO: Social Science Education Consortium. This guide is an excellent resource as it contains much practical information about working with handicapped students in social studies. There are seven major sections to the book, each covering an important area of mainstreaming.

Shaw, T. (Ed.) (1981). *Teaching handicapped students social studies: A resource handbook for K–12 teachers.* Washington, DC: National Education Association. This is another excellent material for teachers to use. It contains many useful suggestions for accommodating handicapped students within the regular education classroom. What is particularly noteworthy is the extensive attention given to the secondary level.

Singleton, L. R. (1979). *Social studies for the visually impaired child* (MAVIS Sourcebook 4). Boulder, CO: Project MAVIS, Social Science Education Consortium. The resource is valuable for teachers who have visually impaired students in their classrooms. Contained within are many specific techniques for adapting materials/equipment and modifying instruction.

Instructional Materials Relevant for Special Groups

Brown Paper School Books, Little, Brown & Co., 200 West Street Waltham, MA 02254. This series is described in the section on science resources. The titles related to social studies are *My Backyard History Book; The Book of Where (How to Be Naturally Geographic);* and *Only Human (Why We Are the Way We Are).*

C. C. Publications Social Studies Series, P.O. Box 23699, Tigard, OR 97223. This is an American history series that primarily uses workbooks as a means of sharing information. Other accompanying instructional materials include software, minibiographies, and historical novels. The thirteen workbooks are written at a low readability level (2.9–3.4 level).

History Alive, Educational Insight, Compton, CA: This material contains a series of classroom plays for social studies. Readability is at the 4–5 grade level.

Quercus materials: *American History Course, World History Course, Government Course*, Quercus Corporation, 2768 Pineridge Road, Castro Valley, CA 94546. The American and world history programs are designed to supplement other textbook materials. The government course is designed to prepare students for passing competency measures in this area. All of these materials are written at the second-grade reading level.

Project MAVIS, Social Science Education Consortium, 855 Broadway, Boulder, CO 80302. This project was funded to adapt social studies curriculum materials for visually impaired students so that they could participate more appropriately in mainstreamed settings. The main thrust was to adapt two commercial series: Houghton Mifflin and Silver Burdett. An assortment of specific changes were made. Six sourcebooks written for teachers were developed.

Your World of Facts, C. C. Publications, P.O. Box 23699, Tigard, OR 97223. This program is described in the section on science resources.

Computer Software

Geography Search, McGraw-Hill, 1221 Avenue of the Americas, New York, NY 10020. This is a simulation that combines concepts and skills from history and geography. It places students as sailors aboard ships searching for gold in the New World. The crew must interpret the data supplied and then make decisions as to what actions to take. Students are required to use a compass, measure latitude and longitude, and develop a map of their voyage.

Hometown: A Local Area Study, Active Learning Systems, P.O. Box 1984, Midland, MI 48640. (Grades 7–12.) This is a data base designed to file information about student's hometowns. Students can study the data collected and determine relationships about their communities.

Revolution and Constitution, Midscape, 3444 Dundee Rd., Northbrook, IL 60062. (Grades 5–8.) This intriguing program involves historical problem solving. Students attempt to name a specific historical event after having examined the locale of this event, studying objects found at the site, and interviewing witnesses. This program causes one to think about the possibilities of teaming this idea with interactive video.

Road Rally U.S.A., Bantam, 666 Fifth Ave., New York, NY 10103. (Grades 5–8.) This engaging software asks students to use maps (both on-screen and off-screen) to go from city to city. As they do this, they learn about these areas that they have visited. It develops map-reading, geography, and problem-solving skills.

Where in the World is Carmen Sandiego? Broderbund, 17 Paul Dr., San Rafael, CA 94903. (Grades 8–12.) This program has received much attention and well-deserved praise. Students become detectives and try to track down the wanted criminal, Carmen Sandiego, and her accomplices who are at large in the world. The students, as international detectives, travel throughout the world in their quest. At each stop, they question witnesses and consult their reference materials. Eventually, they must get to Interpol for an arrest warrant before they can make the arrest. Students must analyze clues, use reference materials (e.g., almanac), and draw inferences. A version that involves travel within the United States is available as well.

Career and Vocational Education

JOHN KREGEL
Virginia Commonwealth University

Chapter Objectives

After reading Chapter 9 the student will be able to

- Demonstrate knowledge regarding the current degree of occupational adjustment on the part of handicapped individuals after they leave public school special education programs
- Define the concepts of career and vocational education and describe the key issues in delivering career and vocational education to handicapped students in integrated programs
- Identify appropriate curriculum content and methods of instruction for providing career and vocational education instruction to handicapped students of all ages
- Identify the appropriate professionals who should be involved in the career preparation of handicapped students and specify their appropriate roles

H andicapped Americans are not participating in the workforce to the same extent as nondisabled citizens. Of more than 225 million people in our country, approximately 36 million are disabled. However, unemployment rates of 50% to 75% for handicapped individuals are consistently reported (U.S. Commission on Civil Rights, 1983). Today, despite a decade of litigation, legislative mandates, and increased public awareness of the rights of handicapped people, millions of potentially employable handicapped adults remain idle. The failure to incorporate these individuals into our nation's workforce wastes a valuable human resource, and the cost of this dependency places a tremendous strain on our nation's economy. Even greater are the human costs of idleness and dependency on the lives of these handicapped people.

Disabled Americans who are fortunate enough to find employment have a difficult time earning a satisfactory wage. Many are underemployed; although they are working, they do not make enough money to support themselves or their families. Sixty percent of all handicapped adults of working age are at or near the poverty level (Bowe, 1978). In 1976, Biklen and Bogden reported that of all employed disabled people, 85% were earning less than $7,000 yearly, and 52% were earning less than $2,000 a year. Ten years later, Kiernan, McGaughey, and Schalock (1986) found that this situation had not changed significantly. Clearly, most handicapped Americans do not earn a salary that allows them to live independent, self-directed lives.

For subgroups within the handicapped population, the employment situation is even worse. For example, 76% of all disabled women are unemployed (Bowe, 1980). In an analysis of the effectiveness of work-study programs for mildly mentally retarded students, Cegelka (1976) discovered that even though these programs may benefit males, they do little to improve the lives of females. Generally, handicapped women are employed less frequently, make less money, and work in less rewarding jobs than disabled men.

Another group for whom the situation is particularly bleak includes individuals who work in sheltered workshops or activity centers. In a phone survey, Bellamy, Rhodes, Bourbeau, and Mank (1986) found that between 80,000 and 100,000 mentally or physically handicapped people were served in adult daycare or activity centers. Many of the centers surveyed did not focus their efforts on vocational training and placement. The U.S. Department of Labor (1979) reported an average annual wage of $666 per year for all clients in sheltered employment in 1976. For mentally retarded individuals in sheltered employment, the average wage was $414 per year.

Individuals with handicaps generally are employed less frequently and make less money than other people in our society. In addition, they are often adversely affected by the types of jobs they hold. Many handicapped adults work in jobs that are classified as unskilled or semiskilled. Bowe (1978) indicates that most handicapped workers labor in jobs that economists term the "secondary labor market." These jobs are characterized by minimum wages, menial skill requirements, high turnover rates, few opportunities for advancement, and vulnerability to hard economic times. Undoubtedly, many handicapped people are able to perform far more sophisticated work than that for which they are trained and placed. The types of jobs generally held by adults with learning disabilities are of equally low status (Association for Children and Adults with Learning Disabilities, 1982; White, Deschler, Schumaker, Warner, Alley, & Clark, 1983). This is often frustrating to the individual, and denies the person the opportunity to obtain personal satisfaction, self-worth, and daily challenges in his or her vocation.

An analysis of the vocational adjustment of disabled adults uncovers a situation that places a heavy burden on our nation's economy. The cost of maintaining disabled individuals in dependent roles, in terms of public income maintenance, has increased tremendously in recent years. The financial costs represent only one aspect of the problem. The human and social costs of imposed idleness and lifelong dependency are incalculable.

The reality of the vocational adjustment of handicapped people is both distressing and frustrating. It is distressing in terms of its impact on the economic and emotional well-being of these people, and frustrating because it does not have to be this way. An abundance of evidence compiled over the last 30 years unequivocally makes the point—handicapped workers are generally good workers; they are productive, safe, and dedicated employees.

In a review of thirteen different studies, Parent and Everson (1986) document the vocational potential of disabled individuals. Most are able to produce at a rate equal to or greater than other employees; generally have lower accident, absenteeism, and turnover rates; and require no special adjustments to the workplace. Advances in training technology have allowed even severely handicapped individuals to move toward competitive job placements (Wehman, Kregel, Shafer, & Hill, 1987). Yet, a number of negative stereotypes about handicapped workers still persist. They are often perceived as more expensive to train, to place, and to maintain in employment. Both employers and vocational educators often feel that handicapped individuals are unable to conduct themselves safely in a work environment. Other perceived shortcomings include a lack of flexibility and ability to adapt to new situations and responsibilities.

Despite convincing evidence that handicapped workers can be valuable assets to business and industry, they remain underrepresented in the American workforce. In addition, they are all too often viewed by their families and the public at large as incapable of contributing to their economic self-sufficiency. Why does this situation persist? The answer does not lie in the mental, physical, or emotional impairment of the handicapped person. Chronic absenteeism, tardiness, alcoholism, or lack of commitment to the business or industry are the factors that "handicap" any individual in terms of fulfilling his or her job responsibilities. These characteristics simply do not describe the majority of handicapped individuals. With appropriate training and support, handicapped individuals can become productive, successful members of a community's workforce.

The Challenge to Teachers

Developing the career potential of handicapped students presents educators with a different type of challenge. The process begins when students first enter the school system and continues after they leave. It involves the efforts of many people over many years. Regular and special educators, related service personnel, administrators, parents, and community members are all involved to varying degrees at different times. The experiences and instruction provided by each professional contribute to the comprehensive vocational development of handicapped students.

When the handicapped student reaches adolescence, the responsibility for vocational preparation falls primarily on vocational educators. Special educators and related service personnel may provide support and assistance as required, but the vocational educator is the individual who possesses the knowledge of the local business community, an understanding of the skills and characteristics required by effective workers, and the instructional strategies that will prepare secondary students effectively for the world of work. Without the direct involvement of vocational educators, it is unlikely that handicapped students can achieve their vocational potential. At the elementary level, regular educators must be directly involved in teaching the important career awareness concepts described in detail later in the chapter. By infusing career education content into the curriculum, handicapped students mainstreamed at the elementary level will acquire a positive attitude toward themselves and their future role as workers.

Effective vocational preparation is clearly a cooperative effort between vocational and special educators. As stated previously, vocational educators must assume primary responsibility for setting vocational goals, designing vocational curricula, and delivering instruction. However, the active cooperation of special educators in the career-preparation process will greatly assist vocational educators and maximize the handicapped student's chances for vocational success. Special educators generally possess useful knowledge regarding ways to modify curricula and instructional activities to meet the needs of students with particular types of handicaps. They usually have had a great deal of contact with individual students and are able to suggest strategies to motivate and instruct them. In addition, special educators frequently have regular contact with the student's parents. Active support provided by the family often plays a key role in the student's vocational success. The special educators can often serve a useful role in eliciting parents' support in the vocational preparation process.

This chapter describes a comprehensive approach to the career preparation of handicapped students. First, basic concepts of career and vocational education are defined and discussed. Second, a five-stage approach to career development is outlined—awareness, exploration, orientation, preparation, and placement—including the major goals and adapted instructional activities appropriate to each stage. Next, guidelines for providing integrated vocational programs and issues in work preparation are described. The final section outlines the process of developing a vocational IEP.

Career and Vocational Education Concepts and Definitions

A major barrier for many handicapped people attempting to become independently employed is their functional exclusion from appropriate vocational training programs. It is generally recognized that vocational training opportunities for handicapped adolescents and young adults have not been satisfactory (Halpern, 1979; Heller, 1981; Wehman & Barcus, 1985). Despite dramatic improvement in vocational services and a clear federal mandate, handicapped adolescents continue to be underrepresented in vocational education and job-training programs. Far too many students continue to be placed into work-study or separate vocational preparation programs operated by special education personnel, which do little to enhance their employability. Handicapped students also are placed into nonskill-oriented prevocational programs that do not equip them with a skill, craft, or trade needed to compete in the open labor market. As a result, millions of handicapped individuals lack the vocational skills necessary to compete for jobs in their communities.

An analysis of prevalence statistics indicates that fewer handicapped students are enrolled in secondary programs than in elementary programs. Generally, the prevalence of handicapped students at the secondary level is less than half that at the elementary level. An even larger decline is found in the number of handicapped students enrolled above the age of 16. A portion of this reduced prevalence can be attributed to special education students returning to regular classes. However, much of the reduction is due to a disproportionately high drop-out rate. In fact, the President's Committee on Employment of the Handicapped (1979) reported a drop-out rate for disabled students five to six times higher than the rate for other high school students. Obviously, many students do not perceive the services they are receiving to be of any value for their future lives. Unfortunately, in many instances this perception is accurate. After an exhaustive review of work-study programs, Brolin and Kolstoe (1978) concluded: "The recognition that neither placement nor promotion of the handicapped could be credited to training programs in public education comes as a sobering discovery" (p. 20). The reasons for the failure of these programs are numerous and complex, but several important factors can be identified. First, the traditional organization of the secondary school has served to limit the alternatives offered to handicapped students. Secondly, many students who could benefit from vocational education programs are not receiving these services. A third factor relates to the inherent limitations of the work-study approach in preparing handicapped students for employment.

Secondary schools have traditionally been organized along departmental and subject matter lines. The academic focus of the secondary curriculum is inappropriate for many handicapped adolescents (Clark, 1975). Yet an academic program is sometimes the only alternative offered to many handicapped students. This practice leads to some students not receiving instruction appropriate to their individual needs. Halpern (1979) identifies two perspectives on providing academic instruction to secondary special education students—the remedial approach and the functional approach. The *remedial approach* is generally used with learning disabled, emotionally disturbed, and physically and sensory impaired students. It attempts to improve students' basic academic skills to enable them to succeed within the regular, content-oriented curriculum. In contrast, the *functional approach*, in use primarily with mentally retarded students, emphasizes the practical application of functional skills. It focuses on preparing handicapped students for roles as producers, citizens, and consumers. Although the advantages and disadvantages of each approach have been widely debated (Clark, 1980), neither approach is generally superior to the other. The individual needs of a given student determine which approach is the most appropriate. Too often, however, only one alternative is available to handicapped students.

The 1963 Vocational Education Act was the first legislation of its type to mention handicapped students specifically. Although no specific monies were allotted, vocational educators were encouraged to make a special effort to serve disabled individuals. The 1968 Amendments to the Vocational Education Act set specific financial requirements. The Amendments provided that 10% of the federal funds coming to states must be spent in programs for handicapped students. To obtain these funds, states were required to match them dollar for dollar. However, as many as fourteen states chose not to match this money and returned it to the federal government. As a result, handicapped students remained largely unserved.

In an attempt to rectify this situation, Congress tightened the matching requirements in 1976. States are now required to spend at least 10% of their total allotment on vocational education for handicapped persons. States are also required to use these funds to the maximum degree possible to assist handicapped persons in participating in regular vocational education programs. These provisions have been retained in the 1984 Carl Perkins Act, the most recent reauthorization bill. However, these regulations have not yet had a significant impact on the number of handicapped students enrolled in vocational education. In 1974–1975, disabled students represented only 1.7% of the total enrollment of vocational education programs (Razeghi & Davis, 1979). The data from 1979 indicate that enrollment increased to only 2.1%. This small increase suggests that more attention should be given to providing services to handicapped individuals in regular vocational education programs (Razeghi & Davis, 1979).

Razeghi and Davis (1979) report that handicapped students enrolled in vocational education are served primarily in segregated programs. Such programs limit the range of occupations for which handicapped students can be prepared. It appears that handicapped students are most often placed in vocational education without any type of support or are confined to separate programs that offer few options for vocational training. Ideally, handicapped students should be placed in regular vocational education programs with the support services necessary to guarantee their success.

A final variable contributing to the overall ineffectiveness of vocational training efforts relates to an overreliance on the traditional work-study approach in the preparation of handicapped secondary students. Although work-study programs are valuable to some students, they severely restrict the range of available career options. Most vocational training occurs on the job, and the coordination between the work and study components is often poorly articulated. In addition, segregated programs often prepare students for low-level, unskilled occupations. Many of these programs focus on occupations such as hotel maids, building maintenance, or dishwashers. These types of employment only perpetuate the cycle of handicapped workers in low-paying jobs that offer little chance for advancement and are not commensurate with their abilities.

A comprehensive vocational preparation program should include specific job-skill training and work experience. Services such as prevocational education, vocational evaluation programs, or sheltered employment are not sufficient in and of themselves. Yet they make up the bulk of many handicapped students' career-preparation programs. The problem is that after receiving all these services, the student still lacks a saleable vocational skill. No program is complete without vocational skill training; that is, equipping students with all the skills required to perform a competitive job in the open labor market. Two major movements of the past decade within general education may provide increased opportunities for handicapped students to acquire practical skills within regular education classes. Career education and the inclusion of handicapped students in vocational education programs have done a great deal to add functional content to secondary curricula. Much still remains to be done in terms of curriculum revision and development of appropriate support services. However, career education and vocational education hold the promise of making secondary curricula more relevant to the needs of students with handicaps.

Career Education

High school curricula alternatives typically provide students choices among college preparatory, general education, or vocational education programs (Scott & Moye, 1978). None of these programs are currently committed to the comprehensive career preparation of individual students. Numerous recent criticisms have been leveled at secondary schools. Many students leave the public school system lacking the skills needed to function in adult roles. Graduates lack the basic academic skills for adaptability (e.g., converting measures, comparative shopping, personal finance, and so on). Students frequently see no relationship between the skills they learn and their future lives, and they often have no saleable job skills. They lack knowledge of the federal government, energy resources, first aid, and family planning. High school is an alienating experience for many students. These criticisms raise serious doubts concerning the relevance and effectiveness of current high school curricula.

Career education is a concept that was introduced in 1971 by then U.S. Commissioner of Education Sidney P. Marland. The concept has evolved over the last 15 years, and the Career Education Incentive Act (1978) provided assistance to school districts to help them develop career education programs. Hoyt (1975) defines *career education* as the "totality of experiences through which one learns about and prepares to engage in work as a part of her or his way of living" (p. 4). Career education was at first interpreted as preparation for a job, and many people viewed it as synonymous with vocational education. But career education was soon viewed as dealing with more than just paid employment.

Hoyt (1975) clarifies the scope of career education through his definition of work:

> "Work" is conscious effort, other than that involved in activities whose primary purpose is either coping or relaxing, aimed at producing benefits for oneself and/or for oneself and others. (p. 3)

This definition of work makes few restrictions in meaning. The term *work* applies to the musician, the athlete, the volunteer, the bricklayer, the homemaker, the custodian, or the do-it-yourself person. Emphasis is placed on career education as preparation for many roles, not merely as worker. Curriculum development is based on a logical analysis of the various life careers in which individuals engage as a part of society—producers of goods and services, members of families, citizens active in the social and political life of society, and participants in recreational pursuits.

Career education for handicapped individuals has received considerable attention in recent years. Several approaches have been developed or advocated that can serve as career education models for handicapped students (Apolloni & Westaway, 1980; Brolin, 1982; Clark, 1980). All models reflect an expanded view of career education; together they provide another source of content for special educators designing curricula for handicapped students in secondary schools. For example, Brolin's (1982) model identifies twenty-two career-preparation competencies clustered in three primary areas—daily living skills, personal-social skills, and occupational guidance and preparation. These competencies are further subdivided into 102 subcompetencies. The Council for Exceptional Children has published a program guide based on these competencies (Brolin, 1978).

Vocational Education

Another area of the secondary school curriculum that has much to offer handicapped students is vocational education. *Vocational education* is defined as

> Organized educational programs which are directly related to the preparation
> of individuals for paid or unpaid employment, or for additional preparation for
> a career requiring other than a baccalaureate or advanced degree. (*Federal
> Register*, 1977, p. 53869)

Vocational education programs have existed in our nation's public schools since
before 1920, when agriculture education, industrial arts, and trade and industrial
education programs emerged with the passage of the Smith-Hughes Act in 1918.
Over the past 50 years, other programs have developed, so that vocational education now encompasses seven distinct service areas:

1. Agriculture education.
2. Distributive education.
3. Health occupations education.
4. Home economics education.
5. Industrial arts.
6. Office occupations education.
7. Trade and industrial education.

Vocational education emphasizes preparation for paid or unpaid employment.
Programs are evaluated on whether graduates take jobs in the vocational areas
for which they were trained. While unpaid employment is mentioned in the
definition to include homemaker preparation through home economics education, the emphasis of vocational education is clearly on preparation for entry-
level semiskilled or skilled employment. Vocational education programs in
secondary schools may also be viewed as preparation for additional employment
training at the post-secondary level through vocational-technical schools, community colleges, or other employment-training programs.

Vocational education programs are designed around a careful analysis of local
economic and employment needs. This approach allows vocational educators to
identify occupational clusters and specific occupations in each cluster to be included in the program. Information is obtained through advisory committee
input, community surveys, and a review of local economic data. Advisory com-
mittees are formed at the program and cluster level. They function to advise
the vocational education program on employment needs and relevance of the
training programs. Local employers, personnel directors, and Chamber of Com-
merce officials may be surveyed to determine the needs of business and industry.
Parents and students are also surveyed to identify programs they would like
to see offered. Reviewing economic and employment studies conducted by state
and federal government can help vocational educators predict future employment trends. Developing curricula from an analysis of local economic conditions
enables vocational education programs to provide graduates the opportunity
for a job related to their training on graduation. The job will be one that will
not become obsolete in the near future.

The Relationship Between
Career and Vocational Education

The relationship between career and vocational education is often confused. Whereas vocational education focuses exclusively on preparation for employment, career education attempts to prepare students for all potential life roles (family member, citizen, consumer, and so on). As such, career education encompasses vocational education. Career education also represents an attempt to refocus all education toward the preparation of students for life beyond education. Whereas vocational education represents a specific curricular area within the school, career education content is infused throughout all areas of the curriculum. For example, competencies in managing personal finances may become the partial responsibility of the mathematics instructor, or the social studies staff may become involved in teaching competencies related to engaging in civic activities. Career education instruction should be a cooperative effort of all individuals involved in a specific student's educational program.

The federal government has recognized that the educational system plays a major role in preparing handicapped students to bridge the gap between education and work. In 1978, the United States Office of Education issued a policy statement mandating that a comprehensive vocational education be made available and accessible to every handicapped citizen. The statement clearly implied that educators have a responsibility to prepare handicapped students for the world of work as well as all other facets of adult life. Vocational education must be *comprehensive*. All segments of the educational system must be involved—elementary, secondary, and adult education. Vocational education, vocational rehabilitation, and professionals in related service areas must be involved in addition to special education personnel.

Handicapped adolescents may well constitute the largest unserved or underserved school-aged population (Halpern, 1979). Inappropriate and inadequate secondary programs are often cited as a major cause of the adult adjustment problems of handicapped individuals (Heller, 1981; Wehman, 1982). Specific problems frequently mentioned include insufficient numbers of vocationally oriented secondary programs for handicapped individuals; reliance on inappropriate, nonfunctional curricula; lack of a continuum of vocational preparation options; and lack of coordination between disciplines and service agencies involved in the career-development process.

It is unfortunate that the vast majority of handicapped Americans are not prepared for vocational activities that are personally and economically rewarding. However, as a result of state and federal legislation, we are now committed to the provision of public school vocational training for all individuals, no matter the severity of their handicaps. This mandate presents a clear challenge to educators providing vocational instruction to handicapped individuals in public schools.

The Five-Stage Instructional Approach to Career Development

Most special educators recognize that the acquisition of language skills, motor skills, and social skills by handicapped children is a developmental process. These skills develop sequentially, meaning that certain skills are acquired before others or that they emerge in a recognizable order. Failure to acquire critical skills at an early age can make the acquisition of more sophisticated skills later in life very difficult. However, many educators fail to recognize that acquisition of career and vocational skills also follows a developmental sequence. Career development is a process that begins in the preschool years and continues through childhood and adolescence. As is the case with motor or language development, the failure to acquire significant skills and concepts at any stage of the career-development process can negatively affect a handicapped individual's oportunity to function successfully as an adult in our society.

This section describes a comprehensive approach to the career development of handicapped students. The proposed model views career development as a five-stage process: awareness, exploration, orientation, preparation, and placement and follow-up. Each stage is discussed in terms of its central focus, the major goals to be acquired, and the adapted instructional activities used to teach the specified goals. It is important to note that the age level identified for each stage suggests when instruction should begin in this area. Career awareness, for example, is emphasized in the elementary grades, but instruction in this area continues throughout the entire career-development process.

Stage 1: Awareness

As most children grow and mature, they experience situations and events from which they form a view of themselves as future workers. They perform chores in their homes, baby-sit or mow lawns in their neighborhoods, or have paper routes. They become aware of the role that work plays in the lives of the people around them. They identify many different workers in their homes, schools, and communities. From these early experiences children begin to form concepts—there are certain activities they enjoy; work is a part of the lives of most adults; and the workplace is different than one's home or classroom.

All children should receive career-awareness experiences that will enable them to set and pursue career goals and to function successfully in a work setting. But many handicapped students reaching adulthood have been denied these developmental experiences, and as a result they are unable to enter employment or adjust to the role of worker successfully. Career-awareness activities, designed to provide handicapped individuals the experiences that will form the basis of future vocational training, should begin when the child enters public education. Although career awareness is emphasized in the elementary grades, instruction in this area continues in middle school and secondary programs. Career-awareness instruction focuses on helping the student acquire positive attitudes toward work and school.

Clark (1979) and Goldstein (1974) have developed comprehensive instructional programs designed to develop the career-awareness skills of handicapped students in elementary schools. Clark, for example, divides career awareness into four areas: values, attitudes, and habits; human relationships; occupational information; and job and daily living skills. Goldstein's social learning approach encourages students to become aware of themselves, their neighborhoods, their schools, their bodies and emotions, and other people in the society. As applied here to handicapped students, career awareness has two major goals at the elementary level: (1) development of mobility skills, environmental awareness, and communication skills; and (2) development of initial work-related concepts and values.

Development of Mobility Skills, Environmental Awareness, and Communication Skills. The development of mobility skills, environmental awareness, and communication skills allows children to participate and interact with their environment. Increased mobility allows handicapped children to explore vocational, recreational, and consumer-oriented settings and provides experiences to be built on during later instruction. Environmental-awareness training equips students with the skills they need to begin to interact with the people encountered in community settings. Children will begin to feel confident in settings such as stores, parks, restaurants, and churches.

The development of communication skills is critical to the establishment of positive human relationships. It is important that educators recognize the school's role in the development of the child's ability to interact with other people. Career-awareness programming should include activities designed to develop skills in establishing and maintaining positive human relationships through effective communication. Skills in communicating with others and developing human relationships frequently have been taught through incidental methods rather than through direct, clear-cut objectives and procedures. Special educators, however, must accept the development of communication skills as a legitimate component of career-awareness programming.

Development of Initial Work-Related Concepts and Values. Handicapped children should receive direct instruction leading to the development of work-related concepts and values, even during the elementary school years. Direct instruction in this area provides children knowledge and experiences that will facilitate vocational training in later years. At the elementary level, children should be introduced to the concept of work.

Work is a part of our lives. Our country is work-oriented. It is important for young handicapped children to learn they can take pride in and receive satisfaction from working. They must experience the satisfaction of learning a new skill, carrying a task through to completion, or doing something for someone else. In addition, handicapped children can begin to realize there are many reasons for working. Pay is only one of the rewards of work. Work may also have the benefit of helping others, the chance to pursue interests and talents, the opportunity to be around people, or the means to gain self-esteem.

Children at the elementary level can also be introduced to the nature of working and the work environment. Work involves responsibility. It is often physically tiring or demands long periods of concentration. Our immediate wishes and desires may need to be postponed until our work is completed. Failing to fulfill our work responsibility affects not only ourselves, but others who are depending on us to complete a task. In fact, all work generally involves interaction with other people. Interaction with supervisors, co-workers, or community members is required in most work settings. Work settings even have their own specialized vocabularies. Children can be introduced to concepts such as worker and supervisor.

Clark (1979) has developed a useful resource for the development and implementation of career-awareness activities for handicapped elementary school students. His *Career Education for the Handicapped Child in the Elementary Classroom* contains a thorough discussion of career education curriculum content at the elementary level, sample goals and objective statements, suggested activities and materials for teaching the content, and suggestions for implementing career education programs in elementary school settings. Table 9.1 outlines Clark's selected goals and objectives statements in the areas of occupational information.

Adapted Activities.   Instruction in the career-awareness area must emphasize concrete experiences to build understanding of important concepts. Much of this content can be taught to students in regular elementary classrooms through in-class discussions and activities that focus on out-of-school experiences. Handicapped children may lack the mobility or social interaction skills to acquire these experiences outside the school setting. Special educators must provide each child an opportunity to experience the responsibility of knowing that others are depending on him or her to complete an assigned task. Activities must be designed to enable the child to experience success in these endeavors. Handicapped children must feel that their abilities and efforts are important, that they can successfully contribute to their families and friends. The elementary child should demonstrate skills in (1) providing personal services (delivering messages, running errands), (2) cleaning (sweeping, mopping), (3) performing routine chores, and (4) developing basic number concepts.

Instructional activities for students in elementary classes should progress

TABLE 9.1
Career-Awareness Goals and Objectives

Goals for Awareness of Occupational Roles

Primary Level (K–3)

1. Students demonstrate a knowledge of basic differences between the roles of paid and unpaid workers.
2. Students demonstrate a knowledge of various worker roles that relate to differences in times for work and differences in amounts of time spent for work.
3. Students demonstrate a knowledge of some of the basic worker role categories (e.g., indoor versus outdoor; rural versus urban; workers concerned with people, things, or ideas).
4. Students verbalize, "I want to be a worker when I grow up–when can I start?"

Intermediate Level (4–6)

1. Students demonstrate a knowledge of the two basic roles in the world of work—producer and consumer.
2. Students demonstrate a knowledge of some examples of occupations characteristic of the roles of producers, consumers, maintainers, disposers, and recyclers.
3. Students demonstrate a knowledge of worker roles by occupational clusters or primary service category.
4. Students demonstrate a knowledge of the consumer role in the world of work by describing where various kinds of goods and services can be obtained.

Goals for Occupational Vocabulary

Primary Level (K–3)

1. Students demonstrate an understanding of the meaning of basic vocabulary related to various producer (worker) roles.
2. Students demonstrate an understanding of the meaning of basic vocabulary related to various consumer roles.
3. Students demonstrate an increase in their occupational vocabulary by being able to identify (by name) the occupations of family members, acquaintances in their neighborhood, and workers in their school.

Intermediate Level (4–6)

1. Students demonstrate a knowledge of the names of occupations within various selected occupational clusters.
2. Students demonstrate an increase in their working occupational vocabulary by being able to identify (by name) workers in the community.
3. Students demonstrate an increase in their working occupational vocabulary by being able to identify (by name) workers in the state and region.

Goals for Occupational Alternatives

Primary Level (K–3)

1. Students develop an identification with workers in various occupations.
2. Students demonstrate knowledge of differences between occupational settings and roles.
3. Students verbalize or communicate some initial choices of occupations.

TABLE 9.1
(continued)

Goals for Occupational Alternatives

Intermediate Level (4–6)

1. Students identify occupations that require the performance of activities they enjoy.
2. Students explore interests that allow for wider choice among occupations or work roles.
3. Students demonstrate an understanding that occupations and life-styles are related.
4. Students demonstrate continuing "choosing behaviors" among occupational alternatives to which they are exposed.

Goals for Basic Information on Realities of the World of Work

---

Primary Level (K–3)

1. Students demonstrate an understanding of the reality that most people in our society are engaged in some kind of work.
2. Students demonstrate an understanding of the need for division of labor within the family, the classroom, and the community.
3. Students demonstrate an understanding that work is part of life and that certain kinds of behaviors are expected when one is working.
4. Students demonstrate an understanding that work nearly always involves someone telling someone else what to do, how to do it, and when to do it.
5. Students demonstrate an understanding that people work for a number of reasons.

Intermediate Level (4–6)

1. Students demonstrate an awareness that, although most people work, there are many people who cannot obtain work or who are not happy in the work they do.
2. Students demonstrate an understanding of how the skills being learned at school relate to skills needed at work.
3. Students demonstrate an understanding of the public nature of most work settings.
4. Students demonstrate an awareness of the importance of time in work settings.
5. Students demonstrate an understanding of the dependence and interdependence of workers and work settings.
6. Students demonstrate an understanding of the existence of "unwritten rules" for workers on how to act, how to talk, what to wear, and so on.
7. Students demonstrate a basic understanding of why some jobs pay more than other jobs.
8. Students demonstrate an awareness that work, like play, can be monotonous or boring after doing it for a period of time, but that it is good to be able to be doing something of benefit for others or oneself.

Source: G. M. Clark (1979), *Career education for the handicapped child in the elementary classroom* (Boulder, CO: Love Publishing Co.), pp. 94–97. Used by permission.

TABLE 9.2

Selected Activities that Teach Occupational Information at the Elementary and Intermediate Levels

Occupational Roles and Alternatives

Elementary Level

Interviewing parents and guardians about their jobs

Drawing pictures of parents or family members at work

Making worker puppets; putting on puppet worker "plays" and watching puppet role playing

Playing with adult hats, uniforms, or costumes

Engaging in semistructured free play with a play store, play office, play clinic, play house, and so on

Making a wall mural of workers by categories or clusters of occupations

Playing occupational jump rope (each pupil has a turn and calls out occupations while jumping; jumping continues until pupil misses or is unable to call out an occupation in rhythm)

Participating in structured dramatic play

Listening to parents, family members, and school workers who come to class and talk about their work

Reading picture and easy-to-read books

Listening to songs or stories about workers

Intermediate Level

Group projects requiring role differentiation and division of labor (e.g., construction projects, newspapers, minirestaurant or tea room, dramatic presentation, or musical show)

Role playing based on new occupational information

Simulating a community to demonstrate dependence/interdependence of workers and work settings

Videotaping a process or sequence of services showing different worker roles

Teaching units on occupational clusters

Planning, writing, and filming a "documentary" on some occupation or cluster

Having community workers talk to the class about their work

Going on field trips to view or interview workers on the job

Conducting community surveys for community occupations

Conducting community surveys for volunteer work opportunities

Sponsoring exhibits by local businesses or industries

Sponsoring a school demonstration or exhibit by junior high school industrial arts classes and high school vocational education programs

from the concrete to the abstract, from the familiar to the unfamiliar. Therefore, experiences should initially focus on environments most familiar to the student—home and school—and move from there to an exploration of the student's community. A variety of instructional techniques may be employed dur-

TABLE 9.2
(continued)

Occupational Vocabulary

Elementary Level
Career bingo (teacher-made boards with names of occupations)
Bulletin broad focusing on occupational vocabulary
Occupational stimulus cards for visually identifying workers by name
Occupational sound stimulus tapes that auditorially identify workers by name
Lids for kids (pupils identify workers by caps, hats, or other headgear)

Intermediate Level
"What's My Line" (use television show game rules or adapt to meet abilities of
    pupils)
Occupational "Password" (use television show game rules but use only occupations
    as words)
Occupational crossword puzzles
Occupational games
"Research" and report on new work roles

Realities of the World of Work

Elementary Level
Have parents assign children a work responsibility at home and complete a Home
    Worker's Checklist
Assign work responsibilities in the classroom and evaluate with a Classroom
    Worker's Checklist
Stories and easy-to-read books
Films and filmstrips
Class project using an assembly-line process

Intermediate Level
Actual operation of a minibusiness (e.g., school supply store, tea room, school bank)
Work and work-training simulation
Simulate a community or microsociety demonstrating effects of economic variations
    ("booms" and recessions), labor strikes, natural disasters, and so on
Assign jobs in classroom or school and evaluate with a Classroom/School Worker's
    Checklist
Rent-a-Kid Day (pupils work for an agreed-upon wage for a specific task on a given
    day)

Source: G. M. Clark (1979), *Career education for the handicapped child in the elementary
classroom* (Boulder, CO: Love Publishing Co.), pp. 99–102. Used by permission.

ing this period, including role-playing, games, simulations, field trips, hands-on
activities, and class visitations by community members. Table 9.2 contains a
listing of selected activities developed by Clark (1979) to teach content in the
area of occupational information to elementary- and intermediate-aged students.

Stage II: Exploration

Career exploration occurs at the elementary level, but its primary emphasis generally comes during the middle school and early high school years. During this phase, the student examines his or her own unique set of abilities and needs, the world of work, and the demands of the local community. Instruction during career exploration focuses on the development of independent living skills and the hands-on exploration of broad occupational areas. It is important for school personnel to be able to design curricula and instructional experiences that facilitate self-exploration. This should include the use of a variety of techniques, experiences, and settings relevant to each individual. The incorporation of community-based instruction is critical during this phase. Specific goals of the career-exploration phase include (1) development of independent living skills and (2) hands-on exploration of broad occupational categories.

The Development of Independent Living Skills.   Independent living skills include all those vocational, domestic living, and recreational skills that enhance an individual's ability to participate in integrated community environments and use generic community services (Bellamy & Wilcox, 1982). Independent living skills are designed to enhance a student's chances for participation in all facets of normal community life. In this sense, the content of the independent living curricular domain is limitless. Commercial materials generally outline broad independent living-skill categories such as home maintenance, money management, clothing care, food preparation, community mobility, and use of public and commercial services (Apolloni & Westaway, 1980; Bender & Valletutti, 1976; Thiel, 1978). Instruction in these areas should begin as soon as a student acquires the basic self-help skills.

Hands-on Exploration of Broad Occupational Categories.   Career-exploration programs are designed to help students examine several broad occupational clusters and engage in a variety of hands-on experiences, both in and out of school. To learn more about occupational possibilities, handicapped students must observe them first-hand to understand their characteristics, try them out in simulated situations, and gain familiarity with the equipment and materials used in specific jobs. The focus of these exploratory activities is not to learn to perform the job but to provide students with information and experiences that will allow them to decide whether they might like to learn the job later during the career-preparation phases.

Adapted Activities.   Career-exploration experiences are generally provided to students in regular classrooms in two ways. The first is the *cluster approach* to career exploration, where students are enrolled in a 9-week or semester-long course to explore a particular occupational service area (home economics, agriculture, industrial arts, business, and so on). Students may rotate through a series of courses during an entire program. The second alternative is the *psycho-social approach* to career exploration. Content in this approach is typically organized into modules based on psychological and sociological factors such as the world of work, work and self, society and work, or decision making and goal setting. It is important for students to be encouraged to try various simulated job tasks and community jobs, develop work habits and behaviors, acquire physical and manual skills, and learn other skills needed in the workplace.

Instructional strategies for teaching independent living skills to handicapped students should include mainstreaming into existing middle and high school classes. Career-exploration courses offered by vocational education are often appropriate for handicapped students. Much career-exploration content may be acquired through infusing the content into other areas of academic programming. Effective techniques for teaching career-exploration concepts include simulated vocational tasks, job-site visitations, and job shadowing. Job shadowing involves a student following an employee on the job to observe exactly what the worker does during a typical day. These activities may begin to provide a practical knowledge base of occupations and the realities of the world of work. The activities may be expanded to allow the student to compare information about jobs and occupations available locally to their own interests and abilities. Following are some suggestions for modified activities in this area.

1. Invite a group of parents and other community members to the class and ask them to describe their jobs, including which aspects are most rewarding and which factors they like least about their jobs. This information will help students to identify the personal values met through work that are of the greatest importance to them.
2. Students might be required to obtain information on one job per week for several weeks during a semester. Information compiled could include job title, company, wages, working conditions, basic job duties, and opportunity for advancement. Group discussions will allow the students the opportunity to compare the various jobs as they relate to their skills and interests.
3. Values clarification exercises may be employed. For example, the students could list their major occupational needs; that is, the needs and values they hold that should be met through work. Students might review a worksheet developed by the teacher that contains a variety of statements dealing with why people work. Students should rank statements, such as "I want a job where I can be outdoors a lot," "I want a job only to make a lot of money," or "I want a job where I can be my own boss," as high or low priority for them. This type of exercise encourages students to begin to formulate the characteristics of jobs of interest to them.

Stage III: Orientation

Career orientation focuses on the general work behaviors, vocational survival skills, and social survival skills necessary for success in job-training programs

TABLE 9.3
Description of Employability Skills

Skill	Description
On-task behavior and consistency of performance	Does the student come to work every day? Does he or she come on time? Does the student attend to the work at hand during work periods? Is the student's work performance the same on a day-to-day basis?
Speed, accuracy, and precision of performance	Does the student produce an amount of work equal to or greater than that produced by other workers in the position? Does the student's performance meet or exceed acceptable industrial standards for accuracy? Is the student's work regarded by their supervisor as of high quality?
Adjustment to repetition	Is the student able to perform the same job duties on a day-to-day basis without loss of speed or accuracy? Is the student able to perform the same job task all day long without losing motivation or interest?
Endurance/stamina	Is the student able to work a regular shift without becoming overly fatigued? Does the student possess all the physical abilities (strength, coordination, and so on) required to perform the job?
Self-confidence	Does the student take pride in the work he or she performs? Does the student have a positive image of him- or herself as a worker?
Need for supervision	Is the student able to perform all aspects of the job independently? Does the student seek assistance from the supervisor when required?

and employment. These skills are also termed *employability skills.* Career orientation also provides students an opportunity to investigate an occupational area in depth before making a decision to prepare for a specific job. For nonhandicapped students, this process usually occurs in the ninth and tenth grades. The specific goals of the career-orientation phase include development of (1) general work behaviors, (2) vocational skills, and (3) social survival skills.

Development of General Work Behaviors.   There are several ways to identify the general work behaviors required to complete job-training programs and enter employment. The first approach is to analyze jobs and vocational curricula to determine the skills required in a particular program. Some vocational education programs have developed criterion-referenced tests based on an analysis of the academic skills required by various training options. Job analyses can determine interpersonal skills and work attitudes required by a specific job setting.

TABLE 9.3
(continued)

Skill	Description
Self-direction	Does the student know what is expected of him or her and when all job tasks should be performed? Will the student complete all job assignments without extensive reminders? Does the student seek out additional work assignments when all work has been completed?
Ability to follow directions	Is the student able to follow directions presented verbally? In written form? Is the student able to follow complex directions?
Acceptance of authority	Does the student interact with the supervisor in an appropriate and pleasant manner? Does the student accept all reasonable directions and assignments given to him or her? Does the student respond appropriately to criticism?
Relationships with co-workers	Does the student interact appropriately with co-workers on the job site? Does the student socially interact during lunch and break times? Does the student socially interact with co-workers during company-sponsored activities outside the work setting (softball team, company picnic, and so on)?
Ability to work under pressure	Is the student able to perform successfully during close supervision? Is the student able to meet all required deadlines?
Conformity to schedule	Is the student able to adjust to a regular work routine? Is the student able to tolerate major disruptions to the work routine?

Source: Adapted from P. Sitlington & D. Wimmer (1980). Vocational assessment, in G. M. Clark & W. White (eds.). *Career education for the handicapped: Current perspectives for teachers* (Boothwyn, PA: Educational Resources), pp. 74–87. Used by permission.

Another method for identifying employability skills is to analyze the problems encountered by nonhandicapped and handicapped individuals entering employment. Scott and Moye (1978) investigated students who had graduated from Georgia's vocational education cluster programs. Graduates and employers felt that the vocational education students needed further instruction in performing work of high quality, communicating in job situations, following directions and taking orders, and acquiring skills for advancement.

A number of special educators have developed listings of the employability skills critical to handicapped students. Sitlington and Wimmer (1978) identify several different categories of skills that they believe are important. Table 9.3 contains a description of several major skills cited by Sitlington and Wimmer. Wehman (1981) provides another useful breakdown of general work behaviors.

Employability skills are analyzed into six categories: (1) proficiency—competence in performing a skill correctly; (2) rate—speed in completing a job; (3) quality—how well a job is completed; (4) perseverance level—repetitive performance of nonfunctional motor behavior; (5) repertoire—number of related skills the student can already perform; and (6) endurance—ability to fulfill the physical demands of a job.

Direct instruction designed to develop general work behaviors provides both short-term and long-term benefits to handicapped students. The ability to perform a variety of work tasks safely and effectively maximizes a student's chances for success in vocational training programs. If properly developed, the career-orientation curriculum can equip students with the work habits identified as critical for future success in work environments.

Development of Vocational Survival Skills.   Any classification of survival skills is in a very real sense an arbitrary task. The term *vocational survival skills*, as used here, refers to behaviors directly related to job performance. Rusch and Mithaug (1980) have developed a comprehensive listing of vocational survival skills. Important among these are the ability to come to work daily and to tolerate an 8-hour work day. Workers must also be able to move safely around the work area, avoiding dangerous areas and wearing safe clothing. If workers cannot come to work regularly or be trusted in the work area, they will be provided little opportunity to work. Other important skills identified by Rusch and Mithaug include tolerance for changes in the regular work routine and new work environment, and the ability to socially interact with other individuals encountered in the workplace.

Development of Social Survival Skills.   The development of social survival skills maximizes the opportunity for handicapped students to acquire and maintain employment. *Social survival skills* address those behavioral deficits that prohibit placement in work environments. The acceptable standard of performance on any social survival skill must be based on an analysis of the entry requirements of local employment settings. Among the more important social survival skills identified by Rusch and Mithaug (1980) are the ability to communicate basic needs, maintain proper grooming and hygiene, respond to directions requiring immediate compliance, and refrain from behavioral disruptions on the job.

Adapted Activities.   The following public school programs can contribute to the development of career-orientation skills in handicapped students.

Introductory Vocational Education Courses.   Introductory courses in vocational education programs permit students to work with the tools, materials, processes, and products peculiar to a given work setting. They provide in-depth, hands-on experiences in performing organizational, creative, and motivational tasks in a single occupational family. With this in-depth investigation, students will be able to decide if they desire to pursue further training in this area.

An effective technique for providing adapted career-orientation instruction to students with handicaps is the use of the *Vocational Assessment and Curriculum Guide* (Rusch, Schutz, Mithaug, Stewart, & Mar, 1982). The guide assesses both vocational and social survival skills and can be normed to local business and industrial standards. The information obtained through the assessment activities can be easily translated into IEP objectives through the use of the curriculum guide. These objectives can become the focus of work experience and career-orientation activities throughout the student's school day.

Regular Academic Courses. Students can acquire the reading, writing, and communication skills that contribute to vocational success in regular academic courses. This requires the incorporation of career development and vocational education content in regular math and reading courses. Regular courses should emphasize the occupational implications of the subject matter.

Special Education Work-Orientation Courses. Special educators in resource rooms and self-contained classrooms can develop units and courses that specifically teach employability skills. Topics could include occupational reading, occupational math, written communication, securing employment, and making career decisions.

Work Experience. Work-experience programs provide handicapped students with direct participation in the world of work. Although these programs should not represent the total vocational education provided to a student, they should complement future skill training. The emphasis in work-experience programs is the acquisition of desirable social skills and general work behaviors. The particular work experience placement may or may not directly relate to a student's career objectives. Work sites can be either off-campus (in the community) or on-campus. If on-the-job work experience is not possible or practical for handicapped students, a simulated work experience may be provided in the classroom.

Simulated Work Settings. If on-the-job work experience is not possible or practical for handicapped students, a simulated work experience may be provided in the classroom. A mock-up or simulation of an actual community or sheltered work station is created in the vocational laboratory and the student learns the task in the simulated setting.

Occupational Guidance. After a student has completed the activities in the exploration and orientation stages of the career-development process, he or she is ready to select a specific occupation or occupational cluster for specific skill training. This implies that counselors should be directly involved with these programs. After each work experience, students should be helped to look at the experience in terms of the following questions.

How did I feel about myself while involved in the work role?

What other jobs in our society might provide similar satisfaction?

What are the different decisions I would have to make to enter this kind of work?

What kind of schooling would prepare me for it?

The guidance and counseling programs should be designed to help students analyze their vocational experiences at each educational level and to assist them at decision-making points in the process.

Stage IV: Preparation

As with the other stages of career development, career preparation is not solely confined to one period of schooling. Like the others, it begins in the early grades and continues throughout life. But, for most handicapped students the high school years are critical for acquiring entry-level employment skills. At this level, career choices, although still tentative, can be more specifically directed toward job skill training.

Whenever possible, students should be able to select from a range of occupational training programs and community job experiences available in their high school. If employability skills have been successfully acquired at earlier stages, instruction at this level can focus on preparation for a specific entry-level job. This section describes the basic characteristics of three approaches to specific job skill training: the job-cluster approach, the specific job-training approach, and the work-experience approach. The advantages and disadvantages of each approach are identified.

Job-Cluster Approach. A *job cluster* may be defined as a group of related jobs. An example of a job-cluster system is shown in Figure 9.1. In the job-cluster approach, students are trained to perform a set of related tasks or jobs. Rather than being prepared for a single, specific job, in the cluster approach the student is taught to perform skills that are found in several related jobs in the same industrial area. This multioccupational approach provides some degree of career choice flexibility. Clusters can be constructed around a family of related occupations that have many tasks or duties in common. Examples of clusters include child care, food service, and auto mechanics. The use of the cluster approach does not eliminate the need for on-the-job training in the community. By itself, it is an inadequate technique. However, when used in combination with other techniques it has the advantage of increased flexibility and the potential to maximize the generalization of newly acquired skills and increase the number of skills that can be acquired in the school prior to community job placement.

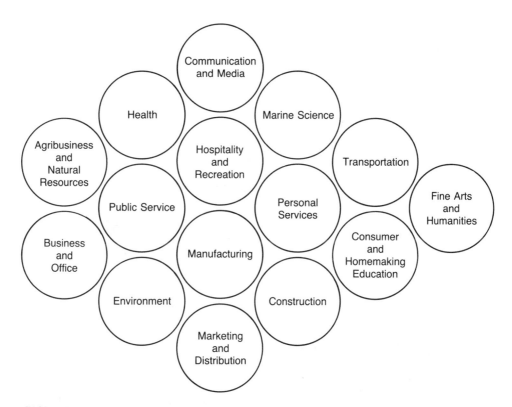

FIGURE 9.1
Job-Cluster System (Source: U.S. Office of Education (1971), *Career educa-tion* [Washington, DC: U.S. Government Printing Office].)

Specific Job-Training Approach.   Specific-job training is a direct approach to the career preparation of handicapped adolescents. In this approach, an appropriate community job is identified for each student, the specific duties and tasks of the job are analyzed, and the student is provided direct instruction on each of the identified skills. Whenever possible, school-based instruction is provided on those tasks that can be successfully replicated in the school environment. When replication is not possible or feasible, direct instruction is provided at the work site.

Work-Experience Approach.   In the work-experience approach, students obtain on-the-job experience through full- or part-time work in a variety of employment settings. This strategy attempts to enhance employability through realistic job experiences. In a typical program, students move through a series of in-school and off-campus work-experience placements.

The work-experience approach provides handicapped students realistic vocational training in integrated community settings. Students are often involved

Cluster-Related Instructional Areas (Course titles and/or major instructional units)	Career Cluster—Automotive and Power Service Occupations			
Auto mechanics	Automobile mechanic helper Used car renovator	Muffler installer Automobile accessories installer Tune-up man	Automobile mechanic Transmission mechanic Automobile service mechanic	
Small engine repair		Gasoline engine repairman Power saw mechanic Outboard motor mechanic Motorcycle repairman		
Auto body repair	Automobile body repairman Helper	Painter, automobile	Automobile body repairman	Shop estimator

FIGURE 9.2
Sample Job-Cluster Specification (Source: L. A. Phelps & R. Lutz (1977), Career exploration and preparation for the special needs learner [Boston: Allyn & Bacon], p. 171. Reproduced by permission.)

in interaction with nondisabled co-workers, customers, and supervisors. When students are placed in off-campus work placements, they are able to sample locally available jobs. The skills they learn may be quite useful when they enter the job market on graduation.

The major limitation of the work-experience approach when used with handicapped individuals lies in the inability of these students to acquire job skills through simple exposure to the work environment. Unless accompanied by intensive job-skill training, it is doubtful the work-experience approach can equip students with all the specific skills required for competitive employment in other than poor-paying jobs in entry-level occupations.

Adapted Activities. Adapting career-preparation activities involves a cooperative effort between vocational and special education personnel. The process of adapting the preparation program begins by analyzing the jobs identified in a career cluster to determine those that may be appropriate for handicapped students in the program. A sample job-cluster specification sheet for the

Cluster-Related Instructional Areas (Course titles and/or major instructional units)	Career Cluster—Automotive and Power Service Occupations			
Heating and air conditioning	Ventilation man Furnace installer & repairman helper Air cond. installer domestic		Furnaceman	
Service station	Automobile service station attendant			
Level:	Laborer Assistant Helper Worker Sorter or packer Loader Attendant Tender	Operator Driver Assembler Clerk Installer Aide	Craftsman Technician Complex operator Supervisor Inspector	Middle manager Foreman Official

FIGURE 9.2 *continued*

automotive and power service occupations cluster (Phelps & Lutz, 1977) is shown in Figure 9.2. After reviewing the cluster, potential jobs may be identified for further analysis.

The content for any vocational program must stem from the tasks performed by workers on the job. A multistep approach to job analysis is often used (Scott and Moye, 1978). Task listings are first developed from written information. There are a number of excellent resources available that provide initial job analyses. This tentative list is then discussed with a group of incumbent workers. They can provide information as to (1) the relevance of the skills listed to the local setting, (2) the most frequently performed tasks, (3) the usual length of time required to perform a task and the quality standards demanded, and (4) the most difficult tasks to learn and perform. The skills listings are grouped into tasks, duties, and jobs. A *task* is a unit of work complete in itself. A *duty* is a group of tasks related to one another that comprises one of the distinct major activities of the work performed. Several duties and a number of tasks make up a *job*. Jobs are the duties and tasks actually performed by workers in a specific occupation.

An illustration is provided in the area of automotive mechanics (see Figure 9.2). First a listing of performance objectives is developed in the area. Completing all objectives will qualify an individual to perform the jobs of automotive mechanic, automotive service mechanic, or automotive mechanic helper. The tasks are organized into the following duties: evaluating and inspecting; performing engine overhaul activities; maintaining and repairing power trains; automatic transmissions; electrical systems; fuel systems; cooling systems; standard and power steering units; braking systems; front ends; automobile air conditioners; and heaters. After deciding which occupations to include in a specific vocational education program, teachers can determine the specific duties and tasks to include in the curriculum, develop instructional packages, and implement instruction. Additional procedures for developing and modifying vocational education programs are discussed later in the chapter.

Stage V: Placement and Follow-up

Career-placement and follow-up services can occur during the last semester of the twelfth grade or even later, depending on the student's readiness for this final stage of career development. This is usually the time when students are given the opportunity to be placed on an actual job as regular workers. This may be either on a full- or part-time basis and may last longer than one semester, depending on a student's individual needs.

A variety of individuals are often involved in the placement and follow-up of handicapped students. Special education teachers, work-study coordinators, vocational education teachers, and vocational rehabilitation counselors may all have a role in placing students with handicaps into employment. Specific services that might be provided include the following.

1. Provision of information to employers to dispel their fears about handicapped individuals.
2. Provision of information to employers and handicapped individuals to assist them in acquisition of adaptive devices that will enable physically handicapped individuals to be competitively employed.
3. Establishment of procedures to search actively for job openings for handicapped students.
4. Provision of assistance as needed to students during interviews and in contacts with personnel officers.
5. Assistance to students during the initial period on the job.

6. Establishment of on-the-job follow-up procedures.
7. Coordination of educational agency placement activities with vocational rehabilitation, state employment services, and other community agencies.

Handicapped students often have a difficult time adjusting to work environments. Reasons for failure in employment settings more often relate to social problems encountered on the job than to failure of the disabled individual to perform the work (Wehman, 1981). Vocational education work-experience coordinators, special education work-study coordinators, and rehabilitation counselors rarely are able to provide the intense monitoring services needed by handicapped students. Consequently, students too often fail in the initial placement, and the result is someone permanently removed from the workforce.

_____ *Case Study* _____

CAREER AND VOCATIONAL EDUCATION

Kenny is an 18-year-old student classified as mildly mentally handicapped enrolled in a twelfth-grade carpentry program. Kenny's measured IQ is 62; recent achievement tests place his reading skills at the second-grade level and his math skills at the third-grade level. Although Kenny is generally shy and withdrawn around other students, he is enthusiastic about his carpentry program and enjoys participating in group construction projects. He hopes one day to work in a furniture factory or in a building construction position.

While in elementary school, Kenny's resource room teacher supplemented his reading and math instruction with materials that focused on career education content. In the eighth grade, he was mainstreamed into an industrial arts class. The class provided Kenny with an opportunity to learn about potential careers in the carpentry area. He had his first opportunity to use basic tools and made several visits to community sites where he was able to observe carpenters working in various settings.

In the tenth grade, Kenny enrolled in the Introductory Carpentry class. There he received an introduction to basic terminology, safety procedures, and use of tools and equipment. Meanwhile, Kenny's resource room teacher was working with him on basic measurement skills and assisting him with the course content. During the second semester of the tenth grade, he was able to spend 2 hours per day, 3 days per week, as a helper in cabinet-making shop. After this experience, Kenny became convinced that carpentry was the career area that he wanted to pursue.

Prior to beginning the eleventh grade, Kenny, his parents, the resource room teacher, the carpentry teacher, the vocational education cooperative

instructor, and a vocational rehabilitation counselor met to design an individualized transition program for Kenny. He enrolled in the carpentry program for the eleventh and twelfth grades. Through the cooperation of the
special education and vocational education teachers, Kenny completed units
in hand and power tools, machine operation, and blueprint reading. During
the second semester of the twelfth grade, Kenny began working in a small
furniture factory, a job identified for him by the vocational education
cooperative instructor.

The instructor is monitoring Kenny's performance on the job carefully.
If problems arise, the instructor will attempt to solve them with the
assistance of the special education teacher. If the team feels that the furniture factory placement is not an appropriate one for Kenny, he will be
referred to the vocational rehabilitation counselor for further evaluation
and training.

Adapted Activities.   Wehman and Kregel (1985) describe a model, called the
supported-work model, for providing intense follow-up services to handicapped
individuals entering employment. Even though the model was originally
developed with handicapped adults in a rehabilitation setting, it has the potential to be adapted for use with school-aged individuals. In the supported-work
model, a job coach is assigned to each individual after they have completed
general employability skills and specific job-skills training. When the individual
is placed into competitive employment, the job coach remains with the individual
all day, every day, until services are no longer required. Then the job coach fades
assistance until the individual is working independently. Table 9.4 outlines the
major activities involved in the supported-work approach to competitive
employment.

Integrated Vocational Programs

There are many issues facing educators attempting to implement work
preparation programs for handicapped students. These issues revolve around
the key provisions of Public Law 94–142. How do we provide an *appropriate
vocational education,* in the *least restrictive environment,* in accordance with
an *individualized educational program* (IEP) to each and every handicapped individual? Each individual possesses his or her own unique set of abilities, aptitudes, and interests. Many different program options exist, each of which may
be effective for a particular student. Obviously, a continuum of career-
preparation options must be developed. Providing alternative programs will help

TABLE 9.4

Checklist of Activities in the Supported-Work Approach
to Competitive Employment

Component Phases	Activities
Program Component I: *Job Placement*	Structured efforts at finding jobs for client and matching client strengths to job needs
	Planning of transportation arrangements and/or travel training
	Active involvement with parents on identifying appropriate job for client
	Communication with Social Security Administration
Program Component II: *Job Site Training and* *Advocacy*	Trained staff provides behavior skill training aimed at improving client work performance
	Trained staff provides necessary social skill training at job site
	Staff works with employers/co-workers in helping client
Program Component III: *Ongoing Monitoring*	Provides for regular written feedback from employer on client progress
	Utilizes behavioral data related to client work speed, proficiency, need for staff assistance, and the like
	Implements periodic client and/or parent satisfaction questionnaires
Program Component IV: *Follow-up and Retention*	Implements planned effort at reducing staff intervention from job site
	Provides follow-up to employer in form of phone calls and/or visits to job sites as needed
	Communication to employer regarding staff accessibility as needed
	Helps client relocate or find new job if necessary

Source: P. Wehman & J. Kregel (1985). A supported work approach to competitive employment of individuals with moderate and severe handicaps. *Journal of the Association for
Persons with Severe Handicaps, 10*(1), 3–11. Used by permission.

each handicapped student receive vocational training that meets his or her
unique needs in the least restrictive setting.

In integrated programs the student participates in the regular vocational
education program with support services directly related to the vocational program provided by special education personnel. Participation with nonhandicapped
students is maximal in this model. Students receive instruction in general work
skills through mainstreaming into introductory courses within the vocational
education curriculum. Career preparation is provided through cluster- or single-

Special students can actively participate in regular education vocational classes.

skill training programs that prepare students for semiskilled or skilled jobs in the local labor market. Work experience is acquired through participation in cooperative training programs that allow students to practice newly acquired skills in local employment settings.

Special education personnel must assume an active support role in the integrated program model. Typical support services may include related services personnel consulting with the vocational education teacher. Tutoring in specific skills may be provided by classroom teachers. In some states a third alternative has been developed to provide support to the handicapped student and vocational education teacher within the vocational classroom. Vocational resource programs were developed to provide support to handicapped students enrolled in regular vocational education programs. The vocational resource instructor serves handicapped students in the vocational clusters. The instructor can provide resource assistance to handicapped students within the vocational lab itself, or may also conduct small-group sessions outside the vocational class. Some instructors conduct classes for the students on their caseload. Although providing students assistance in the regular vocational classes seems to be the most effective approach to the vocational resource program, success has been achieved using a number of different organizational models.

Although vocational resource programs are operating effectively in many states, handicapped students are just beginning to receive services through the programs. The resource instructor is only able to serve a limited number of students. Another limitation of the program is that resource instructors are often not involved in the job placement and follow-up stages of the program. This stage is clearly critical for handicapped students, many of whom need intensive support services during the early stages of job placement that cannot be provided by vocational education or vocational rehabilitation personnel.

Scheduling, curricular, or equipment modifications may be required to enable handicapped students to benefit from integration into vocational education programs. Scheduling modifications may be needed to provide additional time for faculty to assist handicapped students. The school day or school year can be extended. Students may be retained in programs an additional semester or provided instruction on an individualized basis. Flexible scheduling may be initiated to permit students to enter and exit programs as they progress. Curricular modifications enable students to compensate for their handicaps and increase their success within the vocational program. This might involve allowing an additional amount of time to develop a skill, or the use of specially designed instructional methods. Occupations can be analyzed to identify possible modification of instruction or equipment. Effective program modifications allow handicapped students to acquire specific job skills in regular vocational education programs.

Whenever possible, handicapped students should be served in integrated vocational preparation programs. The vocational education approach has obvious advantages over other approaches in terms of the types of jobs participants may acquire and their potential for job mobility and advancement. Vocational education programs use an analysis of local employment needs to determine program offerings. The emphasis in training programs is on the actual skills performed by incumbent workers. In contrast, special education personnel are often forced to train and place students into any job they can find. In many programs, students are placed on jobs that require little training (e.g., grocery clerks), or in placement where all the training is provided on the job.

Even though integrated programs possess several major advantages, placement into these programs must be made with caution. Students are sometimes placed into integrated programs inappropriately. Vocational education programs are usually not designed to prepare individuals for unskilled jobs or to teach general employability skills. Handicapped students mainstreamed into regular programs should be committed to working in the occupational area in which they are trained. In addition, when the vocational education curriculum is modified to accommodate handicapped students, the duties and tasks students learn must totally prepare them for a specific job. There are many ways vocational educators normally modify curricula. However, all these modifications result in students learning skills that will equip them for real jobs in the community. Special educators have been known to say, "Let us place the student in your auto mechanics class. Just teach the student to wash cars and change oil." This is only valid if the student can earn a living in the local community washing cars and changing oil. If no such jobs exist, the vocational education experience becomes only simulated work—it is not appropriate education. And the vocational education classroom is not the least restrictive environment for the student.

As vocational educators become more adept at working with handicapped students, more and more students will be mainstreamed into vocational education programs. Adequate support services will enable them to benefit fully from the programs. Unfortunately, problems relating to admission, curriculum

What You Can Do

- Carry over vocational educational objectives into the content areas.

- Include career and vocational skills in the developmental sequence.

- Remember that career development is a process that begins in the preschool years and continues through childhood and adolescence.

- Provide students with experiences that will enable them to set and pursue career goals.

- Give direct instruction to handicapped students during the elementary school years that will lead to the development of work-related concepts and values.

- Be aware of the stages of career development.

modification, and staff development for special and vocational education teachers persist. Some students who could succeed in integrated programs are being denied access. For other students, instruction in the regular vocational education program will not be appropriate, even if adequate support services are provided. For these students, special education must take direct responsibility for the provision of vocational training.

Issues in Work Preparation

Educators are continually involved in many complex issues as they begin to develop work-preparation options for handicapped students. This section addresses three of these issues: (1) appropriate programs, (2) least restrictive environments, and (3) interagency collaboration.

Appropriate Programs

An *appropriate program* is one from which a student can derive optimal benefit. Different types of programs have been described, any of which might be the appropriate program for a given student. However, *individualization* means that programs must be modified or combined if no one program adequately meets a student's needs.

Clearly, arrangements in which a student receives services from more than one of the programs are possible. Some students may learn to perform specific duties within integrated vocational programs, practice those skills through participation in special vocational programs, reenter the vocational program to acquire additional skills, and then move back to a special vocational program to practice both previously and newly acquired skills. Or a student could receive temporary vocational training in a substantially separate vocational program, enroll in regular vocational education, participate in special or regular work experience, and reenter regular vocational education (Johnson, 1980). Other types of flexible arrangements can be implemented. This flexibility is essential to guarantee that each student's program appropriately meets his or her individual needs.

Least Restrictive Environments

Placement in regular vocational education programs is not only the most "normal" placement for handicapped students but it also holds the greatest potential for preparing students for the world of work. Students trained in vocational education will be ready for more sophisticated jobs and have greater opportunities for job mobility and advancement. However, the least restrictive environment may not always be the appropriate environment for a student. In these instances, the student's right to an appropriate education takes precedence over his or her right of placement in the least restrictive environment. If a separate program most appropriately meets a student's individual needs, then that program is the least restrictive placement for that student. Mainstreaming solely for reasons of social integration cannot be justified.

Some students are denied access to regular education programs because of eligibility requirements that discriminate against handicapped students. In some cases, academic requirements to enter a vocational training program are greater than the academic requirements of the job itself. Perhaps requirements could be modified to adapt the course to handicapped students. If the admissions requirements for entrance into vocational education programs are legitimate, then students need to receive remedial instruction, if feasible, to prepare them to meet entrance requirements.

Interagency Collaboration

Local educational agencies should make every effort to ensure the coordination of services delivered by vocational education, special education, and vocational rehabilitation. Formal agreements have developed at the state and national levels that define the services provided by each discipline. The nature of the services provided by each agency will vary with the age and functioning level of a particular student.

Vocational education will be involved in the career preparation of some handicapped students. For these students, special education may play a supportive or advisory role. Vocational rehabilitation may restrict their involvement to a few mildly handicapped students. The degree or amount of services vocational rehabilitation provides will depend on the student's age. Until the ages of 16 to 18, the rehabilitation counselor may only consult with school system personnel.

Vocational Transition and IEP Development

The need to assist handicapped students to bridge the gap between secondary school and postschool employment or training alternatives has recently received significant attention from the U.S. Department of Education (Will, 1984). This initiative has been termed *transition from school to work* and has been designated as a major federal priority by both the Office of Special Education and Rehabilitative Services and the Administration on Developmental Disabilities. Wehman, Kregel, and Barcus (1985) have defined *transition* as follows:

> Vocational transition is a carefully planned process, which may be initiated either by school personnel or by adult service providers, to establish and implement a plan for either employment or additional vocational training of a handicapped student who will graduate or leave school in three to five years; such a process must involve special educators, vocational educators, parents, and/or the student, an adult service system representative, and possibly an employer. (p. 26)

A number of different theoretical models of the vocational transition process recently have been proposed (Halpern, 1985; Rusch & Chadsey-Rusch, 1985; Wehman, Kregel, & Barcus, 1985). Particularly useful guides have been developed by McKinney, Vreeberg, and West (1986), and Wehman, Moon, Everson, Wood, and Barcus (1988). These models share several common features. First, the models focus on the necessity of quality secondary school programs that emphasize functional curricula and the availability of community-based work experience programs. Second, they emphasize that successful vocational transition is dependent on the availability of adequate postschool employment options that will meet the needs of individual students. Third, the models concentrate on the transition planning process itself, and, specifically, the development of a formal, individualized transition plan for every handicapped student, linked to the student's IEP, and based on input from a variety of professionals, the student, and the student's family.

Providing a comprehensive vocational education to each mentally handicapped individual requires the cooperative planning of professionals from various disciplines and agencies over many years. The career-preparation program options described here attempt to provide instruction in the areas of general work habits, specific job-skill training, work experience, and community activities. Personnel from special education, vocational education, and vocational rehabilitation all have complimentary roles to play in the career-preparation process. The necessity for cooperative planning requires that local officials pay particular attention to issues involving (1) appropriate participants in the IEP process and (2) preparation for the IEP meeting.

IEP Participants

Federal regulations set minimum requirements for participation at IEP meetings. Each meeting to develop, review, or revise an IEP must include the student's teacher, one or both of the student's parents, the student (when appropriate), and a representative of the local education agency qualified to provide or supervise the provision of special education. Although the participants required by the regulations must be included at the IEP meeting, the representation and active involvement of many other individuals is necessary to develop and implement effective individualized education programs. Vocational educators and related services personnel are often actively involved in the IEP development process. At the secondary level, personnel from vocational rehabilitation frequently become involved. As a student nears completion of the secondary program, representatives of agencies providing vocational services to handicapped adults should also participate.

Representatives from numerous agencies and disciplines must do more than merely participate in the IEP development process. They must also engage in cooperative, joint planning activities to ensure the coordination of services and optimal use of resources. Not all these individuals will provide direct services to a particular student. A specific discipline may provide direct services, support services, or consultant services depending on the career-preparation program appropriate for the student. The IEP is the vehicle through which professionals and parents can coordinate their activities and focus their energies on the comprehensive career preparation of the handicapped student.

Special Educators. Special education must assume responsibility for ensuring a quality IEP for every handicapped student. Special educators provide support services to students served in integrated programs. This support may include the direct services of a vocational resource instructor, tutorial support provided by a resource teacher, or intense instruction on skills that will enable a student to enter an integrated program at a later date. Consultant services are provided through information shared with rehabilitation personnel or follow-up services delivered to students entering adult service programs.

Vocational Educators. Vocational educators also perform a multifaceted role in the development of IEPs for handicapped secondary students. In instances where special education is responsible for providing direct instruction, vocational educators can be a tremendous source of information and support. They may effectively assist in identifying the skills required by students for later participation in an integrated program, or provide feedback as to the validity and relevance of the specific job-skill training and work-experience activities included in special programs. When students participate in an integrated program, vocational educators must be directly involved in the development and implementation of the IEP. Vocational education brings to the IEP a variety of occupational offerings that can be coordinated with a student's abilities and interests. If at any time the curriculum or methods of instruction in the vocational class are to be modified, the vocational educator should make the final determination as to how this should be accomplished.

Parents. The role of the parent or guardian of the student in the development of the career preparation aspects of the IEP is to provide information relevant to the student's characteristics, abilities, and special interests. This information should greatly improve an individual's chances for success in a career-preparation program. The process allows parents to become familiar with instructors, administrators, and the career-preparation program. It also enables parents to identify ways in which they can supplement the educational program beyond the school environment.

Related Services Personnel.   Related services personnel often play a significant role in developing the career preparation aspects of the individualized education program. Physical therapists can assist in assessing an individual's physical capacity to perform work. Occupational therapists may design adaptations of regular equipment that will allow an individual to perform a specific job skill. Other important services are provided by speech therapists, social workers, and other related services professionals.

Adult Service Agency Personnel.   Representatives of vocational rehabilitation and adult service programs may appropriately participate in IEP development during various phases of the career-preparation process. Vocational rehabilitation may provide a variety of services, including evaluation services, funding for work experience and vocational training efforts, and placement and monitoring services for some students entering competitive employment. During the final years of the student's participation in the secondary program, active involvement in the IEP development should include representatives of any adult service programs in which the student will be placed after graduation. As a student nears the end of his or her schooling, it is important to ensure that the student can successfully perform a specific job, travel to and from a specific work site, and meet the social demands of a specific vocational environment.

Preparation for the IEP Meeting

In order to make the IEP a functional document, professionals and parents must engage in a series of advance planning activities prior to the meeting at which the IEP is developed. Effective cooperative planning among professionals from different disciplines does not simply occur but evolves through interactions over a period of time. A failure by professionals to appreciate the contributions of other disciplines has in many instances limited the development of effective programs. Special educators, vocational educators, and other professionals must learn to work and plan effectively with each other by investigating the potential contribution of other disciplines and respecting the concerns and limitations of various professionals.

Effective cooperative planning requires professionals to develop an understanding of the roles and responsibilities of other disciplines. This can be accomplished through observation of various programs and joint staff development activities. After all assessment activities have been completed, the student's current level of functioning can be compared to the content of the available career-preparation options. Special education's ability to teach general work skills and knowledge of instructional technology should be matched with vocational education's knowledge of occupational content. The result of the coordinated planning process should be a systematic and sequential outlining of the skills to be acquired and the services to be provided.

The active participation of parents in IEP planning is essential. A pre-IEP conference can provide parents a review of the general IEP process, the specific agenda and decision-making format for the upcoming meeting, and suggested ways to prepare for the meeting. Parents should be encouraged to observe potential programs and actively express their opinions. Interviews can identify parents' priorities for IEP content in a nonthreatening, individual situation prior to the more formal IEP meeting.

Summary

Handicapped individuals are generally employed less frequently, make less money, and work in less satisfying jobs than their nonhandicapped peers. A comprehensive career-preparation program that begins when the child enters the elementary grades and continues throughout the school years is required to allow handicapped persons to obtain and maintain employment successfully on graduation. The career-preparation process described in this chapter has five distinct stages—awareness, exploration, orientation, preparation, and placement and follow-up. Systematic programming at each stage of career development is necessary to enable each individual to maximize his or her career potential.

Mainstreaming handicapped students into career education and vocational education programs offers them the greatest opportunity for ultimate vocational success. Mainstreamed programs provide handicapped students the chance to prepare for sophisticated jobs in integrated settings that more closely approximate the community-based work setting in which students will be required to function. Successfully mainstreaming handicapped students into career and vocational education programs requires the close cooperation of all individuals involved in the career-development process—regular and special educators, related services personnel, parents, and community service providers.

Discussion Questions

1. Describe the current employment outlook for handicapped individuals exiting public school special education programs.
2. Define the concepts of *career education* and *vocation* and discuss their relevance for handicapped students in integrated programs.
3. Describe the central focus and major goals of each of the five stages of the career-development process.
4. Specify the roles and responsibilities of all the professionals involved in the career preparation of handicapped students.

Resources

Brolin, D. E. *Life Centered Career Education: A Competency-Based Approach.* CEC Publications, 1920 Association Drive, Reston, VA 22091. This guide's activities and resources provide secondary special education students experiences necessary for them to acquire the twenty-two competencies in the life centered career education approach. Each of the competencies is broken down into subcompetencies, for which instructional activities, evaluation suggestions, and personnel recommendations are provided.

Vocational Assessment and Curriculum Guide. Exceptional Education, P. O. Box 15308, Seattle, WA 98115. The VACG assesses the vocational and social survival skills necessary for success by students with handicaps in local businesses or industries. Procedures for developing local norms are provided. Individual students may be assessed with the instrument, and the assessment information may be easily translated into IEP objectives through the use of the curriculum guide.

Career Related Instructional (CRI) Materials. Capital Area Career Center, 611 Hagadorn Avenue, Mason, MI 48854. The CRI materials series contain 1,802 programmed learning units designed to provide instruction to special needs learners in the areas of vocation terminology, concepts, tools, equipment, and machinery. The nonconsumable modules are prepared at the third- or fourth-grade reading levels. Modules are developed in ten cluster areas comprising thirty-four occupations. Audiotapes of each module are available for visually impaired or nonreading students enrolled in vocational education programs.

Sarkees, M. D., & Scott, J. L. *Vocational Special Needs.* American Technical Publishers, Inc., 1155 W. 175th St., Homewood, IL 60430. This second edition of the Sarkees and Scott textbook is a major resource for all professionals concerned with mainstreaming students with handicaps into secondary vocational education programs. The book is divided into twelve modules for professionals, focusing on such topics as referral, identification, and placement; vocational assessment; IEP development; interagency collaboration; curriculum modification; and instructional techniques. It also offers a unique chapter focusing on the integration of special needs students into vocational student organizations.

Clark, G. M. *Career Education for the Handicapped Child in the Elementary Classroom.* Love Publishing Company, 1777 South Bellaire Street, Denver, CO 80222. This book provides a variety of information, resources, and assistance for the design and implementation of career education programs for elementary students. It contains a discussion of the major issues of career education and a complete description of career education content. For four content areas—values, attitudes, and habits; human relationships; occupational information; and job and daily living skills—the book provides selected goal and objectives statements, selected activities and materials, and career education programming evaluation checklists.

Wircenski, J. *Employability Skills for the Special Needs Learner*. Aspen Publishers, Inc., 1600 Research Blvd., Rockville, MD 20850. This 720-page manual contains a large number of activities and worksheets designed to teach employability skills to special needs students. Content focuses on five areas—socialization skills; communication skills; financial management skills; values clarification skills; and job procurement and retention skills. The program appears appropriate as a source of supplementary activities for special needs learners in secondary schools.

Parrish, L. & Kok, M. *Procedures Handbook for Special Needs Work-Study Coordinators*. Aspen Publishers, Inc., 1600 Research Blvd., Rockville, MD 20850. The handbook is a comprehensive guide to the development, operation, and evaluation of work experience programs for special needs students. It contains sections dealing with setting up a program, understanding pertinent laws and regulations, public relations skills and identifying and selecting jobs, and evaluating a student's performance while on the job. The handbook also provides examples of forms that may be useful in monitoring all facets of the employment program.

Janus Alternative Basal Texts. Janus Book Publishers, Inc., 3541 Investment Blvd., Suite 5, Hayward, CA 94545. The Janus series provides an array of supplementary resource materials and student workbooks in a variety of areas—career awareness; job-seeking skills; practical living skills; survival guides; financial skills; nutrition; and child care. Teacher's guides are available for the series that provide suggestions for using the materials in varying situations with students with handicaps.

Tools, Equipment, and Machinery Adapted for Vocational Education. Wisconsin Vocational Studies Center, University of Wisconsin–Madison, 964 Education Science Building, 1025 W. Johnson St., 53706. This resource is a catalog designed to assist professionals providing vocational education to persons with handicaps. It contains descriptions and illustrations of modified tools, equipment, and machinery. It also provides photographs and illustrations of adapted devices designed to meet the needs of specific individuals. It surveys both commercially available equipment and specially designed equipment modifications.

McKinney, L., Vreeberg, M., & West, K. *Extending Horizons*. The National Center for Research in Vocational Education, 1960 Kenney Road, Columbus, OH, 43210. This comprehensive guide proposes a model for facilitating the transition of handicapped students from vocational education to employment. It contains sections that focus on (1) procedures for preparing and coordinating school and community teams; (2) in-service training materials; (3) information on career-exploration activities; and (4) suggestions for instructional strategies.

Wehman, P., Moon, M. S., Everson, J., Wood, W., & Barcus, J. *Transition from school to work.* Paul H. Brookes, P. O. Box 10624, Baltimore, 21285-0624. This comprehensive text provides a thorough discussion of the values underlying current emphasis on transition from school to work and outlines a framework for developing a complete transition program. The text focuses on three steps: (1) preparation for transition in secondary school; (2) initiating careful transition planning; and (3) strategies for achieving successful postschool employment.

Chapter 10

Regular and Special Educators' Feedback —A Survey Report

JUDY W. WOOD

Chapter Objectives

After reading Chapter 10 the student will be able to

- Identify and discuss a model for adapting the learning environment
- Provide examples for making classroom adaptations for each component of the model

T his chapter is unique to textbooks on mainstreaming. With the assistance of hundreds of regular and special educators across the nation, an effort was made to survey educators and find out what types of modifications, if any, are being used in mainstreamed classes. The purpose of this survey was to gather for readers information that traditionally cannot be found in other textbooks.

This book presents the reader with (1) an overview of mainstreaming (Chapter 1); (2) the roles and functions of the multidisciplinary team (Chapter 2); (3) the characteristics of handicapping conditions (Chapters 3 and 4); and (4) specific suggestions, by academic areas, for teaching the handicapped students (Chapters 5–9). Chapter 10 goes beyond other texts by providing readers with a first-hand look at what educators are doing in their mainstreamed classes.

The purpose of the chapter is to present data collected from regular and special educators surveyed nationwide. The survey examined the types of modifications educators are using and their suggestions. It took a great deal of time to complete the survey form. However, as a result of hundreds of caring educators, we now have a closer look at what special and regular educators are doing in their classes.

The chapter is divided into two major sections:

1. A description of the population responding to the survey.
2. What teachers are doing in their classrooms in the following areas:
   a. Learning environment.
   b. Teaching techniques.
   c. Presentation of the format of content.
   d. Media use.
   e. Evaluation.

The Population Surveyed

The population for the study consisted of a random sample of 1,000 special education teachers of the mentally retarded, emotionally disturbed, and learning disabled (K–12) and of 1,000 regular education teachers (K–12) selected from across the United States. Approximately 400 of the participants surveyed, or 20%, returned the form. Even though the return rate was low, it was felt that the information is significant since this is the only national survey of its type to be reported. A beginning point for making classroom adaptations is knowing what educators are doing in their classes. With this in mind, this chapter presents a look into classrooms across the nation to observe what teachers are doing and what adaptations they suggest work for special needs students.

The surveyed population reached from the east coast to the west coast with educators from regular and special education responding (see Table 10.1). Both

TABLE 10.1
Description of Educators Surveyed

Category	Regular Education	Special Education	Category	Regular Education	Special Education
Sex:			*Grade level taught*		
Male	39	11	1–3	21	10
Female	61	89	4–6	29	12
Highest degree earned:			7–9	21	10
B.S. or B.A.	33	25	10–12	21	10
M.A., M.S., or M.Ed.	48	21	Combination	15	53
Advanced Certificate	18	9	*In-service training*		
Ph.D. or Ed.D.	0	15	*hours related to*		
Years of teaching			*mainstreaming:*		
experience:			None	61	45
1–5	8	23	1–5	28	34
6–10	18	35	6–10	7	12
11–15	24	25	11–15	0	34
16–20	29	10	16–20	2	3
21–25	11	5	21 or above	2	3
26–30	8	1	*Number of special*		
31–35	0.8	0.5	*education college*		
36–40	0.8	0	*courses:*		
Type of school setting:			0	47	
Urban	27	39	1	16	
Rural	36	35	2	12	
Suburban	31	27	3	8	
Private	5	0	4	8	
Category taught:			5	2	
Mentally retarded		16	6	7	
Learning disabled		37	more	0.8	
Emotionally disturbed		12	*Subject area taught:*		
Combination		33	Language arts	6	
Other		0.5	Mathematics	5	
			Science	9	
			Social studies	15	
			Combination	61	
			Other	5	

groups largely were female and held an undergraduate or masters level degree. Both samples were evenly distributed among urban, rural, and suburban school settings. Of special interest was that 47% of the regular education teachers surveyed had had no college courses in special education.

What Teachers Are
Doing in Their Classes

This section is based on a curriculum-based model for adapting the learning environment (see Figure 10.1). A student's school day may be divided into three major sections: the social/emotional/behavioral environment, the physical environment, and the instructional environment. The section for instruction may be further divided into four sections: teaching technique, media, content, and evaluation. In any one of these major areas, the educator can make a simple adaptation or modification that will make education more appropriate for the special needs student, thereby providing an environment that is the least restrictive. The survey assessed educators as to what they were doing in these areas and what types of adaptations they are making in these same areas.

Adaptations are simple adjustments to teaching, to testing, or to areas within the environment. For example, if a student cannot read the textbook, there are several adaptations to the text that the teacher may use to assist the lower reading level student to learn the material.

For the five areas surveyed, we define the area, provide data on what the teachers are doing, and list suggested adaptations that the teachers are using.

Social, Emotional, and
Physical Environments

The social, emotional, and physical environments include numerous aspects of the school. Socially/emotionally we work with the overall school climate. This includes the attitudes of educators as well as students and ways of improving these attitudes. In addition, we spend a great deal of time helping the special needs students to develop appropriate social skills so that they will be more effective within their environments. Physically, we are concerned with how we schedule and group students as well as providing an environment that is free of physical barriers.

For this survey, we only investigated the type of scheduling that the schools use. The total school day is organized according to the master schedule of the school. According to Wood (1984), "the soundness of this schedule determines the effectiveness of administrative detail, plant facilities, instruction and overall school organization" (p. 61). All educators need a basic knowledge of how the master schedule is organized and the special educator should play an active part in planning the schedule for the mainstreamed student. At the secondary level, the master schedule becomes more complex, thus proper placement of the handicapped student becomes more of a problem. Ultimately, the principal or guidance counselor is responsible for making the master schedule. Whoever does the planning should carefully evaluate the needs of the handicapped student prior to the scheduling process.

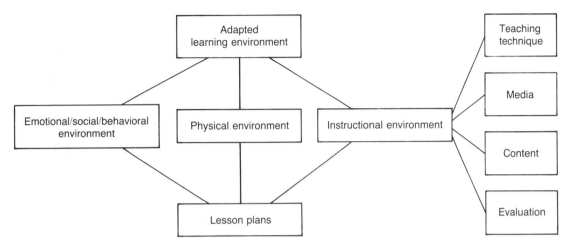

FIGURE 10.1
Curriculum-Based Model for Adapting the Learning Environment. (From Wood, J. W., Project TRAIN, Virginia Commonwealth University, Richmond, VA, 1988.)

In our survey, we focused on six major areas of concern.

1. What type of master schedule is used for placing the mainstreamed student in classes?
2. Is the special education teacher involved in the scheduling of mainstreamed students?
3. Are problems created when the mainstreamed student moves back and forth from the regular to the special classrooms?
4. What are these problems?
5. What are suggestions to these problems?
6. When a special student is placed in the mainstream, how could the special or regular educator assist in making the transition?

Schedule Type, Teacher Involvement, and Problems.   For the first three areas of concern, it was found that hand scheduling for the special needs student is the most common method used. 81% of regular educators as compared to 93% of special education teachers assist in the scheduling process for the special student. Almost half of the teachers felt that problems are created when the mainstreamed student moves from regular to special classes.

Problems in Moving Back and Forth from Regular to Special Classes.   Frequently, when the special needs student is sent to the special class for instruction, problems occur. Table 10.2 presents some of these problems. The responses in Table 10.2 are divided into perceived problems as seen by the regular educators and the special educators. Responses are listed in order of priority of response. Miss-

TABLE 10.2

Problems Created when the Mainstreamed Student Moves Back and Forth from the Regular to Special Classroom

Regular Educator	Special Educator
Parents become upset when their child misses classwork	Difficulty in performing on grade level
Due to inflexible regular class schedules, the mainstreamed student gets only bits and pieces of the lesson	Student does not adapt well when moving from one class to another
When in the special education class, the student misses out on class discussion of other students	Regular teachers feel overworked
	Different teacher expectations
	Student is unable to get along with regular students
When in special education classes, the student misses regular class involvement (movies, speakers, class discussions)	Lack of consistency among regular classes
Scheduling students into classes that move too quickly	Groups are already in session when the special student arrives
Students are not able to cope with change when they enter the room	Student misses work in regular class when he or she comes out for special class
Because student cannot do regular classwork, he or she becomes embarrassed and noisy	Working around scheduled activities, recess, music, and so on
Fools around while moving from regular to special class	Behavior problems in regular classroom
Difficulty integrating the students back into the curriculum when they enter the room	Lack of communication between teachers
Student forgets to bring textbooks, homework, and so on to class	Difficulty remembering when it is time to go to special class
Competitiveness in the regular classroom lessons—the brighter students suffer	Trouble adjusting to change
	Takes too much time getting to class
Mainstreamed student has difficulty functioning in groups	The special and regular class are too far apart
Lack of communication between special and regular teachers	Some students cannot cope with activity in the hallways
Students are excused for certain class projects and assignments	Supervision in hallways is inadequate
Frustrated by the subject matter	Special student is embarrassed when entering the regular class
A different standard and expectation are presented to the special student	
Problem in getting the special needs student to complete the work in the time allotted	

ing class work while out of the regular class, not getting the subjects needed, and getting only "bits and pieces" of the lesson are the major concerns of the regular educator. Not being able to perform on the grade level of the class is seen as a major problem by the special educator. The remaining responses are presented for the reader to get a better picture of the reality of moving students back and forth between classes.

Suggestions for Improvement.   While the respondents had many concerns, they also had several excellent suggestions for the problems with scheduling. Of interest, most regular educators suggested that most mildly handicapped students should remain in the regular class. While this is the focus of this text, this response was timely. All of the suggestions presented in Table 10.3 are excellent for helping the scheduling process flow more smoothly.

TABLE 10.3
Suggestions for Problems in Scheduling

Regular Educator	Special Educator
Leave most of the mildly handicapped students in the regular class	Work on developing the mainstreamed student's social skills
Regular educator spends 2–3 minutes as soon as the special student enters class to focus the student	Provide "time cards" to students who loiter in the halls
Upon entering the room, have the student immediately do an activity with manipulatives	Provide folders for each mainstreamed class in which to keep papers so often lost
Mainstream only for nonacademic areas	Do not isolate special education classrooms
Smaller regular class sizes	Let a special education aid assist in the regular classroom
More paraprofessional help for the regular classroom teacher	Strong administrative support is imperative for successful mainstreaming scheduling
Maintain flexibility	In-service training
Let the regular class teacher send for the special student when ready	Give the special education teacher material that is being used in the regular class
Primary children should receive instruction in the basics in the morning	Teach basics at a slower pace
Let students change classes when all other students are changing classes	Schedule the mainstreamed student into lower-level classes
Assign a buddy for those students having difficulty moving between classes	Match the special education student's learning style to the regular education teacher's teaching style

(continued)

TABLE 10.3
(*continued*)

Regular Educator	Special Educator
Hand schedule students for benefit of classroom teacher's schedule	Schedule mainstreamed students only into classes where the regular educator wants them
Make modifications to the regular education curriculum	Allow special education teachers to teach regular education classes using special methods
Let all teachers who teach a mainstreamed student help plan the schedule collectively (provides for ownership)	Always keep the special education teacher informed on what is going on in the regular class
Keep the lines of communication open	Team teach
Special education teachers should make periodic check-ups on the students	Provide a study skills class where the special education teacher works on homework and tests (this eliminates the special education stigma)
Special education teachers should provide information and assistance	Teach students on their instructional levels
Develop a better understanding of how regular and special education need to support each other to help the children	Provide notes when a student misses class
Provide security for the student	Begin mainstreaming at early elementary levels
Provide in-service training to the teachers	When students are near grade level, place them in a class of both regular and special students and let regular and special education teachers co-teach
Make mainstreamed students feel a part of the regular class	When the student is three to four levels below expected, adaptations of curriculum should be made

Assisting in the Transition.   When asked what the teacher could do to assist the mainstreamed student in making a smooth transition into the regular class, regular and special educators had numerous suggestions. In rank order, these are presented in Table 10.4. Letting both teachers participate in the planning of the mainstreamed student's curriculum and reducing the special student's work load when new concepts are being taught were popular responses. A common theme throughout this response is working together to make mainstreaming work.

Teaching Techniques

According to Jarolimek and Foster (1981), "there is a great deal of disagreement, even among well-informed persons, about what constitutes good teaching and how teaching should take place" (p. 109). Here we present information reflecting the major instructional modes of teaching that teachers use and look further at each of the specific teaching techniques of each mode. For each teaching mode, the frequency of the technique used most often by teachers is reported. This information can be useful to educators in two ways: (1) knowing the teaching mode and teaching technique used most often by teachers provides information for where instructional adaptations should be made, and (2) seeing a discrepancy between the techniques used most often by the regular educator and the special educator helps to understand why a special student may have difficulty in making instructional transitions.

When teachers teach, they do so in one of four major modes of teaching: the expository mode, the activity mode, the inquiry mode, or the demonstration mode. The *expository mode*, most popular among educators, simply means to provide an explanation. The *inquiry mode* involves "asking questions, seeking information, and carrying on an investigation" (Jarolimek & Foster, 1981, p. 116). "Showing, doing and telling" (Jarolimek & Foster, 1981, p. 120) are essential components of the *demonstration mode*. The *activity mode* "can best be described as a set of strategies that involve pupils in learning by doing things that are, for the pupils, meaningfully related to the topic under study" (Jarolimek & Foster, 1981, p. 127).

For each of these modes, the regular educators and the special educators were asked the following questions.

1. Which instructional modes of teaching do you use most often?
2. Which teaching techniques do you use most often in the expository mode, activity mode, inquiry mode, and demonstration mode?
3. Do you have a suggestion for adapting teaching techniques that would be helpful in teaching a mainstreamed student?

Instructional Modes Used Most Often.   Regular educators reported using the expository teaching mode 53% of the time, the inquiry mode 23%, the activity mode 21%, and the demonstration mode 3%. Special educators reported using the activity mode 36%, inquiry 35%, expository 24%, and demonstration 6%. Since the regular educator used the expository mode most often as compared to the activity mode for the special educator, problems might occur for the special student. Students must know how to respond to different modes of teaching and be prepared to function successfully in the mainstream when the teaching modes between the classes differ.

TABLE 10.4
Ways to Assist the Transition to the Mainstream

Regular Educator	Special Educator
Let both the special and regular educator participate in the planning of the curriculum for the mainstreamed student	Reduce work load for the special student when a new concept is taught
Be sure that the special education teacher has a conference with the regular education teacher *prior* to placement in the mainstream	Be sure that special students understand why they are going to the regular class
Let the regular educators get to know the student *prior* to placement	Have definite criteria to be met and mainstreamed
Explain the "reality" of the regular classroom prior to placement	Hold an introductory meeting with special student and teachers so the student can ask questions and become familiar with the new classroom
Communicate with the student	Always have an assigned desk for the mainstreamed student
Assist in developing "positive attitudes" of educators	In-service training is needed for teachers and students
Check on the mainstreamed student's work on a consistent basis	Regular and special teachers should discuss students' capabilities, disabilities, and needs and develop a plan of action
Be sure that the special teacher receives a copy of all regular class assignments	
In chemistry, the special education student needs an aide	Special teachers should assist regular teachers in modifying methods and techniques
Be sure that the regular educator knows the reading levels of the student and what to expect from the student	Staffing concerning scheduling
	Prescreen mainstreamed classes and start prospective mainstreamed students on regular classwork a few weeks prior to placement
Learn and emphasize students' strengths	
Good communication among parents, students, and teachers	The special teacher should make sure all homework is completed
Provide goals and rewards for the student	Do not give up and call a situation hopeless
Advise all regular teachers in ways to work with the special student's needs	Provide study skills classes
Start the special student with mainstreamed subject matter prior to placement	Mainstream the student in small segments
Coordinate assignments	

TABLE 10.4
(*continued*)

Regular Educator	Special Educator
Conference between special education and regular teacher to identify problems and/or plan teaching strategies	
Review student records prior to placement	
Cooperative groups with the class	
Closely supervise the interaction between the special student and the regular student	
Prepare the class for a special student when appropriate	
Treat the special child like a normal child	
Provide an opportunity for all students to participate in all classroom activities when possible	
Have assigned desks for mainstreamed students so they will not have to sit in different places each day	
When appropriate, let the aide make the initial transition to the regular class	
Be flexible regarding time needed to complete assignments	
Try to begin all mainstreaming at the beginning of the school year	

Techniques Used Most Often.　Each major teaching mode—expository, activity, inquiry, and demonstration—has several techniques specific to it alone. Table 10.5 shows the techniques characteristic for each mode and the percent of time that regular and special educators use them. Major techniques include discussion, lecture, and questioning.

Suggestions for Adapting Teaching Techniques.　The survey participants had several excellent suggestions for adapting specific teaching techniques. Table 10.6 presents these suggestions by modes of teaching.

TABLE 10.5
Percent of Time Teaching Techniques (by Mode) Are Used

Expository Mode				Activity Mode			
Regular Educator		**Special Educator**		**Regular Educator**		**Special Educator**	
Discussion	37%	Explanation	57%	Group work	66%	Group work	72%
Explanation	26%	Discussion	20%	Processing	11%	Processing	12%
Lecture	19%	Telling	10%	Construction	6%	Role playing	5%
Telling	11%	Audio recording	9%	Role playing	4%	Construction	5%
Sound filmstrip		Sound filmstrip		Preparing exhibits	4%	Preparing exhibits	2%
Audio recording	7%	Lecture	0.8%	Dramatizing	4%	Dramatizing	2%
Motion pictures		Motion pictures		Other	4%	Other	2%
Recitation		Recitation					
Other		Other					

Inquiry Mode				Demonstration Mode			
Regular Educator		**Special Educator**		**Regular Educator**		**Special Educator**	
Asking questions	66%	Asking questions	59%	Experiments	34%	Modeling	36%
Self-directed study	10%	Self-directed study	21%	Games	22%	Games	25%
Observing	2%	Observing	6%	Modeling	21%	Simulations	11%
Interpreting	5%	Interpreting	6%	Simulations	11%	Experiments	8%
Stating hypothesis	5%	Stating hypothesis	1%	Exhibits	4%	Exhibits	6%
Drawing conclusions	2%	Drawing conclusions	1%	Field trips	4%	Field trips	6%
Classifying	2%	Classifying	1%	Other	4%	Other	6%
Testing hypotheses	2%	Test hypotheses	1%				
Synthesizing	2%	Synthesizing	1%				
Other	2%	Other	1%				

Format of Content Presentation

Frequently, the mainstreamed student can learn the academic content presented in the regular classroom. However, a few of the special needs students have difficulty in understanding the material presented. The presentation of the format of content in regular classrooms can be modified by making simple "adjustments" ongoing with instruction. For example, if a student cannot read the social studies text, he or she is not learning the material presented. The teacher can make numerous adaptations to the text, thus paving the way for a more appropriate education for the special student in the mainstream. If special students could do the work just like everyone else, they would not be in special classes. The regular education class teacher should ask the following questions about the mainstreamed student.

1. Does the student have the skills to complete the required task?
2. If not, does the student have the prerequisite skills for beginning the required task?
3. Does instruction begin at the student's functioning level?
4. Has the student's learning style been determined? (Wood, 1984, p. 118)

If the preceding questions are answered in the affirmative, and the student is still experiencing difficulty with the material, the teacher should adapt the presentation of the format of content for the student.

The following list presents ideas given by the surveyed teachers on ways in which they are adapting the presentation of the format of content for students. The ideas are categorized by academic subject areas. The regular and the special educators' responses are combined. Beside each activity the letter *R* represents a response given by the regular education teacher and the letter *S* represents a response given by a special education teacher.

Language Arts Modifications—Activities

- Create a story from pictures (Wordless Book). This is excellent for students who do not read well but are able to express themselves verbally. (R)
- Instead of having the student do several exercises on parts of speech, only have the mainstreamed student do one-half to one-third of the total assignment. (R)
- Let the better reader read the subject textbook out loud so that everyone can be exposed to the material. (R)
- Always include something the mainstreamed student can do as part of his or her assignment. (R)
- Let students prepare and write their own stories and illustrate them. (R)
- Teaching reading to the nonreader as you would a foreign student—survival conversation. (R)
- Let a child spell a sound, then work from there. (R)
- When assigning spelling words, circle only part of the list. It is better for the student to learn only some words than no words at all. (R)
- Let students learn the *to be* verbs by singing them in a particular order to the song "Jingle Bells." "Be, being, been, am, is, had, do, does, did, can, may, might, must, shall, will, should, would, could" (repeat). (S)

TABLE 10.6

Suggestions for Adapting Teaching Techniques by Major Mode Areas

Regular Educator	Special Educator
Expository Mode	*Expository Mode*
Draw mainstreamed students into discussions so that they can gain confidence and self-worth (*discussion*)	When lecturing, only give material in short sessions of 15–20 minutes. (*lecture*)
Entire class follows words as tape reads. More able students reread text in groups of two or three and answer prepared questions. Less able students work in a group with the teacher and answer and discuss the questions together. (*sound filmstrip*)	Let the students learn using a hands-on approach. (*explanation*)
	When explaining material using the board, the explanations may need to be written in manuscript rather than cursive. (*explanation*)
	Have the student repeat instructions to the teacher. (*explanation*)
Before a class discussion, provide reading material on tape read orally or use video materials. (*discussion*)	While verbally explaining a concept, it is often a good idea to write on the board the important components of the explanation. (*explanation*)
Before, during, and after class discussions, give positive reinforcement to the mainstreamed student to boost self-worth. (*discussion*)	State facts to be internalized aloud and ask all students to restate in a group response. (*lecture*)
Let the more advanced student make a flowchart for class discussion. Both levels of student benefit. (*discussion*)	Develop graphic organizers to assist in following and obtaining desired data. (*lecture*)
	Tape or video record lectures. (*lecture*)
Put an outline of the lecture on the overhead projector to follow during the lecture. (*lecture*)	Provide manipulative, multisensory approaches. (*lecture*)
Provide a written study guide of the lecture after the lesson *(lecture)*.	Let students assume ownership for what they learn. (*lecture*)
When explaining material, restate the information in many ways and use concrete materials. (*explanation*)	Prepare an outline of the lecture. Fill in some major points and let the student fill in the specifics during the lecture. It helps develop listening and outlining skills. You can gradually put fewer main points on the outline as the student becomes more proficient. (*lecture*)
When lecturing, use a diagram or provide the class with a written outline of the key points of the lecture. (*lecture*)	
Activity Mode	*Activity Mode*
Assign a peer buddy during group work. (*group work*)	Highlight parts in a play in yellow to make it easy for the mainstreamed student to keep up with the group. (*dramatizing*)
Be sure that the group in which the mainstreamed student is placed is a comparative and cooperative group. (*group work*)	Use small groups of three or four where a peer is assigned as leader. (*group work*)
Assign each group member a specific job. (*group work*)	

TABLE 10.6
(*continued*)

Regular Educator	Special Educator
Inquiry Mode	*Inquiry Mode*
Provide for specific, short-range goals. (*self-directed study*) Make periodic checks to see if the student is understanding the material studied. (*interpretation*)	Be aware of each student's ability to answer questions of varying difficulty. There is always a question every student can answer. (*asking questions*) Have a guided outline of the steps to follow in reaching conclusions. (*drawing conclusions*) Reinforce students for answering questions. (*asking questions*) Allow another student to serve as a tutor or answer questions for a child trying to study alone. (*asking questions*) Use short sentences and explain vocabulary. (*self-directed study*) Organize the class into sections or groups for small discussion sessions. Then come together for large-group discussion. (*drawing conclusions*) Keep an assignment sheet. (*self-directed study*) Simplify questions to ask one thing. Ask several questions. (*asking questions*) Let the student make a poster or scrapbook showing hypothesis. (*stating hypothesis*)
Demonstration Mode	*Demonstration Mode*
Act out molecular movement for solid, liquid, or gas. Act out light rays being absorbed, reflected, and refracted by walking on tape marks on the floor. (*simulation*) Pair a good, caring student to work with the mainstreamed student. (*experimenting*)	Assign a peer to role model. (*modeling*) Let the student play games before discussing a new concept. (*games*) Use the game "Monopoly" to reinforce subtraction and addition by having students keep bank records and balance their accounts at the end of each play period. (*games*)

- For teaching spelling, have student write spelling word at top of paper and fold. Next, on bottom of paper, write the word—unfold the top to check correct spelling. If word is incorrect, fold up bottom of page and rewrite, checking spelling to top of page. This way the student never continues to see the incorrect work. (S)

- For difficult spelling tests, let students learn two or three words each night and check the next day. (S)
- For poetry writing, even the poorer readers get excited about writing silly rhymes and jingles about themselves, their classmates, and the teacher. These are then typed in booklet form. (S)
- Tape record and make worksheet for new vocabulary words prior to introducing new selection in reader. (S)
- Tape record stories for reluctant readers to read along for meaning before attempting to read alone. (S)
- Prepare a model book report form and allow student to fill in pertinent information. (S)

Mathematics Modifications—Activities

- Enlarge the math book pages so that students do not have to copy the activities before completing them. (R)
- When teaching making change, have a class store that is used daily. (R)
- When you introduce a new skill, present a real-life situation through which the student can learn the skill. (S)
- Use the computer for drill and practice. (S)
- Make a special instruction card for the student to keep in his or her notebook (e.g., steps in long division). (S)
- Always read a subtraction problem from the top down. Be consistent. (S)

Social Studies Modifications—Activities

- When assigning creative projects, have several alternatives to choose from, so that different talents can be used (e.g., an oral instead of a written report). (R)
- Select books at students' individual reading level for topics under discussion. (R)
- Use films, role playing, and other visuals to supplement class discussions. (R)
- To reinforce concepts of government, use mock Congress and trial. (R)
- Allow students to draw or act out concepts being studied. (R)
- Prepare a copy of class notes for the student to correct his or her own copy. (S)
- After teaching a unit or series of concepts, play "Social Studies Around the World." Directions: The teacher asks a factual, true-false, or incomplete question and the student who answers correctly challenges the next student and remains at the front of the class. Students who answer incorrectly return to their seats. Questions proceed in a round-robin fashion until only one student remains and is declared winner. (S)
- Let students create a map of their neighborhood to learn directionality. (S)
- Allow students to tape record a chapter outline instead of writing it. (S)
- Underline the main ideas of paragraphs in the desk copy of a text, using a colored pencil or a marker. (S)
- Student prepares a minibook report on a provided form using classic comic books, current events, historical miniseries, or other television programs as subject matter. (S)

General Modifications—Activities

- Reduce assignment loads (e.g., give fewer math problems or shortened spelling list). (R)
- Make VAKT (visual, auditory, kinesthetic, tactile) packets for an area of study (e.g., puzzles to match vocabulary words; tapes to match test questions). (R)
- Let students use color instead of labeling (e.g., color Iowa blue on U.S. map). (R)
- Task analyze steps involved in projects and give students list of steps to complete (e.g., "Writing a Term Paper." Step 1—Prepare title page with centered title, subject, class, name and date). (S)
- Let students put spelling words, vocabulary, and reading assignments on the computer. The study disks may be used to review for a test, revise notes, or complete homework assignments. (S)
- Allow the student to draw or make something related to the subject instead of doing written homework. (S)
- Tape record textbooks and lectures for students to listen. (S)
- Allow students to earn privileges for completing a designated percentage of the assignment. (S)
- Use brain-storming techniques to review and organize material. (S)
- Use role-playing to reinforce concepts being studied. (S)
- Let students make flashcards (vocabulary, formulas, and so on) to practice content. (S)

Media Use

Media is a vital aspect of the instructional process. Teachers should use a variety of media so that students are reached through a multisensory approach. This section reports the most frequently used media in classrooms.

Frequently Used Media. It was felt that it would be of educational interest to survey teachers and find what type of media is being used most often in the classrooms across the nation. The regular class teacher reported that the overhead projector was used 31% of the time, filmstrip projectors 23%, videotapes 16%, and computers 14%. Special education teachers use the tape recorder 36% of the time and the computer second 25%. Regular class teachers reported that they required students to copy notes from the board 54% of the time as compared to using handouts 26% of the time. Likewise, the special teacher required notes copied from the board 46% and handouts 37%.

Evaluation

Good teaching requires careful instructional planning. It also requires a valid method of evaluating instructional outcomes, usually in the form of a teacher-made test or some other form of evaluation. The last section of our survey investigated the following:

1. The type of tests used most often.
2. The test adaptations used most often.

Test Type Used Most Often.   Table 10.7 reports the type of tests most often used by regular educators and by special educators. It is important for students to know what type of test they will be taking. It is also important for the teacher to know how to provide adaptations for each type of test. The special education teacher should teach the special needs student how to take each type of test.

Test Adaptations Used by Educators.   Test adaptations can be made when the test is being constructed and when the test is being administered. Surveyed teachers were asked to share test adaptations that they had found successful in their classes as they related to test construction and test administration. Tables 10.8 and 10.9 present these adaptations. In Table 10.8, test construction is subdivided into test directions, test items, and test design.

TABLE 10.7
Types of Tests Used Most Often by Educators

Regular Educator		Special Educator	
Test Type	Percent	Test Type	Percent
Multiple choice	31%	Matching	21%
Completion	20%	Multiple choice	19%
Matching	14%	Oral	17%
Essay	9%	Simple recall	16%
True/false	4.8%	Essay	5%
Oral	4.8%	True/false	5%
Simple recall	4.8%	Completion	5%
Fill in	4.8%	Fill in	5%
Other	4.8%	Other	5%

TABLE 10.8
Adaptations for Test Construction

Regular Educator	Special Educator
Test Directions	*Test Directions*
Print instead of write	Teacher or another student read directions or whole test orally
Read orally	
Test Items	*Test Items*
Arrange questions sequentially, from easiest to most difficult	For older students, use essay questions to test written expression (e.g., writing complete sentences)
Eliminate some questions	Use pictures that represent words as cues to questions
Use fewer essay questions	
Provide visual cues to questions (e.g., diagram on chalkboard)	Use carefully worded questions
	Group items logically (e.g., alphabetical order for terms, phonetic pattern groups for spelling)
Test Design	*Test Design*
Test major concepts, not details	Give test as work/study sheet the day before the test; collect before actual test is given
Print or type (large type if available)	
Adjust test to student's reading and language level	Put test on tape
	Place all of one type of question (e.g., multiple choice) on one page
Pre- and posttest	
Provide more spacing on page	Print or type
Individualize test assessing student's personal goals	Shorten test (some items optional)
	Leave more space between questions
Enlarge test paper	Adjust readability level of test to meet student's needs
Use testing recommendations from special teacher, child study team, supplemental teacher, or student.	Clearly duplicate using black ink (vs. purple dittos)
	Provide more space to write because of frequency of fine motor problems
	Print test on computer
	Xerox test copies
	Design the test to test the way student was taught (e.g., if taught for facts, test for facts)

TABLE 10.9
Adaptations for Test Administration

Regular Educator	Special Educator
Check off questions for student to answer	Use peer tutor
Omit questions above student's ability level	Allow nonverbal students to demonstrate or use sign language
Give test orally	
Give test individually	Administer test orally
Allow students to complete only questions they feel competent to answer	Limit number of choices (e.g., on long matching list, select either A, M, or P)
Monitor to see if child is "on track"	Give part of the test in oral form and part in written
Go over directions for each section of test	
No time limits within class period	Give credit for answers based on student's ability
Give more time to complete	Tape record oral answers
Give test in parts; one section one day, another section the next day	Teacher writes down student's oral responses
Give shorter version of test	For test failures, reteach and retest
Allow one-word response rather than a complete sentence	Give student extra time to complete
Adjust grade to reflect student's overall ability	Change test format (e.g., from essay to matching)
Open book tests	Simplify wording of questions
Use more matching or interpretive drawings rather than fill-in-the-blank or essay	Omit difficult test sections
	Give review test before graded test
Use peer tutor or parent helper to assist student in staying on task	Cross out items student has not mastered
Allow special education teacher to administer test	Make flashcards to study for test
	Paraphrase questions
Test in small groups at student's vocabulary level	Put information on computer
	Study quiz disks
Teach test-taking skills	Open note test
Allow student to take test where he or she is most comfortable (e.g., resource room, carrel, floor)	Break test into components given in stages
	Give test at optimal time of day for student
Provide rest breaks	Shorten testing period
Administer test after school	Show students the test the day before so they know what to expect
Vary explanation to meet individual needs	Special education teacher administers for regular teacher
Students develop study cards for test with terms on one side and definitions on the other	Orally repeat questions as needed
	Interpret questions; make diagrams
	Highlight key words
	Provide answers for student to select from

Summary

This chapter is especially designed to complete this text on mainstreaming. It is important to know that thousands of educators across the nation strive each day to provide an education that is appropriate for handicapped students. It is through the sharing of ideas, the continuous seeking of new ideas, and the willingness to implement these ideas that handicapped students will be able to achieve their potential within regular class settings.

The overall themes of the text are keeping special students in regular classes as much as possible and providing instructional alternatives when needed. By providing information on how to work with the special needs student in the regular class, and lastly, by sharing what actually is happening across our nation, it is hoped that working with the handicapped student in regular classes will become the rule, not the exception. Working together to make it work is a worthy goal.

Discussion Questions

1. Take any regular class lesson plan and provide suggestions for making adaptations to the lesson.
2. Take any of the teacher suggestions from the lesson plan and discuss how you would apply the suggestions to a selected academic area.
3. Discuss the advantages of having an understanding of the scheduling problems that might occur within a school.

Appendix

Organizations and Associations

Alexander Graham Bell Institute for the Deaf
3417 Volta Place, N.W.
Washington, DC 20007
(202) 337-5220

American Academy of Neurology
2221 University Avenue, S.E., Suite 335
Minneapolis, MN 55414
(612) 623-8115

American Academy of Pediatrics
141 North West Point
Elk Grove Village, IL 60009-0927
(312) 869-9327

American Association of Psychiatric Services for
   Children
1133 15th St., N.W., Suite 1000
Washington, DC 20005
(202) 429-9713

American Association of School Administrators
1801 North Moore Street
Arlington, VA 22209
(703) 528-0700

American Association on Mental Retardation
1719 Kalorama Road, N.W.
Washington, DC 20009
(202) 387-1968

American Council for the Blind
1010 Vermont Ave., N.W., Suite 1100
Washington, DC 20005
(202) 393-3666

American Educational Research Association
1230 17th St., N.W.

Washington, DC 20036
(202) 223-9485

American Foundation for the Blind
15 West 16th Street
New York, NY 10011
(212) 620-2000

American Humane Association
Children's Division
9725 East Hampden Avenue
Denver, CO 80231
(303) 695-0811

American Medical Association
535 North Dearborn Street
Chicago, IL 60610
(312) 645-5000

American Occupational Therapy Association
1383 Piccard Drive, P.O. Box 1725
Rockville, MD 20850
(301) 948-9626

American Personnel and Guidance Association
5999 Stevenson Avenue
Alexandria, VA 22304
(703) 823-9800

American Physical Therapy Association
1111 N. Fairfax Street
Alexandria, VA 22314
(703) 684-2782

American Printing House for the Blind
1839 Frankfort Avenue
Louisville, KY 40206
(502) 895-2405

American Psychological Association
1200 17th Street, N.W.
Washington, DC 20036
(202) 955-7600

American Rehabilitation Counseling Association
of the American Personnel and Guidance
Association
5999 Stevenson Avenue
Alexandria, VA 22304
(703) 823-9800

American Society for Deaf Children
814 Thayer Avenue
Silver Spring, MD 20910
(301) 585-5400

American Speech and Hearing Association
10801 Rockville Pike
Rockville, MD 20852
(301) 897-5700

American Vocational Association
1410 King Street
Alexandria, VA 22314
(703) 683-3111

Association for Children with Learning
Disabilities
4156 Library Road
Pittsburgh, PA 15234
(412) 881-2253

Autism Society of America
1234 Massachusetts Avenue, N.W., Suite 1017
Washington, DC 20005
(202) 783-0125

Black Child Development Institute
1463 Rhode Island Avenue, N.W.
Washington, DC 20005
(202) 387-1281

Braille Circulating Library
2700 Stuart Avenue
Richmond, VA 23220
(804) 359-3743

Clearinghouse and Research in Child Abuse
and Neglect
P.O. Box 1182
Washington, DC 20013
(703) 821-2086

Council for Exceptional Children
1920 Association Drive
Reston, VA 22091
(703) 620-3660

Council of State Administrators of Vocational
Rehabilitation
P.O. Box 3776
Washington, DC 20007
(202) 638-4634

Cystic Fibrosis Foundation
6931 Arlington Road
Bethesda, MD 20814
(800) 344-4823

Division for the Blind and Physically Handicapped
Library of Congress
1291 Taylor Street, N.W.
Washington, DC 20542
(202) 287-5100

Education Commission of the States
1860 Lincoln Street
Denver, CO 80295
(303) 830-3600

Epilepsy Foundation of America
4351 Garden City Drive, Suite 406
Landover, MD 20785
(301) 459-3700

Gifted Child Society, Inc.
190 Rock Road
Glenrock, NJ 07452
(201) 444-6530

International Reading Association
800 Barksdale Road, P.O. Box 8139
Newark, DE 19714
(302) 371-1600

National Aid to the Visually Handicapped
3201 Balboa Street
San Francisco, CA 94121
(415) 221-3201

National Amputee Foundation
1245 150th Street
Whitestone, NY 11357
(718) 767-8400

National Association for Retarded Citizens
2501 Avenue J
Arlington, TX 76006
(817) 640-0204

National Association of Private Residential
   Resources
6400 H T Corners Place
Falls Church, VA 22044
(703) 536-3311

National Association of Secondary School
   Principals
1904 Association Drive
Reston, VA 22091
(703) 860-0200

National Association of School Psychologists
1511 K Street, N.W., Suite 716
Washington, DC 20005
(202) 638-4750

National Association of State Directors of
   Special Education
2021 K Street, N.W., Suite 315
Washington, DC 20006
(202) 296-1800

National Association of the Deaf
814 Thayer Avenue
Silver Spring, MD 20910
(301) 587-1788

National Braille Press
86 St. Stephen Street
Boston, MA 02115
(617) 266-6160

National Easter Seal Society for Crippled
   Children and Adults
2023 West Ogden Avenue
Chicago, IL 60612
(312) 243-8400

National Education Association
1201 16th Street, N.W.
Washington, DC 20036
(202) 833-4000

National Foundation of The March of Dimes
1275 Mamaroneck Avenue
White Plains, NY 10605
(914) 428-7100

National Headquarters for Mental Health
   Association
1021 Prince Street
Alexandria, VA 22314
(703) 684-7722

National Heart Institute
9000 Rockville Pike
Building 31, Room 4A21
Bethesda, MD 20892
(301) 496-4000

National Hemophilia Foundation
110 Greene Street
New York, NY 10012
(212) 219-8180

National Kidney Foundation
2 Park Avenue, Suite 908
New York, NY 10016
(212) 889-2210

National Multiple Sclerosis Society
205 E. 42nd Street
New York, NY 10010
(718) 986-3240

Orthotic and Prosthetic Specialties, Inc.
9811 Mallard Drive, Suite 112
Laurel, MD 20708
(301) 470-3344

President's Committee on Employment of the
   Handicapped
U. S. Department of Labor
Washington, DC 20210
(202) 523-4000

President's Committee on Mental Retardation
Regional Office Building, #3
7th and D Streets, S.W., Room 2614
Washington, DC 20201
(202) 245-7634

Recording for the Blind, Inc.
215 East 58th Street
New York, NY 10022
(718) 557-5720

Society for Visual Education
1345 W. Diversey Parkway
Chicago, IL 60614
(312) 525-1500

Spina Bifida Association of America
1700 Rockville Pike, Suite 540
Rockville, MD 20852
(301) 770-7222

United Cerebral Palsy Association
66 East 34th Street
New York, NY 10016
(212) 481-6300

References

Abelson, M. A., & Woodman, R. W. (1983). Review of research on team effectiveness: Implications for teams in schools. *School Psychology Review, 12*, 125-136.

Abeson, A. (1976). Legal forces and pressures. In R. L. Jones (Ed.), *Mainstreaming and the minority child* (pp. 15-36). Minneapolis: Leadership Training Institute/Special Education.

Adams, A., Carnine, D., & Gersten, R. (1982). Instructional strategies for studying content areas texts in the intermediate grades. *Reading Research Quarterly, 18*, 27-55.

Adams, D. M., & Bott, D. A. (1984). Tapping into the world: Computer telecommunications networks and schools. *Computers in the Schools, 1*(3), 3-17.

Affleck, J. Q., Lowenbraun, S., & Archer, A. (1980). *Teaching the mildly handicapped in the regular classroom* (2nd ed.). Columbus, OH: Merrill.

Alley, G. R. (1977). Grouping secondary learning-disabled students. *Academic Therapy, 13*, 37-45.

Anderson, K., & Milliren, A. (1983). *Structured experiences for integration of handicapped children.* Rockville, MD: Aspen Systems Corporation.

Anderson, P. S., & Lapp, D. (1979). *Language skills in elementary education* (3rd ed.). New York: Macmillan.

Apolloni, T., & Westaway, A. (1980). *Becoming independent.* Bellevue, WA: Edmark Associates.

Armstrong, D. G. (1984). Helping youngsters grapple with textbook terminology. *The Social Studies, 75*, 216-219.

Asher, S. R., & Taylor, A. R. (1981). Social outcomes of mainstreaming: Sociometric assessment and beyond. *Exceptional Education Quarterly, 1*, 13-30.

Ashlock, R. B. (1986). *Error patterns in computation: A semi-programmed approach* (4th ed.). Columbus, OH: Merrill.

Ashlock, R. B., Johnson, M. L., Wilson, J. W. & Jones, W. L. (1983). *Guiding each child's learning of mathematics.* Columbus, OH: Merrill.

Association for Children and Adults with Learning Disabilities. (1982). ACLD Vocational Committee Survey of LD Adults. *ACLD News Briefs, 145*, 20-23.

Atwood, R. K., & Oldham, R. R. (1985). Teacher's perceptions of mainstreaming in an inquiry oriented elementary science program. *Science Education, 69*, 619-624.

Baca, L. M., & Cervantes, H. T. (1984). *The bilingual special education interface.* St. Louis: Times Mirror/Mosby.

Bagford, J. (1985). What ever happened to individualized reading? *The Reading Teacher, 39*(2), 190-193.

Baker, T., Dixon, N. P., Englebert, B., Kahn, M., Siegel, B. L., & Wood, J. W. (1982). Mainstreaming minimanual: Ten steps to success. *Instructor, 91,* 63–66.

Ball, D. W. (1978). *ESS/special education teacher's guide.* St. Louis: Webster/McGraw-Hill.

Barclay, J. R. (1977). *Appraising individual differences in the classroom: A manual of the Barclay Classroom Climate Inventory* (4th ed.). Lexington, KY: Educational Skills Development.

Barclay, J., & Kehle, T. (1979). The impact of handicapped students on other students in the classroom. *Journal of Research and Development in Education, 12,* 80–92.

Barnard, L. E. (1981). Teaching strategies for middle-level handicapped students. In T. Shaw (Ed.), *Teaching handicapped students social studies: A resource handbook for K–12 teachers* (pp. 29–32). Washington, DC: National Education Association.

Barngrover, E. A. (1975). A study of educators' preferences in special education programs. *Exceptional Children, 37,* 754–755.

Baroody, A. J. (1984). Children's difficulties in subtraction: Some causes and cures. *Arithmetic Teacher, 32*(3), 14–19.

Barton, L. E., Brulle, A. R., & Repp, A. C. (1987). Effects of differential scheduling of timeout to reduce maladaptive responding. *Exceptional Children, 53,* 351–356.

Bean, R. M., & Eichelberger, R. T. (1985). Changing the role of the reading specialists: From pull-out to in-class programs. *The Reading Teacher, 393,* 648–653.

Beattie, J., & Algozzine, B. (1982). Improving basic academic skills of educably mentally retarded adolescents. *Education and Training of the Mentally Retarded, 17*(3), 255–258.

Beck, J. J. (1981). A paradigm for computer literacy training for teachers. *The Computing Teacher, 9,* 27–28.

Bellamy, G. T., Rhodes, L. E., Bourbeau, P. E., & Mank, D. M. (1986). Mental retardation services in sheltered workshops and day activity centers. In F. R. Rusch (Ed.), *Competitive employment issues and strategies* (pp. 257–271). Baltimore: Paul H. Brookes.

Bellamy, G., & Wilcox, B. (1982). *Design of high school programs for severely handicapped individuals.* Baltimore: Paul H. Brookes.

Bender, M., & Valletutti, P. J. (1976). *Teaching the moderately and severely handicapped: Curriculum objectives, strategies, and activities* (Vol. II). Baltimore: University Park Press.

Bender, W. N. (1985). Strategies for helping the mainstreamed student in secondary social studies classes. *The Social Studies, 76,* 269–271.

Berdine, W. H., & Blackhurst, A. E. (Eds.). (1985). *An introduction to special education.* Boston: Little, Brown.

Berdine, W. H., & Cegelka, P. T. (1980). *Teaching the trainable retarded.* Columbus, OH: Merrill.

Biklen, D., & Bogden, R. (1976, October 28). Handicappism in America. *Win.*

Bina, M. J. (1986). Social skills development through cooperative group learning strategies. *Education of the Visually Handicapped, 18,* 27–40.

Birchell, G. R., & Taylor, B. L. (1986). Is the elementary social studies curriculum headed "back-to-basics"? *The Social Studies, 77,* 80–82.

Bittle, R. G. (1975). Improving parent-teacher communication through recorded telephone messages. *Journal of Educational Research, 69,* 87–95.

Blackhurst, A. E., & Berdine, W. H. (Eds.). (1981). *An introduction to special education.* Boston: Little, Brown.

Blankenship, C. S., & Black, M. (1985). *Using student-constructed pictorial aids to increase accuracy in solving word problems.* Unpublished manuscript.

Blankenship, C. S., & Lovitt, T. C. (1976). Story problems: Merely confusing or downright befuddling? *Journal for Research in Mathematics, 7*(5), 290–298.

Block, G. H. (1980). Dyscalculia and the minicalculator: The ALP program. *Academic Therapy, 16*(2), 175–181.

Blosser, P. E. (1986). What research says: Meta-analysis research in science instruction. *School Science and Mathematics, 86,* 166–170.

Boehmer, D. P., & Hofmeister, A. M. (1978). The effect of a monitoring system on the math achievement of the educably mentally retarded. *Journal of Special Education Technology, 2*(1), 13–17.

Bond, C. L., & Dietrich, A. (1981, November). *Survey of teacher attitudes toward the role of the resource program.* Paper presented at the tenth annual meeting of the Mid-South Education Research Association, Lexington, KY. (ERIC Document Reproduction Service No. ED 221 988)

Bott, D. A. (1983). Math performance across six modality combinations: A study of children with learning problems (Doctoral dissertation, University of Florida, 1983). *Dissertation Abstracts International, 45,* p. 1091A.

Bowe, F. (1978). *Handicapping America.* New York: Harper & Row.

Bowe, F. (1980). *Rehabilitating America.* New York: Harper & Row.

Bristow, P. S. (1985). Are poor readers passive readers? Some evidence, possible explanations, and potential solutions. *The Reading Teacher, 39*(4), 318–325.

Brittain, W. L. (1979). *Creativity, art, and the young child.* New York: Macmillan.

Brolin, D. (1982). *Life-centered career education: A competency-based approach.* Reston, VA: The Council for Exceptional Children.

Brolin, D. E., & Kolstoe, O. P. (1978). *The career and vocational development of handicapped learners.* Columbus, OH: The ERIC Clearinghouse on Adult, Career, and Vocational Education, Ohio State University.

Bronicki, G. J., & Turnbull, A. P. (1987). Family-professional interactions. In M. E. Snell (Ed.), *Systematic instruction of people with severe handicaps* (3rd ed., pp.9–38). Columbus, OH: Merrill.

Brophy, J. E. (1979). Teacher behavior and its effects. *Journal of Teacher Education, 71,* 733–750.

Brown, D. (1985). Five tips on using games effectively. *The Reading Teacher, 39*(4), 819–820.

Brown, W. (1982). Classroom climate: Possible effects of special needs on the mainstream. *The Journal for Special Educators, 19,* 20–27.

Bulgren, J. A., & Knackendoffel, A. (1986). Ecological assessment: An overview. *The Pointer, 30*(2), 23–29.

Bullard, P., & McGee, G. (1983, April). *With a little help from my friend: Mastering math facts with peer tutoring.* Paper presented at the annual meeting of the International Convention of CEC, Detroit, MI. (ERIC Document Reproduction Service No. ED 229 999)

Burns, P. C., Roe, B. D., & Ross, E. P. (1984). *Teaching reading in today's elementary schools* (3rd ed.). Boston: Houghton Mifflin.

Buttery, T. J., & Creekmore, W. N. (1985). Planning reading instruction for the mildly handicapped child. *Reading Improvement, 22*(3), 206–212.

Cain, S. E., & Evans, J. M. (1984). *Sciencing: An involvement approach to elementary science methods* (2nd ed., pp. 237–240). Columbus, OH: Merrill.

Caldwell, J. (1985). A new look at the old informal reading inventory. *The Reading Teacher, 39*(2), 168–173.

Callahan, L. G., & Robinson, M. C. (1973). Task-analysis procedures in mathematics instruction in achievers and wider achievers. *School Science and Mathematics, 73*(7), 578–584.

Canady, R. (1980, April). Reading for meaning. *Highlights for Children, 3*(4) (Newsletter: Parenting), 5.

Career Education Implementation Incentive Act of 1977 (P.L. 95–207).

Carlberg, C., & Kavale, K. (1980). The efficacy of special versus regular class placement for exceptional children: A meta-analysis. *The Journal of Special Education, 14,* 295–309.

Carlsen, J. M. (1985). Between the deaf child and reading: The language connection. *The Reading Teacher, 38*(4), 424-426.

Carpenter, T. P., Corbitt, M. K., Kepner, H. S., Lindquist, M. M., & Reys, R. E. (1980). Solving verbal problems. Results and implications from national assessment. *Arithmetic Teacher, 28*(1), 8-12.

Carter, R. D. (1979). *Help! These kids are driving me crazy.* Champaign, IL: Research Press.

Cartwright, G. D., Cartwright, C. A., & Ward, M. E. (1984). *Educating special learners.* Belmont, CA: Wadsworth.

Casteel, G. G. (1981). Notes on teaching history to socially, intellectually, or academically handicapped high school students. In T. Shaw (Ed.), *Teaching handicapped students social studies: A resource handbook for k-12 teachers* (pp. 55-56). Washington, DC: National Educational Association.

Cawley, J. F. (1970). Teaching arithmetic to mentally handicapped children. *Facts on Exceptional Children, 2*(4), 1-8.

Cawley, J. F. (1985). *Cognitive strategies and mathematics for the learning disabled.* Rockville, MD: Aspen.

Cawley, J. F., Fitzmaurice, A. M., Shaw, R. A., Kahn, H. S., & Bates, H. (1979). Math word problems: Suggestions for LD students. *Learning Disability Quarterly, 2*(2), 25-41.

Cazden, C. (1976). How language helps the classroom teacher—or does it? A personal account. *The Urban Review, 9,* 74-90.

Cegelka, P. T. (1976). Sex role stereotyping in special education: A look at secondary work study programs. *Exceptional Children, 42*(6), 323-328.

Center, Y., & Ward, J. (1984). Integration of mildly handicapped cerebral palsied children into regular schools. *The Exceptional Child, 31,* 104-113.

Center, Y., Ward, J., Parmenter, T., & Nash, R. (1985). Principals' attitudes towards the integration of disabled children into regular schools. *The Exceptional Child, 32,* 149-161.

Chandler, A. M. (1970). Mathematics and the slow learner. *Arithmetic Teacher, 17*(3), 196-198.

Chandler, H. N. (1978). Confusion compounded: A teacher tries to use research results to teach math. *Journal of Learning Disabilities, 11,* 361-369.

Charles County Board of Education. (1981). *Math objectives guide: Project CAST.* La Plata, MD: Office of Special Education. (ERIC Document Reproduction Service No. ED 242 146)

Chenfeld, M. B. (1978). *Teaching language arts creatively.* New York: Harcourt Brace Jovanovich.

Chinn, P. C. (1982). Curriculum development for culturally different exceptional children. In C. H. Thomas & J. L. Thomas (Eds.), *Bilingual special education resource guide* (pp. 22-37). Phoenix: Oryx Press.

Chinn, P. C., & Hughes, S. (1987). Representation of minority students in special education classes. *Remedial and Special Education, 8,* 41-46.

Clark, F. L. (1980). *The development of instrumentation to measure regular classroom teachers' attitudes toward mildly handicapped students.* Unpublished doctoral dissertation, University of Kansas.

Clark, G. M. (1975). Mainstreaming for the secondary educable mentally retarded: Is it defensible? *Focus on Exceptional Children, 5*(3), 110-118.

Clark, G. M. (1979). *Career education for the handicapped child in the elementary classroom.* Boulder, CO: Love Publishing.

Clark, G. M. (1980). Career education for handicapped adolescents: A matter of appropriate education. *Exceptional Education Quarterly, 1*(2), 11-17.

Clewell, S., & Haidemenos, J. (1982, April). *Organizational strategies to increase content area learning: Webbing, pyramiding, and think sheets.* Paper presented at the International Reading Association Convention, Chicago, IL.

Cloer, T., Aldridge, J., & Dean, R. (1981-1982). Examining different levels of print awareness.

Journal of Language Experience, 4(1-2), 25-34.

Clore, G. L., & Jeffrey, K. M. (1972). Emotional role playing, attitude change and attraction toward a disabled person. *Journal of Personality and Social Psychology, 23,* 105-111.

Coble, C. R., Matthis, F. E., & Vizzini, C. T. (1982). A project to promote science for the handicapped. *School Science and Mathematics, 82,* 692-701.

Coble, A. (1982). Improving math fact recall: Beating your own score. *Academic Therapy, 17*(5), 547-553.

Cochrane, M., & Ballard, K. D. (1986). Teaching five special needs children in a regular primary classroom using a consultation-collaboration model. *The Exceptional Child, 33,* 91-102.

Cole, J. T., Kitano, M. K., & Brown, L. M. (1981). Concept analysis: A model for teaching basic science concepts to intellectually handicapped students. In M. E. Corrick (Ed.), *Teaching handicapped students science* (pp. 51-53). Washington, DC: National Education Association.

Cone, J. D., Delawyer, D. D., & Wolfe, V. V. (1985). Assessing parent participation: The parent/family involvement index: *Exceptional Children, 51*(5), 417-424.

Connolly, A., Nachtman, W., & Pritchett, E. (1976). *Key Math Diagnostic Arithmetic Test.* Circle Pines, MN: American Guidance Service.

Cook, W., & Wollersheim, J. (1976). The effect of labeling of special education students on the perceptions of contact vs. noncontact with normal peers. *Journal of Special Education, 10,* 187-198.

Corman, L., & Gottlieb, J. (1979). Mainstreaming mentally retarded children: A review of research. In N. R. Ellis (Ed.), *International review of research in mental retardation* (pp. 251-275). New York: Academic Press.

Cosden, M. A., Gerber, M. M., Semmel, D. A., Goldman, S. R., & Semmel, M. I. (1987). Microcomputer use within micro-educational environments. *Exceptional Children, 53,* 399-409.

Costabile, S., & Costabile, R. (1985). How to work with your reading specialist. *The Reading Teacher, 39*(3), 374.

Courtnage, L., & Smith-Davis, J. (1987). Interdisciplinary team training: A national survey of special education teacher training programs. *Exceptional Children, 53,* 451-458.

Creekmore, W. N., & Creekmore, N. N. (1983). Math strategy for MH children. *Academic Therapy, 19*(1), 65-71.

Culatta, R., & Culatta, B. K. (1985). Communication disorders. In W. H. Berdine and A. E. Blackhurst (Eds.), *An introduction to special education* (2nd ed., pp. 141-335). Boston: Little, Brown.

Cullinan, D., & Epstein, M. H. (1986). Communication and sensorimotor disorders. In N. G. Haring & L. McCormick (Eds.), *Exceptional children and youth* (4th ed., pp.161-199). Columbus, OH: Merrill.

Curtis, C. K. (1974). Social studies for the slow learner. *The Clearing House, 48,* 456-460.

Danzer, G. A. (1980). Textbook graphics and maps: Keys to learning. *Social Education, 44,* 101-103.

Dardig, J. C. (1981). Helping teachers integrate handicapped students into the regular classroom. *Educational Horizons, 59,* 129.

Davies, J. M., & Ball, D. W. (1978). Utilization of the elementary science study with educable mentally retarded students. *Journal of Research in Science Teaching, 15,* 281-286.

Deno, E. N. (Ed.). (1973). *Instructional alternatives for exceptional children.* Reston, VA: Council for Exceptional Children.

Diana v. State Board of Education, C-70, 37 RFP, N.D. Cal., 1970, 1973.

Dillard, J. M., Kinnison, L. R., & Peel, B. (1980). Multicultural approach to mainstreaming: A challenge to counselors, teachers, psychologists, and administrators. *Peabody Journal of Education, 57*(4), 76-90.

Dinsmore, J. A., & Isaacson, D. K. (1986). Tactics for teaching dyslexic students. *Academic Therapy, 21*(3), 293-300.

Donaldson, J. (1980). Changing attitudes toward handicapped persons: A review and analysis of research. *Exceptional Children, 46*(7), 504–514.

Donaldson, J., & Martinson, M. C. (1977). Modifying attitudes toward physically disabled persons. *Exceptional Children, 43*, 337–341.

Doris, S., & Brown, R. (1980). *Toleration of maladaptive classroom behaviors by regular and special educators.* Fresno, CA: California State University. (ERIC Document Reproduction Service No. ED 211 456)

Downey, M. T. (1980). Pictures as teaching aids: Using the pictures in history textbooks. *Social Education, 44*, 93–99.

Drabman, R. S., & Patterson, J. N. (1981). Disruptive behavior and the social standing of exceptional children. *Exceptional Education Quarterly, 1*, 45–56.

Drew, C. J. (1973). Criterion-referenced and norm-referenced assessment of minority group children. *Journal of School Psychology, 11*(4), 323–329.

Dreyer, L. G., Futtersak, K. R., & Boehm, A. E. (1985). Sight words for the computer age. *The Reading Teacher, 39*(1), 12–17.

Dunlap, W. P., & Brennan, A. H. (1979). Developing mental images of mathematical processes. *Learning Disability Quarterly, 2*(2), 89–96.

Dunlap, W. P., & McKnight, M. (1980). Teaching strategies for solving word problems in math. *Academic Therapy, 15*(4), 431–441.

Dunn, R., & Dunn, K. (1974). *Practical approaches to individualizing instruction.* West Nyack, NY: Parker.

Dunne, L. A., & Knudsen, O. (1981). My place in space: Painting maps on classroom floors. In T. Shaw (Ed.), *Teaching handicapped students social studies: A resource handbook for K–12 teachers* (pp. 26–28). Washington, DC: National Education Association.

Durkin, D. (1978–1979). What classroom observations reveal about reading comprehension instruction. *Reading Research Quarterly, 14*(4-5), 481–533.

D'Zambo, M., Laflex, E., Glenn, D., Webster, L., & Raiser, L. (1981, April). *Mainstreaming: How we made it work.* Paper presented at the Council for Exceptional Children Annual Conference, New York. (ERIC Document Reproduction Service No. ED 204 953).

Ehman, L. H., & Hahn, C. L. (1981). Contributions of research to social studies education. In H. D. Mehlinger & O. L. Davis (Eds.), *The social studies. Eightieth yearbook of the National Society for the Study of Education* (pp. 60–81). Chicago: University of Chicago Press.

Ekwall, E. E., & Shanker, J. L. (1985). *Teaching reading in the elementary school.* Columbus, OH: Merrill.

Elkins, J. (1986). Self-help for older writers with spelling and composing difficulties: Using the word processor and spelling checker. *The Exceptional Child, 33*, 73–76.

Elliot, D. L., Nagel, K. C., Woodward, A. (1985). Do textbooks belong in elementary social studies? *Educational Leadership, 42*, 22–24.

Emmer, E. T., Evertson, C. M., Sanford, J. P., Clements, B. S., & Worsham, M. E. (1984). *Classroom management for secondary teachers.* Englewood Cliffs, NJ: Prentice-Hall.

Endsley, W. R. (1980). *Peer tutorial instruction.* Englewood Cliffs, NJ: Educational Technology Publications.

Esler, W. K., Midgett, J., & Bird, R. C. (1977). Elementary science materials and the exceptional child. *Science Education, 61*, 181–184.

Esposito, D. (1973). Homogeneous and heterogeneous ability grouping: Principal findings and implications for evaluating and designing more effective educational environments. *Review of Educational Research, 43*,(3), 163–179.

Evans, J. (undated). *Working with parents of handicapped children.* Reston, VA: Council for Exceptional Children.

Evans, S. S., & Evans, W. H. (1986). A perspective on assessment for instruction. *The Pointer, 30* 9–12.

Evertson, C. M., Emmer, E. T., Clements, B. S., Sanford, J. P., & Worsham, M. E. (1984).

Classroom management for elementary teachers. Englewood Cliffs, NJ: Prentice-Hall.

Federal Register. (1977, August 23). Washington DC: Department of Health, Education, and Welfare, Office of Education.

Ferreiro, E., & Teberosky, A. (1982). *Literacy before schooling.* Exeter, NH: Heinemann Educational Books.

Fiedler, C. R., & Simpson, R. L. (1987). Modifying the attitudes of nonhandicapped high school students toward handicapped peers. *Exceptional Children, 53,* 343–349.

Final, M. J. (1967). Attitudes of regular and special class teachers toward the educable mentally retarded child. *Exceptional Children, 33,* 429–430.

Fleischner, J. E., & Hathaway, K. (1984, April). *Arithmetic instruction for LD students.* Paper presented at the 63rd Annual Convention of the Council for Exceptional Children, Anaheim, CA.

Flynn, J., Gack, R., & Sundean, D. (1978). Are classroom teachers prepared for mainstreaming? *Phi Delta Kappa, 59,* 562.

Forester, A. (1980). Learning to spell by spelling. *Theory into Practice, 19,* 186–193.

Freiberg, H. J., Cooper, J. M., & Ryan, K. (1980). *Learning guide: Those who can, teach* (3rd ed.). Boston: Houghton Mifflin.

Fuchs, L. A., & Fuchs, D. (1986). Effects of systematic formative evaluation: A meta-analysis. *Exceptional Children, 53,* 199–208.

Fuson, K. C., & Brinko, K. T. (1985). The comparative effectiveness of microcomputers and flash cards in the drill and practice of basic mathematics facts. *Journal for Research in Mathematics Education, 16*(3), 225–232.

Gable, R. A., Strain, P. S., & Hendrickson, J. M. (1979). Strategies for improving the status and social behavior of learning disabled children. *Learning Disability Quarterly, 2,* 33–39.

Gagne, R. M. (1974). Task analysis—its relation to content analysis. *Educational Psychologist, 11,* 1–18.

Gagne, R. M., & Briggs, L. J. (1979). *Principles of instructional design* (2nd ed.). New York: Holt, Rinehart & Winston.

Gambrell, L. B., Wilson, R. M., & Gantt, W. M. (1981). Classroom observations of task-attending behaviors of good and poor readers. *Journal of Educational Research, 74,* 400–404.

Garcia, J., & Logan, J. W. (1983). Teaching social studies using basal readers. *Social Education, 47,* 533–535.

Gargiulo, R. M. (1985). *Working with parents of exceptional children.* Boston: Houghton Mifflin.

Garnett, K., & Fleischner, J. E. (1983). Automatization and basic fact performance of normal and learning disabled children. *Learning Disabilities Quarterly, 6*(2), 223–230.

Garrett, M. K., & Crump, W. D. (1980). Peer acceptance, teacher preference, and self-appraisal of social status of learning disabled students. *Learning Disability Quarterly, 3,* 42–48.

Gear, G., Peat, I., Sprain, T., Donaldson, C., & Butler, K. (1979). *Billy: The visually impaired child in your classroom.* Birmingham, AL: Alabama University, School of Education; Washington, DC: Bureau of Education for the Handicapped (HEW/OE), Division of Personnel Preparation. (ERIC Document Reproduction Service No. ED 176 456)

Gearheart, B. R., & Weishahn, M. W. (1980). *The handicapped student in the regular classroom* (2nd ed.). St. Louis: Mosby.

Gearheart, B. R., & Weishahn, M. W. (1984). *The exceptional student in the regular classroom* (3rd ed.). St. Louis: Times Mirror/Mosby.

Gentile, L. M., Lamb, P., & Rivers, C. O. (1985). A neurologist's view of reading difficulty: Implications for remedial reading instruction. *The Reading Teacher, 39*(2), 174–183.

Gentry, J. R. (1981). Learning to spell developmentally. *The Reading Teacher, 34,* 378–381.

Gentry, J. R. (1985). Getting kids to write in kindergarten and first grade. *Early Years, 16*(3), 34–35.

Gibson, E. J., & Levin, H. (1975). *The psychology of reading.* Cambridge, MA: MIT Press.

Gickling, E. E., & Thompson, V. P. (1985). A personal view of curriculum-based assessment. *Exceptional Children, 52,* 205–218.

Goldman, S. R., Semmel, D. S., Cosden, M. A., Gerber, M. M., & Semmel, M. I. (1987). Special education administrator's policies and practices on microcomputer acquisition, allocation, and access for mildly handicapped children: Interfaces with regular education. *Exceptional Children, 53,* 330–339.

Goldstein, H. (1974). *Social learning curriculum.* Columbus, OH: Merrill.

Goldstein, S., Strickland, B., Turnbull, A. P., & Curry, L. (1980). An observational analysis of the IEP conference. *Exceptional Children, 46,* 278–286.

Gonzales, E. (1979). Preparation for teaching the multicultural exceptional child: Trends and concerns. *Teacher Education-Special Education, 2*(4), 12–18.

Good, T. (1983). Classroom research: A decade of progress. *Educational Psychologist, 18,* 127–144.

Good, T. L., & Brophy, J. E. (1986). School effects. In M. C. Wittrock (Ed.), *Handbook on research and teaching* (3rd ed., pp. 570–602). New York: Macmillan.

Goodman, H., Gottlieb, J., & Harrison, R. N. (1972). Social acceptance of EMR's integrated into a nongraded elementary school. *American Journal of Mental Deficiency, 26,* 412–417.

Goodman, L., & Miller, H. (1980). Mainstreaming: How teachers can make it work. *Journal of Research and Development Education, 13*(4), 45–57.

Goodman, Y., & Altwerger, B. (1980). *Reading: How does it begin?* Unpublished manuscript.

Goodstein, H. A., Bessant, H., Thibodeau, G., Vitello, S., & Viahakos, I. (1972). The effects of three variables on the verbal problem solving of educable mentally handicapped children. *American Journal of Mental Deficiency, 76*(6), 703–709.

Gottlieb, J. (1981). Mainstreaming: Fulfilling the promise? *American Journal of Mental Deficiency, 86,* 115–126.

Graham, S. (1985). Evaluating spelling programs and materials. *Teaching Exceptional Children, 17*(4), 299–304.

Graham, S., & Miller, L. (1980). Handwriting research and practice: A unified approach. *Focus on Exceptional Children, 13*(2), 5–6.

Graves, D. H. (1983). *Writing: Teachers and children at work.* Exeter, NH: Heinemann Educational Books.

Greene, B. N. (1985). Developing comprehension: Selecting significant details. *The Reading Teacher, 39*(2), 248.

Gregory, G. P. (1979). Using the newspaper in the mainstreamed classroom. *Social Education, 43,* 140–143.

Gregory, G. P. (1980). Modes of instruction. In J. G. Herlihy & M. T. Herlihy (Eds.), *Mainstreaming in the social studies* (Bulletin No. 61, pp. 34–41). Washington, DC: National Council for the Social Studies.

Gregory, J. W. (1979). Test failure and mathematics failure—There is a difference. *Arithmetic Teacher, 27*(3), 50–52.

Gresham, F. M. (1982). Misguided mainstreaming: The case for social skills training with handicapped children. *Exceptional Children, 48,* 422–433.

Grimes, L. (1981). Computers are for kids: Designing software programs to avoid problems of learning. *Teaching Exceptional Children, 14,* 54–57.

Groff, P. (1984). Successful remediation of cursive handwriting. *Journal of Reading, Writing, and Learning Disabilities International, 1*(1), 11–15.

Grossman, H. (Ed.). (1977). *Manual on terminology and classification in mental retardation.* American Association on Mental Deficiency. Baltimore, MD: Garamond/Pridemark Press.

Guerin, G. R., & Marer, A. S. (1983). *Informal assessment in education.* Palo Alto, CA: Mayfield.

Guralnick, M. (1976). The value of integrating handicapped and nonhandicapped preschool children. *American Journal of Orthopsychiatry, 46*, 236–245.

Gurosky, L. (1986, November). *A second grader's revision: One part of the writing process.* Paper presented at the 15th annual meeting of the Mid-South Educational Research Association, Memphis, TN.

Guskey, T. (1981). Individualizing instruction in the mainstream classroom: A mastery learning approach. In *Toward a research base for the least restrictive environment: A collection of papers* (pp. 32–46). Lexington, KY: University of Kentucky.

Hahn, A. L. (1985). Teaching remedial students to be strategic readers and better comprehenders. *The Reading Teacher, 39*(1), 72–79.

Hall, C. W., & Richmond, B. O. (1985). Nonverbal communication, self-esteem and interpersonal relations of LD and non-LD students. *The Exceptional Child, 32*, 87–91.

Hallahan, D. P., Lloyd, J. W., & Stoller, L. (1982). *Improving attention with self-monitoring: A manual for teachers.* Charlottesville, VA: Learning Disabilities Research Institute, University of Virginia.

Hallenbeck, P. H. (1974). Teaching social studies to special children. *Journal of Learning Disabilities, 7*, 18–21.

Halpern, A. S. (1979). Adolescents and young adults. *Exceptional Children, 45*, 518–523.

Halpern, A. S. (1985). Transition: A look at the foundations. *Exceptional Children, 57*(6), 479–486.

Halpern, N. (1981). Mathematics for the learning disabled. *Journal of Learning Disabilities, 14*, 505–506.

Hammill, D. D., Leigh, J. E., McNutt, G., & Larsen, S. C. (1981). A new definition of learning disabilities. *Learning Disability Quarterly, 4*, 336–342.

Hannaford, A., & Sloane, E. (1981). Microcomputers: Powerful learning tools with proper programming. *Teaching Exceptional Children, 49*, 137–141.

Harber, J. (1982). Accepting dialect renderings of existent materials on black English-speaking children's oral reading scores. *Education and Treatment of Children, 5*, 271–282.

Haring, N. G., & McCormick, L. (Eds.). (1986). *Exceptional children and youth* (4th ed.). Columbus, OH: Merrill.

Harris, J., & Aldridge, J. (1983). 3 for me is better than 2 for you. *Academic Therapy, 18*(3), 361–364.

Hart, V. (1981). *Mainstreaming children with special needs.* New York: Longman.

Hartfield, E. M. (1975). Why are they blind? *Sightsaving Review, 45*(1), 3–22.

Hasselbring, T. S., Goin, L. I., & Bransford, J. D. (1987). Developing automaticity. *Teaching Exceptional Children, 19*(3), 30–33.

Hauptman, E. (1983, April). *Communication between special educators and the mainstream teacher.* Paper presented at the 61st Annual International Convention of the Council for Exceptional Children, Detroit, MI. (ERIC Document Reproduction Service No. ED 231 173)

Hawk, P. P., & McLeod, N. P. (1984). Graphic organizers: A cognitive teaching method that works. *The Directive Teacher,* Winter/Spring, 6–7.

Hayden, A. H., Smith, R. K., von Hippel, C. S., & Baer, S. A. (1978). *Mainstreaming preschoolers: Children with learning disabilities.* Washington, DC: U.S. Department of Health and Human Services.

Hedley, L. N., & Hedley, E. (1984). Using computer software to teach writing to children who have difficulty forming letters. *Journal of Reading, Writing, and Learning Disabilites International, 1*(1), 17–19.

Heller, H. W. (1981). Secondary education for handicapped students: In search of a solution. *Exceptional Children, 47*(8), 582–583.

Heller, K. A., Holtzman, W. H., & Messick, S. (Eds.). (1982). *Placing children in special education: A strategy for equity.* Washington, DC: National Academy Press.

Henderson, E. (1985). *Teaching spelling.* Boston: Houghton Mifflin.

Heron, T. E., & Harris, K. C. (1982). *The educational consultant: Helping professionals, parents and mainstreamed students.* Boston: Allyn & Bacon.

Heward, W. L., & Orlansky, M. D. (1988). *Exceptional children* (3rd ed.). Columbus, OH: Merrill.

Hildebrand, V. (1986). *Introduction to early childhood education* (4th ed.). New York: Macmillan.

Hoskisson, K. (1974). Assisted reading and parent involvement. *The Reading Teacher, 27*(7), 714–719.

Howell, K. W., & Kaplan, J. S. (1980). *Diagnosing basic skills: A handbook for deciding what to teach.* Columbus, OH: Merrill.

Hoy, C. (1984). Story problems: Vehicles to develop thinking skills. *Academic Therapy, 19*(5), 567–572.

Hoyt, K. B. (1975). *An introduction to career education: A policy paper of the U.S. Office of Education.* Washington, DC: U.S. Government Printing Office.

Humbert, J. (1982). Some considerations of planning the integration of handicapped children into the mainstream. *Journal of Learning Disabilities, 15,* 73–80.

Hunter, B. (1985). Problem solving with data bases. *The Computing Teacher, 12*(8), 20–27.

Iowa Test of Basic Skills. (1982). New York: Riverside Publishing Co.

IRUC Briefings. (1977). Washington, DC: Information and Research Utilization Center; Physical Education and Recreation for the Handicapped; American Alliance for Health, Physical Education and Recreation.

Jamison, P. J., & Shevitz, L. A. (1985). RATE: A reason to read. *Teaching Exceptional Children, 18*(1), 46–51.

Jarolimek, J. (1981). The social studies: An overview. In H. D. Mehlinger & O. L. Davis (Eds.), *The social studies. Eightieth yearbook of the National Society for the Study of Education* (pp. 3–18). Chicago: University of Chicago Press.

Jarolimek, J., & Foster, C. D. (1981). *Teaching and learning in the elementary school* (2nd ed.). New York: Macmillan.

Johnson, A., & Cartwright, C. (1979). The roles of information and experience in improving teachers' knowledge and attitudes about mainstreaming. *Journal of Special Education, 13,* 453–462.

Johnson, C. A., & Katz, R. C. (1973). Using parents as change agents for their children: A review. *Journal of Child Psychology and Psychiatry, 14,* 181–200.

Johnson, C. M. (1980). *Preparing handicapped students for work: Alternatives for secondary programming.* Reston, VA: Council for Exceptional Children.

Johnson, D. (1982). Microcomputers and dyslexic students. *Educational Computer, 2,* 36–37.

Johnson, D., Maruyama, G., Johnson, R., Nelson, D., & Skor, L. (1981). Effects of cooperative, competitive, and individualistic goal structures on achievement: A meta-analysis. *Psychological Bulletin, 89,* 47–62.

Johnson, D. W., & Johnson, R. T. (1980). *Promoting constructive student-student relationships through cooperative learning.* Minneapolis: National Support System Project.

Johnson, D. W., Johnson, R. T., Waring, D., & Maruyama, G. (1986). Different cooperative learning procedures and cross-handicap relationships. *Exceptional Children, 3,* 247–252.

Johnson, R. T., & Johnson, D. W. (1981). Mainstreaming handicapped students into science classrooms. In M. E. Corrick (Ed.), *Teaching handicapped students science* (pp. 27–32). Washington, DC: National Education Association.

Joiner, L. A. (1979). *A computer-based reading and language arts program for secondary learning disabled students.* Carbondale, IL: Department of Special Education, Southern Illinois University.

Jones, V. F., & Jones, L. S. (1986). *Comprehensive classroom management: Creating positive learning environments.* Boston: Allyn & Bacon.

Jongsma, E. (1985). Research view: Grouping for instruction. *The Reading Teacher, 39*(5), 918–920.

Kameenui, E. J., & Carnine, D. W. (1986). Preteaching versus concurrent teaching of component skills of a subtraction algorithm to skill-deficient second graders: A components analysis of direct instruction. *The Exceptional Child, 33,* 103–115.

Kang, Y. W., & Masoodi, B. A. (1978–1979). Abacus instruction for moderately retarded blind children. *Education of the Visually Handicapped, 10,* 79–84.

Karlin, M. S., & Berger, R. (1969). *Successful methods for teaching the slow learner.* West Nyack, NY: Parker Publishing.

Kauffman, J. M., Gottlieb, J., Agard, J. A., & Kukic, M. B. (1975). *Project PRIME: Mainstreaming toward an explication of the construct* (Project No. IM–71–001). Washington, DC: U.S. Office of Education, Bureau of Education for the Handicapped, Intramural Research Program.

Kauffman, J. M., Hollahan, D. P. Haas, K., Braine, T., & Boren, R. (1978). Imitating children's errors to improve their spelling performance. *Journal of Learning Disabilities, 11,* 217–222.

Kehle, T. J., Bockrath, D. A., & Wood, P. G. (1978). *Effects of mainstreaming on social development of special education students.* Unpublished manuscript. (Available from T. J. Kehle, Kent State University.)

Kehle, T. J., & Guidubaldi, J. (1978). Effect of EMR placement models on affective and social development. *Psychology in the Schools, 15,* 275–282.

Keller, W. D. (1981). Science for the handicapped. *Focus on Exceptional Children, 13*(5), 1–11.

Keogh, B. (1976). Special education in the mainstream: A confrontation of limitations? *Focus on Exceptional Children, 8,* 1–11.

Kevra, B., Brey, R., & Schimmel, B. (1972). Success for slow learners or RX: Relax . . . and play. *Arithmetic Teacher, 19*(5), 335–343.

Kiernan, W. E., McGaughey, M. J., & Schalock, R. L. (1986). *Employment survey for adults*

with developmental disabilities. Boston: Developmental Evaluation Clinic, Boston Children's Hospital.

Kirk, S. A., & Gallagher, J. J. (1983). *Educating exceptional children* (4th ed.). Boston: Houghton Mifflin.

Klumb, R. F. (1985). Peer tutoring is a reward. *The Reading Teacher, 39*(1), 115.

Kopp, O. W. (1967). The evaluation of oral language activity: Teaching and learning. *Elementary English, 44,* 114–123.

Kounin, J. (1970). *Discipline and group management in classrooms.* New York: Holt, Rinehart & Winston.

Kourilsky, M., & Ballard-Campbell, M. (1984). Minisociety: An individualized social studies program for children of low, middle, and high ability. *The Social Studies, 75,* 224–228.

Kroth, R. L. (1985). *Communicating with parents of exceptional children: Improving parent-teacher relationships* (2nd ed.). Denver, CO: Love Publishing.

Kroth, R. L., Whelan, R. J., & Stables, J. M. (1970). Teacher application of behavioral principles in home and classroom environments. *Focus on Exceptional Children, 3,* 1–10.

Krouse, J., Gerber, M. M., & Kauffman, J. M. (1981). Peer tutoring: Procedures, promises, and unresolved issues. *Exceptional Education Quarterly, 1,* 107–115.

Lancioni, G. G. (1982). Employment of normal third and fourth graders for training retarded children to solve problems dealing with quantity. *Education and Training of the Mentally Retarded, 17*(2), 93–102.

Langone, J., Koorland, M., & Oseroff, A. (1987). Producing changes in the instructional behavior of teachers of the mentally handicapped through inservice education. *Education and Treatment of Children, 10,* 146–164.

Larrivee, B., & Algina, J. (1983, April). *Identification of teaching behaviors which predict success for mainstreamed students.* Paper presented at the annual meeting of the

American Educational Research Association, Montreal, Canada. (ERIC Document Reproduction Service No. ED 232 362)

Larry P. v. Riles, 71-2270 US C. 343 F. Suppl 1306 C.N.P. (al 1982).

Larry P. v. Riles, 343 F. Suppl 1306, 502 F. 2d 963 C.N.D. (al. 1979).

Leslie, M. (1980). *Teaching the visually impaired child in the classroom.* MAVIS Sourcebook 3. Washington, DC: Bureau of Education for the Handicapped. (ERIC Document Reproduction Service No. ED 195 464)

Lewis, R. B., & Doorlag, D. H. (1987). *Teaching special students in the mainstream* (2nd ed.). Columbus, OH: Merrill.

Leyser, Y., & Lessen, E. (1985). The efficacy of two training approaches on attitudes of prospective teachers toward mainstreaming. *The Exceptional Child, 32,* 175-183.

Loftus, L., & Walter, V. (1981). *For special educators: Tips for working with regular classroom teachers. For your information.* Washington, DC: Office of Special Education and Rehabilitative Services. (ERIC Document Reproduction Service No. ED 236 903)

Lovitt, T., Rudsit, J., Jenkins, J., Pious, C., & Benedetti, D. (1985). Two methods of adapting science materials for learning disabled and regular seventh graders. *Learning Disability Quarterly, 8,* 275-285.

Lovitt, T., Rudsit, J., Jenkins, J., Pious, C., & Benedetti, D. (1986). Adapting science materials for regular and learning disabled seventh graders. *Remedial and Special Education, 7*(1), 31-39.

Lovitt, T. C. & Curtiss, K. A. (1968). Effects of manipulating an antecedent event on mathematics response rate. *Journal of Applied Behavior Analysis, 1*(4), 329-333.

MacMillan, D. L. (1982). *Mental retardation in school and society* (2nd ed.). Boston: Little, Brown.

MacMillan, D. L., Jones, R. L., & Meyers, C. E. (1976). Mainstreaming the mildly retarded: Some questions, cautions, and guidelines. *Mental Retardation, 14,* 3-10.

MacMillan, D. L., Keogh, B. K., & Jones, R. L. (1986). Special education research on mildly handicapped learners. In M. C. Wittrock (Ed.), *Handbook on research on teaching* (3rd ed., pp. 686-724). New York: Macmillan.

MacMillan, D. L., Meyers, C., & Yoshida, R. (1978). Regular class teachers' perceptions of transition programs for EMR students and their impact on the students. *Psychology in the Schools, 15,* 9-103.

Madden, N. A., & Slavin, R. E. (1983). Mainstreaming students with mild handicaps: Academic and social outcomes. *Review of Educational Research, 53*(4), 519-569.

Mager, R. (1975). *Preparing objectives for instruction* (2nd ed.). Belmont, CA: Feron.

Mandell, C. J., & Strain, P. S. (1978). An analysis of factors related to the attitudes of regular classroom teachers toward mainstreaming mildly handicapped children. *Contemporary Educational Psychology, 3,* 154-162.

Manning, M., & Manning, G. (1981). The school's assault on children. *Childhood Education, 28*(8), 694-700.

Manzo, A. V. (1980). Three universal strategies in content area reading and languaging. *Journal of Reading, 24,* 147.

Maring, G. H., & Furman, G. (1985). Seven "whole class" strategies to help mainstreamed young people read and listen better in content area classes. *Journal of Reading, 28,* 694-699.

Maring, G. H., Furman, G. C., & Blum-Anderson, J. (1985). Five cooperative learning strategies for mainstreamed youngsters in content area classrooms. *The Reading Teacher, 39*(3), 310-313.

Marston, R., & Leslie, D. (1983). Teacher perceptions from mainstreamed versus nonmainstreamed teaching environments. *Physical Educator, 40,* 8-15.

Martin, B. (1970). *Brown bear, brown bear.* New York: Holt, Rinehart & Winston.

Mathias, M., & Johnson, R. A. (1981). Some thoughts on teaching science to the mentally handicapped secondary student. In M. E. Corrick (Ed.), *Teaching handicapped students science* (pp. 75–78). Washington, DC: National Education Association.

Matthes, C. (1977). *How children are taught to read.* Lincoln, NE: Professional Educators Publications.

Maxim, G. W. (1987). *Social studies and the elementary school child* (3rd ed.). Columbus, OH: Merrill.

McAfee, J. M. (1987). Classroom density and the aggressive behavior of handicapped children. *Education and Treatment of Children, 10,* 134–145.

McAloon, A. (1979). Using questions to diagnose and remediate. *Arithmetic Teacher, 27*(3), 44–48.

McClure, A. A. (1985). Predictable books: Another way to teach reading to learning disabled children. *Teaching Exceptional Children, 17*(4), 267–273.

McKinney, L., Vreeberg, M., & West, K. (1986). *Extending horizons.* Columbus, OH: National Center for Research in Vocational Education.

McLeod, T. M., & Armstrong, S. W. (1982). Learning disabilities in mathematic-skill deficits and remedial approaches at the intermediate and secondary level. *Learning Disability Quarterly, 5*(3), 305–311.

Memory, D. M., & McGowan, T. M. (1985). Using multilevel textbooks in social studies classes. *The Social Studies, 76,* 174–179.

Mendrinos, R. B. (1986). Uses of data bases in the classroom. *Computers in the School, 2*(4), 65–70.

Mercer, C. D. (1979). *Children and adolescents with learning disabilities.* Columbus, OH: Merrill.

Mercer, C. D. (1987). *Students with learning disabilities* (3rd ed.). Columbus, OH: Merrill.

Mercer, C. D., & Mercer, A. R. (1981). *Teaching students with learning and behavior problems.* Columbus, OH: Merrill.

Mercer, C. D., & Mercer, A. R. (1989). *Teaching students with learning problems* (3rd ed.). Columbus, OH: Merrill.

Mercer, C. D., Mercer, A. R., & Bott, D. A. (1984). *Self-correcting learning materials for the classroom.* Columbus, OH: Merrill.

Mercer, C. D., Mercer, A. R., & Evans, S. (1982). The use of frequency in establishing instructional aims. *Journal of Precision Teaching, 3*(3), 57–63.

Metropolitan Achievement Test. (1978). New York: Harcourt Brace Jovanovich.

Michael, R. J., & Trippi, J. A. (1987). Educators' view of procedures for grading mainstreamed handicapped children. *Education, 107,* 276–278.

Michaelis, J. U. (1985). *Social studies for children: A guide to basic instruction* (8th ed.). Englewood Cliffs, NJ: Prentice-Hall.

Middleton, E., Mosink, C., & Cohen, S. (1979). Program graduates: Perceptions of need for training in mainstreaming. *Exceptional Children, 45,* 256–263.

Miller, W. H. (1977). *The first R in elementary reading today* (2nd ed.). New York: Holt, Rinehart & Winston.

Mirga, T. (1986). The patterns in our social fabric are changing. *Education Week, 5*(34), 60.

Moger, R. L. (1986). *For the final report of a state educational agency federal evaluation study conducted by the program evaluation and research division, California State Department of Education* (Contract No. G0084C–3505). Washington, DC: U.S. Department of Education.

Morsink, C. V. (1981). *Perspectives of an ivory tower realist.* Lexington, KY: University of Kentucky. (ERIC Document Reproduction Service No. ED 202 836)

Morsink, C. V. (1984). *Teaching special needs students in regular classrooms.* Boston: Little, Brown.

Morsink, C. V., Soar, R. S., Soar, R. M., & Thomas, R. (1986). Research on teaching: Opening the door to special education classrooms. *Exceptional Children, 53,* 32–40.

Mosconi, L. E. (1984). *Effects of a cognitive intervention training program on mathematics achievement.* Unpublished master's thesis, California State College, Bakersfield, CA.

Moses, B. (1982). Individual differences in problem solving. *Arithmetic Teacher, 30*(4), 10–14.

National Coalition of Advocates for Students. (1985). *Barriers to excellence: Our children at risk* (pp. 26–27). Boston, MA: Author.

National Science Teachers Association. (1981). *Selected bibliographies. Reports of the Deans Grants: 4.* Washington, DC: Bureau of Education for the Handicapped. (ERIC Document Reproduction Service No. 224 238)

National Society to Prevent Blindness. (undated). *The Snellen chart.* Schaumburg, IL: Author.

Nazzaro, J. N. (1981). Special problems of exceptional minority children. In J. N. Nazzaro (Ed.), *Culturally diverse exceptional children in school* (pp. 13–52). Washington, DC: National Institute of Education. (ERIC Document Reproduction Service No. 199 993)

Nelson, R. S. (1979). Multiplication games that every child can play. *Arithmetic Teacher, 27*(2), 34–35.

Novak, J. D., & Gowin, D. B. (1984). *Learning how to learn.* Cambridge, MA: Cambridge University Press.

Ochoa, A. S., & Shuster, S. K. (1980). *Social studies in the mainstream classroom, K–6.* Boulder, CO: Social Science Education Consortium.

Oden, W. (1976). Desegregation and mainstreaming: A case of deja vu. In R. L. Jones (Ed.), *Mainstreaming and the minority child* (pp. 53–64). Minneapolis: Leadership Training Institute/Special Education.

Olion, L. D. (1980, April). *Strategies for meeting the needs of the mildly handicapped black adolescent.* Paper presented at the International Convention of the Council for Exceptional Children, Philadelphia. (ERIC Document Reproduction Service No. ED 233 516)

Olson, M. O. (1985). Practicing high frequency words with rebus stories. *The Reading Teacher, 39*(3), 820.

Omizo, M. M., Cubberly, W. E., & Cubberly, R. D. (1985). Modelling techniques, perceptions of self-efficacy, and arithmetic achievement among learning disabled children. *The Exceptional Child, 32,* 99–105.

Omizo, M. M., Cubberly, W. E., Semands, S. G., & Omizo, S. A. (1986). The effects of biofeedback and relaxation training on memory tasks among hyperactive boys. *The Exceptional Child, 33,* 56–64.

Orlansky, M. D., & Rhyne, J. M. (1981). Special adaptations necessitated by visual impairments. In J. M. Kauffman & D. P. Hallahan (Eds.), *Handbook of special education* (pp. 552–575). Englewood Cliffs, NJ: Prentice-Hall.

Ortiz, A. (1984). Texas: A state policy for Hispanic children with special needs. In P. Williams (Ed.), *Special education in minority communities* (pp. 34–53). New York: Milton Keynes, Taylor and Francis, Inc.

Osborn, R., Lance, C., & Hill, G. (1979). Revision of the NCSS social studies curriculum guidelines. *Social Education, 43,* 261–274.

Ottman, R. A. (1981). Mainstreaming: Initial steps in a difficult process. *Educational Horizons, 59*(4), 198–202.

Parent, W., & Everson, J. M. (1986). Competencies of disabled workers in industry: A review of business literature. *Journal of Rehabilitation, 52*(4), 16–23.

Pasanella, A. L., & Volkmor, C. B. (1981). *Teaching handicapped students in the mainstream: Coming back or never leaving* (2nd ed.). Columbus, OH: Merrill.

Patton, J. R., & Oyama, E. (in progress). *Curricular integration through a basal reading series.* Unpublished manuscript, University of Hawaii/Manoa, Department of Special Education, Honolulu.

Patton, J. R., Payne, J. S., Kauffman, J. M., Brown, G. B., & Payne, R. A. (1987). *Exceptional children in focus* (4th ed.). Columbus, OH: Merrill.

Patton, J. R., Polloway, E. A., & Cronin, M. E. (in press). *Science instruction for mildly handicapped students: A status report. Science Education.*

Patton, J. R., Polloway, E. A., & Cronin, M. E. (1987). Social studies instruction for mildly handicapped students: A status report. *The Social Studies, 71,* 131–135.

Paul, J. L., Turnbull, A. P., & Cruickshank, W. M. (1977). *Mainstreaming: A practical guide.* Syracuse, NY: Syracuse University Press.

Payne, R., & Murray, C. (1974). Principals' attitudes toward integration of the handicapped. *Exceptional Children, 41,* 123–125.

Penick, J. E., & Yager, R. E. (1986). Science education: New concerns and issues. *Science Education, 70,* 427–431.

Pfeiffer, S. I. (1980). The school-based interprofessional team: Recurring problems and some possible solutions. *Journal of School Psychology, 18,* 388–394.

Phelps, L. A., & Lutz, R. (1977). *Career exploration and preparation for the special needs learner.* Boston: Allyn & Bacon.

Pieper, E. (1983). A technique for discovering LD adolescents' strategies for solving multiplication facts. *The Pointer, 27*(2), 40–41.

Pieterse, M., & Center, Y. (1984). The integration of eight Down's syndrome children into regular schools. *Australia and New Zealand Journal of Developmental Disabilities, 10,* 11–20.

Pike, C. (1985). *Vocational math: The use of checking accounts.* Unpublished manuscript.

Policastro, M. M. (1985). What's happening: Predicting before, during, and after the picture. *The Reading Teacher, 39*(3), 929.

Polloway, E. A., Patton, J. R., Payne, J. S., & Payne, R. A. (1985). *Strategies for teaching retarded and special needs learners* (3rd ed.). Columbus, OH: Merrill.

Polloway, E. A., Payne, J. S., Patton, J. R., & Payne, R. A. (1989). *Strategies for teaching learners with special needs* (4th ed.). Columbus, OH: Merrill.

Polloway, C. H., & Polloway, E. A. (1981). Survival words for disabled readers. *Academic Therapy, 16*(4). 443–448.

Popp, R. A. (1983). Learning about disabilities. *Teaching Exceptional Children, 15,* 78–81.

Post, L., & Roy, W. (1985). Mainstreaming in secondary schools: How successful are plans to implement the concept? *NASSP Bulletin, 69,* 71–79.

Powers, D. A. (1979). Mainstreaming EMR pupils at the secondary level: A consideration of the issues. *The High School Journal, 63*(3), 102–108.

President's Committee on Employment of the Handicapped. (1979). *Affirmative action for disabled people: A pocket guide.* Washington, DC: U.S. Government Printing Office.

Price, M., News, J., & Stitt, M. (1982). Beyond the three R's: Science and social studies instruction for the mildly handicapped. In T. L. Miller & E. E. Davis (Eds.), *The mildly handicapped student* (pp. 367–390). New York: Grune & Stratton.

Price, P. (1984). A comparative study of the California Achievement Test (forms C and D) and the Key Math Diagnostic Arithmetic Test with secondary LD students. *Journal of Learning Disabilities, 17*(7), 392–396.

Prillaman, D. (1981). Acceptance of learning disabled students in the mainstream environment: A failure to replicate. *Journal of Learning Disabilities, 14,* 344–346.

Raykovicz, M. L., Bromley, K., & Mahlois, M. (1985). The reading tasks as viewed by good and poor readers. *Reading Improvement, 22*(2), 87–91.

Razeghi, J., & Davis, S. (1979). Federal mandates for the handicapped: Vocational education opportunity and employment. *Exceptional Children, 45*(5), 353–359.

Read, C. (1971). Preschool children's knowledge of English phonology. *Harvard Educational Review, 41,* 1–34.

Reese-Dukes, J. L., & Stokes, E. H. (1978). Social acceptance of elementary educable mentally retarded pupils in the regular classroom. *Education and Training of the Mentally Retarded, 13,* 356–361.

Reisman, F. K. (1982). *A guide to the diagnostic teaching of arithmetic.* Columbus, OH: Merrill.

Resnick, L. B., & Ford, W. W. (1981). *The psychology of mathematics for instruction.* Hillsdale, NJ: Lawrence Erlbaum.

Resnick, L. B., Wang, M. C., & Kaplan, J. (1973). Task analysis in curricular design: A hierarchically sequenced introductory mathematic curriculum. *Journal of Applied Behavior Analysis, 6*(4), 679-710.

Reynolds, B., Martin-Reynolds, J., & Mark, F. (1982). Elementary teachers' attitudes toward mainstreaming educable mentally retarded students. *Education and Training of the Mentally Retarded, 17,* 171-176.

Reys, R. E. (1975). Diagnosing and remediating systematic errors in addition and subtraction computation. *Arithmetic Teacher, 22*(2), 151-157.

Richmond, B. O., & Blagg, D. E. (1985). Adaptive behavior, social adjustment, and academic achievement of regular and special education children. *The Exceptional Child, 32,* 93-97.

Roach, J. C., Paolucci-Whitcomb, P., Meyers, H. W., & Duncan, D. A. (1983). The comparative effects of peer tutoring in math by and for secondary special needs students. *The Pointer, 27*(4), 20-24.

Roberts, G. H. (1968). The failure strategies of third grade arithmetic pupils. *The Arithmetic Teacher, 15,* 442-446.

Rodriguez, F. (1982). Mainstreaming a multicultural concept into special education: Guidelines for teacher trainers. Exceptional Children, 49(3), 220-227.

Roffman, A. J. (1983). *The classroom teacher's guide to mainstreaming.* Springfield, IL: Charles C. Thomas.

Roger, C. R. (1961). *On becoming a person.* Boston: Houghton Mifflin.

Rossman, M. (1985). Why kids fail to learn science and what to do about it. *Learning, 12,* 77-80.

Rubin, D. (1985). *Teaching elementary language arts* (3rd ed.). New York: Holt, Rinehart & Winston.

Rusch, F. R., & Chadsey-Rusch, S. (1985).Employment for persons with severe handicaps: Curriculum development and coordination of services. *Focus on Exceptional Children, 17*(9), 1-8.

Rusch, F. R., & Mithaug, D. E. (1980). *Vocational training for mentally retarded adults: A behavior analytic approach.* Champaign, IL: Research Press.

Rusch, F. R., Schutz, R. P., Mithaug, D. E., Stewart, J. E., & Mar, D. K. (1982). *Vocational assessment and curriculum guide.* Seattle, WA: Exceptional Education.

Ryor, J. (1978). 94-142: The perspective of regular education. *Learning Disability Quarterly, 1,* 6-14.

Sabatino, D. A., Sabatino, A. C., & Mann, L. (1983). *Discipline and behavioral management: A handbook of tactics, strategies, and programs.* Rockville, MD: Aspen Systems Corporation.

Sadowski, B. R. (1982, March). *Developing remedial mathematics strategies.* Paper presented at the International Conference of the Association for Children with Learning Disabilities, Chicago. (ERIC Document Reproduction Service No. 238 213)

Salend, S. J. (1984). Factors contributing to the development of successful mainstreaming programs. *Exceptional Children, 50*(5), 409-416.

Salend, S. J., & Viglianti, D. (1982). Preparing secondary students for the mainstream. *Teaching Exceptional Children, 14,* 137-140.

Salvia, J., & Ysseldyke, J. E., (1981). *Assessment in special and remedial education.* Boston: Houghton Mifflin.

Salvia, J., & Ysseldyke, J. E. (1985). *Assessment in special and remedial education* (3rd ed.). Boston: Houghton Mifflin.

Sapon-Shevin, M. (1978). Cooperative instructional games: Alternatives to the spelling bee. *The Elementary School Journal, 79,* 81-87.

Scheffelin, M. M. (1986). *Existing student study team processes in selected volunteer special education local plan areas, school districts, and schools in California: A descriptive evaluation study*. Sacramento, CA: Program Evaluation and Research Division, California State Department of Education.

Schlick, A. R., Gall, M., Riegel, R. H. (1981). Modifying study guides, practice and tests for students with learning difficulties at the secondary level. In T. Shaw (Ed.), *Teaching handicapped students social studies: A resource handbook for K-12 teachers* (pp. 33–44). Washington, DC: National Education Association.

Schmelkin, L. P. (1981). Teachers' and nonteachers' attitudes toward mainstreaming. *Exceptional Children, 48*(1), 42–47.

Schneider, D. O., & McGee-Brown, M. J. (1980). Helping students study and comprehend their social studies textbooks. *Social Education, 44*, 105–112.

Schoen, H. L. (1979). Using the individual interview to assess mathematical learning. *Arithmetic Teacher, 27*(3), 34–37.

Schubert, M. A., & Glick, F. M. (1973). The diagnostic/prescriptive teacher. In E. W. Deno (Ed.), *Instructional alternatives for exceptional children* (pp. 47–57). Reston, VA: Council for Exceptional Children.

Schubert, M. A., & Glick, F. M. (1981). Least restrictive environment programs: Why are some so successful? *Education Unlimited, 3*(2), 11–13.

Schug, M. J., & Kepner, H. S. (1984). Choosing computer simulations in social studies. *The Social Studies, 75*, 211–215.

Schulz, J. B., & Turnbull, A. P. (1984). *Mainstreaming handicapped students: A guide for classroom teachers* (2nd ed.). Boston: Allyn & Bacon.

Schwartz, S. E., & Budd, D. (1983). Mathematics for handicapped learners: A functional approach for adolescents. In E. L. Meyen, G. A. Vergason, & R. J. Whelan (Eds.), *Promising practices for exceptional children* (pp. 321–340). Denver, CO: Love Publishing.

Scott, P., & Moye, M. (1978). *Curriculum management handbook for vocational education administrators*. Atlanta: University of Georgia.

Scruggs, T. E., & Mastropieri, M. A. (1986). Improving the test-taking skills of behaviorally disordered and learning disabled children. *Exceptional Children, 53*, 63–68.

Scruggs, T. E., Mastropieri, M. A., Levin, J. R., & Gaffrey, J. S. (1985). Facilitating the acquisition of science facts in learning disabled students. *American Educational Research Journal, 22*, 575–586.

Semmel, M. J., Gottlieb, J., & Robinson, N. M. (1979). Mainstreaming: Perspectives on educating handicapped children in the public schools. *Review of Research in Education, 7*, 223–279.

Sequential Tests of Educational Progress, Series III. (1979). Reading, MA: Educational Testing Services.

Shaver, J. P. (1981). Citizenship, values, and morality in the social studies. In H. D. Mehlinger & O. L. Davis (Eds.), *The social studies. Eightieth Yearbook of the National Society for the Study of Education* (pp. 105–125). Chicago: University of Chicago Press.

Sheinker, A., & Coble, C. R. (1981). Science for the handicapped: Can we justify it? In M. E. Corrick (Ed.), *Teaching handicapped students science* (pp. 11–14). Washington, DC: National Education Association.

Shepherd, G. D., & Ragan, W. B. (1982). *Modern elementary curriculum* (6th ed.). New York: Holt, Rinehart & Winston.

Silbert, J., Carnine, D., & Stein, M. (1981). *Direct instruction mathematics*. Columbus, OH: Merrill.

Silverman, H. (1980). *How to handle behavior in school*. Lawrence, KA: H & H Enterprises.

Simms, R. B. (1984). Mildly handicapped students in the social studies class: Facilitating learning. *The Social Studies, 75*, 265–267.

Simpson, R. L. (1980). Modifying the attitudes of regular class students toward the handicapped. *Focus on Exceptional Children, 13*, 1–11.

Singleton, L. R. (1979). *Social studies for the visually impaired child* (Sourcebook 4). Boulder,

CO: Project MAVIS, Social Science Education Consortium.

Siperstein, G. N., Bopp, M. J., & Bak, J. J. (1978). Social status of learning disabled children. *Journal of Learning Disabilities, 11,* 49–53.

Sitlington, P. L. & Wimmer, D. (1978). Vocational assessment techniques for the handicapped adolescent. *Career Development for Exceptional Individuals, 1,* 74–87.

Sitlington, P., & Wimmer, D. (1980). Vocational assessment. In G. M. Clark & W. White (Eds.), Career education for the handicapped: Current perspectives for teachers (pp. 74–87). Boothwyn, PA: Educationsl Resources

Skirtic, T. M., Kvam, N. E., & Beals, V. L. (1983). Identifying and remediating the subtraction errors of learning disabled adolescents. *The Pointer, 27*(2), 32–38.

Slade, D. (1984). Helping LD Students make transitions: Six suggestions. *Academic Therapy, 19,* 543–547.

Smith, D. D. (1981). *Teaching the learning disabled.* Englewood Cliffs, NJ: Prentice-Hall.

Smith, P. B., & Bentley, G. (1975). *Facilitator manual, teacher training program. Mainstreaming mildly handicapped students in the regular classroom.* Austin, TX: Education Service Center, Region XII.

Smith, R. M., Neisworth, J. T., & Greer, J. G. (1978). *Evaluating educational environments.* Columbus, OH: Merrill.

SRA Achievement Series. (1978). Chicago, IL: Science Research Associates.

Stallings, J. (1982). Applications of classroom research of the 1970s to mathematics and science instruction. In R. E. Yager (Ed.), *What research says to the science teacher* (Vol. 4, pp. 7–21). Washington, DC: National Science Teachers Association.

Stallings, J. (1983). *Staff development and administrative support.* Nashville, TN: George Peabody College for Teachers, Vanderbilt University, Stallings Teaching and Learning Institute.

Stanford Achievement Test. (1982). New York: Harcourt.

Starr, K., & Bruce, B. C. (1983). Reading comprehension: More emphasis needed. *ASCD Curriculum Update,* pp. 1–4.

Stephens, T. M., Blackhurst, A. E., & Magliocca, L. A. (1988). Teaching mainstreamed students, 2nd ed. New York: Pergamon Press.

Stephens, T. M., & Wolf, J. S. (1980). *Effective skills in parent/teacher conferencing.* Columbus, OH: Ohio State University, National Center for Educational Materials and Media for the Handicapped.

Stowitschek, J. J., Gable, R. A., & Hendrickson, J.M. (1980). *Instructional materials for exceptional children.* Germantown, MD: Aspen Systems Corporation.

Strain, P. S. (1981). Peer-mediated treatment of exceptional children's social withdrawal. *Exceptional Education Quarterly, 1,* 93–105.

Sullivan, J. (1985). Reinforcing language in arithmetic problem solving. *The Reading Teacher, 39*(1), 119–120.

Sulzer-Azaroff, B., & Mayer, G. R. *Applying behavioral analysis procedures with children and youth.* New York: Holt, Rinehart & Winston, 1977.

Superka, D. P., Hawkes, S., & Morrissett, I. (1980). The current and future status of the social studies. *Social Education, 44,* 362–369.

Swezey, R. W. (1981). *Individual performance assessment: An approach to criterion-referenced test development.* Reston, VA: Reston Publishing.

Tapp, G. S., & Barclay, J. R. (1974). Convergent and discriminant validity of the Barclay Classroom Climate Inventory. *Educational and Psychological Measurement, 34,* 439–447.

Taylor, S. E. (1969). *Listening: What research says to the teacher.* Washington, DC: National Education Association.

Temple, C. A., Nathan, R. G., & Burris, N. (1982). *The beginnings of writing.* Boston: Allyn & Bacon.

Teters, P., Gabel, D., & Geary, P. (1984). Elementary teachers' perspectives on improving science education. *Science and Children, 22*(3), 41–43.

Thiagarajan, S., & Stolovitch, H. (1974). *Before and beyond behavioral objectives.* Hartland, MI: Michigan Department of Education, Waldenwoods Conference Center.

Thiel, S. A. (1978). *Inventory of rehabilitation programs for mentally handicapped adults.* Portland, ME: Portland Rehabilitation Center.

Thorkildson, R., Bickel, W. K., & Williams, J. G. (1979). A microcomputer/videodisc CAI system for the moderately mentally retarded. *Journal of Special Education, 4,* 15–23.

Thornton, C. A., & Bley, N. S. (1982). Problem solving: Help in the right direction for LD students. *Arithmetic Teacher, 29*(6), 26–27, 38–41.

Thornton, C. A., Tucker, B. F., Dossey, J. A., & Bazik, E. F. (1983). *Teaching mathematics to children with special needs.* Menlo Park, CA: Addison-Wesley.

Thurman, S. K., & Widerstrom, A. H. (1985). *Young children with special needs: A developmental and ecological approach.* Boston: Allyn & Bacon.

Tobin, K. G. (1980). The effects of teacher wait-time on science achievement. *Journal of Research in Science Teaching, 17,* 469–475.

Trifiletti, J. J., Frith, G. H., & Armstrong, S. (1984). Microcomputer versus resource rooms for LD students: A preliminary investigation of the effects on math skills. *Learning Disability Quarterly, 7*(1), 69–76.

Turnbull, A. P. (1983). Parent-professional interactions. In M. E. Snell (Ed.), *Systematic instruction of the moderately and severely handicapped* (2nd ed., pp. 18–43). Columbus, OH: Merrill.

Turnbull, A. P., & Turnbull, H. R., III. (1986). *Families, professionals, and exceptionality: A special partnership.* Columbus, OH: Merrill.

Turner, T. N. (1976). Making the social studies textbook a more effective tool for less able readers. *Social Education, 40,* 38–41.

Tyo, J. (1980). An alternative for poor readers in social science. *Social Education, 44,* 309–310.

Underhill, R. (1981). *Teaching elementary school mathematics* (3rd ed.). Columbus, OH: Merrill.

Underhill, R. G., Uprichard, A. E., & Heddens, J. W. (1980) *Diagnosing mathematical difficulties.* Columbus, OH: Merrill.

U.S. Commission on Civil Rights. (1983). *Across the spectrum of individual differences.* Washington, DC: U.S. Government Printing Office.

U.S. Department of Education. (1984). *Sixth annual report on the implementation of P.L. 94-142.* Washington, DC: U.S. Government Printing Office.

U.S. Department of Education. (1987). To assure the free appropriate public education of all handicapped children. *Ninth annual report to Congress on the implementation of the education of the handicapped act.* Washington, DC: U.S. Government Printing Office.

U.S. Department of Labor. (1979). *Study of handicapped clients in sheltered workshops* (Vol. II). Washington, DC: U.S. Government Printing Office.

Van Bourgondien, M. E. (1987). Children's responses to retarded peers as a function of social behaviors, labeling, and age. *Exceptional Children, 53,* 432–439.

Vasa, S. F. (1981). Alternative procedures for grading handicapped students in the secondary schools. *Education Unlimited, 3,* 16–23.

Veatch, J., Sawicki, F., Elliott, G., Barnette, E., & Blakey, J. (1979). *Key words to reading: The language experience approach begins.* Columbus, OH: Merrill.

Von Harrison, G., & Guymon, R. E. (1980). *Structured tutoring.* Englewood Cliffs, NJ: Educational Technology Publications.

Walker, H. M. (1979). *The acting out child: Coping with classroom disruption.* Boston: Allyn & Bacon.

Wallace, G., & Kauffman, J. M. (1978). *Teaching children with learning problems* (2nd ed.). Columbus, OH: Merrill.

Wallace, G., & Kauffman, J. M. (1986). *Teaching students with learning and behavior problems* (3rd ed.). Columbus, OH: Merrill.

Warger, C. L., Aldinger, L. E., & Okun, K. A. (1983). *Mainstreaming in the secondary school: The role of the regular teacher.* Bloomington, IN: Phi Delta Kappa. (ERIC Document Reproduction Service No. ED 229 355)

Webster, R. E. (1980). Short-term memory in mathematics-proficient and mathematics-disabled students as a function of input-modality output-modality pairings. *Journal of Special Education, 14,* 67–78.

Wehman, P. (1981). *Competitive employment: New horizons for severely disabled individuals.* Baltimore: Paul H. Brookes.

Wehman, P. (1982). *Vocational training and placement of severely disabled persons* (Vol. III). Richmond, VA: Virginia Commonwealth University.

Wehman, P., & Barcus, M. (1985). Unemployment among handicapped youth: What is the role of the public school? *Career Development for Exceptional Individuals, 8*(2), 90–101.

Wehman, P., & Kregel, J. (1985). A supported work approach to competitive employment of individuals with moderate and severe handicaps. *Journal of the Association for Persons with Severe Handicaps, 10*(1), 3–11.

Wehman, P., Kregel, J., & Barcus, M. (1985). From school to work: A vocational transition model for handicapped students. *Exceptional Children, 52*(1), 25–37.

Wehman, P., Kregel, J., Shafer, M., & Hill, M. (Eds.). (1987). *Competitive employment for persons with mental retardation: From research to practice* (Vol. II). Richmond, VA: Rehabilitation Research and Training Center, Virginia Commonwealth University.

Wehman, P., Moon, M. S., Everson, J., Wood, W., & Barcus, J. (1988). *Transition from school to work.* Baltimore: Paul H. Brookes.

Weill, B. F. (1978). Mrs. Weill's hill: A successful subtraction method for use with the learning disabled child. *Arithmetic Teacher, 26*(2), 34–35.

Weir, S., & Watt, D. (1980–1981). Logo: A computer environment for learning-disabled students. *The Computing Teacher, 8,* 11–17.

Weitzman, D. (1975). *My backyard history book.* Boston: Little, Brown.

Wepner, S. B. (1985). Linking logos with print for beginning reading success. *The Reading Teacher, 39*(3), 633–638.

White, O. R., & Haring, N. G. (1980). *Exceptional teaching* (2nd ed.). Columbus, OH: Merrill.

White, W., Deschler, D., Shumaker, F., Warner, M., Alley, G., & Clark, F. (1983). The effects of learning disabilities on past school adjustment. *Journal of Rehabilitation, 49,* 46–50.

Wieck, C. (1980). Computer resources: Will educators accept, reject, or neglect in the future? *Education Unlimited, 2,* 24–27.

Wiegerink, R., Posante-Loro, R., & Bristol, M. (1978). *Parent involvement in programs for handicapped, parent involvement survey form.* Chapel Hill, NC: Frank Porter Graham Child Development Center, University of North Carolina.

Will, M. (1984). Let us pause and reflect: But not too long. *Exceptional Children, 51,* 11–16.

Willet, J. B., Yamashita, J. J. M., & Anderson, R.D. (1983). A meta-analysis of instructional systems applied in science teaching. *Journal of Research in Science Teaching, 20,* 405–417.

Wiseman, D. E., Van Reusen, A. K., & Hartwell, L. K. (1981). Teaching social studies to low-achieving students in the secondary school. In T. Shaw (Ed.), *Teaching handicapped students social studies* (pp. 57–64). Washington, DC: National Education Association.

Wolfensberger, W., & Zanka, H. (1973). *Citizen advocacy and protective services for the impaired and handicapped.* Toronto: National Institute on Mental Retardation.

Wong, B. Y. L. (1979). Increasing retention of main ideas through questioning strategies. *Learning Disabilities Quarterly, 2,* 42–47.

Wong, B. Y. L. (1985). Potential means of enhancing content skills acquisition in learning disabled adolescents. *Focus on Exceptional Children, 17*(5), 1–8.

Wood, J. W. (1984). *Adapting instruction for the mainstream: A sequential approach to teaching.* Columbus, OH: Merrill.

Wood, J. W., & Carmean, M. (1982). Profile of a successful mainstreaming teacher. *Pointer, 27*(1), 21–23.

Wood, J. W., & Gibson, D. (1984). *Adaptations: A guide for teachers*. Richmond, VA: Project ADAPT.

Woodward, A., Elliott, D. L., & Nagel, K. C. (1986). Beyond textbooks in elementary social studies. *Social Education, 50*, 50–53.

Wright, B. A. (1979, August). *The coping framework and attitude change: A guide to constructive role-playing*. Paper presented at the annual conference of the American Psychological Association, New York.

Wylie, R. (1976). Attitudes of children toward their handicapped peers. *Childhood Education, 52*, 177–183.

Yaffe, E. (1979). Experienced mainstreamers speak out. *Teacher, 96*, 61–63.

Yeager, T. A., & Edwards, C. W. (1980). The textbook: A source for activities. *Social Education, 44*, 113–114.

Young, J. L. (1984). Uncovering the algorithms. *Arithmetic Teacher, 32*(3), 20.

Young, J. L., & Shepherd, M. L. (1983). *The adjustment of the educable mentally retarded to the regular classroom—The teacher's perspective*. Hattiesburg, MS: University of Southern Mississippi. (ERIC Document Reproduction Service No. ED 258 372)

Ysseldyke, J. E. (1983). Current practices in making psychoeducational decisions about learning disabled students. *Journal of Learning Disabilities, 16*, 226–233.

Zintz, M. V. (1977). *Corrective reading* (4th ed.). Dubuque, IA: William C. Brown.

Name Index

Subject Index